D1200085

EMDR AS AN INTEGRATIVE PSYCHOTHERAPY APPROACH

EMDR AS AN INTEGRATIVE PSYCHOTHERAPY APPROACH

Experts of Diverse Orientations
Explore the Paradigm Prism

Edited by Francine Shapiro, PhD

AMERICAN PSYCHOLOGICAL ASSOCIATION
WASHINGTON, DC

Copyright © 2002 by the American Psychological Association. All rights reserved. Except as permitted under the United States Copyright Act of 1976, no part of this publication may be reproduced or distributed in any form or by any means, or stored in a database or retrieval system, without the prior written permission of the publisher.

First Printing: June 2002
Second Printing: November 2002

Published by
American Psychological Association
750 First Street, NE
Washington, DC 20002
www.apa.org

To order
APA Order Department
P.O. Box 92984
Washington, DC 20090-2984

Tel: (800) 374-2721; Direct: (202) 336-5510
Fax: (202) 336-5502; TDD/TTY: (202) 336-6123
Online: www.apa.org/books/
Email: order@apa.org

In the U.K., Europe, Africa, and the Middle East, copies may be ordered from
American Psychological Association
3 Henrietta Street
Covent Garden, London
WC2E 8LU England

Typeset in Goudy by EPS Group Inc., Easton, MD

Printer: United Book Press, Inc., Balto., MD
Cover Designer: NiDesign, Baltimore, MD
Technical/Production Editor: Kristen R. Sullivan

The opinions and statements published are the responsibility of the authors, and such opinions and statements do not necessarily represent the policies of the American Psychological Association.

Library of Congress Cataloging-in-Publication Data
EMDR as an integrative psychotherapy approach : experts of diverse orientations explore the paradigm prism / edited by Francine Shapiro.—1st ed.
    p. cm.
  Includes bibliographical references and index.
  ISBN 1-55798-922-2 (alk. paper)
    1. Eye movement desensitization and reprocessing. 2. Psychic trauma—Treatment. I. Shapiro, Francine.

RC489.E98 E465 2002
616.89′14—dc21

2002018259

British Library Cataloguing-in-Publication Data
A CIP record is available from the British Library.

Printed in the United States of America

To my extraordinary husband
ROBERT WELCH,
who surpassed even my dreams.

CONTENTS

CONTRIBUTORS

CHAPTERS 1 AND 2: OVERVIEW, INFORMATION PROCESSING, AND EMDR

Francine Shapiro, PhD, the originator and developer of eye movement desensitization and reprocessing (EMDR), is a senior research fellow at the Mental Research Institute in Palo Alto, CA. She is the founder and President Emeritus of the EMDR Humanitarian Assistance Programs, a nonprofit organization that coordinates disaster response and pro bono trainings worldwide. She has served as advisor to a wide variety of trauma treatment and outreach organizations and journals. Dr. Shapiro has been an invited speaker on EMDR at numerous major psychology conferences, including two divisions of the American Psychological Association (APA) and the American Psychological Society Presidential Symposium on posttraumatic stress disorder (PTSD). She has written and been the coauthor of numerous articles, chapters, and books about EMDR, including *Eye Movement Desensitization and Reprocessing* and *EMDR*. She is a recipient of the Distinguished Scientific Achievement in Psychology Award presented by the California Psychological Association.

CHAPTER 3: EMDR AND PSYCHOPHYSIOLOGY

Bessel A. van der Kolk, MD, is Professor of Psychiatry at Boston University, where he teaches neuroscience and psychiatry. He is the Past President of the International Society for Traumatic Stress Studies and was coinvestigator of the fourth edition of the *Diagnostic and Statistical Manual of Mental Disorders* Field Trial for Posttraumatic Stress. He is the Medical Director of The Trauma Center in Boston and has been active as a clinician, researcher, and teacher in the area of posttraumatic stress for almost 25 years. His current research focuses on the effects of trauma on memory processes, the relative efficacy of psychological vs. biological interventions in PTSD treatment, and neuroimaging. He has taught at universities throughout the world and has published widely in the field as an author and editor, including the classic texts *Psychological Trauma* and *Traumatic Stress: The Effects of Overwhelming Experience on Mind, Body, and Society*.

CHAPTER 4: EMDR AND DEVELOPMENTAL NEUROBIOLOGY

Daniel J. Siegel, MD, received his medical degree from Harvard University and completed his postgraduate medical education at the University of California–Los Angeles (UCLA). An award-winning educator, he formerly directed the UCLA training program in child psychiatry and has served as a National Institute of Mental Health Research Fellow. He is currently an Associate Clinical Professor of Psychiatry at the UCLA School of Medicine and the Director of the Center for Human Development, an educational organization that focuses on how the development of individuals, families, and communities can be helped by examining the interface of human relationships and basic biological processes. Dr. Siegel is the author of *The Developing Mind: Toward a Neurobiology of Interpersonal Experience*, which has been used by many organizations, including the Sundance Institute, the U.S. Department of Justice, the Vatican, and academic departments worldwide.

CHAPTER 5: EMDR AND PSYCHOANALYSIS

Paul L. Wachtel, PhD, is CUNY Distinguished Professor in the doctoral program in clinical psychology at City College and the Graduate Center of the City University of New York. He did his undergraduate work at Columbia, received his PhD in clinical psychology from Yale, and is a graduate of the postdoctoral psychoanalytic training program at New York University, where he is also on the faculty. Dr. Wachtel is the author of, among other books, *Action and Insight; The Poverty of Affluence; Family Dynamics in Individual Psychotherapy; Therapeutic Communication; Psychoanalysis, Behavior Therapy, and the Relational World*; and most recently, *Race in the Mind of America: Breaking the Vicious Circles Between Blacks and Whites*. He is a cofounder of the Society for the Exploration of Psychotherapy Integration and has been a member of its Steering Committee from its inception.

CHAPTER 6: EMDR AND COGNITIVE–BEHAVIOR THERAPY

A. Desmond Poole, PhD, FBPsS, is Past President of both the British Association for Behavioural and Cognitive Psychotherapies and the European Association for Behavioural Cognitive Psychotherapies. He is Head of the Department of Psychological Therapies, Police Rehabilitation, and Retraining Trust in Belfast, Northern Ireland, and is an Honorary Lecturer in the School of Psychology at Queen's University of Belfast. Dr. Poole was previously an Associate Professor of Behavioural Science in Medicine in the Department of Psychiatry and Behavioural Science at the University of Western Australia and has also been on faculty in the Departments of Psychology and Psychiatry in Trinity College at Ireland's Dublin University. He has published extensively on behavior therapy.

Nancy J. Smyth, PhD, MSW, is Associate Professor and Associate Dean at the State University of New York at Buffalo School of Social Work. She has been active on numerous committees of the Association for the Advancement of Behavior Therapy since 1994, including as Chairperson of Special Interest Groups and Affiliates. She is currently President of the organization's EMDR Special Interest Group and has presented extensively on relevant research parameters. She has published behavioral clinical research on suicidal behavior, addictions, and dual disorders and is currently involved in federally funded research investigating links between addiction and trauma among addicted mothers and their children.

CHAPTER 7: EMDR AND SCHEMA-FOCUSED THERAPY

Jeffrey E. Young, PhD, is on the faculty in the Department of Psychiatry at Columbia University and is Director of the Cognitive Therapy Centers of New York and Connecticut. He is the founder of Schema Therapy and has published widely in the fields of both cognitive and schema therapies; two of his major books are *Cognitive Therapy for Personality Disorders: A Schema-Focused Approach* and *Reinventing Your Life*. He has also served as a consultant on the editorial boards of journals, including *Cognitive Therapy and Research* and *Cognitive and Behavioral Practice*.

William M. Zangwill, PhD, is an associate at the Cognitive Therapy Center of New York. He is Adjunct Clinical Supervisor of Psychology at Yeshiva University and has written chapters on sexuality and on EMDR. Dr. Zangwill specializes in the treatment of PTSD, sexual, relationship, and family problems.

Wendy E. Behary, LCSW, is the founder and director of the Cognitive Therapy Center of New Jersey. She specializes in the treatment of narcissism, couples, and social phobia and has given extensive lectures and training on cognitive and schema therapy.

CHAPTER 8: EMDR AND MULTIMODAL THERAPY

Arnold A. Lazarus, PhD, ABPP, is the Distinguished Professor Emeritus of Psychology at Rutgers University and President of the Center for Multimodal Psychological Services. His many honors include two awards from the APA, the prestigious Cummings PSYCHE Award, the Distinguished Service Award from the American Board of Professional Psychology, and two Lifetime Achievement Awards. He has served as the president of several professional societies and authored well over 200 scientific articles and has authored, coauthored, or edited 16 books, including *Brief but Comprehensive Psychotherapy: The Multimodal Way* and *Marital Myths Revisited.*

Clifford N. Lazarus, PhD, is a licensed clinical psychologist and neuropsychologist with a practice in Princeton, New Jersey, where he is the Director of Comprehensive Psychological Services. He has published numerous scientific articles, book chapters, and two popular books *Don't Believe It for a Minute: 40 Toxic Ideas That Are Driving You Crazy* and *The 60-Second Shrink.* He was honored by the Prescribing Psychologists' Register "For Outstanding Contributions to the Pioneering Efforts of Training in Psychopharmacology for Psychologists."

CHAPTER 9: EMDR AND HYPNOSIS

Stephen Gilligan, PhD, is a licensed psychologist practicing in Encinitas, CA. Dr. Gilligan studied extensively with Milton Erickson and Gregory Bateson. After receiving his doctorate in psychology from Stanford University, Dr. Gilligan became known as one of the premier teachers and practitioners of Ericksonian hypnosis and psychotherapy. Subsequently, he developed his own work of radical awakening, known as *self-relations psychotherapy.* His numerous publications include *Therapeutic Trances: The Cooperation Principle in Ericksonian Hypnotherapy, Brief Therapy* (edited with J. Zeig), *Therapeutic Conversations* (edited with R. Price), *The Courage to Love: Principles and Practices of Self-Relations Psychotherapy,* and *The Legacy of Erickson.*

CHAPTER 10: EMDR AND EXPERIENTIAL THERAPY

Arthur C. Bohart, PhD, is Professor of Psychology at California State University–Dominguez Hills and is also affiliated with Saybrook Graduate School. Dr. Bohart coedited *Empathy Reconsidered: New Directions in Psychotherapy* with Leslie Greenberg. He is also the coauthor of *How Clients Make Therapy Work: The Process of Active Self-Healing* and the coeditor of *Constructive and Destructive Behavior: Implications for Family, School, and Society.*

Leslie Greenberg, PhD, is Professor of Psychology at York University in Toronto, Ontario, and is the Director of the York University Psychotherapy Research Clinic. Dr. Greenberg is the coauthor of *Emotion in Psychotherapy, Emotionally Focused Therapy for Couples, Facilitating Emotional Change,* and *Working With Emotions in Psychotherapy.* He recently coedited the *Handbook of Experiential Psychotherapy.* Dr. Greenberg is a founding member of the Society of the Exploration of Psychotherapy Integration and a Past President of the Society for Psychotherapy Research. He is on the editorial board of numerous psychotherapy journals, including the *Journal of Psychotherapy Integration* and the *Journal of Marital and Family Therapy.*

CHAPTER 11: EMDR AND FEMINIST THERAPY

Laura S. Brown, PhD, is a distinguished scholar and practitioner in the field of feminist therapy. Her book *Subversive Dialogues: Theory in Feminist Therapy* is considered the classic text on the topic, and in 1995 it won the Distinguished Publication Award from the Association for Women in Psychology. Dr. Brown has published four additional books and more than 100 journal articles and book chapters on feminist therapy theory, ethics, and practice, as well as on the topics of trauma treatment, psychotherapy with lesbians, and multiculturalism. In 1995, she was the recipient of the APA award for Distinguished Professional Contributions to Public Service and in 1997 was the recipient of the Sarah Haley Award for Clinical Excellence from the International Society for Traumatic Stress Studies.

CHAPTER 12: EMDR AND FAMILY SYSTEMS

Florence W. Kaslow, PhD, ABPP, is Past President of the Divisions of Family and Media Psychology of APA, the International Family Therapy Association, the Florida Association of Professional Family Mediators, and the American Board of Family Psychology. A member of many journal editorial boards who has authored or edited 20 books and over 160 articles and book chapters, Dr. Kaslow is coauthor of *Painful Partings: Divorce and its Aftermath*, the *Handbook of Relational Diagnosis and Dysfunctional Family Patterns*, and the *Handbook of Couple and Family Forensics*. Currently she is President of the International Academy of Family Psychologists and Chairperson of the Family Psychology Specialty Council.

A. Rodney Nurse, PhD, ABPP, directs the family program at the Boyer Foundation (which treats people with serious mental illnesses) and was formerly the President and Dean of the California Graduate School of Family Psychology. Dr. Nurse edits the "Practice Enhancement" column for the Academy of Family Psychology and is Chair of Forensic Family Psychology for the APA Division of Family Psychology. He is the author of *Family Assessment* and *Personality-Guided Couple Therapy*.

Peggy Thompson, PhD, is a founder and codirector (with Dr. Nurse) of the Collaborative Divorce and Family Psychological Services of Orinda and San Rafael, CA. She has been a licensed psychologist for 25 years and specializes in treating children and families. Dr. Thompson is a coauthor of *Divorce: A Problem to Be Solved, Not a Battle to Be Fought*.

CHAPTER 13: EMDR AND TRANSPERSONAL PSYCHOLOGY

Sheila Krystal, PhD, received her doctorate in Experimental Psychology at Columbia University and held a four-year Postdoctoral Fellowship at the University of California in the Human Development Program at Langley Porter Neuropsychiatric Institute. Since the early 1970s, Dr. Krystal has been a licensed clinical psychologist specializing in meditation and visualization techniques for psychospiritual education and healing. She has published articles in *Maturitas* and the *Journal of Substance Abuse Treatment* and has contributed to numerous transpersonal psychology volumes.

Peter Fenner, PhD, was a married monk in the Tibetan Buddhist Tradition for nine years. He lectures extensively in Australian and American universities in East–West Psychology and is the author of the book *Intrinsic Freedom*.

Phyllis Krystal has been an internationally known workshop leader since the early 1950s. She has developed a system of visualization techniques with archetypal symbols and is the author of eight books on transpersonal psychology, including *Cutting the Ties That Bind*.

John J. Prendergast, PhD, is a practicing psychologist and on staff at the California Institute of Integral Studies. He has published in the *International Journal of Yoga Therapy*.

Kali and Isaac Shapiro, the author of *Outbreak of Peace*, have traveled worldwide since 1992 offering Satsang meetings in the tradition of Ramana Maharshi and H.W.L. Poonja. The Shapiros are considered to be leaders in awakening consciousness in Advaita Vedanta and related nondual approaches to understanding the psyche.

CHAPTER 14: EMDR AND INTEGRATION

John C. Norcross, PhD, is Professor of Psychology at the University of Scranton, editor of *In Session: Journal of Clinical Psychology*, and a clinical psychologist in part-time practice. The author of more than 150 scholarly publications, Dr. Norcross has cowritten or edited 12 books, including the *Authoritative Guide to Self-Help Resources in Mental Health, Psychologists' Desk Reference,* and *Systems of Psychotherapy: A Transtheoretical Analysis.* He was the 2000 President of the APA Division of Psychotherapy, codeveloper of the APA Psychotherapy Videotape Series, and a member of a dozen editorial boards. Dr. Norcross has received many professional awards, such as Pennsylvania Professor of the Year from the Carnegie Foundation and election to the National Academies of Practice.

PREFACE

Life, like a dome of many-coloured glass,
Stains the white radiance of Eternity.

—Percy Bysshe Shelley

Sir Isaac Newton was the first to demonstrate that white light is composed of all of the different light frequencies. He did this by directing sunlight through a prism and observing that the result was a display of the various colors, spread out like a rainbow. Just so do we find the field of psychology. Although psychologists may look at the same human condition, it is seen through the lenses of each school of thought, resulting in various characteristics and therapeutic processes being judged most salient and significant. This prismatic displacement has unfortunately often resulted in internecine warfare, as successive schools struggled first for a place on the landscape and, perhaps, then for dominance over its brethren. Fortunately, the concentration on different aspects has also resulted in the development of profoundly important insights and procedures within each of the various schools by which to further the healing process. The goal of this volume is to display the range of thought of these schools side by side and explore their many contributions.

Luminaries and clinicians of a wide variety of orientations have been asked to view EMDR and its clinical effects through the lenses of their paradigms. Each chapter contains the wisdom of not only a leader or seminal thinker but also a practicing clinician. This gives readers a range of theoretical and therapeutic insight not only into EMDR but also into the very process of change as well as the human condition. It is my hope that this volume will result in a greater appreciation of the integrative nature of EMDR and, more important, of the need for an integration of the field of psychology. For as beautiful as each aspect of the rainbow might be—

as brilliant and resonating one color might appear to any of us—each color is an integral part of the whole.

This allusion is paralleled in an old Indian fable about several blind men and an elephant. The man who held the elephant's trunk thought the elephant was like a snake. The man who touched the elephant's side thought the elephant was like a wall. Another man touched the elephant's leg and thought the elephant was like a tree trunk. But indeed, it was all one elephant. It is equally important, however, to remember that, even with eyes wide open, we can only hope to see the part of the elephant exposed to our view. Only by sharing our perspectives so that we can see each aspect from each angle can we have a full understanding of the whole. I hope that this volume is a step in that direction.

ACKNOWLEDGMENTS

The publication of this book marks the 15th year since I began developing EMDR. During these years, I have met many people who have dedicated their lives to developing ways to contribute to the healing of psychological suffering and have shown a generosity of spirit in sharing their knowledge and offering their support. These, the true leaders of this field, are well represented in this volume. I thank all of the contributors for their time, effort, and vision. In this context, I wish to acknowledge Joseph Wolpe, who I first met in 1988 when he was presenting at the American Psychological Association convention. I had planned to approach him after his talk to see if he might be interested in my findings. As fate would have it, I wound up sitting next to friends of his, and he came over to greet them before starting his talk. When he finished speaking to them, he turned and looked directly at me with an interested expression. I took that opportunity to say, "I'd like to speak to you, if possible. I seem to have found a way to desensitize memories in one session." He simply said, "I'm *very* interested. Please wait for me so we can talk after the lecture."

When we met after the talk, he asked me to demonstrate the procedure, and subsequently he became both mentor and colleague. During that early time, I once told him how it impressed me that he was so open and supportive of a procedure that if proven would displace his own innovation, systematic desensitization. Although a staunch behaviorist who had spent his own time in turf wars, his reply was, "I don't care if it's *psychoanalysis*. If it helps people, I want to know about it." His attitude supported me in viewing any other type of response to innovation as aberrant and stood me well in the ensuing years. Therefore, I here acknowledge Dr. Wolpe's openness and support. He introduced EMDR to the behavioral community, and he had intended to write the behavior therapy chapter in this volume. The book is poorer for his untimely death. For his friendship, I will be always grateful.

This project spanned more than 5 years from inception to fruition. During that time, many individuals provided their personal support, and I am thankful to all of them. Of special note, as always, is the unswerving friendship and integrity of Robbie Dunton. She is a shining light to all who know her. Few of the projects that have been accomplished on behalf of EMDR during the past decade could have occurred without her.

My special gratitude goes also to Louise Maxfield for her important contributions and tireless efforts during this project. Her astute observations, suggestions, and editorial assistance have greatly enhanced the book in many ways. I also thank the reviewers of various chapters for their input. The goal of the book is to introduce readers to the wisdom of the various psychotherapeutic orientations and make their principles and procedures accessible and meaningful to practicing clinicians. This was accomplished with input from Louise Maxfield and from the following people: Uri Bergman, Elizabeth Call, Linda Cohn, Robbie Dunton, Blanche Freund, Deborah Korn, Howard Lipke, Marilyn Luber, Jeri Marlowe, Priscilla Marquis, Allen Rubin, Elizabeth Snyker, Susan Rogers, and Marshall Wilensky. My gratitude also goes to Linda McCarter, Lansing Hays, and Kristen Sullivan of APA Books for shepherding the volume through the publication process.

I also thank once again all the clinicians and researchers who have contributed to the development of EMDR and its responsible dissemination throughout the world. Those who have taken their time to rigorously investigate and refine the procedures understand that without the combination of science and practice, we shortchange our clients. Those who have volunteered to participate in the EMDR International Association and the EMDR Humanitarian Assistance Programs understand that without the addition of heartfelt service, we shortchange humanity. To all of you, I am endlessly grateful.

EMDR AS AN INTEGRATIVE PSYCHOTHERAPY APPROACH

1

INTRODUCTION:
PARADIGMS, PROCESSING, AND
PERSONALITY DEVELOPMENT

FRANCINE SHAPIRO

What is the goal of psychotherapy? Is it the alleviation of symptoms and human suffering, or is it the enhancement of personal development and growth toward a substantial sense of being? Can one be attained without the other? How are *dysfunction*, *health*, and *meaning* defined? Is the evolution of personal consciousness a concomitant of natural development or a convergence of influences? Is the province of psychology best influenced by the study of behavior, cognition, philosophy, or theology? Is it most akin to science or to art?

I believe it can be reasonably stated that no one answer to these questions exists, because each school of psychotherapy has varying definitions of *change* on both personal and process levels. The medium is the message, and clearly a clinician is guided not by technique but by orientation. The client is seen through the lenses of the clinician's paradigm, and the road to health is defined by its boundaries. The way the client enters into the process of therapy and the explicit or implicit definition of goals is an interaction between client and clinician. Is the clinician healer or facilitator, companion or guide? Is truth considered intrinsically derived or is it externally supplied? Is the client permanently damaged or integrally intact?

Perhaps we see what we look for, and the goals of therapy might best be derived from our spiritual leaders. For Mother Teresa the primary goal was to discover the divine "in all its distressing disguises." The goal of this volume is to help us refine our many tools to achieve this end. Most important, it is to assist in integrating the field to best serve humanity "in all its distressing disguises." In this regard a basic tenet of this book is that each school of thought in the field of psychology has an important contribution to make in this service. The central metaphor of the book as expressed in the subtitle and the preface is meant to convey that the entire range of orientations is akin to the rainbow produced by Newton's prism. Although our eyes may be attracted to one color or another, they cannot be weighted differentially. The colors are all part of the makeup of the universal white light.

PURPOSE OF THIS BOOK

The purpose of this book is to guide practicing clinicians and those interested in psychotherapy theory into a greater understanding of the potential for robust treatment. As experts in the major psychological orientations, each chapter author adds an invaluable perspective to this multifaceted process as they lead readers through an examination of their own paradigms and through evaluations of EMDR. Evolving primarily from clinical experience, EMDR is an integrative psychotherapy approach that directly addresses the experiential contributors of pathology. As such, it dovetails nicely with the need of practicing clinicians to treat a wide range of problems. These applications have been developed in direct clinical practice by the integration of EMDR with the specialty wisdom of these various fields. That is, experts and consultants in areas such as substance abuse, dissociative disorders, and somatoform disorders have written protocols and guidelines for the application of EMDR to a variety of complaints. Authors of the various chapters have included clinical descriptions of diverse applications; a comprehensive listing of case reports on various disorders appears in Appendix A, and parameters for future evaluation are included in Appendix C.

As we search for ways to refine our service to humanity, I believe it is vital that science is bent to its service. To aid in the integration of science and practice, a discussion of the controlled research exploring EMDR and its place among the other approaches is contained in Appendix A. Furthermore, although EMDR has been examined by independent investigators in a wide variety of settings, as with any form of psychotherapy, many unanswered questions remain. Consequently, Appendix C offers researchers and students a list of commonly asked questions and suggested parameters for their future investigations. The volume also begins with two eminent theorists in the field of neurobiology who expound on the contribution of the primary sciences in understanding the physiological underpinnings of change, regardless of orientation. But to my mind, although many orientations have not yet been scrutinized by controlled research, they have much to offer. These orientations have been part of the mainstream of psychology during the past century, and their proponents have added greatly to the understanding of the process of change and to the human condition. Chapter topics and authors were chosen to offer a comprehensive spectrum of these approaches.

As described in the text, EMDR has evolved theoretically in the past years, so some of the authors are familiar with the information-processing model and theory of personality, and others are not. Some authors have used EMDR extensively, and others have experimented with it. However, authors of each of the chapters have some personal experience with its clinical outcomes, and it was felt best to allow each to describe EMDR solely on that basis. For rather than an interpretation of theory, of much greater importance is the unfettered examination of clinical procedures and phenomena. It is noteworthy that regardless of their range of experience, the authors have each been able to identify elements and outcomes of EMDR treatment most salient to their world view. As such, each chapter offers a glimpse into diverse orientations that can hopefully explicate EMDR's effects but more importantly, guide diverse clinicians to a more robust and comprehensive practice.

The authors were asked the following questions:

1. What elements of EMDR are representations of traditional thought in your area?
2. How can the positive treatment effects be described?
3. How does EMDR allow individuals practicing your modality to "use what they know?"
4. How does EMDR complement or extend the outcomes of your previous work?
5. What suggestions do you have for strengthening the EMDR protocols (e.g., by exploring new avenues that might be successful as predicted by the principles inherent in your model, or incorporating aspects of the various modalities that are not currently included)?
6. How can EMDR be used as a resource to investigate open questions or interesting areas in your modality of origin?

In summary, the basic thesis of this book is that EMDR is an integrated mode of psychotherapy with incorporated principles, protocols, and procedures that are compatible with all the major psychological orientations. This book includes chapters offering ways to view EMDR through the lenses of experts in these various models. Through these authors' expertise, I hope that EMDR can bridge the gap between various forms of psychotherapy and perhaps allow the information-processing model (which is explained in this chapter) to act as a common language. In this spirit, following are some questions for readers to answer according to their own evaluation and clinical experience:

- Can the clinical phenomena that have served as a hallmark of each orientation be explained through information processing?
- Is each hallmark of change in the various modalities represented in EMDR's clinical outcomes?
- Can we learn from each other without prejudice so that the wisdom of the field can be united to treat each client as a whole person?

No person is expendable, and no one is without worth. Can we make our treatments so comprehensive and so robust that no one will be lost? We will explore these possibilities throughout this volume.

ORGANIZATION OF THIS BOOK

The book begins with an overview of current EMDR theory and practice. This overview offers my perspective as the developer of the approach under examination. The two opening chapters set the groundwork for the remainder of the text. They provide an explanation of EMDR as an approach to psychology that includes a theory of personality development and a specific view of treatment and change processes. They also offer readers who are unacquainted with EMDR an explanation of the clinical phenomena, principles, and procedures that the subsequent authors interpret. For those acquainted with EMDR, they explain the latest refinements of thought in the area of personality development and therapeutic change.

The chapters that follow offer diverse views, ranging from the neurobiological through the primary orientations, roughly in the order in which they were introduced to the field of psychology. As such and with added reason, one of the final chapters deals with the existential and transpersonal aspects of change. The book begins with the biological, so I believe it is only fitting that it ends with the transcendent. This decision is purely one borne out of my personal world view that although the reduction of overt suffering and shifts in biochemistry are important elements of change, the primary goal of therapy is to empower a whole and radiant human being capable of love and service. Regardless of religious or spiritual orientation, I believe that the greatest boon we can offer to any individual is to help permit a life of minimal fear and greatest love.

Arguably the most eloquent spokesperson for this viewpoint is Victor Frankl. In his seminal work, *Man's Search for Meaning* (1959/1984), he argued that the avoidance of existential despair and true satisfaction in life can be found only in the ability to find in everyday events the greater sense of purpose for one's existence and by being able to choose one's attitude in any circumstance. Both of these pivotal ideas have direct pertinence to clinicians and clients. It should not be surprising that Frankl's tenets are so relevant to the context of the treatment of trauma—whether large or small—because they are based on his experiences during the World War II Holocaust, one of the most traumatizing experiences in human history.

With respect to the importance of having a higher purpose in life, it may be said that most clinicians enter the field of psychology with a desire to alleviate suffering. They interact with their clients at a profound and intimate level in an attempt to meet this goal. However, if the goal is not achieved because of factors such as clinical failures and minimal improvement, compassion fatigue is a likely outcome. Therefore, it seems that one of the best ways to prevent compassion fatigue is to use those tools that have the greatest possibility of clinical success. An important goal of this volume is to provide sources of change across the clinical spectrum and across orientations that may have been hitherto locked from view because of adherence to one theoretical world view.

Clinical treatment itself echoes Frankl's second tenet—the freedom to choose one's attitudes regardless of circumstances. It is exactly this freedom that the client often lacks, and therefore, a primary goal of treatment is to restore, or engender for the first time, this needed capacity. How can a client best achieve the ability to choose his or her attitude within a given environment, rather than being primarily *reactive* to it? I believe this is particularly pertinent because primary drivers of fear and anxiety distort the present and can cause a self-fulfilling prophecy of pain and despair. Breaking this personal cycle of desolation and despair is arguably one of the goals of any of the orientations explored in this book.

EMDR AND INFORMATION PROCESSING

The abilities to obtain or construct meaning from experiences and be able to interpret these experiences in a flexible manner are two of the hallmarks of mentally healthy individuals, whereas the absence of these capacities—the hampered ability "to choose one's attitude"—typifies those with posttraumatic stress disorder (PTSD), the first group of clients treated with EMDR. Clinical experience has clearly shown that when an individual is locked into a particular interpretation of reality, the source of the problem is the interaction of the present situation with disturbing memories. For example, combat veterans may react with violent rage in the present because a coworker's incompetence triggers memories of comrades who died in Vietnam because of negligence. For them, albeit on a preconscious level, *incompetence* means impending disaster. Such "preconstructed," rigid schema and reaction patterns appear to be manifestations of unprocessed information in which negative affect dominates (Shapiro, 1995, 2001; Shapiro & Forrest, 1997). In essence, the individual reacts dysfunctionally to current situations because of automatic responses that were first elicited by past events and have become physiologically encoded. Current research has emphasized the biological underpinnings of trauma response (e.g., van der Kolk, 1996), and the physiological concomitants of the disorder may account for the relative imperviousness of PTSD to conventional clinical methods (Hyer, 1994; Seligman, 1995; Shalev, Bonne, & Eth, 1996; Solomon, Gerrity, & Muff, 1992).

If the clinical use of EMDR has shown clinicians anything during the past decade, it is that PTSD is an excellent benchmark for the problems that underlie most pathologies. That is, dysfunctional physiological encoding of perceptions is not limited to the obvious trauma victims but is actually a contributor to most problems that bring clients into therapy. What makes a person believe "I'm not lovable, or worthwhile"? What leads a client to declare, "I can't succeed" or "I'll be abandoned"? Unless we believe that it comes from an alien virus, clinicians, regardless of orientation, generally agree that the basis of the problems comes at least in part from earlier life experiences.

A behaviorist may ignore the earlier event and concentrate on the present symptoms. A cognitive therapist may concentrate on the beliefs presently displayed. A psychodynamic therapist may explore the interpretations of the earlier experiences. An experiential therapist may orchestrate a reenactment of the event, and so forth. Regardless of whether the event is placed in foreground or background, all the therapists would agree that some previous events have contributed to the present problem. As an approach, EMDR places the attention squarely on these etiological events, which become the central focus of both theory and practice.

As a distinct orientation, EMDR therapy is guided conceptually and practically by an adaptive information-processing model (Shapiro, 1991, 1995, 2001). It is posited that the physiological systems of the brain that attend to the assimilation of experience are no different from other body systems. That is, if the body is cut, it has a tendency to close and heal. This movement toward health and balance is sustained unless there is a block or repeated traumatization. Once the recurrent assault is stopped or the block removed, the body again moves toward healing. This movement toward a positive state can also be seen in the physical system that governs the integration of perception and the psychological (cognitive and affective) concomitants of "mind."

Specifically, it is proposed that inherent in all of us is a physiological information-processing system that integrates the perceptions of sensory input and the cognitive components of experience into an associated internal memory network to allow for ecological, healthful, balanced functioning. Optimally, individuals are allowed to choose their current attitudes and actions because the immediate responses are appropriate to current life conditions. All the contributors to a happy and fruitful existence are available when one is able to trust one's own perceptions, bond, experience joy and intimacy, and achieve a sense of greater purpose, service, and connection, however those may be defined. This experience is possible because a physiological mechanism is in place to take any perceptual experience, including disturbance, to a higher level of mental health.

For instance, "George" may have a disagreement with a colleague at work and initially react with anger, negative self-talk, and physical tension. However, he goes home and thinks about it, talks about it, and dreams about it, and after a while it does not bother him any longer. One can say that it has achieved an *adaptive resolution*. That is, what is useful has been learned—stored in the brain with appropriate affect so that it is capable of guiding him in the future. What is useless—the cognitive discord, negative emotions, physical arousal, and tightness—are discarded. When George next sees the colleague, he will respond in a balanced manner that is informed by his insights and internal connections. However, when a trauma occurs, this internal information-processing system may become imbalanced. Without the appropriate internal connections being made, little learning and resolution takes place. The initial perceptions are stored as they were at the time of the original experience, along with all the distortions engendered by the high arousal. A central tenet of EMDR treatment is that if these memories remain unprocessed, they become the basis of current dysfunctional reactions.

The obvious example of unprocessed events contributing directly to current dysfunction can be found in clients suffering from a distinct trauma such as rape or combat—the "Criterion A" events needed to diagnosis posttraumatic stress disorder. The intrusions necessary for the diagnosis of PTSD in those who have experienced a rape may include intrusive images of the rapist, often along with the smell and touch of the rapist's body. In addition, the person has feelings of terror, possibly alternating with feelings of shame and numbness. Unhealed, those who have been raped are trapped in the event of the past, truly unable to choose their present attitude. Even if a beloved and trusted partner unexpectedly touches them in the same way the rapist did, they may startle, cringe, and be flooded with the feelings associated with the rape. For the EMDR therapist, the present dysfunction is caused by a lack of processing of the event.

It is not that they "learned" to feel helpless. In the present moment they are helpless because the perceptions (the stored experience) of the earlier event override them emotionally and physically and trap them into being reactive rather than appropriately responsive to their partner's touch.

The EMDR processing of a rape takes a client emotionally, cognitively, and physiologically through a rapid learning curve that may start with a summation of the self ranging from "I'm worthless. I should have done something" to "I did well . . . He had a knife at my throat and I got out alive . . . The shame is his, not mine"—and from a shame-based feeling of "I'm damaged goods" to a sense of "I'm a resilient and strong woman." The movement is one of psychic growth to a new sense of identity, not merely a simple symptom reduction. The obvious indicators of symptom remission, such as fear and anxiety desensitization, and subsequent lack of intrusions are all natural by-products of the reprocessing of the event.

PERSONALITY DEVELOPMENT AND REORGANIZATION

The assimilation of the event into the associative memory network and accommodation of the client's previous identity to encompass it can be considered the basis of personality development. A clinician using EMDR as a distinct approach is taught to consider personality not as an immovable mountain but rather as an accumulation of characteristic internal patterns and responses. Each of these characteristics is believed to be an interaction between genetic predisposition and experiences. If the responses are appropriate, they are considered to be engendered by adequately processed childhood experiences that have laid the groundwork for adaptive behaviors. If the responses are dysfunctional, they are considered to be engendered by inadequately processed experiences that are activated by current conditions.

These dysfunctional pivotal, or touchstone, memories contain the perceptions that were encoded at the time of the event—images, thoughts and sounds, emotions, physical sensations, and the metaperceptions or self-beliefs. Changes may occur because of sequential reexperiencing. However, just as an unhealed person may have memories of a rape that have been largely unaltered since the day the rape occurred (Lee, Vaillant, Torrey, & Elder, 1995; van der Kolk, Greenberg, Boyd, & Krystal, 1985; van der Kolk, Hopper, & Osterman, 2001), these pivotal early experiences may be encoded with fundamentally unaltered childhood perceptions, regardless of the current age of the client. These earlier perceptions may be accurate depictions of reality, or they may be intrinsically distorted because of the engendered affect, or an interaction of the experience and previously encoded dysfunction. Regardless, inappropriate fears of abandonment, lack of love, fear of failure, and all the ubiquitous psychic pains that mar a person's present existence can generally be traced to early childhood experiences physically stored in the brain. Those individuals who have PTSD are comparatively the lucky ones. They have the intrusive images that allow them to be aware of the genesis of their fears. Other clients have only the thoughts, emotions, or associated physical sensations released into consciousness; they are gripped by the past without knowing how or why.

Astute clinicians know these facts intuitively because they have noted that their clients lapse into the demeanor or tones of childhood when speaking of certain problems and concerns. The condition of childhood is one of powerlessness in a world of giants. An internal locus of control is a thing of fantasy—not ecology. That these childhood affects are literally stored in the brain becomes obvious when one deliberately accesses an unprocessed childhood event. For instance, in every workshop I have given in the past 5 years, I have asked, "Who in the audience remembers having been humiliated some time in grade school?" Easily 95% of the participants raise their hands, regardless of the country or venue in which the workshop is being conducted. I then say, "Close your eyes, and notice how your body feels. Now, bring up the humiliation from grade school, and notice what happens in your body. Notice the thoughts that come up about it." During the debriefing, many people note that their body cringed or they felt the rising heat of some of the emotions they experienced at the time of the original event. Others had the same thoughts they remember having at that time.

In all of these instances, we would say that the early memory has not been processed. When the audience members considered the characteristics of the event, they may have found that the tendrils of the past had wrapped around their present. Perhaps the event contributes to current problems with authority, a fear of being scrutinized in public, or difficulties walking into a room or meeting a group of people. The stored emotion and physical sensations of the early event arise and are reexperienced in the present when a similar event occurs.

Simply put, the present is perceived through the lenses of the past. Anything that happens to us in the present has to physiologically link up in the memory network with past events to be understood or recognized. The perceptions of observing a cup in the present link up with our previous "cup" experiences in order to know what do with it. If the appearance is too dissimilar, its function will not be realized. Furthermore, if a person's childhood included experiences of being hit on the head with a cup, then the past childhood fear may be presently associated with the current perception of the cup. The fear may arise in the mind and body without the person knowing why, but it would be real and palpable in the present. Rather than (or, in certain instances, in addition to) simple conditioning, the information-processing paradigm posits that it is the early perceptions of the events that are stored and triggered.

Not only is fear engendered from certain childhood experiences, but all the complexity of the stored childhood perception may be experienced in the present. A man may feel frightened and intensely humiliated when confronted with an angry authority figure because his stored early memories include being beaten by his father. A woman may feel helpless or incessantly angry in a current relationship because of a domineering sibling. The level of intelligence, education, or spiritual development is unimportant in this equation. Essentially, discrete development of a particular characteristic response has been arrested at the level of the childhood event. The responses are due simply to the emergence of the dysfunctional stored material which makes the past, present. These habitual patterns of response and perception become identified as personal characteristics. As pervasive responses, they are identified as personality traits. Nevertheless, each is the sum of its parts and as such, every etiological event and those that have accreted around it can be directly targeted and treated.

Clients who have experienced a single-event trauma or a single class of events are relatively easy to treat with EMDR. Controlled research has found that approximately 85% to 100% of those with this class of civilian PTSD can be effectively treated in the equivalent of three 90-minute sessions (e.g., Ironson, Freund, Strauss, & Williams, 2002; Marcus, Marquis, & Sakai, 1997; Rothbaum, 1997; Wilson, Becker, & Tinker, 1997). Concentrating on a single event or one that represents a distinctly similar cluster of experiences can allow the positive treatment effects to generalize and integrate within the rest of the adaptive networks. However, if a child was pervasively humiliated, abused, and violated throughout childhood, the entire personality may be configured in this arrested form. The emotions and physical sensations of myriad childhood events can be triggered by a wide variety of circumstances. Consequently, nonadaptive responses and behaviors emerge consistently without volition or conscious awareness of their genesis.

Although an adult, the client may be characteristically responding as a child, whether the person is avoiding social contact, unable to distinguish boundaries, dissociating to escape perceived danger, or reacting with ongoing fears of abandonment or helplessness. However, one of the tenets of the information-processing model is that personality constructs change as pivotal memories are sufficiently processed. With adequate preparation, as processing occurs, the adult perspective emerges as a concomitant of the learning that takes place. Unprocessed, or undigested, events are metabolized; what is useful is assimilated, and what is useless is discarded. Although this learning process is not three-session therapy, the experience of clinicians who specialize in personality disorders is that the treatment time is significantly decreased (Manfield, 1998).

Where complex dysfunctional configurations underlie personality disorders, EMDR is used, in addition to processing dysfunctionally stored memories, to incorporate positive affects and experiences in order to fill the gaps and deficits caused by developmental windows that may have closed before needed aspects of personal growth and socialization had taken place. Specifically, traumatized children may have been unable to learn to trust their perceptions, identify appropriate boundaries, develop object constancy and the other multiple characteristics needed to bond, and experience a healthful and joyous life. For these clients, processing dysfunctional memories is insufficient and often initially contraindicated because they do not have enough positive and adaptive networks to allow an adequate assimilation of the event.

Processing itself is the appropriate association of experience and its assimilation into functional comprehensive networks. For clients with extensive abuse and neglect histories, this learning and adaptive resolution cannot take place because they have insufficient internal resources and positive experiences to transform the initial dysfunction. As a consequence of clinical observation, it was fortunately discovered that focused information processing allows negative affects, imagery, beliefs, and sensations to become weaker and less valid, while positive affects, imagery, beliefs, and sensations strengthen and become more robust (Shapiro, 1989a, 1991, 1995). Consequently, EMDR has been used to strengthen positive resources (Korn & Leeds, in press; Leeds, 1998; Leeds & Shapiro, 2000; Phillips, 2001; Shapiro, 1991, 1995, 2001) in preparation for processing dysfunctional material and to incorporate positive templates for current and future functioning (Shapiro, 1999, 2001).

EMDR's ability to enhance affects and imagery and build resiliency for processing requires greater investigation to determine the way it can best aid the development of the psychic infrastructure needed to overcome years of childhood neglect and abuse. Once again, this goal underscores the need for a greater integration of orientations. The wisdom of the psychodynamic and child development communities is needed to identify the experiences pivotal to producing a healthy, joyous, and loving adult. These experiences need to be engendered and enhanced within the therapeutic process. Whereas neurobiological deficits have been identified in those who have experienced profound deprivation and abuse (Perry, 1997; Perry, Pollard, Blakley, Baker, & Vigilante, 1995; Schore, 1994, 1997, 2001; Siegel, 1999), the degree to which EMDR can be used to remediate these problems should be explored (Schore, Siegel, Shapiro, & van der Kolk, 1998; Shapiro, 2001, 2002). The degree to which not only the suffering of victims, but also subsequent potential perpetrator activity can be reduced has major implications on local and global levels (see Appendixes A, B, C).

Incorporated into an overview of the EMDR treatment is the notion that relatively few clients are permanently damaged, since the information-processing system is intrinsic and adaptive. Once the appropriate memories are accessed and the information-processing system is stimulated and maintained in a dynamic form, the stored perceptions generally transform into an adaptive resolution. This underscores the notion that no client is expendable and, the hope that with enough conjoint effort to pool the collective wisdom of the field, no client has to be left behind.

NATURE AND NURTURE

Determining which events may cause lasting, negative effects deserves intensive investigation. For example, recall the example of people who remember being humiliated in childhood. Certainly, all the participants did not have negative reactions. Some found that they smiled at their own antics or had spontaneous thoughts, such as "That person shouldn't have been teaching" or other appropriate adult responses to a historically past event of little importance. We would say that these people have sufficiently processed the events. Rather than having encapsulated within them the childhood affect, physical responses, and perspectives, these events have already been successfully integrated within an adaptive network. The nature of the experience might have been the same, but the result of the interaction was different.

Many factors may explain the range of impact. Perhaps similar negative events have different effects on various individuals because of genetic predispositions, the number and type of preceding events that may have engendered a greater resiliency, or a corrective emotional experience that may have occurred within a window of opportunity immediately following the event. For instance, perhaps a person who was teased in school had a friend immediately provide comforting words, whereas another may have merely been ostracized. Perhaps some people have a predisposition to higher reactivity just as some have weaknesses in cardiac or respiratory systems. Perhaps some people had previous experiences that have sufficiently bolstered their self-esteem, whereas others had experiences that supported the notion they were not good enough. Perhaps the environment played an important role in a particular event. For example, a child may have been awakened unexpectedly early the day of the event and was therefore particularly tired and so was more profoundly affected. As the eloquent Vince Lombardi is reported to have said, "Fatigue makes cowards of us all."

Whatever the reason, it is not only clear that individuals respond differently to similar events but also that there can be no clear definition of "*trauma*" other than "any event that has a lasting negative effect on the self or psyche." Therefore, part of the EMDR work is to process any negatively contributing experience. Substantially, any event can be a trauma. We may designate the Criterion A events that define a PTSD diagnosis as "Big T" traumas because they are easily recognizable. However, any of the ubiquitous experiences of childhood can qualify as a "Small t" trauma (Shapiro, 1995, 2001; Shapiro & Forrest, 1997). What may seem to an adult to be of negligible importance may have been extremely important for a developing child. In fact, if a person remembers the scene of a childhood humiliation, it is clear that to the child it was not an insignificant event. In fact, to extend even further into the realm of speculation, it is possible that the reason so many of these childhood experiences have a lasting effect is that the information-processing system became overwhelmed by survival fear. This concept is certainly recognizable as the precursor of diagnosed PTSD. However, as an underlying cause of so many adult-related complaints, it may simply mean that being humiliated in childhood is the evolutionary equivalent of being "cut out of the herd," which stimulates arousal corresponding to fears of survival.

The same may be true of the events that can be categorized as catalyzing fears of abandonment, lack of love, or inability to succeed. Underneath all of these fears may lurk a simple survival instinct. Given the evolutionary imperative of parental care and nurturing during childhood and perhaps an intrinsic need for group assimilation and identification, any event that threatens coherence can cause these experiences to be stored with a fight-or-flight arousal that signifies danger. As previously noted, this encapsulation of the childhood perspective remains substantially intact until the event is subsequently processed to an adaptive resolution. Therefore, even though what was potentially dangerous for a child is no longer dangerous for the adult, it is the stored perceptions that dominate. There seems to be little physiological differentiation between the triggered fear inherent in the stored past event and a reality-based fear evoked in the present.

The lack of differentiation between the somatic response of past and present is pivotal to the nonadaptive feedback loop enveloping the client. For instance, a woman may have been verbally abused and hit by her mother all through childhood. If these experiences were not processed, the physical sensations of danger that were previously appropriate are physiologically stored. As an adult, just the sight of the mother or anyone resembling the mother could bring up the same physiological feelings of danger and not only color the present perception of reality but also reinforce the previous experience. Locked into the same configuration that was stored in childhood, the same feelings of abuse could be experienced, and she would not be able to assert herself, walk away, set boundaries, or evoke any of the positive reactions of a healthy adult. The past becomes repeated in the present and reinforces itself by second-order conditioning of any associated stimuli, in addition to an elicitation of current autonomic responses related to danger; indeed, because of the dysfunctional responses, the client cannot defend herself. Although the woman may attempt to gain cognitive control, she has no ability to choose the autonomic responses in the present. They are biochemically dictated by the stored past events.

Although EMDR is not a treatment of choice for disorders that are purely organic (such as systemic deficits related to learning disabilities and certain forms of depression), what may seem to be the result of neurological imbalances requiring medication is often merely experientially stored traumata. For example, one woman in her 60s experienced chronic depression her whole life (Shapiro & Forrest, 1997). The depression lifted after the processing of a memory in which her mother pointedly favored her brother and left her feeling as though "the stars and the sun had dropped out the sky." Because she lived in a country where women were generally regarded as second-class citizens, she had ample opportunities for this previous memory to be triggered and reinforced, which resulted in lifelong depression and feeling of repression—even after she had grown, had married, had moved to another country, and was no longer subject to the previous restraints.

It is posited in EMDR's information-processing theory that in situations such as those of the woman just described, depression can deepen and become less manageable over time because more and more experiences are being stored in the same dysfunctional network. Regardless of whether new "objectively" traumatizing events occur, the previous experiences of helplessness and hopelessness are stored and triggered in the present. The feelings of despair and depression that arise color the perceptions of the present and are themselves sequentially stored. As new experiences emerge and trigger the associated memories, the load gets greater and greater as each new experience of helplessness is stored with its own set of dysfunctional affects. Consequently, the negative self-perceptions of one who is helpless and hopeless become reinforced and stored in turn, which exacerbates the affect state termed *depression*. This intermixture of past and present is a feedback loop based on stored somatic responses, which causes the person to be more traumatized each time the responses are experienced. Thus, a childhood event that might be considered unimportant by adult standards can give rise to increasing symptomology because of this sequence.

The ubiquitous nature of "Small t" experiences and their contribution to various diagnostic categories has become clear during the past decade with EMDR. For example, body dysmorphic disorder is characterized by a severely distorted view of personal appearance. The client may believe that a limb or facial feature is obviously and intensely repulsive, but nothing appears problematic to an objective observer. The dysfunctional perspective is responsible for many unnecessary "corrective" surgeries and suicides borne of despair. It is traditionally considered a relatively difficult disorder to treat, and proposed treatment regimens are long and have varying success rates (Neziroglu, McKay, Todaro, & Yaryura-Tobias, 1996; Veale et al.,

1996; Wilhelm, Otto, Lohr, & Deckersbach, 1999). Nevertheless, when EMDR was used for seven consecutive people with the disorder, five of the seven clients had a complete remission of symptoms within one to three sessions (Brown, McGoldrick, & Buchanan, 1997). The standard EMDR protocol was used to target the first time the clients remembered experiencing their belief that something was wrong with them.

For example, a woman had a 24-year history of believing that she was covered with unsightly hair (Brown et al., 1997). Her social life and general functioning had deteriorated over time, and she spent hours each day looking in the mirror and plucking out every visible hair before she was willing to appear in public. The belief, emotion, and physical reactivity to her appearance changed after three EMDR sessions and were maintained at a 1-year follow-up. The identified target was the etiological event: Her aunt had made a disparaging remark about her underarm hair.

What biochemical interaction of nature, nurture, and environmental pressure was necessary to cause this remark to overwhelm the client's information-processing system? The factors that allow these types of experiences to be encoded in a way that alters a client's perceptions for the succeeding decades are worthy of future investigation. Nevertheless, only the internal reorganization attendant to the rapid processing of the event was necessary to allow a complete remission and return to adaptive functioning. Essentially, this case typifies the EMDR approach to pathology. It is assumed that an etiological event is dysfunctionally encoded in the memory system. During processing, the relevant connections and associations generally reveal themselves to the client, and the person experiences a rapid transmutation from dysfunctional perception, affect, and physical arousal to healthy perceptual and emotional states.

ASSOCIATIVE NATURE OF MEMORY

The rapid processing that EMDR affords generally reveals to the client's consciousness the interconnectedness of memories. As previously noted, recognition, understanding, and learning all require that experiences in the present link up in associated memory networks with experiences of the past. The associative nature of consciousness has been well documented in science and in literature. The novels of Henry James and his hallmark delineation of processive consciousness can sensitize readers to their own memory processes. An increased awareness of the associative nature of memory can also be accomplished by simply attempting to meditate. Try as they might, beginning meditators find that merely concentrating on "nothing" or their own breathing is futile. The mind wanders off into its own direction. One thought leads to another and another until the meditator finally remembers the purpose of sitting quietly is to meditate. These associative memory channels are the heart of EMDR because the instigation of processing allows clients to rapidly associate along the pathway needed to clear the dysfunction (Shapiro, 1989a, 1989b, 1999, 2001). The following transcript of a client with PTSD (Popky & Levin, 1994) illustrates the process.

CASE STUDY

"Lynne" is in her mid-30s and is seeking therapy to get rid of the fears she developed from an earthquake she experienced 2 years ago. Psychological testing has indicated a diagnosis of PTSD and a clinically significant *Impact of Event* scale score of 41. She remembers being troubled by previous earthquakes, but she became extremely afraid and had intrusive thoughts only after the last one. One of her earthquake experiences took place when she was in college. Her professor had just put her under hypnosis when the earthquake struck.

The therapist has assisted Lynne with identifying a disturbing image (hiding in a doorway) and a negative belief, which is, "I'm helpless—out of control." The positive belief she would prefer to have is, "I can handle what comes up." On a scale of 1 to 7, in which 1 is completely false and 7 is completely true, Lynne currently considers the positive statement to be a 2, or almost completely false. She also states that she is feeling a high level of anxiety (an 8 on a scale of 0 to 10 subjective units of disturbance [SUD], in which 0 represents no disturbance and 10 represents the worst disturbance she can imagine; Wolpe, 1958). With the therapist's guidance, Lynne concentrates on the image, negative belief, and physical sensations she is feeling, and then the therapist guides her in sets of eye movements. After each set, the therapist gives her brief instructions and asks her to talk about what comes to mind. The transcript that follows describes the first reprocessing session. The sets of eye movements and instructions are designated by **********. Statements in [brackets] are additional clinical aspects that may be particularly interesting for the reader.

****

Therapist: Blank it out and take a deep breath. What are you noticing now?

[After each set of eye movements, Lynne is given this sequence of instructions before she is asked to talk about her experience.]

Lynne: Ah. Sort of a softness in my body. I'm . . . more aware . . . my legs feel really heavy. Sort of a sinking kind of feeling in my legs—they just feel kind of woozy.

[A hallmark of EMDR therapy is that sensations that were part of associated events might arise in the client's body. Because one of the associated memories of earthquakes included being placed under hypnosis, the feeling Lynne identifies in her legs may be related to the hypnosis or a childhood event that she later describes.]

Therapist: Concentrate on that.

Lynne: Okay.

****

Therapist: What are you getting now?

Lynne: Umm. The first thing that occurred to me was just a tape that I listened to about the people who work on trains and have to watch people get smashed by trains. That's the first thing that occurred to me. Ah, ah . . . then I just started being more aware of my body again. Not having another thought.

[Other associations related to lack of control begin to arise.]

Therapist: Okay. Concentrate on that.

Lynne: Okay. Mmm.

****

Therapist: What are you noticing now?

Lynne: Um. More tiredness in my upper body. Um . . . softness. Sadness . . . kind . . . sadness . . . sad, kind of sad, melancholy feeling.

[It is important to note that the anxiety Lynne originally identified as accompanying the memory is often a catch-all phrase for various emotions that are under the surface.]

Therapist: Concentrate on that.

Lynne: Okay.

****

Therapist: What . . . now?

Lynne: Um. I just flashed on the earthquake happening. The one that happened in '89 where I was in the class and I was under and the earthquake happened. I thought about it.

[Although the first earthquake she experienced is the one being directly targeted, the second associated earthquake also emerges into consciousness.]

Therapist: Think about that.

****

Lynne: Just feeling really tired. My body feeling, noticing my body, really tired.

Therapist: Okay. Concentrate on that.

****

Lynne: (laughing) I was thinking about running around my house when I was 6. My brother and I were running around the house, and I wanted to be a boy, and he told me if I ran around the house enough times, I would be a boy. And I was disappointed because it didn't happen.

Therapist: Okay. Think about that.

Lynne: (laughing) Okay.

****

Lynne: Yeah, I was thinking about my sense of betrayal with my brother that he molested me and how I really admired him. (crying)

[Although on the surface, the first memory of her brother that emerged seems to be humorous, the deeper issue of betrayal becomes revealed. Indeed, even in the first instance, she trusted him, and he lied to her.]

Therapist: Concentrate on that. Just let whatever happens happen. Just notice.

Lynne: Okay. (deep breath)

****

Lynne: Yeah. (crying) I was just thinking about ... Something occurred to me like "duh": How much—that it shook my sense of reality.

[The exquisite internal memory connections are revealed: An earthquake, in which the ground is literally shaken, was associated with the internal sense of chaos created in her childhood when those she trusted betrayed her. In both instances, what should have been a firm foundation was shaken.]

Therapist: Notice that.

Lynne: Okay.

****

Lynne: I was thinking about playing cards with my dad across the table from one another.

Therapist: Okay. Concentrate on that.

****

Lynne: I was thinking about my dad taking me to buy a coat and buttoning the button of my coat . . . and pinching my nipple when I was like, 11, and how absolutely stunned I was with that.

[Once again, although the first memory of her father seemed to be innocuous, an additional association of betrayal is revealed. Every client is briefed regarding the fallibility of memory. A person cannot know whether a memory is historically accurate without present corroboration. However, in EMDR therapy, it is assumed that whatever emerges is meaningful for the client, whether it is the result of actual assaults, vicarious traumatization, dream images, or fantasy. Therefore, without any judgment on the part of the clinician, the reprocessing simply continues.]

Therapist: Okay. Let's go with that.

****

Lynne: Ah. I was having more of a thought. Not an image or anything. Just a thought of . . . oh. Now, something came up just now . . . which one do I go with?

Therapist: Whatever one you want.

[This is a fine example of the client-centered, nonleading aspects of EMDR.]

Lynne: Yeah. What comes really clear—is getting sick when I was around the same age. Getting really sick with a pain in my side and nobody being able to figure out what it was and being rushed to the hospital. I really couldn't lower my leg, and no one could decide what was wrong with me. I had a really bad pain in my side, and then they just decided that I had some kind of mental problem. I guess that was the only way that I could express it. (crying)

[Note the associations of this memory to the concepts of lack of control and shaken reality. She knew she had a bad pain, but no one believed her. Their conclusion was that she could not trust her own perceptions. Again, she was betrayed and had no firm ground on which to stand. In addition, note that the childhood problem with her leg might be associated with the sensations in her leg that emerged during the first sets of eye movement. Often the source of the physical sensations that come to a client's consciousness are not revealed until the later stages of processing.]

Therapist: Concentrate on that.

****

Lynne: Ah. Gosh, I was just thinking what a chaotic place it was to live in and what an unsafe place it was to be.

[Her memories of her childhood home resonate with a sense of chaos and lack of safety.]

Therapist: Think about that.

****

Lynne: I was thinking of my mom and dad fighting and throwing things at one another while we were supposed to be in bed asleep. Hiding under the bed and trying to go to sleep and being afraid.

[The image of the frightened child hiding under the bed resonates with the initial image of hiding in the doorway surrounded by the chaos of falling objects during the earthquake.]

Therapist: Focus on that.

****

Lynne: I was thinking about how I wanted to protect my dad from my mother. 'Cause it just seemed really crazy.

Therapist: Think about that.

****

Lynne: It kind of came back up to the earthquake in '87 and jumping out of the shower and running in and grabbing my son Tim out of the crib and running with him downstairs and trying to protect him.

[This is an interesting parallel—protecting both her son and her father.]

Therapist: Good. Think about that.

****

Lynne: I was thinking about needing to protect Tim when he's with his dad. His dad is bipolar. He's diagnosed now and on lithium. How I used to really worry about letting him be with his dad and protecting him from his dad at the same time.

[This brings up numerous intriguing questions regarding the association of family of origin and subsequent relationships. Lynne comes from a family in chaos whose stability was consistently being shaken, and she has married a husband with bipolar disorder, which in its own way mimics the reality of her family—the shifting emotions and sense of lack of safety. In addition, she has once again been placed in the role of protector.]

Therapist: Okay. Concentrate on that.

****

Lynne: I was thinking about a birthday party that I had for Tim when he was 2 and just watching him walk around kind of really blank.

[After approximately 4 additional associations, the therapist brings Lynne back to the initial target.]

Therapist: Okay. Let's get back to that original incident. How disturbing is it to you now, on a scale of 0 to 10, with 10 as the most disturbing?

Lynne: Right now, right now, I can't really feel it in my body. Let me try to go back into and think of it. Right now, you know, it sounds weird, but it really feels pretty flat right now.

[Once the earlier events are processed, the physical sensations and emotions are no longer problematic. Subsequent responses during memory retrieval underscore its resolution.]

Therapist: Does it?

Lynne: It's like, you know, I can see it. Truly I can see it, but it doesn't really have a feeling component right this second.

Therapist: Okay. That's like a 0?

Lynne: Yeah, it's like there's just nothing there right now.

[After further processing and strengthening of the positive belief, the therapist again asks Lynne to think of the earthquake. The goal is to determine what spontaneously comes to her mind. This reveals how the information of the event is currently physiologically stored in the brain.]

Therapist: Okay, so when you think of that original incident . . .

Lynne: Uh-hum.

Therapist: Standing in the doorway with Tim . . .

Lynne: Yeah.

Therapist: How's that for you?

Lynne: Well, what occurs to me is, yeah, that was an earthquake. (laughing) Yeah, that was an earthquake all right.

As a result of the processing, the SUD decreased from 8 to 0, and *Impact of Event* score decreased from 41 to 0. Both scores remained the same at 1-month, 3-month, and 1-year follow-ups. Although impossible with this research participant, a full course of EMDR treatment would have included attention to all of the memories that emerged during this session. Nevertheless, the extent to which the processing of individual targets can result in a generalization of positive treatment effects is something that needs to be extensively researched. In addition, as demonstrated by this transcript, the ways in which events and beliefs are associated in physiologically stored memory networks can provide decades of extensive investigation on the levels of neurobiology and process evaluation (see Shapiro, 2001, for a more extensive review).

Of course, clinicians reading this transcript who have a psychodynamic perspective should have no trouble identifying the genesis of Lynne's fears in her early childhood memories and her apparent free association and cathartic response. Although beginning with a present disturbance, the past associations came to mind with no urging or predetermination by the therapist. From a different vantage point, a behaviorist would identify the association of stimulus/response conditioning patterns. A cognitivist would identify a defining thread in her beliefs: "I'm not in control, and I'm not safe in my world." An experiential therapist would identify the client-centered aspects of the therapy, a systems therapist would recognize the interactional ramifications, and a body-oriented therapist would note the interconnection of physical sensations and perceptual reality. However, what is not clear from the transcript is that all of these paradigms are specifically integrated in the EMDR procedures that are guided by the information-processing model. The procedures are more fully explored in the next chapter.

REFERENCES

Brown, K. W., McGoldrick, T., & Buchanan, R. (1997). Body dysmorphic disorder: Seven cases treated with eye movement desensitization and reprocessing. *Behavioural & Cognitive Psychotherapy, 25,* 203–207.

Frankl, V. E. (1959/1984). *Man's search for meaning.* New York: Washington Square Press.

Hyer, L. (1994). The trauma response: Its complexity and dimensions. In L. Hyer (Ed.), *Trauma victim: Theoretical issues and practical suggestions* (pp. 27–91). Muncie, IN: Accelerated Development.

Ironson, G. I., Freund, B., Strauss, J. L., & Williams, J. (2002). A comparison of two treatments for traumatic stress: A pilot study of EMDR and prolonged exposure. *Journal of Clinical Psychology, 58,* 113–128.

Korn, D. L., & Leeds, A. M. (in press). Preliminary evidence of efficacy for EMDR resource development and installation in the stabilization phase of treatment of complex posttraumatic stress disorder. *Journal of Clinical Psychology.*

Lee, K. A., Vaillant, G. E., Torrey, W. C., & Elder, G. H. (1995). A 50-year prospective study of the psychological sequelae of World War II combat. *American Journal of Psychiatry, 152,* 516–522.

Leeds, A. M. (1998). Lifting the burden of shame: Using EMDR resource installation to resolve a therapeutic impasse. In P. Manfield (Ed.), *Extending EMDR: A casebook of innovative applications* (pp. 256–281). New York: Norton.

Leeds, A. M., & Shapiro, F. (2000). EMDR and resource installation: Principles and procedures for enhancing current functioning and resolving traumatic experiences. In J. Carlson & L. Sperry (Eds.), *Brief therapy strategies with individuals and couples* (pp. 469–534). Phoenix, AZ: Zeig/Tucker.

Manfield, P. (Ed.). (1998). *Extending EMDR*. New York: Norton.

Marcus, S. V., Marquis, P., & Sakai, C. (1997). Controlled study of treatment of PTSD using EMDR in an HMO setting. *Psychotherapy, 34,* 307–315.

Neziroglu, F., McKay, D., Todaro, J., & Yaryura-Tobias, J. A. (1996). Effect of cognitive behavior therapy on persons with body dsymorphic disorder and comorbid axis II diagnoses. *Behavior Therapy, 27,* 67–77.

Perry, B. (1997). Incubated in terror: Neurodevelopmental factors in the cycle of violence. In J. Osofsky (Ed.), *Children, youth and violence: Searching for solutions* (pp. 124–149). New York: Guilford.

Perry, B., Pollard, R., Blakley, T., Baker, W., & Vigilante, D. (1995). Childhood trauma, the neurobiology of adaptation, and "use-dependent" development of the brain: How "states" become "traits." *Infant Mental Health Journal, 16,* 271–290.

Phillips, M. (2001). Potential contributions of hypnosis to ego-strengthening procedures in EMDR. *American Journal of Clinical Hypnosis, 43,* 247–262.

Popky, A. J., & Levin, C. (1994). [Transcript of EMDR treatment session.] MRI EMDR Research Center, Palo Alto, CA.

Rothbaum, B. O. (1997). A controlled study of eye movement desensitization and reprocessing for posttraumatic stress disordered sexual assault victims. *Bulletin of the Menninger Clinic, 61,* 317–334.

Schore, A. N. (1994). *Affect regulation and the origin of self: The neurobiology of emotional development.* Hillsdale, NJ: Erlbaum.

Schore, A. N. (1997). Early organization of the nonlinear right brain and development of a predisposition to psychiatric disorders. *Development and Psychopathology, 9,* 595–631.

Schore, A. N. (2001). The effects of early relational trauma on right brain development, affect regulation, and infant mental health. *Infant Mental Health Journal, 22,* 201–269.

Schore, A. N., Siegel, D. J., Shapiro, F., & van der Kolk, B. A. (1998, January). *Developmental and neurobiological underpinnings of trauma.* Plenary panel presented at Understanding and Treating Trauma: Developmental and Neurobiological Approaches Conference, Los Angeles.

Seligman, M. E. P. (1995). *What you can change and what you can't.* New York: Fawcett.

Shalev, A. Y., Bonne, O., & Eth, S. (1996). Treatment of posttraumatic stress disorder: A review. *Psychosomatic Medicine, 58,* 165–182.

Shapiro, F. (1989a). Efficacy of the eye movement desensitization procedure in the treatment of traumatic memories. *Journal of Traumatic Stress Studies, 2,* 199–223.

Shapiro, F. (1989b). Eye movement desensitization: A new treatment for posttraumatic stress disorder. *Journal of Behavior Therapy and Experimental Psychiatry, 20,* 211–217.

Shapiro, F. (1991). Eye movement desensitization and reprocessing procedure: From EMD to EMDR: A new treatment model for anxiety and related traumata. *Behavior Therapist, 14,* 133–135.

Shapiro, F. (1995). *Eye movement desensitization and reprocessing: Basic principles, protocols and procedures* (1st ed.). New York: Guilford Press.

Shapiro, F. (1999). Eye movement desensitization reprocessing (EMDR) and the anxiety disorders: Clinical and research implications of an integrated psychotherapy treatment. *Journal of Anxiety Disorders, 13,* 35–67.

Shapiro, F. (2001). *Eye movement desensitization and reprocessing: Basic principles, protocols and procedures* (2nd ed.). New York: Guilford Press.

Shapiro, F. (2002). EMDR twelve years after its introduction: Past and future research. *Journal of Clinical Psychology, 58,* 1–22.

Shapiro, F., & Forrest, M. (1997). *EMDR.* New York: Basic Books.

Siegel, D. J. (1999). *The developing mind: Toward a neurobiology of interpersonal experience.* New York: Guilford Press.

Solomon, S. D., Gerrity, E. T., & Muff, A. M. (1992). Efficacy of treatments for posttraumatic stress disorder. *Journal of the American Medical Association, 268,* 633–638.

van der Kolk, B. A. (1996). Trauma and memory. In B. A. van der Kolk, A. C. McFarlane, & L. Weisaeth, (Eds.), *Traumatic stress: The effects of overwhelming experience on mind, body, and society* (pp. 279–302). New York: Guilford Press.

van der Kolk, B. A., Greenberg, M., Boyd, H., & Krystal, J. (1985). Inescapable shock, neurotransmitters, and addiction to trauma: Toward a psychobiology of posttraumatic stress. *Biological Psychiatry, 20,* 314–325.

van der Kolk, B. A., Hopper, J. W., & Osterman, J. A. (2001). Exploring the nature of traumatic memory: Combining clinical knowledge and laboratory methods. *Journal of Aggression, Maltreatment, and Trauma. 4,* 9–31.

Veale, D., Gournay, K., Dryden, W., Boocock, A., Shah, F., Willson, R., et al. (1996). Body dysmorphic disorder: A cognitive behavioural model and pilot randomised controlled trial. *Behaviour Research and Therapy, 34,* 717–729.

Wilhelm, S., Otto, M. W., Lohr, B., & Deckersbach, T. (1999). Cognitive behavior group therapy for body dysmorphic disorder: A case series. *Behaviour Research and Therapy, 37,* 71–75.

Wilson, S. A., Becker, L. A., & Tinker, R. H. (1997). Fifteen-month follow-up of eye movement desensitization and reprocessing (EMDR) treatment for PTSD and psychological trauma. *Journal of Consulting and Clinical Psychology, 65,* 1047–1056.

Wolpe, J. (1958). *Psychotherapy by reciprocal inhibition.* Stanford, CA: Stanford University Press.

2

EMDR TREATMENT: OVERVIEW AND INTEGRATION

FRANCINE SHAPIRO

EMDR is not viewed as a panacea but rather as a comprehensive approach to be applied to experiential contributors of disorder and self-enhancement. The information-processing model that governs EMDR practice invites clinicians to view the overall client picture to identify the past events that contribute to the dysfunction, the present events that trigger disturbance, and the skills and internal resources that need to be incorporated for healthy and adaptive living in the future. The approach to the clinical picture is termed the *adaptive information-processing model* (Shapiro, 2001a). It was previously termed the *accelerated information-processing model* (Shapiro, 1995) because the rapid learning and transmutation of characteristics can take place without the time limitations accepted and imposed on the previous traditional therapies.

One of the reasons for the approach's rapid effects, however, is that EMDR has evolved into a synthesis of the traditional orientations. It is not that any one element is credited for healing but rather that the complex and integrative procedures and protocols incorporate elements of all the major psychological traditions (Shapiro, 1995, 1999, 2001a; Zabukevec, Lazrove, & Shapiro, 2000).

EMDR was not derived from a theoretical perspective or from research experiments. It was initiated by my observation that spontaneously generated eye movements seemed to have a direct effect on my thoughts (Shapiro, 1989). Because the discovery has been addressed in detail in other publications (e.g., Shapiro, 1989, 1995, 2001a; Shapiro & Forrest, 1997), I do not provide a full description in this text. Suffice it to say, I was not the first person to notice these effects. They had previously been documented by well-known dream researchers who were investigating the effects of eye movements in the waking state (Antrobus, Antrobus, & Singer, 1964). In a series of controlled experiments, it was determined that during disturbance, rapid shifts in eye movements are correlated with shifts in cognitive content. Nevertheless, little was made of this observation 40 years ago because no one was investigating the subjective outcomes of these eye movements or their treatment effects.

Since that time, EMDR therapists have discovered that various types of dual-attention stimulation such as hand taps and tones are capable of having the same effects (see Appendixes A and C). In fact, there is a good possibility that the primary common denominator is the attentional element rather than any particular muscle movement (see Lipke, 2000; Shapiro, 1995, 1999, 2001a, 2002; Siegel, chapter 4, this volume; Stickgold, 2002).Therefore, the name *eye movement desensitization and reprocessing* is unfortunate in many ways. The term *eye movement* is unduly limiting, and the same can be said for the term *desensitization*. Having initially developed the procedures with a behavioral orientation, I first thought that all that was occurring was a desensitization of anxiety. The resulting conditioning model was useful but eventually gave way to one that encompassed more of the clinical phenomena and resulted in a greater ability to successfully predict treatment outcomes. However, the addition of the term *reprocessing* caused its own confusion, in that some people have come to believe that it applies merely to cognitive elements, as opposed to the desensitization of affect. In fact, as explored in the following section, *reprocessing* includes multidimensional change in all psychological domains.

Building on early observations (Shapiro, 1989), ongoing clinical work pointed the way to an information-processing model as it became clear that the anxiety reduction was merely a by-product of the learning that was taking place. In addition, whereas the initial behavioral model dictated attention to the present symptoms and stimuli, the application of EMDR soon taught me the wisdom of the psychodynamic formulation. That is, while targeting a client's present disturbing situation as was done in the previous chapter's transcript, the client generally began a rapid association to previous etiological events. Other clients became merely more disturbed. However, when I invited them to stop and look for early experiential contributors and targeted those events, not only did the disturbance generated by the previous events rapidly decrease, but a return to the present stimulus would find that it was generally no longer disturbing. Both behavioral and psychodynamic traditions were equally embraced and honored by formulating the information-processing model, which explained the treatment effects in terms of the association of memory networks.

Based on clinical experiences, the EMDR protocols therefore call for an initial targeting of the etiological event, and then the present stimuli that may still be problematic because of second-order conditioning. As noted in chapter 1, the etiological event is viewed as encapsulating the perceptions that were inherent at the time of the experience. These unprocessed, dysfunctionally stored perceptions are seen as the foundation of the present pathological response. However, the behavioral conditioning model is well represented, in that due to contemporaneous re-experiencing through voluntary and involuntary memory retrieval, a variety of environmental and proprioceptive triggers become sensitized and may need to be separately processed (see Shapiro, 1995, 2001a).

The cognitive tradition was initially incorporated into EMDR as a way to assess the treatment effects (Shapiro, 1989). If the targeted event was verbally assessed, would it be with a believable negative or positive statement? An important contribution of cognitive therapy (Beck, 1976; Ellis, 1962) has been the recognition that beliefs impact behavior and that altering cognitions can result in change. Certainly, in many instances cognitive reorientation and coping skills are sufficient to remediate a given situation. Consequently, these practices have been integrated into the EMDR protocols. However, for the EMDR treatment of etiological events and triggers, beliefs are not given primacy as causes or change agents but rather are viewed as interpretive of the stored affect. That is, the beliefs are generally viewed as a verbalization of the stored perceptions. Likewise, the incorporation of self–other constructs, which are a hallmark of psychodynamic therapy, are mirrored in the use of the negative and positive cognitions, which reflect: "Who am I in relation to the event?" "How do I judge myself because of my participation?" However, from an information-processing perspective, the global self-interpretive belief is a metaperception in that it is a verbalization of the stored sensory experience, which represents the event. It is assumed that the formulated belief and language itself are unnecessary for traumatization. Certainly beliefs can contribute to the stored negative affect. Obviously, however, infants can be traumatized at precognitive stages, and children at preverbal stages (for detailed descriptions of nondeclarative memory systems, see LeDoux, 1996; Squire, 1992).

In EMDR treatment, it is the stored perceptions of the etiological event, which are largely defined by the predominant affect, that are considered to be at the core of the dysfunction. That is, the affective response to a survival threat can occur independently of a higher cortical analysis of the stimulus as dangerous (LeDoux, 1996). In EMDR, affect is viewed as the composite experience of the physiological response. Even the designation of a specific emotion is considered to be merely a cognitive label that delineates or interprets the response in relation to societal or contextual descriptors. That is, the range of affect is the full and subjective array of physiological responses to internal and external cues. Just as the words *red*, *blue*, and *green* cannot describe the wide variegation of all possible hues (e.g., the subtle distinctions between different combinations of blue and green), language that delineates a specific emotion is too limiting to express the full range of affective experience. This is one reason that the emphasis in EMDR is placed on body sensations rather than on language. Its emphasis on affect also underscores the relationship between EMDR and the experiential therapies.

Given the limitations of language and the delineation of independent memory systems, in the processing of a stored etiological memory the verbalized belief is considered to be a manifestation of the stored perceptions and not the cause of the disturbance. In fact, most clients know their affective response is inaccurate and unreasonable, or they would not have sought therapy. It is this affective–cognitive split that is the key to much dysfunction. Nevertheless, beliefs that are at the core of the field of cognitive therapy have great therapeutic utility and are incorporated within the EMDR protocols. For instance, they are used to identify targets for processing and for stimulating the negative and positive memory networks (see Shapiro, 2001a). The same is true of all the orientations represented in this book. Each orientation brings to EMDR a unique contribution and is considered integrally important to the overall treatment effects. Although distinct in its approach and theory of development, EMDR can be considered a nexus that draws on each major orientation.

EIGHT PHASES OF TREATMENT

Basically, EMDR is considered to be a constantly refining and evolving treatment approach. While honoring the distinct contributions of each major psychological orientation, EMDR integrates them and seeks to develop the most robust and comprehensive treatment possible. Consequently, clinicians of all orientations will find some aspect of their own favored modality in EMDR. Further, pending additional rigorous investigations of the proposed neurobiological underpinnings of experientially based disorders, it is hoped that the adaptive information-processing model can potentially serve as a theory for integrative practice which will be able to explain, explore, and elicit the clinical phenomena both sought for and most valued in each of the individual approaches. However, the model is not the method. Whether or not the information-processing formulation is adopted, EMDR procedures can be utilized within the framework of a multitude of orientations. For, as briefly explicated in this section, the various phases of EMDR treatment embody aspects of all the traditional modalities. This overview identifies the therapeutic phases and procedures that are referenced by the chapter authors. For those readers already familiar with the EMDR procedures, it should serve to clarify some common misconceptions and provide updates on theory and practice.

The overall goal of EMDR therapy is to achieve the most profound and comprehensive treatment effects possible while maintaining a stable client within a balanced social system. It is therefore imperative that the EMDR clinician address the entire clinical picture and judiciously proceed with each phase of stabilization, metabolization, and reintegration (Herman, 1992a, 1992b). Client preparation, appropriate selection and prioritization of processing targets, procedural fidelity, and clinical sensitivity are all integral aspects of successful EMDR therapy. However, although procedures such as taking a client's history, preparation, and re-evaluation are common designations for aspects of treatment in all orientations, the content of the phases is distinct for each practitioner's paradigm. For example, a psychodynamic practitioner would ask different questions while taking a client's history than a cognitive–behavioral therapist or an experiential therapist. Likewise, EMDR clinicians focus on different information to orchestrate optimal information processing. This distinction is true in each of the eight phases.

Phase 1: Client History and Treatment Planning

The goal of the first of the eight EMDR phases is to thoroughly screen and assess clients' readiness to benefit from therapy and identify the optimal clinical goals. In this process, it is important to determine whether they are acquiring any secondary gains from their stated problem. If so, these issues are addressed by formulating a concrete plan of action that includes the use of explicit behaviors for addressing any reality-based fear issues. In the next part of this phase, the therapist appraises the entire clinical picture (e.g., dysfunctional behaviors, symptoms, characteristics) to identify and prioritize for sequential processing the therapeutic targets that seem to set the basis for the pathology. This phase includes an assessment of the strength of the clients' inner resources and a delineation of the positive experiences and present support systems. These factors are used to stabilize the clients and on an as-needed basis to aid subsequent processing (see Shapiro, 2001a, for a complete delineation of phases and procedures).

As previously noted, the term *processing* in the context of EMDR treatment refers to active learning. In EMDR, it is assumed that human beings possess an information-processing system that is capable of responding to and resolving everyday minor emotional disturbances. However, a traumatic event can lead to an imbalance in this system, causing the associated information (e.g., memories, visual images, somatic and other perceptual experiences) to seem locked in, or frozen, in the form it took at the time of the event, impervious to the normal resolving powers of the brain. Thus, this state-dependent information remains in what can be referred to as *neurobiological stasis*, in which the neurological connections that would normally allow its resolution fail to occur (van der Kolk, Greenberg, Boyd, & Krystal, 1985; van der Kolk, Hopper, & Osterman, 2001). Processing (or reprocessing) is thus defined in EMDR as the act of stimulating the information-processing system so that the associations required for learning can be forged.

To achieve an adaptive resolution, three criteria must be met. First, the clients must succeed in extracting from the earlier experience its practical lessons (e.g., an awareness of the situations and people they should avoid in the future), develop a new self-awareness, and release the self-denigrating and useless psychological baggage (e.g., debilitating emotional disturbances, unpleasant sensations, fallacious cognitions) that accompany the targeted experience. Second, clients must acquire (or reacquire) the ability to experience the appropriate affect with respect to the traumatic event. Finally, clients must demonstrate that they are capable of effectively guiding their future actions. In other words, have the clients experienced enough personal growth to allow them to enjoy life, bond, work, love, and experience a sense of personal connectedness and balance?

The aim of EMDR is not only to target and resolve the pathological memories, emotions, perceptions, and cognitions associated with the traumatic event but also to address the present situations that evoke emotional disturbances and to educate the clients about the specific skills and behaviors required for a healthy life. On the basis of much clinical evidence concerning the generalization of therapeutic effects, it has become clear that it is unnecessary for every one of a client's dysfunctional memories to be targeted by the therapist. If a group of similar experiences (e.g., several related instances of molestation by the same person) can be identified, it may be necessary to treat only one of them. However, if a client has experienced various separate and dissimilar traumatic events, generalization of treatment effects should not be expected, and each event needs to be reprocessed separately (see Shapiro, 1995, 2001a).

As described in the transcript of Lynne, the woman who was traumatized by an earthquake (see chapter 1), numerous childhood events can be targets for treating the overarching theme of helplessness and lack of control. Although positive treatment effects would be expected because of a generalization among the associated memories, a thorough intervention would target the pivotal events, including the molestation, somatic complaints, and relationship issues. Given Lynne's childhood history and her resulting emotional and behavioral characteristics, she would probably need education in areas such as establishing appropriate boundaries, developing appropriate relationships, and assertiveness skills, in addition to the memory processing. The education could be incorporated into the therapy by first teaching her a skill and then using EMDR processing to assist her with the learning process. These steps create what are termed *future templates* —they invite clients to imagine and cognitively and affectively experience positive future outcomes in previously disturbing situations.

The concentration on clients' current symptoms could be considered a cognitive behavioral formulation. However, the emphasis on reprocessing the earliest memories that set the pathology in motion is more akin to the psychodynamic tradition. Furthermore, in addition to the initial attention to specific symptoms, clinicians ask their clients to identify the 10 most disturbing memories from their childhood. Not only does this information allow clinicians to identify various patterns of dysfunction, but if these events are still disturbing, it is assumed that they have not been fully processed. As these early memories are processed, clients ordinarily show positive changes in generalized affect and increased self-esteem. New positive behaviors generally manifest, and a new sense of well-being is generated.

In addition to the experiences identified as specific contributors to present symptoms, the 10 most disturbing experiences are processed with any others that are reported on subsequent evaluations to contain a negative affect. Optimally, comprehensive treatment with EMDR (Shapiro, 1995, 2001a) includes the processing of all disturbing earlier events to maximize treatment outcomes in affective, cognitive, somatic, behavioral, and interpersonal domains. As noted in chapter 1, the assimilation of the previously unprocessed early experiences allows a comprehensive shift from childlike to adult perspectives.

The information-processing formulation has been so clinically successful, it was recently suggested that clinicians compile a genogram (McGoldrick, Gerson, & Shellenberger, 1999) of all relevant interpersonal relationships and chart all known past traumas during the initial compilation of the client's history (Kitchur, 2000). Once this is done, the memories are reprocessed in chronological order. The chronological approach is posited to allow an overall developmental consolidation within a family systems context. The standard EMDR model (Shapiro, 1995, 2001), which specifically identifies etiological events, is then used to directly attend to any residual symptoms. This strategic developmental model relies on the adaptive information processing to activate and associate the appropriate networks for personal development. However, sufficient client stabilization and integration in a carefully evaluated approach (Herman, 1992b; Shapiro, 1995, 2001a) is always considered a prerequisite for EMDR memory processing.

The comparative efficiency and effectiveness of the standard and strategic approaches to compiling a client's history and target sequencing need to be researched on the basis of clinical outcomes, utility, and process variables. However, from an information-processing vantage point, the integration of both approaches seems to hold great promise for symptom reduction, personal enhancement, and growth. In both approaches, all the disturbing events are processed, which should result in the same global outcomes; however, the sequencing of targets is different. Assuming that certain treatment conditions and caveats apply, at very least the utility of the genogram for taking a client's history and the clinician-friendly chronological approach have the potential to increase EMDR treatment outcomes. This may be particularly true for therapists who have difficulty identifying negative self-attributions or for those who are uncomfortable with a case conceptualization involving a more symptom-based etiological approach. However, in all cases, the comprehensive three-pronged approach, which evaluates past, present, and future targets, is used (see Shapiro, 2001a).

Phase 2: Preparation

In the second phase, the therapist establishes the appropriate therapeutic relationship, sets achievable client expectations, educates clients about their symptomatology and the necessity of actively participating in treatment, and trains clients to use a set of coping skills and self-control techniques aimed at rapidly eliminating disturbance and eliciting positive affects (see Shapiro, 1995, 2001a). Techniques include "Safe Place" and "Lightstream," which use variations of guided imagery to rapidly eliminate negative somatic responses. Because many clients, especially those with anxiety disorders and a history of trauma, are likely to display avoidance behavior at the outset of treatment, this issue must be addressed before embarking on serious attempts at reprocessing. The self-control techniques that are taught during this phase are an important aspect of therapy because they serve as a means of terminating incomplete sessions and maintaining the psychological stability of clients during and between treatment sessions. An additional aspect of this phase is to instruct clients (a) in the usefulness of certain metaphors (e.g., to imagine themselves as being on a train and to think of the disturbance they may be experiencing as merely the scenery passing by), (b) to maintain a balance between the role of observer and participant, and (c) when necessary, to use a "stop signal," in order to provide them with a sense of mastery over the events and feelings that are taking place during a treatment session.

An important recent addition to the EMDR repertoire is the use of resource development and installation procedures in Phase 2 (Korn & Leeds, in press; Leeds, 1998; Leeds & Shapiro, 2000). During the history-taking phase, clients are carefully assessed to determine whether they have sufficient ego strength and resiliency to engage in memory processing. If a client is not ready for the memory-metabolizing stage of therapy, the clinician leads the client in a series of exercises that include the use of EMDR for ego strengthening and development. Positive memories are evoked and processed with EMDR to enhance the positive affects such as courage or safety so that they are more accessible to the client (see also Shapiro, 1995, 2001a). During the preparation phase, the clinician strengthens the therapeutic alliance so that it is firmly rooted in trust and a sense of security. These positive experiences can also be enhanced through the EMDR processing to set the groundwork for the memory work.

Although EMDR has not been thoroughly researched in diagnostic categories other than PTSD, extensive clinical experience has indicated its benefits provided that it is combined with the accumulated wisdom of the field. For instance, the EMDR work would be incorporated with that of Linehan (1993) and Herman (1992a, 1992b) in the treatment of clients with complex PTSD and personality disorders. The works of Fine (Fine, 1991; Fine & Berkowitz, 2001), Chu (1998), Kluft (1985, 1996), Putnam (1989, 2000), Loewenstein (1991), etc. are important for the appropriate utilization of EMDR in the treatment of dissociative disorders. In all cases, the Preparation phase is crucial and is extended until sufficient stabilization has taken place (International Society for the Study of Dissociation, 1997).

Phase 3: Assessment

During the third phase, the therapist and client jointly identify the memory, trigger, or future template (and its associated mental image, beliefs, emotions, and physical sensations) that will serve as the primary target for that session. After establishing this target, baseline responses are measured. A great deal of clinical experience over the years has refined the specific components of the Assessment phase and the order in which they are addressed. First, in the case of traumatic memory, clients identify the representative or most striking mental image associated with the experience. The image has two important purposes. First, it represents an easily accessed manifestation of the stored experience that is associated with the clients' fears. Second, it is a circumscribed representation of the target. When clients mentally retrieve the image, they are able to maintain psychological equilibrium with the assistance of the previously learned self-control skills.

In the next step of Phase 3, clinicians help the clients formulate a negative belief (i.e., the irrational cognition that they most closely associate with the traumatic event). For example, "I'm helpless" could be the negative belief associated with being molested or in a car accident. Although the cognition is the verbalization of the self-limiting belief that arises as the memory is accessed, it is considered to be irrational because the event is in the past and the clients currently have choices and freedom to act. The goals of this part of the phase are to assist the clients in (a) recognizing the irrational aspects of their cognitive interpretation of the traumatic event, (b) verbalizing what they may have heretofore experienced only as "speechless terror" (Rauch et al., 1996), and (c) identifying an additional component of the memory network by which the feared information can be activated.

In the third step of Phase 3, clinicians help clients formulate a positive belief especially suited to the target. A positive cognition in the cases mentioned previously might be "I'm now in control" or "I now have choices." The goals of this procedure are to (a) illuminate for the clients the nature of their current trauma-induced cognitive distortions, (b) introduce information that contradicts the clients' negative emotional experiences, and (c) provide the clients with a "light at the end of the tunnel," which can encourage and motivate them to persevere with the treatment. The positive cognitions that are most likely to lead to substantial positive treatment effects are those that are both ecologically valid (i.e., apply to the client's everyday world) and likely to generalize to the greatest range of associated information (see Shapiro, 1995, 2001a). The appropriateness of the chosen positive cognition and an assessment of a given session's progress can be measured by the validity of cognition (VoC) scale (Shapiro, 1989, 1995, 2001a). The VoC scale is a 7-point Likert scale in which 1 represents a statement that is *completely false* and 7 represents a statement that is *completely true*. Clients are asked to judge how true the positive cognition feels on a "gut" level, because many clients already intellectually know their thoughts are irrational. The information from the VoC scale provides clients and clinicians a baseline by which to assess therapeutic progress. Assuming that this feedback is positive, it is also likely to promote further client treatment adherence.

After the positive cognition has been identified, the image and the negative belief are explicitly paired to increase access to the stored traumatic memory. The emotion, a measure of the subjective units of disturbance (SUD; Wolpe, 1958; where 0 = *no disturbance* and 10 = *the worst disturbance they can imagine*), and location of physical sensation are then identified by the client. Consequent to the identification of the emotion, clinicians are able to (a) provide clients with the appropriate verbal support, (b) anticipate any client beliefs that might impede processing and must be addressed, and (c) establish a response baseline. The latter is important, because it might be assumed that if a client's SUD level remains unchanged over the course of a given session and no specific emotion has been identified, the session has been unsuccessful. However, it is not uncommon for a large number of emotions to be accessed and processed by clients during an individual session. Therefore, although the SUD level may remain the same at the end of the session, clients may have made clinical progress because their type of emotional experience has changed (e.g., they switch from feeling shame to feeling anger). For example, in the case study of Lynne and the earthquake (discussed in the previous chapter), her relevant image was one of hiding in a doorway. Her negative belief was, "I'm helpless," and her positive belief was, "I can handle things." Lynne's VoC score was 4, she identified anxiety as her relevant emotion, her SUD score was 8, and her body sensations were located in her hands and stomach. Although her emotion was initially identified as anxiety, as noted in the transcript, numerous emotions including sadness were processed during the session.

It is considered very important in EMDR treatment for the physical sensations attendant to memory retrieval to be identified by clients. It appears that there is a physical resonance to the cognitive process that can serve to focus clients' attention and expedite processing. Congruent with the client preparation instructions to "just notice" (i.e., observe, not manipulate), the changes of information that take place during processing, clients are not asked to describe the concomitant physical sensations but merely to identify their location. Typically, these physical sensations are associated with either the emotional content of the memory (e.g., fear, shame, anger) or the physical experience of the event itself (e.g., a knife against the throat, physical blows). Neurobiological research has indicated that state-dependent information storage characteristic of implicit memory typically includes, as part of the unresolved traumatic material, the affect and physical sensations experienced at the time of the event (see van der Kolk, chapter 3; Siegel, 1999; van der Kolk, 1994). Clinical observations of EMDR sessions (see Lovett, 1999; Shapiro, 1995, 2001a; Shapiro & Forrest, 1997; Tinker & Wilson, 1999) have similarly demonstrated that the resolution of this traumatic material includes the elimination of these physical sensations (and their associated affective states).

Another outcome of helping clients identify the physical sensations concomitant to their trauma is that it focuses their attention on a less threatening and therefore potentially less judgmental manifestation of the stored experience. Rather than running the risk that clients will become overwhelmed by negative self-recriminations or disturbing pictures, clinicians ask them merely to attend to the location of the physical sensations, an act that often facilitates processing. In addition, when clients come to view their responses as simply "the behavior of the nervous system"—for which they are obviously not personally responsible—they frequently appear comforted as well as motivated to continue treatment.

Phase 4: Desensitization

In the next three phases of EMDR, the dual-attention stimulation in the form of repeated sets of eye movements, tones, or taps is presented along with various procedural elements designed to facilitate information processing (see Shapiro, 1995, 1999, 2001a). Clients are instructed to simultaneously maintain in consciousness the identified image, negative belief, and physical sensations. By so doing, they access the stored traumata as the initial set of bilateral, rhythmic stimulations are introduced. (For a discussion of this component, see Appendixes A and C.) This phase was named *desensitization* during a time in which the primary indicator of treatment was clients' psychological disturbance as assessed by means of the SUD scale described previously (Shapiro, 1989). However, upon moving to an information-processing model, evaluation of treatment effects during this phase has come to include factors in cognitive, somatic, as well as affective domains.

The rapid processing during Phase 4 includes the elicitation of insights and associations, alterations of the sensory experiences, and increases in the client's sense of self-efficacy. Based on the results of numerous previous clinical observations, the EMDR procedures are designed to induce the most rapid information processing possible while insuring that clients feel psychologically safe and in control of both the therapeutic process and its outcome. For instance, clients are asked to focus on a target while the eye movements (or other rhythmic stimuli) are introduced. Instead of being instructed to rigidly maintain the target in consciousness, they are merely told to "let whatever happens, happen." This invitation to remain open to anything that occurs is aimed at (a) reducing any perceived performance pressure, fear of failure, or other form of anxiety on the part of the client and (b) creating an environment conducive to spontaneous associations, which facilitates the emergence of salient, trauma-relevant material (Rogers & Silver, 2002; Shapiro, 1995, 2001a). These practices are congruent with psychodynamic, experiential, and interpersonal traditions.

Immediately after the end of a given set of dual-attention stimulations, clients are told to "Blank it out (or "Let it go") and take a deep breath. What do you get now?" These instructions give clients the opportunity to self-administer their exposure to the material, maintain mastery over the disturbing emotional target, and ultimately activate the information without interrupting the arousal and state-dependent processing assumed to be occurring at this time. The deep breath serves as only a temporary distraction by which clients are momentarily separated from their disturbance and allows them to verbalize it more readily in order to chart treatment progress.

It is important to note that clients are not told to relax or given any other instruction that might disrupt their state-dependent information because the goal is for them to focus directly on the information as it is *currently* stored. Clinicians adhere to certain procedural guidelines, including those necessary to thoroughly address the memory network (Shapiro, 1995, 2001a). However, they remain flexible about where the client's internal attention is directed at the onset of each subsequent set of external stimuli. Based on the clients' verbal and nonverbal responses, clinicians redirect this focus and vary the duration, repetition rate, and type of stimulation from set to set and use various procedures as needed (see Shapiro, 1995, 2001a).

The patterns of memory processing and generalization effects that have emerged from numerous EMDR sessions have been used to guide the clinical application of procedures (see Shapiro, 1995, 2001a; Shapiro & Forrest, 1997). Clinicians are assisted by rules of intervention that encourage maximum client feedback and self-direction, together with an emphasis on the importance of obtaining consistent therapeutic improvements from one set of stimulation to the next. If processing seems to have stalled, as indicated by a lack of change between stimulation sets, numerous variations of movement and specific procedural instructions can be used to get the process moving again (see Shapiro, 1995, 2001a).

It is important to note that mid-session therapeutic progress is not assessed by SUD level but rather by changes in clients' reported images, thoughts, and sensations. SUD ratings are avoided during processing to minimize the possibility of influencing clients' responses by "demand characteristics" and because they are not needed to assess the ongoing changes. Rather, the measurement of a SUD level is typically delayed until the client is no longer revealing disturbance when accessing the material, and processing appears to have reached its culmination. At that point, clients generally have a SUD level of 0, which is an indication to clinicians that the next phase—Installation—can commence. It is recommended that both quantitative and qualitative assessments of clients' stress levels be administered because it is very important that the positive cognition not be introduced prematurely (see Shapiro, 1995, 2001a).

Phase 5: Installation

The primary goal of Phase 5 is to incorporate and strengthen the positive cognition that has been previously designated as a replacement for the client's original negative self-belief. It is not unusual during the Desensitization phase (Phase 4) for the strength of the positive belief to increase or another one to arise that is actually more therapeutically beneficial than the one that was identified in Phase 3 (the Assessment phase). In any event, the most enhancing positive cognition possible is identified and paired with the previously dysfunctional material simultaneously with the sets of stimulation until a VoC of 7 is achieved. The only situation in which a lower VoC is considered acceptable is when there is evidence that such a robust cognition is not realistic or is inappropriate as assessed in relation to the client's current social groups. For example, when Lynne processed the earthquake, her desired cognition was, "I can handle anything that comes up." Clearly, this cognition would be inappropriate at a 7, or "completely true," level since things could certainly arise in life that she might be unable to handle. A sign of the positive treatment effect was that the positive cognition was only able to rise to a VoC of 6—indicating the ecological validity of her subjective evaluation. Only when this point in therapeutic treatment has been reached is the next phase introduced. Alternatively, a positive cognition such as, "It's over. I'm safe now," could have ecologically risen to a level of 7.

Phase 6: Body Scan

In the Body Scan phase, clients notify their therapist of any residual disturbance in the form of body sensations. If present, clients focus on these sensations during subsequent reprocessing. Frequently, these body sensations allow access to additional experiences in need of processing. Only when all disturbing body sensations have ceased is treatment considered complete.

Phase 7: Closure

It is very important that clients be in a state of emotional equilibrium at the end of a given therapeutic session, even if for some reason reprocessing has not reached completion. In the Closure phase, one or more of the various self-control techniques that clients learned during the Preparation phase (Phase 2) are used to obtain this equilibrium. It is also important that clients be debriefed so that they understand what they have experienced in terms of the information-processing model and that additional material can continue to arise in between sessions.

Clients are also requested to maintain a journal and record any positive or negative emotional experiences. The format in which the journal is kept helps them remain alert to the same information gathered in the Assessment phase (i.e., images, cognitions, emotions, sensations) and is used to facilitate the process of accessing appropriate targets in future sessions. Once they have recorded in their journal a particular emotional upset such as feeling out of control during a family fight, they are instructed to use one of their self-control techniques to reestablish a state of psychological well-being. It appears that the acts of recognizing and recording reaction patterns encourages in clients a sense of self-mastery and observation that they are able to implement during subsequent exposure to real-life disturbing conditions. Clearly, these activities, which have firm roots in the cognitive–behavioral tradition, facilitate clients' between-session psychological stability. In addition, clients are requested to use a designated relaxation or guided imagery technique daily. Prerecorded audiotapes are often used for this purpose. This practice, consistent with hypnotic and transpersonal traditions, helps establish a baseline of relaxation and may reduce general physiological arousal.

Phase 8: Re-evaluation

The Re-evaluation phase opens every EMDR session in order to check on treatment maintenance and identify potential new targets for processing. Clients access previous targets to determine whether any new perspectives have arisen that need attention or whether additional processing is necessary. The journal is also examined. During this phase, clinicians investigate the entire clinical picture and are guided by their clients' responses through the various EMDR protocols (see Shapiro, 2001a). The degree to which an EMDR treatment has been successful for a given client can only be determined by follow-up evaluations. These follow-up sessions show the extent to which reprocessing and behavioral effects have endured. As previously noted, the goal of EMDR therapy is to produce the most comprehensive and profound treatment effects possible in a relatively short period while simultaneously maintaining client stability within a balanced system. As such, an assessment of interpersonal responses and systems issues needs to be thoroughly evaluated.

ADAPTIVE INFORMATION PROCESSING

As explained in the previous section, the overall EMDR procedures contain aspects that are often highlighted in various psychological orientations. For instance, imagery is used to access the targeted information, a procedure that has its roots in the earliest of hypnotic traditions. Attention to negative and positive beliefs is congruent with a cognitive therapy framework, just as the focus on emotions and physical sensations is highlighted in the experiential modes. Likewise, the use of the composite is consistent with multimodal therapy, and the use of baseline rating scales is part of the behavioral heritage. The Preparation phase incorporates a client-centered approach consistent with feminist, experiential, and transpersonal psychotherapy and imagery-based self-control techniques that are derived from the hypnotic and cognitive traditions. In the processing phases, the spontaneous elicitation of early memories is consistent with psychodynamic therapy, and the monitoring of the level of stored affect and physical response evinced is consistent with the physiological theory of state-dependent storage. The impact of the events, which is revealed during the processing, sheds light on intrapsychic, interpersonal, mind–body, and interactional–systems aspects of the clinical picture. The net result underscores the need to synthesize the wisdom within the overall field of psychology by combining the extant modalities within an integrative framework. The information-processing model is an attempt to move in that direction, since all treatment effects highlighted in the various orientations either arise spontaneously or are deliberately orchestrated.

Mimicking Spontaneous Processing

The case study of Lynne and the earthquake (see chapter 1) illustrates the way that EMDR processing can often proceed with minimal direction from the therapist. The emergence of insights, associations, and positive affects and the decrease of anxiety and body sensations all occurred spontaneously as the information-processing system was stimulated. As previously stated, the goal of EMDR is to set in motion an intrinsic information-processing system to transform the dysfunctionally stored perceptions and allow rapid learning to take place. This rapid learning occurs as the appropriate associations are made. For Lynne, affective change and insights occurred as the processing of the targeted earthquake spontaneously revealed connections to early childhood events. These insights and emotional changes are not considered the agents of change but rather the manifestations of change.

The central thesis of EMDR therapy is that the physiological storage of earlier life experiences is the key to understanding behavior, personality, and attendant psychological phenomena. According to this view, the perceptual information of past experiences, both negative and positive, is conceptualized as stored in memory networks. Natural learning takes place as unimpeded adaptive associations are made. However, if a trauma occurs the system can become imbalanced and the experience is stored dysfunctionally. If an experience is dysfunctionally stored, it has within it the original perceptions, including disturbing emotions, and physical sensations that were experienced at the time.

Part of the dysfunction is the storage of the experience in neurobiological stasis so that the appropriate connections cannot take place. A combat veteran may be able to forgive everyone else for killing—but he cannot forgive himself. A firefighter may know that all his comrades did a good job but believe he did not. A molestation victim may know that no child is responsible for being molested but nevertheless blame herself. The intellectual beliefs and appropriate knowledge are stored in one network, while the disturbing event is stored in another. The two cannot link up. Hence the ubiquitous metaphorical disconnection between heart, or gut, and head.

EMDR processing allows the appropriate linkups to occur. As we saw previously in Lynne's transcripts, her pronounced disturbance after a recent earthquake was rooted in her past experiences. During processing, the knowledge that she had been betrayed and her "reality shaken" became connected for the first time with her molestation experience, although she had been molested many years before. In this instance, her own internal connections were made spontaneously. Sometimes, however, the clinician has to assist the process by the use of a *cognitive interweave* (Shapiro, 1991, 1995, 2001a). In this procedure the clinician will deliberately elicit the next bit of useful information that would have been expected to associate spontaneously in unimpeded processing. This therapist-elicited information can take the form of imagery, movement, or verbalizations. However, the goal of the intervention is to mimic spontaneous processing as closely as possible and then get out of the way so that clients can continue following the internal pathways necessary for resolving their dysfunction.

As described in chapter 1, EMDR therapy incorporates the tenet that people have an inherent drive toward health and adaptation (Maslow, 1970; Rogers, 1951). As such, the information processing generally proceeds spontaneously if the dysfunctional target is properly accessed and the information-processing system is activated. The rapid shifting of perceived cognitions and affects is attributed to the sequential linkage of adaptive networks. These networks progressively infuse information into the targeted network until adaptive resolution is achieved. Therefore, if the dysfunctional perceptions inherent in a targeted network do not transmute after successive sets of stimulation, then an adaptive network is deliberately stimulated by the therapist. In this way, the next bit of appropriate information is deliberately elicited so that it can be assimilated into the target network during the next stimulation set.

The more closely the deliberate activation mimics spontaneous processing, the more productive it is. In fact, a general rule is that when processing stalls, the clinician can restart it by deliberately promoting what occurred spontaneously for other clients during unimpeded processing. Therefore, the more knowledge clinicians have of particular populations, the more prepared they are to resolve processing blocks. The following section describes the use of three different cognitive interweaves and their processing effects. The section also discusses three generic emotional and cognitive stages that people who have been traumatized generally pass through as their dysfunctionally stored memories are processed. These are also the stages in which processing is apt to become blocked, particularly for those who have experienced childhood traumas (Shapiro, 1991, 1995, 2001a). Examples are also provided of the change processes and clinical phenomena ordinarily identified with various clinical orientations.

Case Study

The following transcript illustrates the use of the cognitive interweave during the Desensitization phase of an initial processing session. Karen was molested as a child by her uncle and is seeking therapy because of pronounced PTSD symptoms. Although Karen is now almost 40, she is still bothered by intrusive symptoms, panic reactions, and a high level of anxiety. As usual in EMDR treatment, she has identified an image, a negative and positive cognition, an emotion, and a physical sensation. The image she has identified is being held by her uncle in the basement. She feels intense fear, and has exhibited a state of terror that translates as a 10 on the "0–10" SUD scale. Repeated sets of eye movements have not succeeded in decreasing her disturbance, so the clinician has initiated a cognitive interweave, using at different times a statement or question to help Karen elicit the next bit of adaptive information necessary to continue processing (for comprehensive description of techniques and parameters see Shapiro 1995, 2001a). Karen needs only to hold the elicited information in her mind, without wholeheartedly embracing or accepting it, during the subsequent set. Her response after the set reveals whether and to what degree the information has been assimilated. The clinician must offer or evoke the information in a client-centered manner. Demand characteristics, or the introduction of inappropriate information generally results in more, not less, disturbance.

To illustrate the clinical practice, we will use the same procedure as in the previous transcript: ********** indicate a set of eye movements, and comments in [brackets] indicate editorial points of interest.

****

Therapist: Let the feelings be there. Let whatever comes up, come up. It's okay. . . . Blank it out—deep breath. . . . What do you get now?

Karen: He just wouldn't let me go, and I know that he knows that I want to go. He keeps talking to me.

Therapist: So whose fault is it? Whose responsibility is it?

[This question is a cognitive interweave because it elicits the adaptive information that places responsibility and blame on the uncle rather than on Karen. Because this information did not arise spontaneously, the clinician elicits it deliberately. This point is particularly pertinent because people who have been abused often blame themselves for the abuse and are unable to set the appropriate boundaries between themselves and others. This boundary and delineation is a fundamental developmental stage that must be established. Psychodynamic therapists most easily identify the ramifications of this stage of processing for appropriate object relations.]

Karen: His.

Therapist: Right. Stay with that and follow.

****

Therapist: What do you get now?

Karen: He's bad. He's bad, and I've got to get away.

[Karen has now identified the appropriate boundary, and the terror has subsided to fear. This decrease in emotion can be interpreted in various ways. It may be that because the appropriate boundary was missing, the danger was intrinsic and hence inescapable. It may be that due to an identification with her uncle's activity, her sense of "wrongness" demands punishment. However, regardless of the subjective therapeutic interpretation, those who have experienced trauma generally experience a decrease in affect when they make the appropriate connections regarding responsibility. Clearly, no 6-year-old girl is responsible for being molested by an adult. If the cognitive interweave had not been effective, then the therapist could have used various imagery, movement, or cognitive assessments (see Shapiro, 2001a, for a review). However, because the therapist was able to help Karen make the appropriate connection with the adaptive information, the therapist allows the processing to proceed.]

Therapist: Stay with that now.

****

Therapist: What do you get now?

Karen: I just feel really light.

[This is a common response to a rapid affective shift.]

Therapist: Stay with that.

****

Therapist: What do you get now?

Karen: All I can picture is him. All I can picture is him. (fear)

Therapist: Where is he now?

Karen: In the basement.

[The client answers from the perspective of her accessed 6-year-old's memory. The clinician uses another cognitive interweave to elicit another piece of information—that in the present, the uncle is not dangerous.]

Therapist: Where is he today?

Karen: He lives in Texas . . .

Therapist: How dangerous is he now?

Karen: Not at all.

Therapist: Think of that.

[Karen now feels a sense of safety, which is the second generic stage of trauma processing (Shapiro, 1991, 1995, 2001a). However, the information processing is not complete until the client has a totally adult perspective. This perspective incorporates an internal locus of control.]

****

Therapist: What do you get now?

Karen: I just get angry and disgusted at him.

[Having elicited the adaptive information that was available to Karen but not assimilated into the memory network that held the childhood molestation memory, she progresses from feeling fear to having a more adaptive, adult perspective. The processing causes a transmutation to new affects. These new affects are targeted to ensure that they are also fully processed. Although anger and disgust can be adaptive, they may also be linked to fear and self-recrimination.]

Therapist: Stay with that.

****

Karen: I feel that I want to tell him that I know what he did to me.

Therapist: Tell him.

[This is an important stage of individuation and is to be encouraged in most clients. The verbalization of the emotion and its specific form of vocalization are comfortable steps for experiential therapists. However, this case study shows an example of spontaneous processing, and Karen leads the way.]

Karen: "Uncle Larry, I know what you did to me. And it was wrong and you hurt me. And you scared me. And you did not even care about me. And it was wrong."

[The therapist notes that the words have a distinctly childlike tone. Therefore, in subsequent sets, Karen is asked to repeat the statement until she can say it with an adult timbre and tone. Elicitation of the adult perspective is at the heart of adaptive information processing. The assimilation of the targeted network allows the evolution of Karen's consciousness from an encapsulated, childlike perspective into an appropriate level as the processing proceeds organically.]

****

Karen: I'm okay.

Therapist: That's right. That's right. Stay with that.

****

Therapist: What do you get now?

Karen: I didn't cause it.

Therapist: That's right. Stay with that.

****

Therapist: What do you get now?

Karen: It's okay now. I just wanted to let him know that I knew.

Therapist: Stay with that.

****

Therapist: What do you get now?

Karen: I don't feel so lonely anymore.

[From an information-processing perspective, it is important for the therapist to take the approach of facilitator rather than guide because clients progress through their own memory network to the place they need to go. If the clinician directs the treatment, as clinicians do in behavioral or cognitive therapy, Karen might not arrive at and process the emotion of loneliness, which is apparently a remnant feeling of the 6-year-old who was molested alone in the basement and warned not to tell anyone about it. This sense of isolation and alienation is the next affect to emerge that needs processing.]

Therapist: Stay with that.

****

Therapist: What do you get now?

Karen: Relief. I feel relieved.

Therapist: Stay with that.

****

Therapist: What do you get now?

Karen: I feel like it's okay. It won't happen again.

Therapist: Stay with that.

****

Therapist: What do you get now?

Karen: I feel safer.

Therapist: Stay with that.

****

Therapist: What do you get now?

Karen: I'm just more calm—relaxed.

Therapist: So you know you can act on what you know is right, and you're now in control.

[The therapist uses a cognitive interweave to summarize the adult perspective and elicit the awareness of an internal, rather than external, locus of control.]

****

Karen: I really feel okay and not to blame.

Therapist: Stay with that.

****

Therapist: What do you get now?

Karen: I feel happier.

Therapist: Stay with that.

****

Therapist: What do you get now?

Karen: More connected—I feel more whole.

Therapist: Stay with that.

****

Therapist: What do you get now?

Karen: I feel like I'm in control. Like an adult . . . like more in control.

[Note that the clinician never used the word *adult*, and yet Karen reports that the sense of self has progressed to that level.]

Therapist: Stay with that.

****

Therapist: What do you get now?

Karen: Peace. Just a real calmness. Really relaxed.

[Reprobe.]

Therapist: What happens when you think of Larry again?

[The therapist reprobes to elicit the memory that is currently physiologically stored. Now, approximately 15 minutes since the feeling of intense terror was engendered when accessing the memory, the client responds quite differently.]

Karen: It's a memory.

Therapist: Stay with that.

****

Therapist: What do you get now?

Karen: I sort of feel sorry for him—a sadness.

Therapist: What do you feel sorry for him about?

[The therapist checks for new associations. Is the sadness ecologically simply the emotion associated with an unhappy past event—sadness that the world is this way? Is it based on some form of self-recrimination?]

Karen: I'm not quite sure. Why he would do that? What would make him want to do that?

Therapist: Stay with that.

****

Therapist: What do you get now?

Karen: Not much of anything. I feel really removed from him—not connected. I do not get much of anything.

Therapist: And how do you feel about yourself?

Karen: A lot better—I feel really released. I don't know—all of this tension that was built up inside—and I can finally release it. It feels really good.

[The therapist now debriefs Karen about the session and ensures Karen knows that more processing can occur after the session.]

Therapist: Great—good. It's in the past. Great. So over the next week things can continue to process even more. Because basically what we've done is we've taken something that was frozen in time—that was locked in the nervous system the way it originally happened, and that's why you continued to cycle through it—the same feelings that were coming up at the time—actually almost reliving the experience. We've opened up the barrier to what was locked up. That's why it's been able to process out. So now we are in present time. So again, when you think of it—how does it come out? How does it feel?

[By debriefing Karen, the clinician is also momentarily distracting her from the event. As the memory of the event is accessed again, the clinician carefully notes what spontaneously comes to Karen's mind, which is an indication of how the memory is currently stored.]

Karen: I'm still feeling this residue of sadness, and I'm not sure where it's connected.

Therapist: Stay with that.

****

Karen: I know what it is!

Therapist: What's that?

Karen: I'm feeling sadness for my little girl.

Therapist: What about your little girl?

Karen: The little girl that experiences things. And me as a mother nurturing her, and holding her, and saying it's okay.

[It is not unusual for the sad and needy image of an assaulted child to emerge for clients after they have processed the image of the "bad child that caused the molestation."]

Therapist: Stay with that. Let it all come out.

****

Karen: I feel so much love. I really do. It's like now I can love this little person inside me and say it's okay.

[This emergence of self-love is an important aspect of healing. Note that Karen is spontaneously reporting these new positive affects even though she is in the Desensitization phase. As noted previously, insights, association, personal strengthening, and growth are all part of this phase of treatment.]

Therapist: Stay with that.

****

Karen: You want me to tell my little girl . . .?

[The therapist nods and encourages the client to express what has naturally arisen.]

Karen: "I understand. I know the pain, the fear you must have felt. You aren't to blame. You did not cause it. You could not make him stop. It's okay."

Therapist: Stay with that.

[Note that the client is reiterating from an adult perspective the emotional and cognitive understanding that she was not responsible for the molestation.]

****

Karen: I'm here now. And I'm here to protect you. And I love you.

[Note that the client has reaffirmed all three plateaus of processing: (a) She was not responsible, (b) she is safe now, and (c) as an adult she now has power and choices.]

Therapist: How does it feel?

Karen: It feels real good.

After approximately 30 minutes of processing a major molestation memory that has been a deciding factor in Karen's development, this middle-age woman has reached a new plateau of self-understanding and self-love. That outcome is the hallmark of EMDR therapy: a complete and comprehensive reprocessing of early memories to a level of present adult functioning. Karen will never look the same, act the same, or think the same way again. She has consolidated all the lessons about this event. She knows she was not responsible, is safe in the present, and as an adult now has choices. She is capable of taking her place in the world.

Can all major traumatic memories be reprocessed in one, two, or three sessions? Certainly not! Nevertheless, a vast majority of memories can be. As noted in the controlled research, 80% to 90% of the individual memories are capable of these rapid reconfigurations. The memories are not erased; they are associated with the appropriate memory networks necessary for rapid learning. This assimilation of memories is part of the personal growth process. The personality changes as the new learning is accommodated. Rather than configuring their personalities around the negative affects of previous trauma, clients incorporate a sense of renewal and take on the characteristics of, as one client explained, "a strong and resilient person." Another client stated, "It was nice to go from survivor to thriver."

Another important aspect of this transcript is that the factors needed to adjudge positive effects according to any of the major orientations are represented: insights, change of construct of self and others, shifting of beliefs, and changes in physical arousal, stimulus response, self-esteem, and self-efficacy. To reiterate, processing is not simple desensitization. Learning takes place, meaning that what is useful is incorporated and stored with appropriate affect to guide the person in the future. What is useless is discarded. A sign of successful treatment is not a 0 SUD level; it is the emergence of positive affects such as self-love and all the attributes necessary to lead a healthy and joyous life.

FUTURE EXPLORATIONS

The positive treatment effects illustrated in the previous transcript are recognizable by practicing clinicians of any orientation. What may seem improbable to some, however, is the accelerated rate at which they occur. Despite this potential skepticism, the controlled research base of EMDR is quite persuasive in this regard (see Appendixes A and C). It should be kept in mind that a basic tenet of the adaptive (or accelerated) information-processing model is that change can occur at a much faster rate than traditionally assumed. The model also predicts that these effects will be both substantial and lasting. For a clinician or theorist to fully accept this concept may require personal experience applying or receiving the treatment.

Such rapid and complete change may also seem reasonable if one thinks of EMDR's effects in terms of the acquisition of new neural connections across narrow synaptic gaps.

Although both clinical anecdotal reports and controlled research have borne out the rapidity and maintenance of clinically significant EMDR treatment effects, of equal importance is the nature of this therapeutic change. As noted previously, clinical outcomes are an interaction of client, clinician, and method. Therefore, the goals of therapy for any given client are often greatly influenced by the clinician's paradigm and personal world view. With EMDR, the reduction of symptoms, while a worthy goal, should be viewed simply as the starting point. Identified traumas or phobias can be considered a doorway of opportunity inasmuch as it is at this point that the client seeks therapy because life has become unmanageable. Although it is possible to use EMDR to simply remove the overt symptoms, I believe that doing so and merely returning the client to a "life of quiet desperation," represents a disservice. Often, clients' initial goals are based upon limited perspectives and they are unaware of life's possibilities. An integrative approach recognizes the potential for multidimensional change and thus it becomes the responsibility of clinicians to explore far-ranging goals and refine their clinical repertoires to achieve them.

Using an information-processing model as a guide, EMDR practice recognizes the indissoluble link between mind and body. Indeed, while not defining consciousness, it recognizes that our clients' greatest aspirations and potentials cannot be accomplished if they are imprisoned by static brain states. It can be argued that the brain is subject to the same laws of cause and effect, and of healing, as the rest of the body. Physical systems can be overloaded by survival fears, arresting psychological development, and blinding consciousness in affects of fear and anxiety; however, healing is also possible. It seems likely that the comprehensive treatment needed to transform the lives of troubled clients to ones of joy and well-being should be characterized by the indicators of change found in all of the various modalities. Thus, it seems reasonable that clients in need can best be served by the integration of the complete wisdom of our field. As a step in this direction, luminaries and master clinicians of the primary psychological orientations will use the coming chapters to espouse their views and implementation of EMDR. The final chapter will summarize and identify similarities in their theory and practice.

Although I do not agree with every interpretation voiced in the following chapters, it is my hope that ultimately we can all be guided by the rigorous evaluation of controlled research, rather than by subjective judgment. In an integrative approach, there is always the danger of the inclusion of certain practices that dilute, rather than enhance, treatment effects (Shapiro, 2001b). On the other hand, it is the innovative practice that advances our field. To adequately interpret potential contributions, we will need to upgrade research standards and forge a greater link between the realities of clinical practice and the exigencies of experimental evaluation. The tension between science and practice is well known in our field. However, I believe that the integration of these two paradigms is also vital for the field of psychology to fully mature (see Shapiro, 2001a, 2002, in press).

In summary, for researcher, theoretician, and clinician alike, I believe it to be vital that we expand our practices and theories to encompass the wisdom of the entire range of therapeutic orientations. To that end, we should try to remember that we each maintain only one vantage point of a vast expanse of reality. In light of the long history of dissension among various schools of thought and clinical traditions, a useful goal for our field should be inclusion, not exclusion. The vast array of human suffering and psychological problems worldwide demands our attention and utmost care. Yet, despite our best intentions, the poignancy of the human condition is that we are always limited in our view. As noted by Albert Einstein, "The theory decides what we can observe." Given our own unique perspectives, we must depend upon and help each other to develop the most effective solutions.

REFERENCES

Antrobus, J. S., Antrobus, J. S., & Singer, J. (1964). Eye movements, accompanying daydreams, visual imagery, and thought suppression. *Journal of Abnormal and Social Psychology, 69*, 244–252.

Beck, A. T. (1976). *Cognitive therapy and the emotional disorders.* New York: International Universities Press.

Chu, J. A. (1998). *Rebuilding shattered lives: Treating complex post-traumatic and dissociative disorders.* New York: Wiley.

Ellis, A. (1962). *Reason and emotion in psychotherapy.* Secaucus, NJ: Citadel.

Fine, C. G. (1991). Treatment stabilization and crisis prevention: Pacing the therapy of the multiple personality disorder patient. *Psychiatric Clinics of North America, 14*, 661–676.

Fine, C. G., & Berkowitz, A. S. (2001). The wreathing protocol: The imbrication of hypnosis and EMDR in the treatment of dissociative identity disorder and other maladaptive dissociative responses. *American Journal of Clinical Hypnosis, 43*, 275–290.

Herman, J. L. (1992a). Complex PTSD: A syndrome in survivors of prolonged and repeated trauma. *Journal of Traumatic Stress, 5*, 377–391.

Herman, J. L. (1992b). *Trauma and recovery.* New York: Basic Books.

International Society for the Study of Dissociation. (1997). *Guidelines for treating dissociative identity disorder (multiple personality disorder) in adults.* Northbrook, IL: Author.

Kitchur, M. (2000, December). The strategic developmental model for EMDR: A sequential treatment strategy for diverse populations, facilitative of developmental recapitulation, with implications for neurobiological maturation. *EMDRIA Newsletter*, pp. 4–10.

Kluft, R. P. (1985). The natural history of multiple personality disorder. In R. P. Kluft (Ed.), *Childhood antecedents of multiple personality* (pp. 197–238). Washington, DC: American Psychiatric Press.

Kluft, R. P. (1996). Multiple personality disorder: A legacy of trauma. In C. R. Pferrer (Ed.), *Severe stress and mental disturbance in children* (pp. 411–448). Washington, DC: American Psychiatric Press.

Korn, D. L., & Leeds, A. M. (in press). Preliminary evidence of efficacy for EMDR resource development and installation in the stabilization phase of treatment of complex posttraumatic stress disorder. *Journal of Clinical Psychology*.

LeDoux, J. E. (1996). *The emotional brain: The mysterious underpinnings of emotional life*. New York: Simon & Schuster.

Leeds, A. M. (1998). Lifting the burden of shame: Using EMDR resource installation to resolve a therapeutic impasse. In P. Manfield (Ed.), *Extending EMDR: A casebook of innovative applications*. New York: W. W. Norton.

Leeds, A. M., & Shapiro, F. (2000). EMDR and resource installation: Principles and procedures for enhancing current functioning and resolving traumatic experiences. In J. Carlson & L. Sperry (Eds.), *Brief therapy strategies with individuals and couples* (pp. 469–534). Phoenix, AZ: Zeig/Tucker.

Linehan, M. M. (1993). *Cognitive–behavioral treatment of borderline personality disorder*. New York: Guilford Press.

Lipke, H. (2000). *EMDR and psychotherapy integration*. Boca Raton, FL: CRC Press.

Loewenstein, R. J. (1991). An office mental status examination for complex chronic dissociative symptoms and multiple personality disorder. *Psychiatric Clinics of North America, 14*, 567–604.

Lovett, J. (1999). *Small wonders: Healing childhood trauma with EMDR*. New York: Free Press.

Maslow, A. H. (1970). *Motivation and personality*. New York: Harper & Row.

McGoldrick, M., Gerson, R., & Shellenberger, S. (1999). *Genograms in family assessment* (2nd ed.). New York: W. W. Norton.

Putnam, F. W. (1989). *Diagnosis and treatment of multiple personality disorder*. New York: Guilford Press.

Putnam, F. W. (2000). Dissociative disorders. In A. J. Sameroff & M. Lewis (Eds.), *Handbook of developmental psychopathology* (2nd ed., pp. 739–754). New York: Kluwer Academic/Plenum.

Rauch, S., van der Kolk, B. A., Fisler, R., Alpert, N. M., Orr, S. P., Savage, C. R., et al. (1996). Symptom provocation study of post traumatic stress disorder using positron emission tomography and script-drive imagery. *Archives of General Psychiatry, 53*, 380–387.

Rogers, C. R. (1951). *Client-centered therapy*. Boston: Houghton-Mifflin.

Rogers, S., & Silver, S. M. (2002). Is EMDR an exposure therapy? A review of trauma protocols. *Journal of Clinical Psychology, 58*, 43–59.

Shapiro, F. (1989). Efficacy of the eye movement desensitization procedure in the treatment of traumatic memories. *Journal of Traumatic Stress Studies, 2*, 199–223.

Shapiro, F. (1991, December). Stray thoughts. *EMDR Network Newsletter, 1*, 1–3.

Shapiro, F. (1995). *Eye movement desensitization and reprocessing: Basic principles, protocols and procedures.* New York: Guilford Press.

Shapiro, F. (1999). Eye movement desensitization and reprocessing (EMDR): Clinical and research implications of an integrated psychotherapy treatment. *Journal of Anxiety Disorders, 13*, 35–67.

Shapiro, F. (2001a). *Eye movement desensitization and reprocessing: Basic principles, protocols and procedures* (2nd ed.). New York: Guilford Press.

Shapiro, F. (2001b). The challenges of treatment evolution and integration. *American Journal of Clinical Hypnosis, 43*, 183–186.

Shapiro, F. (2002). EMDR twelve years after its introduction: A review of past, present, and future directions. *Journal of Clinical Psychology, 58*, 1–22.

Shapiro, F. (in press). EMDR and the role of the clinician in psychotherapy treatment. Towards a more comprehensive integration. *Journal of Clinical Psychology.*

Shapiro, F., & Forrest, M. (1997). *EMDR.* New York: Basic Books.

Siegel, D. J. (1999). *The developing mind: Toward a neurobiology of interpersonal experience.* New York: Guilford Press.

Squire, L. R. (1992). Memory and the hippocampus: A synthesis from findings with rats, monkeys, and humans. *Psychological Review, 99*, 195–231.

Stickgold, R. (2002). EMDR: A putative neurobiological mechanism of action. *Journal of Clinical Psychology, 58*, 61–75.

Tinker, R. H., & Wilson, S. A. (1999). *Through the eyes of a child: EMDR with children.* New York: Norton.

van der Kolk, B. A. (1994). The body keeps the score: Memory and the evolving psychobiology of posttraumatic stress. *Harvard Review of Psychiatry, 1*, 253–265.

van der Kolk, B. A., Greenberg, M., Boyd, H., & Krystal, J. (1985). Inescapable shock, neurotransmitters, and addiction to trauma: Toward a psychobiology of posttraumatic stress. *Biological Psychiatry, 20*, 314–325.

van der Kolk, B. A., Hopper, J. W., & Osterman, J. A. (2001). Exploring the nature of traumatic memory: Combining clinical knowledge and laboratory methods. *Journal of Aggression, Maltreatment, and Trauma. 4*, 9–31.

Wolpe, J. (1958). *Psychotherapy by reciprocal inhibition.* Stanford, CA: Stanford University Press.

Zabukevec, J., Lazrove, S., & Shapiro, F. (2000). Self-healing aspects of EMDR: The therapeutic change process and perspectives of integrated psychotherapies. *Journal of Psychotherapy Integration, 10*, 189–206.

3

BEYOND THE TALKING CURE: SOMATIC EXPERIENCE AND SUBCORTICAL IMPRINTS IN THE TREATMENT OF TRAUMA

BESSEL A. VAN DER KOLK

With sufficient experience, the brain comes to contain a model of the world; at the same time, it also is constantly looking for new ways of putting things together, for new categories to create. (Calvin, 1990, p. 261)

So we shall view memories as entities that predispose the mind to deal with new situations in old, remembered ways—specifically, as entities that reset the states of parts of the nervous system. (Minsky, 1980)

It is precisely because there is no immediate accommodation that there is complete dissociation of the inner activity from the external world. As the external world is solely represented by images, it is assimilated without resistance (i.e., unattached to other memories) to the unconscious ego. (Piaget, 1962)

Research in laboratories devoted to memory research has clearly shown that memory is an active and constructive process: The mind constantly reassembles old impressions and attaches them to new information. Memories, instead of precise recollections, are transformed into stories that people tell themselves and others to convey a coherent narrative of their experience of the world. Rarely do people's minds generate precise images, smells, sensations, or muscular actions that accurately replicate previous experiences. In fact, most well-known memory researchers, such as Elizabeth Loftus, Dan Schachter, and John Kihlstrom, have emphatically denied that the mind is capable of precisely reproducing the imprints of prior experience.

However, learning from individuals who have been diagnosed with posttraumatic stress disorder (PTSD) confronted us with consistent reports from traumatized patients that particular emotions, images, sensations, and muscular reactions related to the trauma became deeply imprinted on their

57

minds. These traumatic imprints seem to be reexperienced without appreciable transformation for months, years, and even decades after the actual event occurred (Janet, 1889, 1894; van der Kolk & Fisler, 1995; van der Kolk, Hopper, & Osterman, 2001; van der Kolk & van der Hart, 1991).

It appears that it is precisely this failure to transform and integrate the sensory imprints associated with a trauma that causes people with PTSD to behave as if they were living in the past, even though they may be quite aware that their reactions are out of proportion to a current stimulus. However, because of people's infinite capacity for rationalizing irrational feelings and behaviors, people who have been traumatized often do not realize that their feelings or actions are not relevant to the present. The discrepancy between people's irrational feelings and behaviors and their rationalizations for them is a function of human consciousness. Among other things, consciousness protects people from becoming aware of the true meaning of the messages being conveyed by the areas of the brain specializing in self-preservation and danger detection.

The extraordinary capacity of the human mind to distort experiences is illustrated in the longitudinal study of the psychological and physical health of 200 Harvard undergraduates who participated in World War II (Lee, Vaillant, Torrey, & Elder, 1995). When the men were interviewed about their experiences 45 years later, those who did not have PTSD had considerably altered their original accounts: The most intense horror of the events had been bleached. In contrast, those who had been traumatized and developed PTSD had been unable to modify their war memories and essentially preserved them, intact, for 45 years.

Thus, although it is "normal" to distort one's memories, people with PTSD seem unable to put traumatic events behind them and minimize their impact. The process that prevents memories from becoming integrated into the large conglomeration of one's autobiographical memory stores is *dissociation*—the failure to integrate all elements of the experience into a coherent whole. Because dissociation prevents traumatic memories from becoming integrated, the memories lead a relatively independent existence from the remainder of a person's conscious experience. If a person's problems with PTSD are being caused by dissociation, treatment needs to consist of *association*.

However, the traumatic memories that need to be *associated* are not primarily represented by a person's verbal account of the past but by the fragmented sensory or emotional elements of the traumatic experience that are triggered when a person with PTSD is confronted with enough sensory or emotional elements related to the trauma. When these elements are activated, the entire neural net in which the memory is stored is stimulated, causing the person to relive the old but terrifying event (Lang, 1985; Pitman et al., 1990; van der Kolk & van der Hart, 1991).

Thus, the core pathology of PTSD is that certain sensations or emotions related to traumatic experiences keep returning in unbidden ways and do not fade with time. This does not mean that the *stories* that traumatized people tell to *explain* what is going on do not change: Narratives are a function of the interaction between the speaker and the listener. The words that people use to explain what they are feeling and sensing depends heavily on the context in which the story is told—the cues and feedback received from the environment and the language that is culturally acceptable for explaining internal experience. In large part, treating PTSD consists of helping patients overcome the traumatic *imprints* that dominate their lives, which are the sensations, emotions, and actions that are not relevant to the demands of the present but are triggered by current events that keep reactivating old, trauma-based states of mind.

Until recently, clinicians had limited knowledge of how to help people integrate such disintegrated traumatic imprints. Traditionally, before the advent of contemporary methods of treatment outcome evaluation, many clinicians, from Pierre Janet to Milton Erikson and his followers, considered hypnosis to be the treatment of choice. Unfortunately the efficacy of hypnosis for the treatment of PTSD was never systematically studied. Eye movement desensitization and reprocessing (EMDR) was the first of the new therapies that suggested the prospect of rapidly and effectively integrating traumatic memories. EMDR has a number of advantages over hypnosis, including that it could easily be put into a treatment protocol, which makes it relatively simple to conduct treatment outcome research. Since it was first articulated by Francine Shapiro in the late 1980s, EMDR has received intense scientific scrutiny and has been found to be a very effective treatment for PTSD (e.g., Chemtob, Tolin, van der Kolk, & Pitman, 2000).

SUBCORTICAL NATURE OF TRAUMATIC MEMORIES

The power of old memories to haunt the present with uncontrollable intensity and precision confronts clinicians with the fundamental question of how the mind processes data that are emotionally overwhelming. After people have been traumatized, certain feelings, sensations, or actions can, without apparent rhyme or reason, generate a predictable set of emotional or physical responses that are utterly irrelevant to what is occurring in the present. These reactions seem to occur in people with PTSD because neuronal networks in the brain are activated by sensations, emotions, or feelings that correspond to the sensations, emotions, or feelings that were experienced during the trauma. A sensory or motor response is then activated that would have been relevant on the original occasion (such as fight, flight, or freeze), but it fails to resolve the hurt, pain, terror, or helplessness that the person is experiencing, just as it failed to do so during the trauma itself (Kardiner, 1941).

By definition, an experience is *traumatic* when it defines the way people organize their subsequent perceptions. In the first comprehensive theory of traumatic stress, Janet (1889) proposed that the stress is the result of people experiencing "vehement emotions" at the time of a trauma. The intensity of the emotions makes it very difficult to put the entire experience into a satisfactory narrative. Janet was the first to propose that the inability to fully observe and "own" a traumatic event causes memory failure. The event is organized not as a coherent, integrated part of one's self but as disconnected emotions, visual perceptions, or kinesthetic sensations that are reinstated when people are exposed to sensations or emotions that remind them of those events.

Janet proposed that at least two different memory systems are involved in intense emotional experiences. One is an autobiographical memory system that is verbal and serves a social function—communication of one's experiences to others. The other memory system, which today is referred to as *implicit memory*, contains the sensory and emotional imprints of particular events that determine the value that people attach to those imprints (van der Kolk & van der Hart, 1991). Janet suggested that these two memory systems function relatively independently of one another.

Today, researchers could argue that subcortical areas of the brain— the primitive parts that are not under conscious control and have no linguistic representation—have a different way of remembering than the higher levels of the brain in the prefrontal cortex. Under ordinary conditions, these memory systems are harmoniously integrated. Under conditions of intense arousal, the limbic system and brain stem may produce emotions and sensations that contradict one's attitudes and beliefs and cause people to behave "irrationally."

Contemporary research has shown that high levels of arousal interfere with frontal-lobe function (Arnsten, 1998; Birnbaum, Gobeske, Auerbach, Taylor, & Arnsten, 1999) and that reliving a traumatic experience interferes with adequate Broca's area functioning (i.e., the brain region needed to verbalize feelings; Rauch et al., 1996). This dysfunction and the altered functioning of other brain regions needed for proper appraisal of incoming stimuli (e.g., hippocampus, thalamus, cingulate and dorsolateral prefrontal cortex) seem to be responsible for organizing trauma imprints as fragmented sensory and emotional traces (van der Kolk & Fisler, 1995; van der Kolk et al., 1996, 2000).

When people remember a particular event, they generally do not also relive the physical sensations, emotions, images, smells, or sounds associated with that event. Ordinarily, all the remembered aspects of experience coalesce into one coherent narrative that captures the essence of what happened. As people remember and tell others about an event, the story is likely to gradually change with time and telling. The implicit memories of traumatic events have a very different quality. When traumas are recalled, people actually have the experience again; they are engulfed by the sensory or affective elements of past traumas.

Traditional psychotherapy has focused mainly on constructing a narrative that explains why a person feels a particular way, with the expectation that understanding its context will cause the symptoms (e.g., sensations, perceptions, emotional, and physical reactions) to disappear. As Sigmund Freud explained in *Remembering, Repeating, and Working Through* (1914): "While the patient lives it through as something real and actual, we have to accomplish the therapeutic task, which consists chiefly of translating it back again in terms of the past."

Freud and Trauma

After visiting the Salpêtrière Hospital, Freud adopted the concepts about hysteria then accepted at that institution (James, 1894). In 1893, he and his new mentor, Joseph Breuer, wrote a seminal paper entitled *On the Psychical Mechanism of Hysterical Phenomena: Preliminary Communication* (1893), in which they identified most of the critical questions about the relationship among trauma, memory, and the therapeutic process. After noting that patients with hysteria often do not have a narrative memory of traumatic events, they claimed that "hysterics suffer mainly from reminiscences." The question was: What was it about memories of trauma that makes them impervious to the normal wearing away processes typical of all memories? Breuer and Freud postulated that, under ordinary conditions, an emotionally upsetting event is put to rest by an appropriate physical reaction. The reaction is accompanied by an autonomic or muscular discharge, which somehow promotes the mental integration of the experience into autobiographical memory stores. Like Janet, they felt that it was crucial to move beyond emotionally upsetting experiences by associating the experience with other memories that were stored in the mind. This association would create a larger psychological context for the particular experience. When proper integration occurs, the event comes to serve as a guide for future actions.

In their paper, Breuer and Freud (1893) postulated that when people find an adequate physical expression to alleviate their emotional distress, such as an act of revenge, they eventually can leave the trauma behind. Breuer and Freud essentially proposed, many years before the concept was introduced in psychology (Maier & Seligman, 1976), that the origin of traumatic neuroses lies in "inescapable shock." However, they did not consider physical action to be the only way for people to overcome emotional imprints of past experiences. They stated that *verbally expressing* the emotional and factual elements of the experience allows people eventually to put these intense experiences behind them. With this statement, Breuer and Freud paved the road for psychotherapy's use of "the talking cure" in the next century.

However, the basic assumption that finding words to express the facts and feelings associated with traumatic experiences can reliably lead to a resolution turns out to be wrong (van der Kolk & Fisler, 1995). It might be more valid to propose that performing the actions that would have overcome one's sense of helplessness at the time of the experience that became traumatic and expressing the sensations associated with the memory of trauma effectively helps people overcome their traumas.

Breuer and Freud (1893) were struck by another characteristic of extremely upsetting experiences—that people often have difficulty expressing the event verbally or may even be completely unable to do so. Whether this is a result of intentionally forgetting the event, involuntary dissociation, or active suppression and avoidance is not the critical therapeutic issue. The net result is that patients often cannot talk about the very issues that need to be processed to come to terms with what has happened and go on with life. Thus, the hidden nature of the traumatic imprints vexed clinicians in many schools of psychotherapy. The big issue that needed to be addressed was how to create associative networks that would allow people to integrate and own the reality of what had happened to them without forcing them to relive the event over and over again. In other words: how to make these unconscious imprints conscious.

Initially, Freud used hypnosis. However, after becoming concerned with the problem of suggestibility, he resorted to the technique of free association, hoping that by slips of the tongue and deeper understanding of dreams and other dissociative processes, patients and analysts could gain deeper access to the unconscious. At the same time, Freud discovered that unconscious mental assumptions and interpersonal experiences would be relived in the transference relationship. Henceforth, psychoanalytical therapy came to rest on the twin pillars of understanding and reenactment: understanding the patients' thought processes as they were revealed in free association and in dreams and the reenactment of previous interpersonal schemas and derivatives of attachment relationships within the transference.

The Processing of Experience

Humans continuously filter, interpret, transform, and derive meaning out of incoming sensory input, which may come from inside the body (e.g., muscular or visceral activity, chemical reactions, breathing, and fatigue) or from the environment (e.g., images, tactile sensations, scents, sounds). These sensations are meaningless unless they are interpreted and attached to other sensations, configurations, and a larger scheme of meaning. A basic task of the human mind is to evaluate the significance of all incoming information and integrate its emotional and cognitive significance. During this process, the mind needs to rapidly scan millions of possible connections and associations to create the proper interpretation about their existential relevance. It then needs to create a response that not only produces internal satisfaction but also is in harmony with the demands and expectations of the environment.

From birth, interpersonal processes provide the meaning and context of sensations and emotions. Newborns are continuously exposed to internal and external stimuli that they do not understand or know how to change. Babies depend on their caregivers to change the way they feel and are programmed to cry out to attract attention. They leave it to their caregivers to figure out how to relieve their distress, which they do by acting (e.g., feeding, changing diapers) and by providing comfort with their presence, by touching them, by making sounds (prosody), and through movements (e.g., rocking).

If they are well cared for, children associate body signals, distress, and various ways of feelings better. Consequently, they learn to use their own body signals and emotions as guides for action. As primates, human beings are programmed to seek out others for the soothing and regulation that they cannot provide for themselves. People seek help when they are either unable to understand and cope with uncomfortable feelings and physical sensations or when they lack internal schemes to serve as guides for relief. This makes people prone to expect others to provide relief as well as to blame other people as the source of their distress. Dependency may easily lead to the sort of tensions and misunderstandings with which everybody, particularly the parents of small children and therapists of individuals who have been traumatized, are intimately familiar. If comfort does not alleviate their distress, people keep looking for other means of relief. This relief may range from helplessly clinging to others, ingesting drugs or alcohol that alter the way they feel, or engaging in physical acts such as purging or self-mutilation that cause shifts in their internal world.

Regardless of the quality of early caregiving experiences, people's body awareness remains the very foundation of their consciousness. People continuously try to understand the meaning of their sensations, and most of the time they can comfortably put them into the context they belong. As people mature, they develop an ever greater capacity to create mental associations to particular physical sensations preventing the emergence of anxiety. However, when the meaning of physical sensations is associated with extreme fear, arousal, or numbing, people may be unable to manage them. These sensations cannot be associated with potential solutions, so people either panic or shut down emotionally in an effort to ignore it or push it away.

TRAUMA AND PHYSICAL SENSATIONS

The imprints of trauma are unique in causing them to be carved into memory as sensations that are likely to be interpreted within the narrow definitions imposed by the person's traumatic past. For example, combat veterans may have intense physical responses to the sound of firecrackers in the summer but not in the winter because the temperature is different than it was during the war. People who have been sexually abused may react to certain physical sensations they associate with being physically violated even when no harm is done. After a person develops PTSD, the mind loses its flexibility and becomes a black hole, "like the rain drops falling on the roof are collected down the rain spout" (Tank & Hopfield, 1987, p. 106; Pitman & Orr, 1990). Because PTSD creates a type of frozen sensory world, the therapeutic challenge is to open patients' minds to new possibilities so that they can encounter new experiences with openness and flexibility rather than interpreting the present as a continuous reliving of the past.

A primary characteristic of PTSD is the inability to properly place certain physical sensations into the context of current experience. Instead, people with PTSD tend to become terrified and react accordingly. The traumatized person is unlikely to be aware of the physical sensations that precipitate fearful emotions and threatening actions. They are not consciously aware that their reactions are being caused by a reminder of something that occurred in the past. It is as if people who have been traumatized lack a central organizing force to help them place traumatic triggers in their proper context in time and space and may believe that they will never end and that they can do nothing to make them stop.

When they experience such intense emotions, people follow the human inclination to make meaning out of what they feel. In their attempt to create a context, traumatized people try to figure out what in their current environment makes them feel this way; they search for some current stimulus "out there" that explains why they are so upset. They tend to blame themselves and think they are not normal. However, the attempt to find an explanation for these sensations in the present is likely to result in the people attributing their reactions to the wrong stimulus.

The Neurobiology of Trauma

Although the basic psychological formulations of the way the mind processes traumatic experiences had largely been formulated by the end of the 19th century and were rediscovered episodically throughout the 20th century (van der Kolk et al., 1996), it has only been in the past 20 years that we have gained a real understanding of how the brain mediates these processes. In turn, understanding these brain processes has started to help clinicians refine the psychotherapeutic interventions that are necessary to overcome trauma.

Numerous studies have shown that people with PTSD, when confronted with reminders of the original trauma, have psychophysiological reactions and neuroendocrine responses indicating they have been conditioned to respond as if they are being reexposed to the actual trauma itself. In other words, their bodies continue to react as if they are being traumatized in the present even though the event may have occurred many years in the past. As Kardiner explained in 1941, "their focus of attention is narrowed down to stimuli related to threat" (p. 27). When confronted with a sufficient number of sensory elements that match the sensory imprints from the original trauma (e.g., being touched the particular way, smelling certain scents, seeing particular images), patients with PTSD activate biological systems as if they are being traumatized all over again.

One of the many biological systems that has been identified as being affected by traumatic experiences is the part of the limbic system that is centrally involved in interpreting the emotional significance of experience: the amygdala. Research in recent years has shown that the limbic system plays a significant role in causing individuals with PTSD to interpret relatively innocuous reminders as harbingers of the trauma's return. A part of the limbic system, the amygdala, serves as the "smoke detector" that interprets whether incoming sensory information is a threat. The amygdala forms emotional memories in response to particular sensations such as sounds and images that have become associated with physical threats. These emotional interpretations are thought to be "indelible," or extraordinarily difficult to extinguish (LeDoux, 1996). Therefore, the challenge of any effective psychotherapy is to decondition the amygdala from interpreting innocuous reminders as a return of the trauma.

The Tyranny of Language

In a previous paper (van der Kolk, 1994), I outlined how it is likely that in traditional, insight-oriented psychotherapy, people learn to *understand* that certain emotional or somatic reactions belong to the past and are now irrelevant. This may help them *override* automatic physiological responses to traumatic reminders but not *abolish* them. Although this insight provides people with a deeper understanding of the reasons they feel the way they do, insight of this nature is unlikely to be capable of reconfiguring the alarm systems of the brain.

In a neuroimaging study utilizing positron emission tomography (PET) scans, Rauch et al. (1996) showed that when people relive their traumatic experiences, they have decreased activation of Broca's area and increased activation of the limbic system in the right hemisphere of the brain. This suggests that when people with PTSD are reliving their trauma, they have great difficulty putting the experience into words. In fact, relatively increased activation of the right hemisphere compared with the left implies that when people relive their trauma, they are imbedded in the experience—they are *having* the experience—but lack the capacity to analyze what is going on in space and time.

Experience has shown that asking people to put their trauma into words while they are in the process of reliving it can be enormously upsetting and sometimes even impossible. Reliving the trauma without being firmly anchored in the present often leaves people with PTSD more traumatized than they were before. Recalling the trauma can be so painful that many patients choose not to expose themselves to situations in which they are asked to do so, including to exposure therapies.

Research with such therapies has shown that if people are capable of sticking with treatment and are willing to relive the trauma using words and expressing feelings in a safe, therapeutic context, it is very likely that they will overcome their PTSD (Foa et al., 1999; Resick & Schnicke, 1992). However, these forms of treatment also have very large dropout rates (Ford & Kidd, 1998; Pitman et al., 1991; Spinazzola, Hopper, & van der Kolk, 2000), probably because patients feel too overstimulated by experiencing the trauma without rapid relief. Therefore, when treating PTSD, one central challenge is determining the way to help people process and integrate their traumatic experiences without making them feel traumatized all over again. In the language of neuroscience, the challenge is determining how to process trauma so that it is *quenched* rather than *rekindled* (Post, Weiss, Smith, Li, & McCann, 1997).

CLINICAL DILEMMAS FOR THERAPISTS OF PATIENTS WHO HAVE BEEN TRAUMATIZED

Clinicians treating individuals with PTSD are confronted with a number of issues that complicate their capacity to provide effective psychotherapy.

1. *Speechlessness.* Traumatized individuals often lack the capacity to communicate in words the essence of what has happened to them. Instead, the imprints of their trauma consist of sensations and perceptions that may have no verbal equivalents. Confronted with sensations that reinstate a traumatic state, people with PTSD simply *have* their feelings, maladaptive behaviors, and uncomfortable bodily sensations without knowing where they come from. Although words may provide validation, a context, and a capacity to provide an *explanation* for the origins of their sensations and emotions, they

are unlikely to neutralize the emotional associations of their sensations and make them go away. In addition, many traumatized individuals experience alexithymia, an inability to interpret the meaning of their bodily sensations. They simply may not *know* what they feel.

2. *Retraumatization*. When they recall trauma, many people with PTSD become so emotionally distressed that the recollection feels like a retraumatization. As a result, many individuals with PTSD avoid psychotherapy.

3. *The relationship*. Many people with PTSD have had their trust shattered by others and are reluctant to make themselves vulnerable to other human beings, particularly when it involves issues that make them feel frightened and ashamed. Many clinicians assume that a safe therapeutic relationship is the cornerstone of any therapeutic enterprise. Most clinicians believe that establishing a relationship with patients that allows them to let down their defenses and abandon their distrust is essential for accessing memories of the most painful and shameful elements of their past. At the same time, clinicians working with traumatized individuals are all too familiar with the fragility of the therapeutic relationship in PTSD. The frequent disruptions of trust, the abrupt terminations, the numerous different therapists who have been asked to provide relief—over time, the intense transference dilemmas in which love and hate in all their original intensity can make therapeutic (i.e., reflective and analytical) work virtually impossible. Perhaps the therapeutic relationship should provide a context in which patients are encouraged to actively mobilize their defenses, even within their relation with the therapist. Only when patients possess adequate defenses can memories be accessed without retraumatization.

4. *Avoidance*. Many traumatized individuals who are in psychotherapy are able to construct a narrative of the trauma that satisfies their need to communicate the essence of what they went through but that leaves out some of the critical elements of the experience. It may be exactly those elements— the sensations that patients actively avoid confronting and reliving in the therapy relationship—that are most prone to return as flashbacks, nightmares, and behavioral reenactments.

5. *Physiological conditioning*. Even after people remember the entire trauma, understand the way they reenact it in their daily lives, reestablish trusting interpersonal relationships, and create ever larger islands of safety and competence, people with

PTSD may still react physiologically to reminders of the trauma as if they are back in the past.

The Therapeutic Challenge

Given these various dilemmas, the ideal treatment should help people process the past without their re-experiencing it. Such treatment could decondition people from having the physiologically inappropriate responses that were created during the trauma but that are no longer relevant under ordinary conditions. While the ideal treatment should take place in the context of a respectful therapist–patient relationship, it should not force the patient to relive the pain, disappointment, and shame derived from previous interpersonal betrayals within that relationship. Moreover, effective treatment should minimize the time spent reliving the past and experiencing its concomitant emotional devastation and help patients to live fully in the present, without the residual dissociation, and hyperarousal, characteristic of PTSD.

Top-Down Versus Bottom-Up Emotional Processing

More than a century ago, William James (1894) formulated the James–Lang theory of consciousness, which held that changing emotions are the result of perceiving changes in bodily states. In other words, consciousness is fundamentally a product of the interpretations that the mind attaches to the physical sensations that accompany shifts in bodily states. One central finding of contemporary neuroscience, as described by such authors as Antonio Damasio (1999), Jaak Panksepp (1998), and Steven Porges (1995, 2000), is that sensate experience indeed plays a critical role in generating emotional states.

Damasio (1999) stated that "the collection of neural patterns which constitute the substrate of a feeling arise in two classes of biological changes: changes related to body state and changes related to cognitive state" (p. 29). Most forms of traditional psychotherapy have focused largely on changes related to the interplay between emotions and thought. When a person is upset, the therapist attempts to grasp the meaning of what gives it such emotional power, while events in a patient's life are examined for their emotional significance. Most types of therapy have essentially ignored changes related to bodily states, or the sensate dimension of experience.

Infants first learn to interpret their physical sensations in the context of their physical interactions with their mothers. The only tool that a mother has to modulate the emotional states of a baby involves physical sensations: rocking; feeding; stroking; changing sources of physical discomfort, such as wet diapers; making soothing noises; and engaging in other comforting physical interactions. The infant is a "subcortical creature . . .

[who] lacks the means for modulation of behavior which is made possible by the development of cortical control" (Schore, 1994, p. 30). This is strikingly similar to what happens to traumatized people who also appear to be at the mercy of their sensations, physical reactions, and emotions. This physiological hyperreactivity is characteristic of PTSD (van der Kolk, 1987). Even as they mature, human beings continue to rely on the feedback from their somatic state to signal whether any particular stimulus is dangerous or agreeable. Even though they vastly expand their repertoire of soothing activities, people continue to rely on being able to establish physical (sensate) homeostasis to establish a sense of "flow," or "being grounded."

Many different brain systems are involved in the harmonious integration of mental functioning. Self-regulation starts at the level of the brain stem—a part of the brain that is essentially hidden from conscious experience and cannot really be modified by reason.

Once people are traumatized and develop PTSD or if they were abused and neglected as children and therefore have not been involved in a healthy "regulatory dyad" (of which a healthy mother–child interaction is the prototype), they lose the capacity for effective regulation of emotional states. This inability to regulate their emotions, which is expressed as a hypersensitivity to unpleasant experiences, is easily perceived as existential threats. Problems with emotion modulation lead to reliance on actions, such as the fight, flight, or freeze responses, or pathological self-soothing, such as self-mutilation, bingeing, starving, or the ingestion of alcohol and drugs, to regulate internal homeostasis.

Fisher, Murray, and Bundy (1991) have stated the following:

> The brain functions as an integrated whole but is comprised of systems that are hierarchically organized. The "higher-level" integrative functions evolved from and are dependent on the integrity of "lower-level" structures and on sensorimotor experience. Higher (cortical) centers of the brain are viewed as those that are responsible for abstraction, perception, reasoning, language, and learning. Sensory integration and intersensory association, in contrast, occur mainly within lower (subcortical) centers. Lower parts of the brain are conceptualized as developing and maturing before higher-level structures; development and optimal functioning of higher-level structures are thought to be dependent, in part, on the development and optimal functioning of lower-level structures. (p. 16)

When a person perceives a threat, this activates preordained, fixed physiological and motor sequences, such as the startle reflex and various expressions of the fight, flight, or freeze response. The simplest sequences are involuntary reflexes, which originate in the spinal cord (e.g., the knee-jerk reaction). These responses are the most rigidly fixed, whereas more complex response patterns are influenced by early experiences, such as the automatic motor responses (e.g., walking and running) that are developed at a young age.

The degree to which these lower responses can be inhibited depends in part on one's relative level of emotional arousal, which depends on the activation of brain stem arousal centers. Under ordinary conditions, one can suppress one's anger or irritation or ignore the sensation of hunger, even while the appropriate physiological processes associated with these states, such as increased blood pressure, the secretion of saliva, and contraction of stomach muscles, continue. This inhibition is called *top-down processing* (LeDoux, 1996, p. 272). Higher (neocortical) levels of processing can and often do override, steer, or interrupt the lower levels, or interfere with emotional and sensorimotor processing (Ogden & Minton, in press).

Much adult activity is based on top-down processing; higher cortical areas act as a control center. Neocortical areas such as the orbitofrontal cortex, the medial frontal cortex, and the dorsolateral frontal cortex hierarchically inhibit subcortical activity (e.g., Schore, 1994). It is as though most of the time people hover above their somatic and sensory experiences, knowing they are there but not allowing them to dominate their actions. Under ordinary conditions, consciousness allows people to achieve relative homeostasis and control the machinery of emotion, attention, and regulation of body states. Along these lines, Damasio (1999) claimed,

> We use our minds not to discover facts but to hide them. One of the things the screen hides most effectively is the body, our own body, by which I mean, the ins and outs of it, its interiors. Like a veil thrown over the skin to secure its modesty, the screen partially removes from the mind the inner states of the body, those that constitute the flow of life as it wanders in the journey of each day.
>
> The . . . elusiveness of emotions and feelings is probably a symptom, an indication of how we cover the presentation of our bodies, how much mental imagery masks the reality of the body. Sometimes we use our minds to hide a part of our beings from another part of our beings rather than concentrating resources on the internal states. It is perhaps more advantageous to concentrate one's resources on the images to describe problems out in the world, on the options for their solution and their possible outcomes. But this has a cost. It tends to prevent us from sensing the possible origin and nature of what we call self. (p. 28)

Bottom-up processing is a different way of processing information. Young children and threatened adults cannot inhibit emotional states that have their origin in physical sensations. Top-down processing is based on cognition and is operated by the neocortex, which allows for high-level executive functioning by observing, monitoring, integrating, and planning. It can only effectively function if the input from lower brain levels is inhibited.

Traditional psychotherapy relies on top-down techniques to manage disruptive emotions and sensations, which are approached as unwanted disruptions of "normal" functioning that need to be harnessed by reason rather than as reactivated, unintegrated fragments of traumatic states. Top-down processing focuses on inhibiting rather than processing (i.e., integrating) unpleasant sensations and emotions. Ogden and Minton (in press) described bottom-up processing as follows:

> Patients are asked to mindfully track the sequence of physical sensations and impulses (sensorimotor processes) as they progress through the body and to temporarily disregard emotions and thoughts that arise until the bodily sensations and impulses resolve to a point of rest and stabilization in the body. The bottom-up element of the process consists of people learning to observe and follow the unassimilated sensorimotor reactions (primarily, arousal and defensive reactions) that were activated at the time of the trauma.

Bottom-up processing, by itself, does not resolve trauma, but if the patient is directed to track and articulate sensorimotor experience while consciously inhibiting emotions, content, and interpretive thinking, it can gradually be assimilated.

Awareness, as opposed to avoidance, of one's internal states allows feelings to become known and to be used as guides for action. Such mindfulness is necessary if people are to respond adaptively to the current requirements for managing their lives. By being aware of and tolerating their sensations, people have new options for solving problems. This allows people to not react reflexively but to find better ways to adapt. "Consciousness establishes a link between the world of automatic regulation and the world of imagination—the world in which images of different modalities (thoughts, feelings, and sensations) can be combined to produce novel images of situations that have not yet happened" (Damasio, 1999, p. 258).

LEARNING ABOUT EMDR

Five years ago, a friend and colleague, Steve Lazrove, visited me and showed me two videotapes of him using EMDR to treat patients with complex PTSD. Until that time, I had been highly skeptical of this new technique that converted so many mental health professionals. I considered it yet another fad, rather like transcendental meditation or est. However, in the videotapes, I witnessed the obvious intense physiological reactions and psychological distress of people recalling their traumatic experiences entirely disappear after a few sessions of EMDR. Within a few sessions, an event that initially seemed to be relived with timeless intensity merely became a story of the past, devoid of much interest. Because I had tried for many years to help patients gain control over their traumatic memories and had not achieved treatment results remotely as effective as those on the videotapes, I decided to take the EMDR training. I was most intrigued with what happened during the EMDR sessions, both as subject and as object.

In my own session, I thought about the recent closing of my Trauma Clinic and the intense distress I continued to feel. During the EMDR session, I had a rapid succession of hypnopompic images of my family child-hood, scenes that appeared to contain some elements of the closing of the clinic. After 30 minutes of processing these images, the distress I felt as I recalled the announcement of the clinic closing had considerably diminished.

The next element of the EMDR training consisted of my administering EMDR to a therapist colleague who wanted to address some painful adolescent incidents with his father but did not want me to know any of the details about what had happened and the distress he felt about it. I was struck by the intense affect that seems to be precipitated by the EMDR session and the almost total absence of verbal interchange between him and me. In fact, he was quite hostile to me throughout the entire EMDR session. At the end of our episode, he told me that he found meeting with me so unpleasant that he would never refer a patient to me. He also told me that he felt that he had resolved the very painful issues with his father.

I left my EMDR level I training greatly preoccupied with three impressions about EMDR, which have continued to fascinate me to this day:

1. EMDR seems to loosen up free associative processes, giving people very rapid access to memories and images of their past and possibly allowing them to, in some way, associate current painful life experiences with previous life events that have been successfully mastered.
2. EMDR seems to be able to accomplish its therapeutic action without forcing people to articulate in words the source of their distress. In other words, it seems to be possible for EMDR to be effective even when people remain in a relative state of speechlessness.
3. EMDR may be beneficial even in the absence of a trusting relationship between the patient and therapist.

Since my training, all these initial impressions have been confirmed by further experience, and at least one additional surprise has been added. It seems that EMDR is capable of softening the pain of past experiences while it can also enhance feelings of pleasure and serenity associated with others.

FURTHER EXPERIENCES WITH EMDR

After we completed our first collaborative neuroimaging efforts of people having traumatic memories (Rauch et al., 1996), we became very interested in pursuing the possibility of imaging how the brains of people with PTSD may change after effective treatment. When the clinicians at the Trauma Center began to show videotapes of patients with PTSD that seemed to demonstrate dramatic improvements after only a few sessions of EMDR, we decided to embark on a pilot study of treatment outcome using EMDR in which we would use changes in brain function as one of the outcome measures. We recently completed that study and will report the full data set elsewhere. However, in the study, we found that 8 of the 12 enrolled subjects had more than a 30% decrease in their Clinician Administered PTSD Scale (CAPS) scores after three sessions. Generally, these decreases in PTSD scores were accompanied by a concomitant decreased physiological reactivity to a personalized trauma script.

Our brain scan images suggest that several study subjects had decreased prefrontal lobe activation when they were exposed to their personalized trauma script before treatment. After three sessions of EMDR, subjects seemed to have an increase in prefrontal lobe activation. This would reflect increased frontal lobe functioning, which would facilitate being able to make sense of incoming sensory stimulation. This increased frontal capacity appears to be reflected in the change in our subjects' accounts of their traumatic memories. Following EMDR treatment, their narratives of the trauma had a much more symbolic quality than before. For example, after EMDR treatment, one subject reported the following:

> I remember it is it as though it was a real memory, but it was more distant, more manageable. It did not have the vividness that I'm used to having. Typically, I drowned in it, but this time I was floating on top. I had a certain horror in calling up the memory. I did not feel as helpless. I had the feeling that I was in control, that I was not going to drown.

Similarly, before treatment, one subject said, "I saw myself really skinny and naked in the shower. I just see me, with my skin kind of glistening. He was dressed, and I wasn't." After the EMDR treatment, the same subject said, "It wasn't as vivid. I did not see myself on the floor, skinny and wet and frightened. I just kind of listened to the tape and didn't see anything, until he has me against the wall." After EMDR treatment, another subject reported, "This time it was like a cohesive unit. I felt each and every step of it before. Now, it is like an event. It is like a whole, instead of fragments, so it is more manageable." These sorts of changes in personal narratives suggest that EMDR is capable of helping people generate associations between previously dissociated, fragmented sensory impressions.

EMDR AS ACCELERATED INFORMATION PROCESSING

The central challenges of psychotherapy have always been the quest to help patients gain control over feelings that are usually blocked off but intrude on behavior and emotion in unbidden ways. Over the years, different schools of psychotherapy have attempted to use different techniques to facilitate access to those feelings and promote harmony between emotions, cognitions, and behavior. Two well-known tools to promote such associations within the psychoanalytic tradition have been hypnosis and free association. Psychoanalysis found the understanding and analysis of dreams to be an important tool for helping people understand and make associations between different life events, motivations, and affect experiences. For reasons that are not currently understood, EMDR seems to provide a third avenue to facilitate such linkages, a method that appears to work much faster than any other nonpharmacological tool that has hitherto been employed.

Although patients have very different experiences during EMDR treatment and even patients themselves may have very different experiences from one session to the next, many patients report very rapid access to material that they had not consciously linked to their current quandaries. Some patients are much more articulate than others about the images and thoughts that come to their minds during EMDR sessions.

INTEGRATIVE CAPACITY OF EMDR: TRANSCRIPT OF ONE SESSION

Following is an example of the capacity of EMDR to help patients integrate their experiences. A transcript allows the reader a chance to evaluate the therapeutic process, which cannot be captured in rating scales or by other quantitative methods. This transcript is of one EMDR session with a 24-year-old woman, during her fourth treatment session. She had been in individual psychotherapy for 3 years with a therapist she trusted and who she felt understood her, but she felt she had stopped making progress. She functioned well in her current professional position but had severe impairments in her interpersonal relationships, which she ascribed to a long history of paternal incest and numerous other incidents of sexual abuse by her father and his friends. She had never maintained a sustained, close, interpersonal relationship and was terrified of being involved in intimate relationships with men or women.

At the end of each set of eye movements, the therapist says, "Take a deep breath," which is followed by, "What do you get now?" or "What comes to mind now?" Carefully tracking emotional changes in the patient, he says, "Stay there" or "Feel that" when the patient seems to have arrived at a new level of emotional arousal or has discovered a new emotionally significant theme. Other than those sentences, the therapist merely remains silent and attentive, staying out of the way of the patient's associations. These sentences and sets of eye movements by the therapist are represented by "Initiates sequence."

Patient: I realize that I have scars—from when he tied my hands behind my back. The other scar is when he marked me to claim me as his, and there (points) are bite marks.

I remember being doused in gasoline—he took Polaroid pictures of me—and then I was submerged in water. I was gang raped by my father and two of his friends; I was tied to a table, I remember them raping me with Budweiser bottles.

Therapist: Initiates sequence.

Patient: Never again! I went to model mugging [a self-defense program for rape victims]—it was great! They really kicked butt! I saw them backing off. I yelled, "Don't you see you are hurting me? I am not your girlfriend."

Therapist: Initiates sequence.

Patient: I'm picturing my life now—my big me holding my little me—saying, "You are safe now."

Therapist: Initiates sequence.

Patient: I have pictures of a bulldozer flattening the house I grew up in. It's over!

Therapist: Initiates sequence.

Patient: I rented the movie *A Bastard Out of Carolina*. I saw how little I was—and the brutalization of the little girl. It was not my fault.

Therapist: Initiates sequence.

Patient: I have an image of two me's—this smart, pretty, little girl —and that little slut. All these women who could not take care of themselves or me, or their men—leaving it up to me to service all these men.

Therapist: Initiates sequence.

Patient: I am thinking about how much I like Jeffrey. (He is in Europe now.) Thinking that he might not want to hang out with me. Thinking "I can't handle it." I have never been someone's girlfriend before, and I don't know how.

Therapist: What are the basics that you feel you don't know?

Patient: All the roles were so conditional. Now, there is a person who just wants to be with me—it is too simple. I don't know how to just be still and be myself around men. Sexually, I am petrified.

Therapist: Initiates sequence.

Patient: (crying profusely) I had an image of Jeffrey and me sitting in the coffee house. My father comes in the doorway. He starts screaming at the top of his lungs, and he is wielding an ax; he says, "I told you, you belong to me"—he puts me on top of the table—then he rapes me, and then he rapes Jeffrey. After Impact Model Mugging I will know how to fight him off—but not yet.

(crying) How do you, can you be "open" with somebody when you have visions of your dad raping you, and then raping us both?

Therapist: What are you feeling in your body when you say that?

Patient: I feel it in my forearms, in my shoulders, and my right chest. I just want be held.

Therapist: Initiates sequence.

Patient: I heard Jeffrey say, "It's okay, that he was sent here to take care of me. And that it was not anything that I did and that he just wants to be with me for my sake."

Therapist: What do feel in your body now?

Patient: I feel really peaceful. A little bit shaky—like when you're using new muscles. Some relief. He knows all this already.

I feel like I'm alive and that it is all over. I have the feeling that I do not need to be frozen anymore, because I am bigger and smarter than he. But I am afraid that he has another little girl and that makes me very, very sad. I want to save her.

Therapist: Initiates sequence.

Patient: I need to throw up. I had to throw up a lot as little girl. I have intrusions of lots of smells—bad cologne, alcohol, and the smell of vomit. I believe I need to do something with this. There is a reason that I am so smart and have not become a drug addict or a prostitute. There is a sense of purpose in all this.

Therapist: Initiates sequence.

Patient: I really feel my mom here now. It is really nice. It feels like she wants me to forgive her. I have the sense that the same thing happened to her when she was a little girl. She has been dead for 6 years now. But she is okay now, and she is really proud of me.

Therapist: Initiates sequence.

Patient: I can really feel what it was like to hug her. (Cries for several minutes) I can really feel her bones—she is apologizing to me over and over. She's telling me that this happened to her—that it was my grandfather. (Cries profusely) She's also telling me that my grandmother is really sorry for not being there to protect me. That she tried to protect me by sending me Richard.

I just want to get all the memories out, I just want to get it out and over with.

Therapist: Initiates sequence.

Patient: I am remembering the gang rape in the garage. Feeling a tongue in my mouth. Felt my grandmother being there, holding my hand. That gave me a warm and safe sensation.

Therapist: Initiates sequence.

Patient: I feel like it's over. I felt my grandmother holding me in my current age—telling me that she is so sorry she married my grandfather. That she and my mom are making sure that it stops here. (Smiles and laughs)

Therapist: Initiates sequence.

Patient: I have an image of pushing my father out of the coffee house with Jeffrey locking the door behind him. He stands outside. You can see him through the glass—everybody makes fun of him.

[Wrap up. End of session.]

EMDR AND THE TRANSFORMATION OF EXPERIENCE

This session illustrates how a person is able to use EMDR to transform her experiences and integrate her memories of what happened to her, combine them with her wishes and imaginations, to move toward a subjective sense of completion and control. She initially discusses stark images, bodily sensations, and other imprints of horrendous childhood experiences, the reality of which were never questioned and do not need to be because this is her subjective experience—one that dominates her perceptions of the present. With little input from the therapist during the EMDR session, she is able to combine these images and sensations with her desire to go on with her life.

The three elements of EMDR that struck me during my own initial experience are the same remarkable elements I noted in this EMDR session: (a) the lack of or minimal input from the therapist; (b) the relatively few words used to describe the details of the traumatic experience; and (c) the activation of new images and thoughts that have, at best, weak associations to the core elements of the trauma.

What Does EMDR Do?

(a) *EMDR promotes the activation of images and thoughts with only weak associations to core elements of the trauma.* The apparent capacity of EMDR to activate a wide variety of unexpected sensations, feelings, images, and thoughts that are ordinarily not accessed in conjunction with other memories strikes me as the single most remarkable feature of this procedure. This capacity for association may be how people ordinarily integrate daily experiences into the totality of their self-experience. Freud searched for ways in which to activate subconscious connections and came to rely on free association as the best method available to him. It is possible that EMDR, as Francine Shapiro (1995) claims, indeed promotes accelerated information processing, the very characteristic that Freud was looking for when he invented the method of free association. This lack of association and the persistence of stark, unmodified, and unsymbolized imprints of sensory and affective elements of the trauma are characteristic of traumatic memories (van der Kolk & Ducey, 1989).

Stickgold (2002) has pointed out the similarity between the associative process produced by EMDR and what seems to occur in rapid eye movement (REM) sleep. He points out how REM sleep activates cholinergic activity in the brain. He proposed that cholinergic activity during REM sleep promotes the loose association between various elements of experience. It is these loose associations that give dreams their irrational quality but also promote the sprouting of associative networks that open up the possibility of multiple, flexible associations. Unlike traumatic memories, which cause one sensation to precipitate very specific associated memories, in REM sleep (seemingly like in EMDR), associative networks are highly flexible. In some way EMDR appears to foster the integration of trauma-related sensations into new associations that are not necessarily connected with the traumatic past. (I hope that this topic will be the future subject of a whole new line of inquiry.)

(b) *The therapeutic alliance is not central to the ability to process information, but therapeutic attunement is.* For effective therapy to occur, it must provide some degree of safety and structure. These are necessary to prevent the activation of interpersonal projections of threat or rescue. Therapy must help people fully experience their sensations and emotions without projecting them onto the environment or reactivating a sense of helplessness and lack of control. Effective therapy helps people accept trauma-related feelings for what they are: reminders of the past.

The basic human position is a social one: that danger comes from outside, and that we can manage emotions and sensations by controlling and effectively responding to the external world. People tend to project internal states of disorganization or fear onto the outside to defend themselves and regain a sense of power and control. Being unable to tolerate and utilize physical sensations and emotional states increases anxiety and the urge to control. A controlling person is an anxious person. Being able to manage one's sensations as distinct, finite chunks that change as one attends to them creates a sense of mastery and ownership. This control over sensory experience is the beginning of establishing new islands of safety and purpose, in which a person comes to trust the processes of the body instead of trying to fight and dominate them.

When people feel safe, they tend to have pleasurable physical sensations accompanied by feelings of openness and expansion. These sensations, in turn, open up new possibilities. Previous experiences involving safety, comfort, and soothing give people a reservoir of pleasurable and safe memories. When they feel threatened and under stress, people with these memories can evoke those feelings and apply them, at least temporarily, to deal with stress at hand.

The opposite process happens to traumatized people. They often are unable to distinguish between internal and external. Their challenge is to gain awareness of the threatening sensations they experience and place them where they belong—in the proper time and place. These sensations need to be organized so that they harmonize with current reality.

Successful therapy activates and repairs these damaged internal regulatory processes by facilitating the organization of inchoate trauma-related sensations into new metaphors and new contexts. If the central deficit in PTSD is a decreased ability to associate new information with existing experience—which causes them to hyperassociate current sensations to past pain—the task of therapy is to help patients form new associations that do not lead to a reliving of the past. This is not the same as telling stories. It consists of *physically* experiencing new possibilities by welcoming and allowing these split-off bodily feelings to run their course. Having experiences that contradict previous associations may stimulate such flexibility.

One of the hallmarks of interpersonal traumatization is that people who have experienced abuse and betrayal are likely to interpret a host of current interactions as a reactivation of the past. They easily become distrustful, frightened, aggressive, suspicious, or withdrawn in response to even minor provocations. The clarification and understanding of traumatic re-experiencing within the transference relationship often becomes a central aspect of many psychotherapeutic endeavors with chronically traumatized individuals. Even when patients are rationally convinced of the benign intentions of the therapist, minor misunderstandings or transgressions often can trigger full-blown re-experience of trauma-related affects, images, and sensations.

While meticulous attention to these transference pitfalls is essential for successful therapy outcome, the relationship itself is unlikely to be able to thoroughly rearrange the patient's conditioned emotional responses and associated physiological abnormalities. The notion that a caring relationship between therapist and patient can provide a corrective emotional experience that can undo the damage of the past is fraught with problems. Any technique that can help people deal with their traumatic experiences and does not necessarily involve relying on a trusting relationship may circumvent the ubiquitous threat of traumatic re-enactment.

CONCLUSION

Although knowledge of the elements of the way trauma affects the mind and body is more than a century old, that body of knowledge has been gradually refined. One of the refinements is the understanding that trauma is not primarily imprinted on people's consciousness but instead becomes deeply imbedded in people's sensate experiences. Talking and insight may help people regain a sense of mastery, but they are unlikely to change people's sensate experiences that form the engines of continuous traumatic reliving. The process that started with showing that bilateral eye movements can help people rapidly and effectively process traumatic sensations and emotions and their associated attributions of self and other was a remarkable step to explore new ways of helping people move beyond the tyranny of the past.

At this point we can only speculate about EMDR's mechanisms of action, and we are only beginning to explore the precise elements of therapeutic action. Aside from its remarkable therapeutic efficacy, this novel treatment changes our most fundamental paradigms about how therapy changes psychological programs. Providing bilateral stimulation obviously does not directly affect consciousness; it is likely to act on subcortical processes that have little or nothing to do with insight and understanding.

The efficacy of EMDR as a therapy is relevant for the exploration of the basic underlying mechanisms of posttraumatic stress, such as how trauma affects subcortical processes of emotion regulation, arousal modulation, threat information, and memory processes. It promises to shed light on the fundamental question of how the mind comes to integrate experience in a way that prepares it for future threats while distinguishing between what belongs in the present and what belongs in the past.

Only careful observations, controlled experimentation, and their integration with the knowledge base of multiple other disciplines, such as neuroscience, learning theory, and developmental psychopathology, will allow us to fully appreciate the richness of this new method of psychotherapy that shows such promise to help people move beyond the tyranny of their traumatic histories.

REFERENCES

Arnsten, A. F. (1998, June 12). The biology of being frazzled. *Science, 280,* 1711–1712.

Birnbaum, S., Gobeske, K. T., Auerbach, J., Taylor, J. R., & Arnsten, A. F. (1999). A role for norepinephrine in stress-induced cognitive deficits: alpha-1-adrenoceptor mediation in the prefrontal cortex. *Biological Psychiatry, 46,* 1266–1274.

Breuer, J., & Freud, S. (1893). On the psychical mechanism of hysterical phenomena: Preliminary communication. In J. Strachey (Ed. & Trans.), *Standard edition of the complete psychological works of Sigmund Freud* (Vol. 2, pp. 1–181). London: Hogarth.

Calvin, W. H. (1990). *The cerebral symphony.* New York: Bantam Books.

Chemtob, C. M., Tolin, D. F., van der Kolk, B. A., & Pitman, R. K. (2000). Eye movement desensitization and reprocessing. In E. B. Foa, T. M. Keane, & M. J. Friedman (Eds.), *Effective treatments for PTSD: Practice guidelines from the International Society for Traumatic Stress Studies* (pp. 139–155, 333–335). New York: Guilford Press.

Damasio, A. (1999). *The feeling of what happens.* New York: Harcourt, Brace.

Fisher, A., Murray, E., & Bundy A. (1991). *Sensory integration: Theory and practice.* Philadelphia: Davis.

Foa, E. B., Dancu, C. V., Hembree, E. A., Jaycox, L. H., Meadows, E. A., & Street, G. P. (1999). A comparison of exposure therapy, stress inoculation training, and their combination for reducing posttraumatic stress disorder in female assault victims. *Journal of Consulting and Clinical Psychology, 67,* 194–200.

Ford, J., & Kidd, T. (1998). Early childhood trauma and disorders of extreme stress as predictors of treatment outcome with chronic posttraumatic stress disorder. *Journal of Traumatic Stress, 11,* 743–761.

Freud, S. (1959). Remembering, repeating and working through. In J. Stachey (Ed. & Trans.), *The standard edition of the complete psychological works of Sigmund Freud* (Vol. 12, p. 145). London: Hogarth Press. (Original work published 1914)

James, W. (1894). Book review of Janet's "État Mentale des Hysteriques" and of J. Breuer & S. Freud's "Ueber den Psychischen Mechanismus Hysterischer Phaenomene." *Psychological Review, 1,* 195–199.

Janet, P. (1889). *L'automatisme psychologique.* Paris: Alcan.

Janet, P. (1894). Histoire d'une idée fixe [The history of a fixed idea]. *Revue philosophique, 37,* 121–163.

Kardiner, A. (1941). *The traumatic neuroses of war.* New York: Hoeber.

Lang, P. J. (1985). The cognitive psychophysiology of emotion: Fear and anxiety. In A. H. Tuma & P. Maser (Eds.), *Anxiety and the anxiety disorders* (pp. 131–170). Hillsdale, NJ: Erlbaum.

LeDoux, J. (1996). *The emotional brain.* New York: Simon & Schuster.

Lee, K. A., Vaillant, G. E., Torrey, W. C., & Elder, G. H. (1995). A 50-year prospective study of the psychological sequelae of World War II combat. *American Journal of Psychiatry, 152,* 516–522.

Maier, S. F., & Seligman, M. E. P. (1976). Learned helplessness: Theory and evidence. *Journal of Experimental Psychology, 105,* 3–46.

Minsky, M. (1980). K-lines: A theory of memory. *Cognitive Science, 4,* 117–133.

Ogden, P., & Minton, K. (in press). Sensorimotor sequencing: One method for processing traumatic memory. *Traumatology.*

Panksepp, J. (1998). *Affective neuroscience: The foundations of human and animal emotions.* Oxford, England: Oxford University Press.

Piaget, J. (1962). *Play, dreams, and imitation in childhood.* New York: Longmans, Green.

Pitman, R. K., Altman, B., Greenwald, E., Longpre, R. E., Macklin, M. L., Poire, R. E., et al. (1991). Psychiatric complications during flooding therapy for posttraumatic stress disorder. *Journal of Clinical Psychiatry, 52,* 17–20.

Pitman, R. K., & Orr, S. (1990). The black hole of trauma. *Biological Psychiatry, 26,* 221–223.

Porges, S. W. (1995). Orienting in a defensive world: Mammalian modifications of our evolutionary heritage. A polyvagal theory. *Psychophysiology, 32,* 301–318.

Porges, S. W. (2000). Emotion: An evolutionary by-product of the neural regulation of the autonomic nervous system. The integrative neurobiology of affiliation. *Annals of the New York Academy of Sciences, 807,* 62–77.

Post, R. M., Weiss, S. R. B., Smith, M., Li, H., & McCann, U. (1997). Kindling versus quenching: Implications for the evolution and treatment of posttraumatic stress disorder. In R. Yehuda & A. C. McFarlane (Eds.), *Psychobiology of posttraumatic stress disorder. Annual New York Academy of Sciences, 821,* 285–295.

Rauch, S. L., van der Kolk, B. A., Fisler, R. E. A., Nathaniel, M., Orr, S. P., Savage, C. R., et al. (1996). A symptom provocation study of posttraumatic stress disorder using positron emission tomography and script-driven imagery. *Archives of General Psychiatry, 53,* 380–387.

Resick, P. A., & Schnicke, M. K. (1992). Cognitive processing therapy for sexual assault victims. *Journal of Consulting and Clinical Psychology, 60,* 748–756.

Schore, A. (1994). *Affect regulation and the origin of the self: The neurobiology of emotional development.* Hillsdale, NJ: Erlbaum.

Shapiro, F. (1995). *Eye movement desensitization and reprocessing: Basic principles, protocols, and procedures.* New York: Guilford Press.

Spinazzola, J., Hopper, J. W., & van der Kolk, B. A. (2000, November). *Treatment outcome research in PTSD: Patient selection and dropout rates.* Paper presented at 14th annual conference of the International Society for Traumatic Stress Studies, Washington, DC.

Stickgold, R. (2002). EMDR: A putative neurobiological mechanism of action. *Journal of Clinical Psychology, 58,* 61–75.

Tank, D. W., & Hopfield, J. J. (1987). Collective computation in neuronlike circuits. *Scientific American, 257*(12), 62–70.

van der Kolk, B. A. (1987). *Psychological trauma.* Washington, DC: American Psychiatric Press.

van der Kolk, B. A. (1994). The body keeps the score: Memory and the evolving psychobiology of posttraumatic stress. *Harvard Review of Psychiatry, 1,* 253–265.

van der Kolk, B. A., & Ducey, C. P. (1989). The psychological processing of traumatic experience: Rorschach patterns in PTSD. *Journal of Traumatic Stress, 2,* 259–274.

van der Kolk, B. A., & Fisler, R. E. (1995). Dissociation and the fragmentary nature of traumatic memories: Overview and exploratory study. *Journal of Traumatic Stress, 8,* 505–525.

van der Kolk, B. A., Hopper, J. W., & Osterman, J. A. (2001). Exploring the nature of traumatic memory: Combining clinical knowledge and laboratory methods. *Journal of Aggression, Maltreatment, and Trauma, 4,* 9–31.

van der Kolk, B. A., Pelcovitz, D., Roth, S., Mandel, F., McFarlane, A. C., & Herman, J. L. (1996). Dissociation, somatization and affect dysregulation: The complexity of adaptation to trauma. *American Journal of Psychiatry, 153,* 83–93.

van der Kolk, B. A., & van der Hart, O. (1991). The intrusive past: The flexibility of memory and the engraving of trauma. *Imago, 48,* 425–454.

4

THE DEVELOPING MIND AND THE RESOLUTION OF TRAUMA: SOME IDEAS ABOUT INFORMATION PROCESSING AND AN INTERPERSONAL NEUROBIOLOGY OF PSYCHOTHERAPY

DANIEL J. SIEGEL

This chapter provides an overview of an interdisciplinary approach to understanding the nature of the developing mind and how the unresolved effects of trauma may be resolved within psychotherapy. Following is a brief background of my introduction to eye movement desensitization and reprocessing (EMDR) and Francine Shapiro, the founder and a leading pioneer in the field of EMDR.

Shapiro and I met for the first time at a trauma conference at which we were both members of the panel of lecturers.[1] It was exhilarating to see the parallels in our conceptual thinking despite the marked differences in the origins of our models. Her work in developing EMDR and the growing

---

[1] Lifespan Learning Institute, "Understanding and Treating Trauma," M. Solomon, coordinator. Los Angeles, CA, January 1998.

clinical and research interest in it as a method of treatment provided the background for her to develop the concept of an accelerated information-processing foundation for EMDR's mechanism of action.

My work comes from an interdisciplinary approach that combines numerous independent fields, including attachment theory and research, cognitive neuroscience, complexity theory, developmental psychology and psychopathology, genetics, psycholinguistics, and the study of trauma. By weaving the findings from these varied disciplines together with clinical work as a child psychiatrist, I developed a conceptual framework that was published as a book, *The Developing Mind: Toward a Neurobiology of Interpersonal Experience* (Siegel, 1999). This chapter offers a brief overview of this work and highlights ways in which this interpersonal neurobiology approach may help in understanding some possible mechanisms underlying trauma and its resolution.

This chapter is only a condensation and initial introduction to this interdisciplinary perspective and is adapted from a more general discussion of trauma (Siegel, in press). A more extensive presentation and thorough discussion of the research background and details about the specific scientific reasoning and references that form the foundation for this framework can be found in the textbook (Siegel, 1999) and related publications.[2] With this framework as a foundation, the chapter highlights possible parallels with some of the processes that may be involved in various forms of effective psychotherapy. The chapter specifically focuses on EMDR as an example of a clinical method that may promote accelerated information processing and the resolution of trauma.

INTERPERSONAL NEUROBIOLOGY OF THE DEVELOPING MIND AND UNRESOLVED TRAUMA

The field of mental health is in a tremendously exciting period. Recent findings from cognitive neuroscience have revealed some new insights into how mental processes emerge from the activity of the brain. Independent advances in the science of development, especially longitudinal studies in the field of attachment, have shed new light on how early experiences influence such fundamental processes as memory, emotion, and the regulation of behavior. The often isolated fields of neurobiology and attachment have a fascinating set of convergent findings relevant to the understanding of trauma. Examination of these and other areas of research can offer new ways of understanding how the developing mind is shaped

---

[2]See Siegel 1995, 1996, 1999, and 2002. The ideas in this chapter have been adapted from these publications and the summary of *The Developing Mind* found in the 1998 *Signal* publication, Vol. 6, No. 3–4, of the World Infant Mental Health Association.

by the interaction of interpersonal experience and neurobiological processes in the creation of the human mind.

The mind develops throughout life as people interact with others in their environment. The genetically influenced timing of the emergence of specific brain circuits during the early years of life makes this a time of particular importance for the influence of interpersonal relationships—with parents and other caregivers—on how the structure and function of the brain will develop and give rise to the organization of the mind. Overwhelmingly stressful experiences may have their greatest impact on the growth of the mind at the times when specific areas of the brain are in rapid periods of development and reorganization. For this reason, the early years of life may be a time of enhanced opportunity as well as vulnerability. Trauma during the early years may have lasting effects on deep brain structures responsible for such processes as the adaptation to stress and the encoding of memory. As explained in the chapter, specific states of mind can also be deeply engrained as a form of a traumatic memory; these states can also be a lasting effect of early traumatic experiences.

How does experience affect the brain? How can human relationships, supportive or traumatizing, influence the activity and development of the brain? What are the mechanisms by which interpersonal experience can actually shape neuronal activity and growth? These questions have led me to become immersed in a pursuit of a "neurobiology of interpersonal experience": a way of understanding the neurobiological processes by which the mind emerges from the activity of the brain during interactions with other brains—with other minds. Some of the more devastating effects of trauma occur because of relationship-based experiences, such as domestic violence or child abuse. Being grounded in a neuroscience of relationships can allow those in the field of mental health to approach their work with a deeper understanding of the central importance of interpersonal experience in creating the subjective life of the mind.

Mind, Brain, and Experience

What is the mind? How do the processes of the mind emerge from the neuronal activity of the brain? Although it cannot be seen with or without a microscope, the mind does have an organization to its processes that can be described and studied. Mental processes such as memory, emotion, attention, behavioral regulation, and social cognition can be understood by examining the nature of brain activity. Recent technological advances have permitted new insights into the nature of the mind. For example, the modern view of the brain and its response to experience has shed some light on how experience directly affects gene function, neuronal connections, and the organization of the mind.

The brain is composed of a massively complex network of about 10 to 20 billion interconnected neurons. The activity of neurons occurs in a network of activation—a certain portion of a spiderweb type of neural network active across time. It is the specific pattern of this brain activity across time that determines the nature of the mental processes created at a given moment; the timing and the location of neural activation within the brain determine the information contained within the neural net patterns, or *neural maps*. Activity in sensory regions may mediate perception, and the specific nature of this firing may signify the different aspects of perceptual information (e.g., a visual stimulus, auditory input, tactile sensation). Information carried within perceptual regions often becomes integrated into a larger cross-modal perceptual system. Such an integrating process is an example of how the brain functions as a hierarchical set of layers of relatively distinct component elements or processing modalities with neuronal activity that may become clustered together into a functional whole.

The brain as a system is composed of hierarchical layers of component parts that can be examined at several analytical levels: single neurons, neuronal groups, circuits, systems, regions, and hemispheres. At birth, the brain is the most undifferentiated of any organ in the body. As development unfolds, neural pathways are created as synapses are formed, which allows for these component parts to become differentiated and be responsible for such functions as attention, perception, memory, and emotional regulation. A large number of genes encode for the timing and general details of how circuits are to develop early in life. However, the creation, maintenance, and elaboration of neural connections may often also require that they be activated in a process sometimes called *experience-* or *activity-dependent development*. Experience activates specific neuronal connections and allows for the creation of new synapses and the strengthening of existing ones. In some cases, lack of use leads to impaired synaptic growth and to a dying-away process called *pruning*, in which connections are lost and neurons may die. Such a pruning process seems to be a major event during the adolescent years, in which the huge increase in synaptic density created during the early years is then pruned to the lower densities of the adult years. How genetically encoded information interacts with environmental and interactive elements to determine the nature of this important adolescent pruning period is a topic for future investigations.

The differentiation of the brain during the early years of life depends on genetic information and proper experiential stimulation. For this reason, the early years of life—during establishment of the basic brain circuits that mediate such processes as emotional and behavioral regulation, interpersonal relatedness, language, and memory—are the most crucial for people to receive the kinds of experiences that enable proper development to occur. Attachment studies suggest that these experiences involve the interactions between the child and the environment. In particular, interactions in the environment of the social world are important—the world in which the child lives. These types of interactions are more significant than the type of sensory bombardment provided by some parents in the form of visual or auditory stimulation who feel pressured to "build better brains" in their children. As the chapter explains, the experiential food for the mind takes the form of collaborative communication instead of sensory overload.

But how does experience actually influence neurons and the genes that encode, in part, their growth and development? Research has demonstrated that genes have two major functions: (a) Genes store information in their *template* function, and (b) genes are expressed in their *transcription* function, which produces specific proteins that can alter cell structure and function (Kandel, 1998). The activation of neurons during an experience leads to the creation of new synaptic connections by activating genes that produce the proteins necessary for neuronal growth and synapse formation. Genes do not exist in a vacuum and may require experience for their expression. Genes can be activated by an experience, revealing the biological reality that experience directly shapes brain structure via gene activation. In the end, experience affects the mind by altering the synaptic connections within the brain. Brain development is a result of several processes, including the extensive growth of synapses that are strengthened, maintained, or allowed to die away; the creation of new synapses in response to experience and its activation of neurons; the alteration of neurotransmitter release and receptor density and sensitivity; and the myelination of neural sheaths, resulting in increased conduction speed of the action potential down the length of the axon, thus functionally increasing the connectivity of neurons.

Recent findings in neurobiology suggest that the brain may continue to develop across the life span. Such development may involve the ongoing modification of synapses or the possible growth of new neurons. In some cases, neurons that integrate widely distributed areas in the brain may continue to grow beyond the early years of life (Benes, 1998). During this exploration of the nature of trauma, the focus needs to remain on how traumatic experiences may alter synaptic connections in a way that impairs subsequent functioning in unresolved states. As described in the following section, one proposal is that trauma directly impairs the capacity to integrate a range of cognitive processes into a coherent whole. Recent studies of anatomical structures of the brains of children who were abused have revealed an associated reduction in overall brain size and impairments in the development of the corpus callosum, the bands of neural tissue that transfer information between the two halves of the brain (De Bellis, Keshavan, et al., 1999).

The Mind: Patterns in the Flow of Energy and Information

Various disciplines explore the mind and its ability to process information and regulate the function of the individual in adapting to the environment. They consider the mind to emerge from and also regulate the self and the physiological processes from which it emerges. The mind is considered to be a process that is fundamental to each person.

A dictionary definition of the *psyche* includes the terms *soul, intellect, spirit,* and *mind.* While attempting to put these various perspectives into a broader framework, it has been useful to have a working definition that considers the mind to be emerging from the patterns of the flow of energy and information within individuals and between individuals. In this way, the mind is created by neurobiological processes within individuals and interpersonal interactions between individuals.

Brain activity processes information within its energized neural patterns. Information is processed in the brain through patterns of neural activity that represent aspects of the internal or external world. These mental symbols, codes, or images are conceptualized as being embedded within patterns of neural net firing, which are sometimes called *neural net profiles* or *neural maps.* For example, when people recall a visual image, such as the house in which they grew up, the firing of a pattern of neural circuits within their visual system is similar but not identical to the pattern or map that fired when they were actually there years ago. Memory, like other mental processes such as ongoing perception, is an actively constructive process that draws on a range of neural systems and is shaped by a wide variety of external and internal factors. Within the brain, the pattern of activation (energy) of distributed neurons acts as a symbol (information) of some experienced event that is constructed by the mind.

Information is represented in the mind through the flow of neural activity across various spatially distributed circuits. The way in which these representations become functionally linked and have additional effects, such as contrasting, clustering into categories, and extraction of general properties, is the essence of information processing. The resultant neural activity becomes a mental symbol itself and creates a cascade of representational processes that are at the heart of the flow of cognition.

Trevarthen (1996) and Tucker, Luu, and Pribram (1995) have described the ways in which the right and left hemisphere are dominant for the mediation of distinct modes of representational processing. Even before birth, the brain reveals an asymmetry in its structure and development. In infants, the right hemisphere dominates growth during the first 3 years of life. It is thus likely to be more vulnerable to the effects of trauma during this crucial period. Recent discoveries over the past several decades have generated many fascinating notions about the divided brain and mental processes. For the purposes of this chapter, I highlight those findings that are particularly relevant to trauma and its resolution. Most of these findings are from the majority of individuals who have the characteristic left-hemisphere (language function) dominance, which is typical of right-handed individuals and the majority of left-handed people. The left hemisphere is dominant for the semantic aspects of language, syllogistic reasoning (drawing cause–effect relationships), and linear analysis. The right hemisphere is usually dominant for nonverbal aspects of language (e.g., tone of voice, gestures), facial expression of affect, the perception of emotion, the regulation of the autonomic nervous system, the registration of the state of the body, and social cognition (including the process called *theory of mind*).

Some researchers have suggested that the right hemisphere is able to experience more intense emotionally arousing states of mind. Furthermore, the retrieval of autobiographical memories seems to be mediated by the right hemisphere. In addition, the registration and the regulation of the body's state seem to be predominantly mediated by the right hemisphere. Recent studies of people having flashbacks suggested that these people have an intense activation of the right-hemisphere visual cortex and an inhibition of left-hemisphere speech areas (Rauch et al., 1996). As discussed in the following section, general impairments in representational integration, including the bilateral integration of information processing between the right and left hemispheres in particular, may be a core deficit in those with unresolved traumatic memories. Therapeutic interventions that enhance neural integration and collaborative interhemisphere function may be especially helpful in moving unresolved traumatic states toward resolution. The strategic activation of specific information-processing modalities may be a possible mechanism of action in the creation of coherent narratives (Siegel, 1999), which is an outcome in various approaches to the treatment of individuals with posttraumatic stress disorder (PTSD), including cognitive–behavior therapy (CBT), psychodynamic psychotherapy, and EMDR. As discussed in a later section of this chapter, specific elements of the EMDR method may be selectively activating representational processes that are dominant in each hemisphere. Their simultaneous activation may cause the brain to link these otherwise isolated processes into a functional whole.

An overview of the relationship between attachment and mental health reveals that the most disturbed form of attachment, called *disorganized/disoriented attachment*, is associated with the most disturbed developmental outcome (Lyons-Ruth & Jacobwitz, 1999). Children with this form of attachment are more likely to have emotional, social, and cognitive impairments later in life. It has been proposed that the experience of these children involves frightened, frightening, or disoriented behavior on the part of the parent (Main & Hesse, 1990). Two important findings are that (a) these children are prone to develop dissociative symptoms (Carlson, 1998), and (b) the parents' autobiographical narrative of their own childhood has features consistent with unresolved trauma or grief (Hesse, 1999). The adults' attachment classification, which is based on the adult attachment interview (AAI), is described as *unresolved/disorganized* (Hesse, 1999). In this situation, the aspect of attachment raises a crucial clinical red flag of warning regarding the intergenerational transmission of trauma. These findings also raise the important issue of what effects *unresolved* trauma has on the functioning of the mind and brain. These issues are a primary focus of *The Developing Mind* (Siegel, 1999).

Memory

Recent discoveries in the development and neurobiology of memory have yielded some exciting and relevant insights into the nature of how the mind responds to experience and influences later functioning (Milner, Squire, & Kandel, 1998). Two major forms of memory have been described: implicit and explicit. *Implicit memory* includes a range of processes such as emotional, behavioral, perceptual, and possibly somatosensory memory. These forms are present at birth and involve circuitry that does not require focal attention for encoding. People do not have the sense that they are "recalling something" when retrieving an implicit memory. This sensation is considered to be a part of the *explicit-memory* experience, which requires the maturation of brain areas such as the hippocampus, which does not occur until after the first year of life. For example, an infant bitten by a dog may have an emotional response of fear when seeing a dog in the future but may have no sense that a specific memory is being recalled.

At less than a year of age, implicit memory is available but explicit memory is not because of the genetically programmed timing of maturation of different circuits in the brain. Implicit memory is *not* the same as unconscious memory. The effects of the recall are indeed within conscious awareness but are only experienced in the present and not with the subjective sense that something is being recalled. These implicit forms of memory are thought to exist in areas of the brain that subsume their functions, such as the amygdala and other areas of the limbic system (emotional memory), basal ganglia and motor cortex (behavioral memory), and the sensory cortex (perceptual memory). These regions are relatively well developed at birth and capable of responding to experience by alterations in the synaptic connections within their circuitry—the essence of memory encoding.

Another important aspect of implicit memory is the ability of the mind to form *schema*, or mental models of experience. These generalizations can encompass various experiences and sensory modalities and reflect the brain's inherent capacity to function as an anticipation machine— deriving from ongoing experience an anticipatory model of what may occur in the future. Making mental models conscious may be a part of a self-concept. The process may be revealed during EMDR during the negative self-belief or self-statement phase of the method. Mental models can also be seen within "read-between-the-lines" themes of the narratives that structure both people's life stories and the manner in which they live their daily lives. For example, a mental model that others cannot be trusted can emerge when one tells a story of an experience of perceived betrayal, and it can also influence behavior as revealed in how a person is willing to be vulnerable within intimate relationships.

Explicit memory requires focal attention for its encoding and seems to activate a region of the brain called the *medial temporal lobe*, which includes the hippocampus. The postnatal maturation of parts of the hippocampus may explain the reason explicit memories do not exist until after the first year of life. When people retrieve an explicit memory, they have the subjective sense that they are recalling something. Explicit memory includes two major forms: (a) semantic (factual) and (b) episodic (autobiographical). The episodic form of memory has the unique features of having a sense of self and time. Recent brain imaging studies have suggested that episodic memory is mediated by numerous regions, including an area of the brain called the *orbitofrontal cortex*. The maturation (synapse formation and myelination) of this and related parts of the prefrontal cortex during the preschool years may be the neurobiological basis for the emergence and continued development of autobiographical memory and self-awareness during childhood and beyond. Wheeler, Stuss, and Tulving (1997) used the phrase *autonoetic consciousness* to refer to the ability of the mind to know the self and carry out "mental time travel"—seeing the self in the past, present, and possible future. The development of the orbitofrontal regions during the first years of life may help researchers understand the onset of this autonoetic capacity during the toddler and preschool periods. The possible ongoing development of this region may also explain the ways in which experience continues to shape the way people come to understand themselves and their world.

A tremendously exciting convergence of findings regarding the orbitofrontal region suggests numerous highly relevant processes are subsumed by this coordinating area of the brain. Located in the prefrontal cortex just behind the eyes and sitting at the junction of the limbic system (which includes the anterior cingulate cortex, hippocampus, and amygdala), the associational regions of the neocortex, and the brain stem, this convergence area receives input from and has neural pathways to a wide array of perceptual, regulatory, and abstract representational regions of the brain. In this manner, the orbitofrontal cortex integrates information from widely distributed systems and regulates the activity of processes ranging from memory representations to the physiological functions, such as heart and respiration rates. The orbitofrontal cortex (a) has been suggested to be dependent on attachment experience for its growth and mediation of emotionally "attuned communication"(Schore, 1994, 1996); (b) plays a primary role in mediating autonoetic consciousness (Wheeler et al., 1997); (c) monitors the state of the body, regulates the autonomic nervous system, and serves as a primary circuit of stimulus appraisal which evaluates the meaning of events (Damasio, 1994); and (d) seems to be an important region subsuming social cognition and theory-of-mind processing (Baron-Cohen, 1995). Interestingly, it seems that it is the orbitofrontal cortex on the right side of the brain that is dominant for most of these processes. Each of these basic aspects of the developing mind is mediated by the same self-regulating, experience-dependent circuits, which initially differentiate during the early years of life.

The following proposal regarding bilateral neural integration, memory consolidation, and the resolution of trauma is based on numerous independent, empirically derived views regarding memory, brain function, and the clinical findings from those with PTSD. This hypothesis has been offered as a possible integration of a range of convergent findings and awaits future empirical studies to support its proposals.

The background findings relevant to this hypothesis include the following:

1. Tulving, Kapur, Craik, Moscovitch, and Houle (1994) proposed a "hemisphere encoding and retrieval asymmetry" hypothesis postulating that autobiographical memories involve encoding by the left orbitofrontal region and retrieval by the right.

2. Explicit memory is thought to proceed through a series of encoding stages that include (a) the initial registration in sensory memory (which lasts less than half a second), (b) encoding into working memory (which lasts 30 seconds), (c) encoding into long-term memory (which lasts days, months, or years), and (d) the consolidation of elements of long-term memory into permanent memory. The last step may take days or months to occur. The representations are then integrated into a network within the associational cortex (independent of the hippocampus) so that they can be retrieved at a later date (McClelland, 1998).

3. REM sleep is essential for the consolidation of memory. Emotional elements of past events are woven together with thematic components of memory to achieve a reintegration, or consolidation, of memory representations.

I have proposed that the autobiographical narrative process may be a fundamental part of cortical consolidation. A dream can be considered to be an emotionally driven narrative process that incorporates elements of distant and more recent past events, ongoing perceptions, and random activations in the reorganization (not new encoding) of existing memory traces. This reveals how memory retrieval can be a form of memory modification (Bjork, 1989). Unresolved trauma can be considered an impairment of this memory consolidation process. Such an impairment may be revealed within the REM sleep disturbances and nightmares that are so prevalent in people with PTSD and in the incoherent narratives and intrusive implicit elements of memory that torment their internal subjective world and interpersonal relationships.

Following is the proposal: Unresolved trauma involves the impairment of integration of representational processes within the brain. This impairment can have various effects on those with PTSD and may make them vulnerable to developing inflexible, reactive states of heightened emotion that lack self-reflection. At the core of unresolved trauma is an impairment in a core process of neural integration. One expression of this impairment is the blockage of memory consolidation (and the resolution of the trauma). Memory consolidation occurs normally via a proposed bilateral activation process in which the right hemisphere is activated and creates an autonoetic retrieval state. The transfer of information from the right hemisphere to the left hemisphere enables the left to use these representations as part of its autonoetic encoding state. In essence, the reactivated autobiographical representations (in the right hemisphere) become the basis for newly reorganized autobiographical encoding (in the left hemisphere). Dreams function within REM to enable this consolidation process to occur. Narratives reflect an internal, nonverbal process of neural integration that may become ultimately expressed in words. Coherent narratives, whether nonverbal or language-based, emerge from such a bilateral integration process. The process of bilateral integration can thus be proposed to be one of the core elements in resolution.

The narrative process that is so fundamental to many forms of psychotherapy may also facilitate (as well as reveal) this integration between the hemispheres. However, the core issue is representational integration. These representations, or mental images, may manifest in an array of modalities, from various forms of perception (e.g., sight, hearing) to words. It is thus quite likely that the therapeutic progress (increased integration) may give rise to increased coherence of autobiographical narratives. This view suggests that mere verbal expression of an internal experience may not be the core feature of successful therapy. Such sharing and expression may need to include a range of representational modalities divided at the most basic level into the nonverbal and the verbal. A sense of safety and the emotional connections created by a secure attachment in a therapeutic relationship may be essential for these integrative processes to finally occur within the mind of a person who has been traumatized. Future research is needed to examine whether this proposed neural integration and resolution process is associated with alterations in neural function and changes in specific integrative neural circuits, such as those in the corpus callosum, prefrontal cortex, and anterior cingulate regions.

Emotion

Researchers have addressed the topic of emotion by examining levels of psychological function, attachment theory, and, more recently, neurobiological substrates of emotional development. The proposed interpersonal neurobiological approach examines the fundamental role of emotion by drawing on various levels of analysis, from neuronal processes to interpersonal relationships, in viewing the individual mind as a system. Similarly, the relationship between individuals is proposed to be the way two minds function together as a dyadic system. This perspective allows clinicians to move back and forth between neuronal activity and mental function and between individual and dyadic processes.

Although a wide range of details are included in the ways researchers attempt to define emotion, many authors highlight numerous common features (Garber & Dodge, 1991; Sroufe, 1996). Emotion is often considered to be a way in which the mind appraises the meaning of a stimulus, a response to engagement with the world, and a way to prepare the self for action. Emotion is also considered to comprise many levels of manifestation, including subjective, cognitive, physiological, and behavioral components.

A fascinating recursive finding regarding the regulation of emotion has been noted by several authors. Emotion is regulated and is regulatory. In other words, the process of having an emotion regulates other mental processes and is itself regulated by mental processes. This view supports the more recently held perspective that no discernible boundaries exist between people's thoughts and feelings. Emotion influences and is influenced by a wide range of mental processes. That is, emotion, thought, perception, memory, and action are inextricably interwoven. Perception is the brain's preparation for action: Perception cannot exist without the potential for action on incoming stimuli. Thus, regions mediating perception are directly influenced by those that respond, internally and behaviorally, to perceptual representations.

Likewise, modern views of the brain circuitry subsuming emotional processes support the theory that all brain layers are influenced by the emotion-generating regions. In fact, recent theories of the neurobiology of emotion suggest that the limbic region, which includes the orbitofrontal cortex, anterior cingulate, hippocampus, and amygdala, has no clearly definable boundaries. This finding of widely distributed neural integration suggests that the functional integration of a wide array of anatomically segregated processes, such as perception, abstract thought, and motor action, may be a fundamental role of the brain. Such an integrative process may be at the core of what emotion does and is. As I have proposed, trauma may directly impair the core integrative capacity of the mind. Therefore, trauma may cause neuronal patterns to become engrained, which restricts the ability of the brain to functionally cluster independent modes of information processing. Such a restriction may involve a single brain (e.g., functional isolation of one hemisphere) or more than one brain (e.g., rigidly constrained interpersonal communications among those who experienced intrafamilial child abuse). With this perspective, resolution of trauma requires a movement toward freeing the innate tendency of the mind to integrate its functions.

The brain as a system can be thought of as a set of differentiated neuronal groups and circuits that can be clustered into a functionally integrated set of activations. Edelman (1992) described the importance of these clusters of interacting parts. The clusters have a *value system* that can reinforce, or select, certain stimuli and neuronal responses and give them more value than others. A range of neuromodulatory systems, including the limbic regions, may be such value systems. A value system must extensively innervate far-reaching areas of the brain, enhance the excitability and activation of neurons, and influence the plasticity of neurons (i.e., their capacity to strengthen and form new neuronal connections). Using these criteria, the limbic regions may be categorized as a primary source of value for the brain. The central location of limbic structures, especially the orbitofrontal cortex and anterior cingulate, may allow these areas to play a crucial role in the neural integration of neocortical, limbic, and deeper structures (which are responsible for states of alertness and body functions).

Regarding the neuronal functions directly related to emotion, researchers believe several important domains of mental processes are interdependent. Stimulus appraisal (the evaluation of meaning), neural circuit activation, social communication, bodily state, and autonomic regulation each seem to be mediated by a closely linked system of neural circuits. Interestingly, these elements of the self seem to be fundamentally linked to the neural substrates of various forms of consciousness (Damasio, 1999). Emotion, body state, and a core consciousness of the self emerge from the same brain circuitry. The significance of this finding is that it explains aspects of communication within attachment relationships. Communication is the primary experience that regulates and organizes the development of the brain circuits that mediate self-regulation and social relatedness. A sense of self emerges directly from interactions with others (Stern, 1985). Early in life, when an infant's brain is developing the circuitry responsible for these domains, attachment relationships help the experience-dependent growth of crucial neuromodulatory regions responsible for emotional regulation (Schore, 1994). Trauma during this early period, especially for those who may be genetically vulnerable to the effects of stress on unfolding brain structures, may have devastating effects on the development of the basic mental processes that create the self. As discussed previously, the overwhelming stress of early abuse seems to be associated with significant alterations in brain development and function (De Bellis, Baum, et al., 1999; De Bellis, Keshavan, et al., 1999).

Sharing information about one's emotional state is a direct route by which one mind connects to another. The brain's evaluation of the meaning of events (the information) links to the activation of neural circuits (the energy). The internal experience of emotion becomes the music of the mind—the rhythmic flow of energy and information through the neural circuitry. The sharing of emotion between people that is typical in those with secure attachment relationships is the way in which the flow of energy and information occurs between individuals' minds, a process that often involves nonverbal exchanges. Nonverbal signals may be one way in which the right hemisphere of one person can connect with the right hemisphere of the other person. The right hemisphere may have a far greater role than the left in the regulation of body and emotional state and in mediating social and emotional communication. This attunement of right-to-right hemisphere may be crucial in establishing the secure attachment environment that may be essential for effective therapy. The therapeutic process thus can be considered an avenue for therapists to serve as a type of attachment figure, part of an interactive relationship that coregulates internal states and eventually allows the patients to more autonomously self-regulate their emotional states.

Within neural circuits, the systems that mediate the perception of social communication, especially the nonverbal messages from facial expressions, gestures, and tone of voice, are closely linked to those that appraise the meaning of stimuli and regulate the activation of the autonomic nervous system. These circuits seem to be predominantly in the right hemisphere. Thus, information and energy flow are directly regulated by the regions that carry out and perceive interpersonal communication.

It is with this new awareness that researchers and clinicians can discover the mechanisms underlying the long-held clinical belief in how powerful human relationships are in organizing our continually emerging minds. The nonverbal behavior of a psychotherapist is crucial for establishing a sense of safety and security within the fragile and vulnerable conditions of therapeutic work. The distinct but equally important logical and verbal output controlled by the left hemispheres of patients and therapists connect in a different way during the therapeutic process. This process is discussed in a later section.

States of Mind and Self-Regulation

The capacity of the mind to organize itself can be explored by examining the nonlinear dynamics of complex systems, or complexity theory.

Modern applications of this systems view of the human mind have yielded some powerful ideas for understanding development. In essence, these applications suggest numerous relevant concepts: self-organization, the movement toward increasingly complex states of activation, and the regulation of the activation state of a system by internal and external factors called *constraints*. In early development the parent's mind alters the present state of the child's mind and helps form the neural circuits that will enable the child's brain to regulate itself in increasingly sophisticated ways. Interaction between parent and child thus promotes self-organization in the interactive moment and the creation of self-organizational neural capacities for the future. Parental behavior that produces disorganization within a child's mind thus may create not only an impairment in functioning in the moment but, if repeated, a tendency to disintegrate in the future. Such a form of self-dysregulation may be at the heart of dissociation (Siegel, 1996).

The organization of attachment relationships may reveal characteristic ways in which a parent's state of mind becomes linked to a child's. For example, a securely attached child–parent relationship may easily result in dyadic states in which their minds join and function as a single adaptive and flexible system. Such a system can be considered to be highly integrated and highly differentiated, creating maximum complexity of the system's flow of states across time.

This feature of complexity theory has profound implications on numerous levels. One implication is that integration occurs when differentiated components are functionally coupled. In the case of secure attachments, this coupling may allow for a balance in the patterns of regularity and novelty within the flow of states of the pair that enables the achievement of maximal complexity. Such a balance manifests as attuned, or contingent, communication. According to complexity theory, the balance allows the system to achieve the most flexibility and stability.

Children with disorganized attachments may have experienced abrupt shifts in state on the part of the parent that can result in fear and disorientation and abrupt shifts in the child's own state of mind. The hypervigilant stance of these children may involve highly coupled communication with poor differentiation that may minimize the level of complexity achievable by the dyad. Parents may seem unable to perceive their children's distress and are thus unable to provide interactive regulatory experiences that could enable the children to use the parents to create tolerable levels of arousal. As mentioned previously, repeated experiences within disorganized attachments have been shown to be associated with dissociation (i.e., mental processes fail to become integrated into a coherent whole; Carlson, 1998; Main & Morgan, 1996; Ogawa et al., 1997).

Integration

Integration, which can be considered to be a central self-organizing mechanism that links the many disparate aspects of internal and interpersonal processes, can be defined as the functional coupling of distinct and differentiated elements into a coherent process or functional whole. This concept has been used by a wide range of researchers, including those studying group behavior (interindividual integration), development across the life span (individual integration), and brain functioning (neural integration). Within a coherently integrated process, adaptive and flexible states are achieved as individual components remain highly differentiated *and* become functionally united. The states are considered to be moving toward conditions that maximize complexity.

The interweaving of findings from attachment research, complexity theory, and neurobiology yield some intriguing possibilities. One idea is that the mind functions as a system that develops the ability to self-organize and uses the modulation of internal and external constraints. Internal mechanisms include neuromodulatory processes that enable the mind to regulate its states of activation, representational processes, and behavioral responses. Such a well-developed capacity for neuromodulation would be mediated by circuits capable of integrating a range of neural processes, from abstract representations to bodily states. As previously discussed, these circuits may confer value to stimuli and are functionally connected to the systems that mediate interpersonal communication.

Coherent narratives and flexible self-regulation may reflect the mind's integrative process. When the mind of one person freely and collaboratively exchanges energy and information with another mind, interpersonal integration has occurred. Such adaptive and flexible states flow between regularity and predictability on the one hand and novelty and spontaneity on the other to yield a maximum degree of complexity. Such dyadic states develop during the interactions of securely attached children and their parents. The mind, or the flow of energy and information, is thus conceptualized as an inherently integrating system. This system may be viewed from a wide range of analytical levels—from groups of neurons, to dyads, to families, and even to communities. Such a view may allow researchers to synthesize their understanding of the brain's neurobiology (internal constraints) and provide insight into the interpersonal functioning (external constraints) of people within dyads and larger social groups.

Another application of integration is involved in those with unresolved trauma or grief. Unresolved states can be thought of as an ongoing barrier of the mind to achieving coherent integration. Lack of resolution thus implies a person has blockage in the flow of information and energy within the mind. The lack of resolution may manifest itself as an impairment in a person's capacity to coherently transfer energy and information to another person's mind. This theory helps explain the reason the most robust predictor of disorganized attachment is a parent's unresolved state of mind (which is revealed in the adult attachment narrative). The various forms of dissociation that can accompany lack of resolution are examples of failed integration. For example, people with unresolved states may experience the intrusion of elements of implicit memory, such as emotions, behaviors, and perceptions, but have no associated explicit memory of past traumatic experiences (Siegel, 1995). Such dissociations (or *dis-associations*) of mental processes may be at the core of clinical dissociation and an outcome of trauma and previous disorganized attachments.

The concept of integration also plays a role in the way people tell their life stories. The structure of the narrative process itself may have at its core the integration of mental health and emotional resilience. Within the brain, the neural integration of the processes dominant in the left hemisphere with those dominant in the right may produce a bihemispheric integration that enables many functions to occur, ranging from perceptual processes to motor coordination. Another process that may depend on bilateral integration is coherent narrativization. The left hemisphere functions as the interpreter, searching for cause-and-effect relationships in a linear, logical mode of cognition. The right hemisphere mediates autonoetic consciousness and the retrieval of autobiographical memory. Also dominant on the right side of the brain is the social cognition, or theory-of-mind, module of information processing. Coherent narratives can thus be thought of as a product of the integration of left- and right-hemisphere processes. The drive to explain cause-and-effect relationships resides in the left hemisphere, and the capacity to understand the minds of others and of the self within autonoetic consciousness reside in the right hemisphere. Therefore, a person's ability to develop a coherent narrative reflects the mind's ability to integrate its processes across time and across the representational processes of both hemispheres.

Perhaps impediments to the mind's capacity for integration, internal and interpersonal, are at the core of unresolved traumatic experiences. Perhaps such an integrative capacity is at the heart of mental health. Finding ways to facilitate an integrative process within and between individuals may enable clinicians to help others grow and develop.

INFORMATION PROCESSING AND THE RESOLUTION OF TRAUMA

The following sections of the chapter explore some ideas about information processing and the resolution of trauma that may be relevant to the effective treatment of individuals with unresolved trauma—specifically, ideas that are relevant to the method of psychotherapy used in EMDR. As

Shapiro has noted, the phrase *eye movement desensitization and reprocessing* is more historical than descriptive and inadequately summarizes the method used in EMDR. However, the name is still used as a result of general familiarity. Shapiro has suggested that the fundamental process at the root of EMDR's effects is a form of *accelerated information processing*. The nature of EMDR's efficacy and specificity, EMDR's essential components, and the exact ways in which the method works each need to be examined carefully in controlled research paradigms. From the information-processing perspective, EMDR is a method that uses basic aspects of mental representational processing that may be present in other forms of effective psychotherapy. Therefore, this chapter focuses on the use of accelerated information processing in EMDR, although it may already be used in numerous other effective approaches such as CBT and may be incorporated or expanded into existing and future approaches to the psychotherapy of those who have been traumatized. This chapter discusses a conceptual framework that is based on the previously discussed interpersonal neurobiological view. This framework may apply to the connections among information processing in the brain, the impact of trauma, and the mechanisms of action of psychotherapeutic intervention. This discussion involves hunches about information processing, neurobiology, and the resolution of trauma that need to be validated by specific research in the future.

Insights From the Academy

Before discussing the possible mechanisms of trauma and its resolution, it is helpful to consider some general principles of clinical practice. At a recent combined annual meeting of the American Academy of Child and Adolescent Psychiatry and the Canadian Academy of Child Psychiatry, several educational sessions focused on how clinicians determine which therapeutic strategies to use for their patients. One of these sessions (Whalens, 1999) included several of the most current thinkers in the research and practice of how to treat children and adolescents with various psychiatric disturbances, such as attention deficit disorder, depression, Tourette's syndrome, obsessive–compulsive disorder, bipolar disorder, anxiety disorder, and thought disorders. Many of these leaders in the field examined some basic principles of clinical care that parallel some of the controversies in the field of trauma treatment. Following is an outline of some topics that are relevant to the issues in this chapter:

1. *Risk–benefit analysis:* The decision to treat a patient with a certain modality or strategy should always involve an assessment of the potential risks and benefits of the approach.
2. *Scientific–clinical rationale:* Decisions about whether to treat a patient with specific approaches should incorporate the latest

scientific research on their mechanisms of action and their clinically demonstrated efficacy and safety.

3. *Statistical vs. individual tailoring of therapeutic approach*: Carefully controlled studies examining the statistical probability of treatment response and treatment side effects need to be carried out and guide treatment choices when possible. Placebo-controlled, double-blinded studies are extremely important considerations in the determination of which treatment elements may be producing a clinical response.

4. *Unclear mechanisms of action*: Some researchers can only hypothesize about the possible mechanisms of action of certain therapeutic agents and then pursue study of their specific modes of action. Clinical approaches may work even if researchers do not know their exact mechanisms of action.

5. *Individualized treatment*: Consideration of the individual patient may affect treatment decisions involving statistical analyses of the "generalized patient." For example, unusual side effects and both positive and negative treatment outcomes may not be predicted by standardized studies.

The use of antidepressant medications for treating preadolescent children helps to illustrate some of the previous points. It had long been known that these medications were extremely helpful for treating adults with major depressive disorder. The decision to use these medications for adolescents and preadolescents was based on the simple logic that "if it works for older individuals, it is likely to work for younger ones." In carefully designed studies, this logic generally was proved to be true for the adolescents but not for the younger patients. After this finding was repeated, clinicians who treated children were faced with a dilemma: should they subject children to the unknown side effects of medications when studies had shown that the medications' effects were no better than a placebo? Generally, clinicians are advised to use other forms of treatment, including the CBT and interpersonal therapy approaches, and other forms of psychotherapeutic intervention such as family therapy. However, some children do not respond to these methods, so the clinician is forced to consider alternative treatments. As is the practice in the thoughtful clinical community and as is advised by the leading research clinicians in the field, sometimes clinicians must choose a treatment modality for an individual even when research involving grouped statistical samples has found that the treatment group showed no more improvement than the control group. Fortunately, such interventions seem to alleviate the suffering of some of these children.

The preceding example highlights a general principle. Researchers must attempt to conduct carefully controlled studies to determine which treatments work for particular patients. Nevertheless, clinicians must embrace the idea that in some instances, necessary statistical procedures in certain studies may actually exclude particular individuals or situations that could indeed benefit from the studied approaches. The same may be relevant in trauma treatment. Whereas numerous individuals may not need a particular intervention, a few may benefit immensely from it.

Depending on its timing in an individual's development, trauma may have a unique impact on the mind. Therefore, clinicians may expect to note marked differences in the effects of overwhelming stress on the developing brain. For example, De Bellis, Baum, et al. (1999) demonstrated that children who were abused had impaired development of specific regions of the corpus callosum; the research did *not* show hippocampal effects, which were found in studies of individuals who were traumatized later in life. This finding may be important because it may indicate that individuals who have been traumatized may have quite distinct patterns of effects and may need different aspects of therapy for treatment to be effective.

Finally, clinicians must keep in mind, the importance of the "First do no harm." approach They must weigh the risk–benefit ratios carefully, always remembering that not treating a patient may also be risky. For some individuals, a safe treatment approach that has been statistically shown to not have a statistically demonstrated effect should not automatically be eliminated from possible treatment options. CBT and EMDR may both be effective methods of treatment for individuals with PTSD. As carefully designed future dismantling studies may reveal, the sensory stimulation component of EMDR may be unnecessary for a successful treatment of many individuals. Knowing how the nonsensory components of the EMDR method and the mechanisms of CBT help heal patients can only help clinicians understand how to treat their patients. However, use of the sensory stimulation for certain individuals may improve the treatment efficacy. For example, the stimulation may be beneficial for patients whose therapeutic progress has stalled and who need an approach that is individually tailored, similar to the situation often encountered with preadolescents who have significant mood disturbances. Clinicians should try to keep an open mind about the importance of clinical research and these clinical care principles as they work to understand and help their patients.

Unresolved Trauma

The discussion in the first part of this chapter suggests that traumatic experiences affect individuals by overwhelming the innate capacity of the mind to respond to stressful events. *Overwhelming* indicates that the brain's ability to process the incoming data is impaired. The flow of information and energy (the essence of the mind) in the brain leads to a dysfunction in the movement toward maximizing complexity. Excessive brain responses, resulting in the release of stress hormones and other chemicals such as catecholamines, norepinephrine, and epinephrine, can have deleterious effects on the functioning of numerous brain systems (De Bellis, Baum, et al., 1999; De Bellis, Keshavan, et al., 1999). Affected brain systems include the medial temporal lobe with the hippocampus, which may be especially susceptible to transient and long-term impairments due to high levels of cortisol. For example, individuals with chronic PTSD have been found to have hippocampi with smaller volumes than control groups (Bremner & Narayan, 1998). The impact of overwhelming stress on this system may cause inhibition of explicit-memory processing in the setting of intact implicit encoding. As discussed, this process may be at the heart of dissociative reactions to stress and may be mediated by specific impairments in the neural circuits that integrate information in the brain.

Overwhelming events, or traumatic experiences, may also have more global effects on the mind. People with excessively restrictive and controlled states of mind or chaotic and disorganized states of mind are examples of this global effect. Patterns in the flow of energy and information become ingrained and manifest as these restrictive or chaotic states, revealing a lack of trauma resolution. As discussed, such an impairment in the system's movement toward complexity directly interferes with its ability to adapt to changes in the internal or external environment. Such impaired flexibility leads to dysfunction in the internal and interpersonal worlds of the individual.

Lack of trauma resolution also manifests as an impairment in the innate capacity of the mind to integrate energy and information flow. *Integration* can be defined as the functional clustering of independent subcomponents into a cohesive whole at a given moment in time. Integration also exists across time and enables the mind to achieve coherence across its many states. Within the brain, neural integration can involve a wide range of layers of components, including clusters of neurons, neural circuits, systems, and hemispheres. With names such as *vertical, lateral, dorsal–ventral,* and *spatiotemporal integration,* the nature of this neural process can be described in quite specific detail. At the core of neural integration is the process called *emotion.* Emotion is inherently integrative; it links subcomponents together in a functional whole. Emotion is also a fundamental part of self-regulation. Therefore, the proposal that unresolved trauma exerts its effects by impairing integration implies that lack of resolution is a form of self-dysregulation and a lack of emotional equilibrium. Integration, self-regulation, and emotion are thus inextricably intertwined neural processes that are impaired in unresolved traumatic conditions.

The Resolution of Trauma

According to the chapter's discussion, one can deduce that the general approach to psychotherapy for individuals with unresolved trauma is to attempt to enhance the mind's innate tendency to move toward integration, both within the brain and within interpersonal relationships. The measure of efficacy for such an approach is an enhancement in self-regulation and emotional processing. In addition to the dissolution of the many and varied symptoms of PTSD, one could also predict numerous other fundamental changes in the individual's functioning. From a systems perspective, therapeutic improvement would be revealed as a more adaptive and flexible mind capable of responding to changes in the internal and external environment. Mood stability would replace emotional lability. An increased capacity to experience a wider range and intensity of emotions would emerge, as would a greater tolerance for change. Resolution would also be indicated by the individual's movement toward more differentiated abilities while simultaneously participating in more joining experiences. This increased individual differentiation and interpersonal integration would reflect the mind's movement toward increasingly complex states. Overall, these changes would reflect not only the freedom from posttraumatic symptomatology but also the enhanced capacity of the individual to achieve integration (internal and interpersonal) and thus more adaptive and flexible self-regulation.

This enhanced integration would result in more coherent autobiographical narratives of specific traumatic events and the life of the individual as a whole. Narratives include personal stories and the ways in which the individual's life is lived, or *narrative enactment*—the way life decisions are made and the quality in which daily life is experienced.

The Interpersonal Experience of Psychotherapy

In general, psychotherapy can be seen as the basis for a form of attachment relationship, one in which the patient seeks proximity to (i.e., wants to have physical and emotional closeness with) the therapist, has a safe haven (is soothed when upset), and achieves an internal working model of security (called a "secure base") derived from the patterns of communication between therapist and patient. Healing within psychotherapy can thus be defined as the ways in which the innate, hard-wired attachment system of the brain is used to enable a patient's mind to achieve more functional self-regulation. As with attachment in general, interactive regulation is first required to enable the mind to achieve more autonomous (and adaptive) self-regulation. The patterns of communication that have been found to be the most effective in creating secure attachments are those that involve reciprocal, contingent, collaborative communication. This type of communication involves the give and take of signals between the two members of the interacting pair. Right-to-right and left-to-left hemisphere communication patterns involve nonverbal and verbal components, respectively.

At the core of effective therapy of many forms may be the manner in which the patient and therapist are able to engage in collaborative communication. For individuals with unresolved trauma, this therapeutic attachment relationship enables the patient's mind to enter terrifying states and process information that previously may have led to excessively restrictive or chaotic patterns in energy and information flow. This interpersonal communicative experience may cause these rigidly constrained or disorganized states, which are at the core of unresolved trauma, to be dramatically—and permanently—altered. It is not essential that patients verbalize all the details of their trauma but rather that they be given a sense of safety, allowing such traumatic states to be re-experienced, communicated if possible, and altered into more adaptive patterns in the future. What emerges from such a process are new levels of integration of information and energy flow. If such a process involves the bilateral integration of information across the hemispheres, an increased coherence of autobiographical narratives may result. Note that the creation or communication of such a narrative may not be essential for resolution but rather may be an expression of resolution.

Accelerated Information Processing and EMDR

EMDR as a method contains very specific elements that may be essential for it to enable patients to resolve their trauma. As Shapiro explained, if EMDR were just about moving the eyes back and forth, people would just need to turn on their windshield wipers and their traumas would be resolved. Instead, like any method of effective psychotherapy, EMDR involves quite specific elements that build on the interpersonal setting described. This section includes highlights of some of the specific component elements of the EMDR approach and proposals of some neurobiological mechanisms that may be at work. As mentioned previously, these ideas are hunches that need careful research to establish their validity. Investigating which elements of EMDR are essential for effective outcomes is also an area of study that may help elucidate the mechanisms of the resolution process.

Focal Attention

When a therapist says to a patient, "Think about [something]" or "Put that image in the front of your mind," the therapist is asking the individual to activate a process called *focal attention*. This form of intentional, conscious attention focuses a kind of attentional spotlight on a set of representations activated at a specific moment in time. Focal attention seems to be a part of the working-memory process, which is considered to be the "chalkboard of the mind." Working memory is thought to be mediated by numerous circuits, especially the dorsolateral prefrontal cortex and the anterior cingulate. Representations activated at a given moment are thought to be linked to the activity of these regions.

The conscious component of working memory may involve a range of elements, including the thalamocortical system and its forty cycles per second (40 Hz) sweep of activity across the brain (Llinas, 1990). Another theory is that when a critical level of integrative clustering occurs, representational processes become a part of conscious awareness (Tononi & Edelman, 1998). Damasio (1999) presented a view of consciousness that examines the ways in which the brain creates neural maps representing the response of the self to interactions with objects in the internal or external world. Focus on the objects results from enhanced neural mapping of the entity that is interacting with the self.

As discussed previously, this sense of core consciousness is intimately connected to the creation of emotion. Therefore, emotion can be thought of as an integrating neural process that emerges as people engage their selves with the world (internal and external). Each perspective may help explain different aspects of consciousness and focal attention. This chapter uses the perspective that involves the dorsolateral prefrontal cortex, a 40-Hz thalamocortical sweep, representations of the interacting self, and the achievement of a certain level of functional clustering (integration) to bind representational processes into consciousness.

The involvement of focal attention seems to be a requirement for the processing of information into explicit memory. This process requires the hippocampus for initial encoding into long-term memory. As discussed, this process may have been impaired in those with unresolved states. Thus, the therapeutic use of focal attention on images of trauma is no casual thing. Using the process of focal attention on representations of past experiences and their associated states of mind can begin to create the opportunity for new forms of information processing.

The therapeutic focus of attention on multiple layers of representational processes, including images, emotions, bodily sensations, global linguistic statements, and perceptions generated from recollections, is a unique and important process. This multilayered focus of attention produces a new information-processing configuration in the brain. By doing so, this therapeutic strategy leads to a new associational matrix of the varied representational elements. Within the setting of a secure, empathic therapeutic relationship, such a multilayered process fosters the creation of new memory associations. This new combination may be essential for the consolidation (and resolution) of unresolved memories of trauma—a process that likely involves the integration of memory representations that had previously been isolated within the unresolved traumatic state.

Orientation, Arousal, and Appraisal

One of the first components of an emotional response is the orientation of the mind to a stimulus and its representations in the brain. By having patients focus attention on an image, their emotions, their bodily state, and their negative self-cognitions, therapists promote a multilayered focus of attention and activate the essential components of emotional processing. This process is also no casual event. As mentioned, emotion is intricately interwoven with the brain's capacity for integration and self-regulation. Within the EMDR approach, the multilayered and densely focused process of activating each element can be especially powerful in numerous ways. These attentional processes may involve an array of functionally differentiated elements of cognitive processing, some of which may have been dis-associated within the unresolved trauma condition.

These representational processes may also have anatomically distributed sites that mediate their function. An autobiographical image is likely generated from the posterior regions of the right hemisphere. When patients respond to the request to verbalize a negative or positive self-cognition, their response probably involves complex layers of mental models and specific elements of autobiographical memory, which become linked to the left hemisphere's semantic-memory and language-processing centers. Such a process produces a "fact about the self" as viewed from a self-standpoint. The focal attention on feelings may also be primarily mediated by the nonverbal right side of the brain as the feelings are generated from various limbic regions including the amygdala. The body scan encourages patients to check the status of their body. This ability is more highly integrated in the right hemisphere through a somatosensory system that registers (and regulates) the homeostatic state of the chemical milieu, internal body organs (e.g., lungs, heart, intestines), and the changing state of the skeletal system musculature (Schore, 1994, 1996). The somatosensory system is thought to involve a range of subcortical and cortical areas, especially the orbitofrontal and anterior cingulate regions (Damasio, 1999). Focusing attention on all of these elements may thus involve the dorsolateral prefrontal cortex, anterior cingulate, orbitofrontal, and thalamo-cortical circuit on each side of the brain.

The movement of the eyes from side to side may also directly activate the attentional focus of the basic orientation response (Corbetta et al., 1998). Other forms of alternating sensory stimulation, such as auditory or tactile, may also orient attention. Whether the specific mechanisms of activating attention used in EMDR are actually necessary or are (a) part of a more generalized process of orientation and (b) part of the initiation of emotional response needs to be clarified in future research.

In unresolved traumatic states, these various representational processes may have remained quite functionally independent—an isolation that may have preserved the individual's ability to function during and after traumatic experiences. In therapy, perhaps for the first time, these representational processes are being activated simultaneously in the brain. In these orienting processes, the activation occurs at the same time as the initiation of focal attention. Such a synchronized activation may be necessary but not sufficient to begin the process of neural integration. This representational situation of multilayered focal attention by itself does not necessarily lead to a lasting form of integration. The nature of the processing that occurs during the simultaneous activation of these previously functionally isolated representational processes can make a significant difference in the direction of information processing and therapeutic outcome.

In the model of emotions described in *The Developing Mind*, the process from initial orientation (of attention) to subsequent arousal and appraisal of the mental representations is the essence of primary emotional states. These primary emotions are the background emotional processes (Damasio, 1999) that are the initial activation patterns that then may become expanded into more complex (specific, or categorical) emotions. Primary emotions, reflected in the profiles of energy activation in the brain, are at the core of how the mind evaluates the significance and meaning of a stimulus. These are the initial aspects of emotional processing. I have proposed (1999) that the neural mechanisms likely involve neuromodulatory circuits (discussed previously) that have numerous properties: (a) They increase the excitability and activation of neurons, (b) they enhance neural plasticity via the growth of synaptic connections, (c) they are widely distributed throughout the brain and enhance integration through their extensive enervation of distinct brain regions, and (d) they are thus fundamental to self-regulation.

The fundamental role of emotion in all aspects of life is highlighted during therapy when the patient's orientation is focused on a particular set of representations. This focus of attention then influences the direction of the emotional processing of the varied layers of subjective mental life, from ongoing perceptions to autobiographical representations. Initial orientation is followed by the arousal and appraisal process; the individual then has an internal sense of good (approach) or bad (withdrawal). As the process emerges, these primary emotional states may expand into the categorical or universal emotions of fear, sadness, anger, joy, surprise, disgust, and shame. Such internal states may manifest as externally expressed affect. Regardless of the external communication level, the patient's internal experience of these emotional states reflects the subjective core of the information-processing flow and the achievement of new levels of integration during therapy. Therefore, effective psychotherapy can be considered fundamentally to be an emotionally engaging and transforming experience that enables new levels of representational integration to occur. Recall that emotion is inherently integrative. Therefore, impaired integration, as indicated by the emotional dysregulation characteristic of unresolved states, may move toward balanced self-regulation during emotionally involving therapy.

States of Mind

The simultaneous clustering of functionally distributed representational processes enables the brain to be in a particular state of mind. In those with unresolved trauma, particular activation of elements in focal attention may create a semistable (fragile and transient) state, which is usually unconsciously avoided or becomes intrusive, overwhelming, and disabling outside of therapy—that can now be a primary focus of treatment. The brain is being primed—that is, being made more likely to activate new associations of representational processes. In fact, the therapist's strategic clustering of these elements (e.g., images, cognitions, feelings, bodily sensations) creates a unique state of mind that may foster new directions of information processing.

As discussed previously, impediments to the acquisition of new processing forms can be embedded in either an excessively restricted, rigid pattern in the flow of states or a chaotic, flooding, and disorganizing flow of states. Either condition can lead to an impairment in the adaptive, flexible response to internal or external factors. Inflexibility is the greatest challenge at this point in therapy. This inflexibility may be what causes patients to "get stuck" or "go blank" during life and during therapy. Patients may experience the inability to think clearly or to move forward in their interactions with the therapist. This pattern is a manifestation of rigid characteristics of the brain's information-processing and energy flow. This rigidity is an ingrained pattern in dire need of change.

One way to alter these rigid patterns, which would allow patients to move on, is through use of the new multilayered simultaneous activations within focal attention and working memory. These activations contain intense emotional elements that may be amenable to change. A secure patient–therapist relationship may create a sense of safety that makes the discomfort, anxiety, fear, or terror more tolerable. During the sensory stimulation sets (e.g., eye movements, sounds, tactile stimulation), many patients have described a relaxation response characterized by calm, tranquil sensations that seem to be a direct result of the bilateral stimulation.

An informal assessment of nonbilateral alternating sensory stimulation (i.e., tactile sensation involving one side of the body or vertical rather than horizontal eye movements) and nonalternating stimulation (i.e., focusing on a stationary object) does not produce the same sense of focused attention or relaxation. If more controlled research conditions systematically establish that this finding is generally true, then perhaps bilateral stimulation during therapy may be helping patients use focal attention to address traumatic elements while simultaneously soothing the intensely negative associated feelings. Overall, the process would enable multiple layers of focal processing, alter the subjective experience of the state of mind, and enable such states to be better tolerated. The re-encoding of the representational elements in a less distressful setting would associate a less intense emotional charge with the reconstructed memory. Future retrieval of the traumatic memories would involve a newly reorganized memory configuration that would be more tolerable. Repeating the process of activation, multilayered focal attention, encoding, reactivation, and encoding would reorganize the memory into a more tolerable, integrated, and perhaps resolved configuration that no longer has such devastating effects on the flexibility of the system's flow of states.

Bilateral Stimulation

In addition to its possible relaxing effects, the effects of the alternating and bilateral stimulation used during EMDR may have general and quite specific effects on the processes of the mind that facilitate the resolution of trauma for certain individuals. Dismantling studies are important in delineating which aspects of a therapeutic method may be essential for positive outcomes in the pooled groups of participants necessary for statistical analyses. Although early dismantling studies may demonstrate that a certain aspect of a technique is not necessary for a statistically significant improvement overall in patient status, clinicians should remember that more subtle aspects of an approach may directly improve the subjective experience of an individual; these benefits may be more difficult to quantify or could have been lost in pooled statistical analyses. Further research needs to clarify whether the form of sensory stimulation used in EMDR truly adds some specific benefit to the therapeutic process and, if so, for which patients it is effective. The EMDR protocol even without sensory stimulation affects a multilayer representational process that may be at the core of EMDR's efficacy.

If alternating stimulation is in fact beneficial for a given patient, researchers need to address whether the stimulation's bilateral nature is important. If it is established that the alternating and the bilateral aspect of the stimulation do provide either qualitative or quantitative benefits for certain individuals, such as internal sense of relaxation, faster resolution, or other important but less quantifiable benefits, then the following mechanisms are possible explanations of the way bilateral stimulation works.

As described in the first half of this chapter, the traumatic impairments to neural integration may have many layers of effects. One layer is the isolation of the representational processes of the right and left hemispheres. These two regions are asymmetrical in the developing embryo and give rise to quite distinct modes of constructing reality (Trevarthen, 1996; Tucker et al., 1995). As I proposed previously in the chapter, the process of integrating the modalities from the left and from the right hemispheres may enable traumatic memories to be processed in a new way, one that fosters resolution. This process may be a component of the emotionally attuned communication and coconstruction of narratives that are a foundation of numerous forms of therapy. Therefore, both nonverbal and verbal communication enable patients and therapists to resonate with each other in a way that promotes internal resonance, or integration, within each person's mind and across each person's hemispheres.

Patients and therapists are both affected by the experience of psychotherapy. My own experience as a psychotherapist before learning about EMDR suggests that this proposed process of bilateral integration may be at the heart of trauma resolution. Coherent narratives emerge from such an integrative process, possibly expressing (or demonstrating) and promoting trauma resolution. After learning EMDR and applying it in a few individuals' therapy sessions, it is my impression that the method enables more rapid progression in some situations. Certain patients whose progress was stalled because of particular issues were helped by EMDR. EMDR is not magic; however, it does seem to promote rapid development of a highly focused form of integration. Although EMDR has been extremely useful for some of my patients, for others it was unhelpful and even distracting. I used nonbilateral or nonalternating sensory stimulation for some patients who had had positive responses, and they reported no longer feeling the described sense of relaxation and focus. Although these examples are clearly nonblinded, single cases that do not qualify as scientific data, they are important and informative subjective accounts of individuals who had been traumatized and were undergoing treatment. Additional carefully designed studies may help researchers clarify individual responsiveness and identify which elements of EMDR are essential for particular patients.

My view is that bilateral stimulation for certain patients enables fixed or chaotic states to achieve new levels of integration that foster rapidly reorganizing patterns in the flow of states across time. Likewise, one view of development is that it involves the organization, disorganization, and reorganization of patterns in the flow of states of mind. Therefore, development requires periods of disequilibrium to move forward. In people with unresolved trauma, such forward movement has stopped. Restrictive or chaotic states preclude adaptive development. Therapeutic interventions that create new associations of representations related to traumatic experiences are a beginning. I propose that the bilateral stimulation may be catalyzing global changes in the flow of states across time based on these representational activations. Such bilateral integration may indeed be present in emotionally attuned, coconstructing therapeutic relationships—without any use of sensory stimulation. Bilateral sensory stimulation may accelerate the therapeutic acquisition of new levels of neural integration and trauma resolution.

The bilateral stimulation sets used during EMDR may instantiate a simultaneous autonoetic retrieval (right) and encoding (left) state (Tulving et al., 1994). Readiness for reorganization of memory processing has been prevented by the unresolved condition. REM disturbances and nightmares may reflect this impairment. As the elements of multilayered focal attention (e.g., images, thoughts, feelings, body sensations) prime the system, the rhythmic activation of left and right hemispheres (which may be stimulated by eye movements, with eyes to left activating the right brain and vice versa, or alternating auditory or tactile stimulation) enables the inherent encoding and retrieval states of each hemisphere to directly alter the experience of autonoetic consciousness. This proposal is based on the suggestion that activity in the opposite side of the brain is associated with sensory stimulation, such as sounds or tactile sensations, or motor activity, such as eye movements (not what the eyes are seeing, but actual motion—activation via the extraocular muscles of the cranial nerves necessary for eye motion) (Kinsbourne, 1972, 1974). In addition, this idea is supported by the general finding that people look to the left when retrieving an autobiographical memory (a process that activates the right hemisphere, especially the orbitofrontal and posterior regions of the cortex; Wheeler, Stuss, & Tulving, 1997).

During repeated stimulation sets, some patients describe the process of recalling their memories as if they were passengers on a train watching the scenery go by, an observation that is quite consistent with current knowledge of autobiographical memory. People have the ability to recall memories as if they are observers or participants, possibly reflecting their noetic and autonoetic reflections on personally experienced events, respectively. Some researchers have suggested that the noetic, semantic, or factual elements of memory are stored predominantly in the left hemisphere, whereas autobiographical representations (i.e., the sense of the self in the past, not just the recall of an experience) are stored in the right hemisphere (Wheeler, Stuss, & Tulving, 1997). As discussed previously, flashbacks seem to involve the intense activation of the right hemisphere (the visual cortex) while the left hemisphere (the speech area) is deactivated. The bilateral stimulation sets may force the activation of both hemispheres to allow integration of autobiographical and semantic representations of traumatic events. For some patients, facilitation of the synchronous process of representational activation involving the circuits of each hemisphere may be sufficient to produce excellent results; bilateral sensory stimulation may be unnecessary. In some cases, the bilateral stimulation—especially eye movements with the eyes open—may actually hinder a patient's ability to visualize important mental images. Bilateral integration may be at the heart of resolution, but the therapeutic strategies necessary to achieve the resolution may vary depending on the needs of a given individual.

With or without sensory stimulation, bilateral activation induced by the psychotherapeutic process of encouraging representations from both sides of the brain seems to evoke a noetic/autonoetic encoding and retrieval state that enables memory to be processed more quickly. Because the structure of memory may include a wide range of explicit components, such as periods of life, thematic elements, specific experiences, and evaluative components, as well as the implicit elements of emotion, behavioral impulse, perception, and bodily sensation, the therapeutic processing of traumatic memories may involve the integration of a wide array of mental processes. These activated representations can then be functionally linked to each other in truly new combinations that are likely mediated by the creation of new synaptic linkages. Effective therapy not only involves a momentarily intense emotional experience but also probably involves lasting changes in brain structure and function.

A region of the prefrontal cortex—the orbitofrontal cortex—seems to play a key role in the encoding and retrieval of autobiographical memory. As a region of the brain in the unique position of receiving and sending information from and to a wide range of important regions, such as the association cortex, the limbic regions, and the autonomic nervous system via subcortical circuits, the orbitofrontal cortex may be a crucial part of neural integration. It has been found that this region is essential in attachment, autobiographical memory, representation and regulation of bodily state, social cognition, and the expression and regulation of emotion (Damasio, 1994; Schore, 1994; Siegel, 1999). The orbitofrontal cortex's role in these processes highlights its probable importance in the resolution of trauma. The orbitofrontal cortex may largely control the brain's modulation of states of mind, allowing the mind to be more flexible, tolerate a wider range of emotional states, gain access to and consolidate autobiographical memory, and enable more complex levels of interpersonal relationships. Considering that neural integration could be the root of trauma resolution, it is wise to consider the role of the integrative orbitofrontal region in mediating the acquisition of mental coherence.

Resolution: Response Flexibility, Autonoetic Consciousness, and Integration

In *The Developing Mind*, I suggest that the term *response flexibility* can be used to describe an important integrative process also mediated by the orbitofrontal region. Response flexibility is the brain's capacity to respond to changes in the internal or external environment with a flexible and an adaptive range of behavioral or cognitive responses. Numerous studies highlight the orbitofrontal region's central role in this ability (Mesulam,

1998; Nobre, Coul, Frith, & Mesulam, 1999). This process may require the orbitofrontal region to use its integrative capacities to functionally link elements from widely distributed input and output circuits. As discussed previously, this region's unique position allows it to link the major regions of the brain, including the associational cortex, limbic circuits, and brain stem areas. The orbitofrontal region enables the more complex, higher-order processing of the neocortex to be integrated with the lower-order functions of the deeper structures. Autonoetic consciousness may be one example of this higher mode of integrative processing—one that permits mental time travel and a deep sense of self-awareness.

One extension of this view is that the mind is capable of a mode of information processing that does not involve the higher mode of processing. In the lower mode (or, as some of my patients prefer to call it, the *low road*) of processing, response flexibility is suspended along with other integrative functions such as autonoetic consciousness and impulse control. In this lower mode, behaviors become reflexive, and the mind becomes filled with deeply engrained, inflexible response patterns. Emotions may flood the mind and impair the ability to have rational thoughts and behave appropriately and compassionately. Trauma may make the lower mode of processing more likely to occur. Although everyone may be vulnerable to entering such states under certain stressful circumstances, those with unresolved trauma may make entry into such states more frequent and more intense and more likely to occur with minimal provocation. Recovering from this condition when it has progressed beyond a certain point may be especially difficult for people with unresolved traumatic conditions. They may remain "on the low road" longer and be on it more often.

The neurobiology of the lower mode of processing may involve the state-dependent inhibition of the orbitofrontally mediated neural integration of neocortical input with that of the limbic and brain stem regions of the brain. In other words, the orbitofrontal cortex and higher thought process of the neocortex are functionally cut off from the lower regions. Behaviors then become driven by these "lower" structures and may include intense emotions (such as anger) as well as reactivations of implicit memory (with automatic behaviors). This condition may be experienced by people who are having flashbacks or intense emotional responses to trauma-related stimuli from the external or internal environment. The condition can produce excessive emotional reactions, inner turmoil, dread, or terror, and an ensuing sense of shame and humiliation. Individuals may be prone to exhibiting infantile rage and aggressive, intrusive, or outright violent behavior. Interpersonally, the condition directly impairs people's ability to maintain collaborative communication. The tendency to have an impairment in response flexibility and autonoetic consciousness may be the root of the behavior of parents who have unresolved trauma. They often are frightened or engage in frightening behaviors, leading to disorganized attachments in their offspring. Lower-mode states do not allow for the sensitive, contingent communication that secure attachments require. Herein may lie the core elements in the intergenerational transfer of trauma as its devastating effects leave a wake of pain across the boundaries of space and time that separate one mind from another (Siegel & Hartzell, in press).

As psychotherapeutic interventions promote neural integration, the integrative orbitofrontal region may become more actively involved in the global functioning of the individual. This outcome may be especially evident during the activation of representations related to traumatic memories. In those with unresolved states, trauma-related stimuli may activate a cascade of mental representations that inhibit response flexibility and autonoetic consciousness. As discussed previously, this impairment may take the form of either excessively rigid or disorganized patterns in the flow of states of mind across time. The blockage of orbitofrontally mediated integration during trauma-related conditions may be responsible for impaired response flexibility. Resolution would thus involve the repair of impediments to flexible self-regulation.

Psychotherapeutic processes may facilitate the resolution of trauma by altering the constraints on the flow of an individual's states of mind. At the most basic level of analysis, this alteration in the neural firing pattern is likely to be mediated by changes in synaptic strengths among widely distributed neurons. These changes may be especially evident in the function of the neuromodulatory circuits. The growth of new synaptic connections and of neurons may be revealed by the integrative fibers of regions such as the hippocampus that have been recently shown to develop throughout the life span (Benes, 1998). The corpus callosum, and the orbitofrontal, cerebellar, and anterior cingulate regions are other integrative areas that may respond positively to new development stemming from effective treatment and trauma resolution.

The global effects of resolution are indicated by how the mind functions as a complex system, allowing for more complex energy and information flow within itself and to other minds. Thus, the healing process is far more than the modification of distress intensity associated with traumatic memories. Instead, trauma resolution can be thought of as a way to enable the mind to regain the natural process of integration across time and states of mind. Successful resolution creates a deep sense of coherence. The resulting enhanced autonoetic consciousness allows individuals to be more flexible as they reflect on the past, live fully in the present, and have an active sense of the self in the future. This new level of mental coherence helps people develop autobiographical narratives that make sense of past experiences and the impact of those events on present functioning. Their minds are also able to regain a sense of hope for the future. People transform from passive trauma victims into active authors of the ongoing story of their lives. However, integrating coherence is an ongoing process, not a final achievement. It is a process that enables people to experience the spontaneous and flexible flow of energy and information in the mind and in meaningful and invigorating connections with others.

REFERENCES

Aitken, K. J., & Trevarthen, C. (1997). Self–other organization in human psychological development. *Development and Psychopathology, 9*, 653–678.

Baron-Cohen, S. (1995). *Mindblindness: An essay on autism and theory of mind.* Cambridge, MA: MIT Press.

Bauer, P. J. (1996). What do infants recall of their lives? Memory for specific events by one-to-two-year-olds. *American Psychologist, 51*, 29–41.

Benes, F. M. (1998). Human brain growth spans decades. *American Journal of Psychiatry, 155*, 1489.

Bjork, R. (1989). Retrieval inhibition as an adaptive mechanism in human memory. In H. L. Roediger & F. I. M. Craik (Eds.), *Varieties of memory and consciousness: Essays in honor of Endel Tulving* (pp. 283–288). London: Wiley.

Bremner, J. D., & Narayan, M. (1998). The effects of stress on memory and the hippocampus throughout the life cycle: Implications for childhood development and aging. *Development and Psychopathology, 10*, 871–888.

Carlson, E. A. (1998). A prospective longitudinal study of disorganized/disoriented attachment. *Child Development, 69*, 1107–1128.

Corbetta, M., Akbudak, E., Conturo, T. E., Snyder, A. Z., Ollinger, J. M., Drury, H. A., et al. (1998). A common network of functional areas for attention and eye movements. *Neuron, 21*, 761–773.

Damasio, A. (1994). *Descarte's error: Emotion, reason, and the human brain.* New York: Grosset/Putnam.

Damasio, A. (1999). *The feeling of what happens: Emotion and the body in the making of consciousness.* New York: Harcourt, Brace.

De Bellis, M. D., Baum, A. S., Birmaher, B., Keshavan, M. S., Eccard. C. H., Boring, A. M., et al. (1999). A. E. Bennett Research Award. Developmental traumatology. Part I: Biological stress systems. *Biological Psychiatry, 45*, 1259–1270.

De Bellis, M. D., Keshavan, M. S., Clark, D. B., Casey, B. J., Giedd, J. N., Boring, A. M., et al. (1999). A. E. Bennett Research Award. Developmental traumatology. Part II: Brain development. *Biological Psychiatry, 45*, 1271–1284.

Edelman, G. (1992). *Bright air, brilliant fire.* New York: Basic Books.

Garber, J., & Dodge, K. A. (Eds.). (1991). *The development of emotion regulation and dysregulation.* Cambridge, England: Cambridge University Press.

Hesse, E. (1999). The adult attachment interview: Historical and current perspectives. In J. Cassidy & P. Shaver (Eds.), *Handbook of attachment* (pp. 395–433). New York: Guilford Press.

Kandel, E. R. (1998). A new intellectual framework for psychiatry. *American Journal of Psychiatry, 155,* 457–469.

Kinsbourne, M. (1972). Eye and head turning indicates cerebral lateralization. *Science, 176,* 539–541.

Kinsbourne, M. (1974). Direction of gaze and distribution of cerebral thought processes. *Neuropsychologia, 12*(2), 279–281.

Llinas, R. R. (1990). Intrinsic electrical properties of mammalian neurons and CNS function. *Fidia Research Foundation Neuroscience Award Lectures, 4,*175–194.

Lyons-Ruth, K., & Jacobwitz, D. (1999). Attachment disorganization: Unresolved loss, relational violence, and lapses in behavioral and attentional strategies. In J. Cassidy & P. R. Shaver (Eds.), *Handbook of attachment: Theory, research, and clinical applications* (pp. 520–554). New York: Guilford Press.

Main, M., & Hesse, E. (1990). Parents' unresolved traumatic experiences are related to infant disorganized status: Is frightened and/or frightening parental behavior the linking mechanism? In M. Greenberg, D. Cicchetti, & M. Cummings (Eds.), *Attachment in the preschool years* (pp. 161–182). Chicago: University of Chicago Press.

Main, M., & Morgan, H. (1996). Disorganization and disorientation in infant strange situation behavior: Phenotypic resemblance to dissociative states. In L. K. Michelson & W. J. Ray (Eds.), *Handbook of dissociation: Theoretical, empirical, and clinical perspectives* (pp. 107–138). New York: Plenum Press.

McClelland, J. L. (1998). Complementary learning systems in the brain: A connectionist approach to explicit and implicit cognition and memory. *Annals of the New York Academy of Sciences, 843,* 153–178.

Mesulam, M. M. (1998). Review article: From sensation to cognition. *Brain, 121,* 1013–1052.

Milner, B., Squire, L. R., & Kandel, E. R. (1998). Cognitive neuroscience and the study of memory. *Neuron, 20,* 445–468.

Nobre, A. C., Coull, J. T., Frith, C. D., & Mesulam, M. M. (1999). Orbitofrontal cortex is activated during breaches of expectation in tasks of visual attention. *Nature Neuroscience, 2,* 11–12.

Ogawa, J. R., Sroufe, L. A., Weinfield, N. S., Carlson, E. A., Egeland, B. (1997). Development and the fragmented self: Longitudinal study of dissociative symptom atology in a nonclinical sample. *Development and Psychopathology, 9,* 855–880.

Rauch, S. L., van der Kolk, B. A., Fisler, R. E., Alpert, N. M., Orr, S. P., Savage, C. R., et al. (1996). A symptom provocation study of posttraumatic stress disorder using positron emission tomography and script-driven imagery. *Archives of General Psychiatry, 53,* 380–387.

Schore, A. N. (1994). *Affect regulation and the origin of the self: The neurobiology of emotional development.* Hillsdale, NJ: Erlbaum.

Schore, A. N. (1996). The experience-dependent maturation of a regulatory system in the orbital prefrontal cortex and the origin of developmental psycho-pathology. *Development and Psychopathology, 8,* 59–87.

Shapiro, F. (2001, March). *EMDR as an integrative therapy.* Presentation at the Healing Trauma Conference, San Diego, CA.

Siegel, D. J. (1995). Memory, trauma, and psychotherapy: A cognitive science view. *Journal of Psychotherapy Practice and Research, 4,* 93–122.

Siegel, D. J. (1996). Cognition, memory, and dissociation. *Child and Adolescent Clinics of North America, 5,* 509–536.

Siegel, D. J. (1999). *The developing mind: Toward a neurobiology of interpersonal experience.* New York: Guilford Press.

Siegel, D. J. (in press). An interpersonal neurobiology psychotherapy. In M. Solomon & D. J. Siegel (Eds.), *Healing Trauma.* New York: Norton.

Siegel, D. J., & Hartzell, M. (in press). *Parenting from the inside out.* New York: Penguin-Putnam.

Sroufe, L. A. (1996). *Emotional development: The organization of emotional life in the early years.* New York: Cambridge University Press.

Stern, D. N. (1985). *The interpersonal world of the infant.* New York: Basic Books.

Tononi, G., & Edelman, G. M. (1998). Consciousness and complexity. *Science, 282,* 1846–1851.

Trevarthen, C. (1996). Lateral asymmetries in infancy: Implications for the development of the hemispheres. *Neuroscience and Biobehavioral Reviews, 20,* 571–586.

Tucker, D. M., Luu, P., & Pribram, K. H. (1995). Social and emotional self-regulation. *Annals of the New York Academy of Sciences,* 213–239.

Tulving, E., Kapur, S., Craik, F. I. M., Moscovitch, M., & Houle, S. (1994). Hemispheric encoding/retrieval asymmetry in episodic memory: Positron emission tomography findings. *Proceedings of the National Academy of Sciences (USA), 91,* 2016–2020.

Whalens, T. (1999, October). *Institute Chair, Institute on Advanced Psychopharmacology: Contemporary issues in clinical care.* Annual meeting of the American Academy of Child and Adolescent Psychiatry, Chicago.

Wheeler, M. A., Stuss, D. T., & Tulving, E. (1997). Toward a theory of episodic memory: The frontal lobes and autonoetic consciousness. *Psychological Bulletin, 121,* 331–354.

SUGGESTED READING

Bowlby, J. (1969). *Attachment and loss: Vol. 1. Attachment.* New York: Basic Books.

Fonagy, P., & Target, M. (1997). Attachment and reflective function: Their role in self-organization. *Development and Psychopathology, 9,* 679–700.

Hofer, M. A. (1994). Hidden regulators in attachment, separation, and loss. In N. A. Fox. (Ed.), The development of emotion regulation: Biological and behavioral considerations. *Monographs of the Society for Research in Child Development, 59*(240), 192–207.

Main, M. (1991). Metacognitive knowledge, metacognitive monitoring, and singular (coherent) versus multiple (incoherent) models of attachment: Findings and directions for future research. In C. M. Parkes, J. Stevenson-Hinde, & P. Marris (Eds.), *Attachment across the life cycle* (pp. 127–159). London: Routledge.

Main, M. (1995). Attachment: Overview, with implications for clinical work. In S. Goldberg, R. Muir, & J. Kerr (Eds.), *Attachment theory: Social, developmental and clinical perspectives* (pp. 407–474). Hillsdale, NJ: Analytic Press.

5

EMDR AND PSYCHOANALYSIS

PAUL L. WACHTEL

Eye movement desensitization and reprocessing (EMDR) originated as an application of a cognitive–behavioral point of view. Its further evolution, procedures, and professional reception, and even its approach to evaluating and checking its efficacy have been powerfully influenced by its cognitive–behavioral origins. As discussed in this chapter, EMDR's origins have important implications for the way that EMDR continues to be pursued and understood, accounting for some of its important strengths and for some of the ways in which the method's full potential remains to be developed.

As EMDR has continued to evolve, it has moved beyond the boundaries of being a strictly cognitive–behavioral approach and has become an *integrative* approach that in fact incorporates aspects of numerous orientations (Shapiro, 1995).[1] Still, integrations have their "flavors" (Wachtel, 1993), and those flavors usually reflect the original orientation of their developers before they incorporated a more integrative point of view. Messer (1992) has argued (see also Stricker & Gold, 1996) that approaches to psychotherapy integration that are usually described as reflecting *theoretical*

---

[1] It is worth noting in this regard that Francine Shapiro, the originator of EMDR, is a member of the Society for the Exploration of Psychotherapy Integration.

integration (Arkowitz, 1997) may be better understood under the rubric of *assimilative integration*. As therapists move toward assuming a more integrative stance, they *assimilate* new ideas or methods into the framework with which they began. In the process the framework itself changes, but it is usually not difficult to distinguish integrative efforts—even genuine and rather thoroughgoing integrative efforts—that were based on a cognitive–behavioral viewpoint from those originating from a psychodynamic point of view. In this sense, although EMDR is clearly an integrative approach, it is an integrative approach with a strong cognitive–behavioral flavor.

In this chapter, EMDR is examined and considered from a different vantage point. For some time, I too have been engaged in developing an integrative approach to therapy (e.g., Wachtel, 1977, 1987, 1991a, 1993, 1997; Wachtel & Wachtel, 1986). However, apropos the previous paragraph, my integrative efforts have a different flavor; they are rooted most deeply in the psychodynamic tradition, not the cognitive–behavioral.

As a consequence of my psychodynamic vantage point, my view and use of EMDR differ somewhat from the "classic" approach to EMDR. This chapter is thus likely to reflect clinical and theoretical views that differ in important ways from those of many of this book's other authors. However, my discussion does not constitute a *critique* of EMDR. I began using EMDR and am writing this chapter because I am intrigued by EMDR—by its clinical potential, the experiences it seems to generate, and the challenges to theory and research that it presents. My goal is to expand our ways of viewing and thinking about EMDR, and to consider the ways in which EMDR can be enriched by a psychoanalytic perspective and vice versa.

For an integration or combination of EMDR and psychoanalysis to be viable, two conditions must be satisfied. The differences must not be so fundamental and unbridgeable that any effort to bring the two approaches together is inherently incoherent and contradictory. At the same time, the differences must not be so trivial or superficial that putting them together adds little or nothing. The interface between EMDR and psychoanalysis meets both these conditions, and the chapter will attempt to demonstrate this as it proceeds.

CHANGES IN PSYCHOANALYSIS: THEIR BEARING ON THE INTERFACE BETWEEN PSYCHOANALYSIS AND EMDR

Both psychoanalysis and EMDR have evolved and changed over time, and in part it is those changes that have created the possibility for useful interactions between the two approaches. Over time, certain significant changes in the psychoanalytic approach have created more fertile ground for the inclusion of EMDR in the practice of psychoanalytic therapists. As is described in detail elsewhere (Wachtel, 1997), the opposition by psychoanalysts to including active interventions from approaches such as be-havior therapy was rooted in misunderstandings about the nature of be-havior therapy and perhaps in a misunderstanding of psychoanalysis as well —in the sense that analysts considered only a narrow range of the potential theoretical options for understanding the observations the psychoanalytic method generates, and as a consequence certain ideas were viewed as in-trinsic to psychoanalysis which were not. That is, although a variety of theoretical approaches were capable of encompassing the full spectrum of observations important to psychoanalytic therapists and thinkers, some ap-proaches were "privileged" by the mainstream psychoanalytic community and others were therefore not recognized or appreciated as genuinely psy-choanalytic.

Over time, however, newer versions of psychoanalytic thought have emerged that place psychoanalytic clinical observations in a different the-oretical context and open new possibilities for combining the strengths of complementary clinical and theoretical approaches. In the interpersonal and relational strands of psychoanalytic thought (see, e.g., Aron, 1996; Mitchell, 1988, 1993) and particularly in the cyclical psychodynamic ap-proach (Gold & Wachtel, 1993; Wachtel, 1993, 1997; Wachtel & McKin-ney, 1992), which was specifically formulated to integrate the observations and methods derived from psychoanalytic work with those from cognitive–behavioral and systemic approaches, many possibilities exist for reconciling what had previously seemed to be incompatible hypotheses and methods. EMDR fits quite well within this emerging multidimensional synthesis, a point that is elaborated as the chapter proceeds.

At the same time, it is important to recognize that in some ways the evolution of psychoanalysis has taken psychoanalysis in directions that *in-crease* the differences between psychoanalysis and EMDR. In certain re-spects, EMDR is most similar to the very earliest versions of psychoanalytic practice. The strong reliance on free association, attention to what spon-taneously emerges (Wachtel, 1982b) from the patient's unguided expression of internally generated thoughts and images, the relatively minimal inter-ference by the therapist, who largely stayed silent while allowing the pa-tient's own material to unfold—these were for many years a dominant characteristic of the psychoanalytic approach. These characteristics ap-proximate certain aspects of EMDR practice in ways that distinguish EMDR from *both* behavior therapy *and* psychoanalysis as they are most typically practiced today. In that sense, EMDR can be thought of as a kind of return to the "roots" of psychoanalysis (albeit from a quite different direction) at a time when psychoanalysis itself is increasingly pruning and replanting some of those roots.

The point is not to suggest disparagingly that EMDR is similar to old fashioned psychoanalysis. To begin with, newer is not always better. In a world characterized by a marketing orientation to almost everything (including, very substantially these days, psychotherapy), there is much reason to be skeptical about the virtues of newness per se. Although I myself am a proponent of some of these newer directions in psychoanalytic thought, the fact that they are new does not in itself make them valuable. Moreover, EMDR clearly differs substantially from *any* version of psychoanalysis, whether practiced in Freud's Vienna or today's Manhattan.

How much EMDR resembles psychoanalysis—early *or* late—is not the issue. Behavior therapy bears little resemblance to psychoanalysis, yet, I have argued, it is fruitfully integrated with a psychoanalytic approach (Wachtel, 1977, 1997; see also Frank, 1999). The important question is whether the recent changes in psychoanalysis have further smoothed the way for an interface between psychoanalysis and EMDR or whether they present further obstacles. The answer is "both."

Beyond Orthodoxy

One characteristic of psychoanalysis in recent years with important implications for the possibility of integration or combination is the increasing openness of the psychoanalytic community itself. The very term *orthodox*, once so commonly applied to certain versions of psychoanalysis (versions which for a time even constituted the mainstream of psychoanalytic thought), now sounds rather dated. Even practitioners whose approach most closely resembles that venerable set of practices would now most likely groan at the use of such a term.

Psychoanalysis bears much less resemblance to a religious movement than it once did, rendering terms like *orthodox* oddly quaint. At one time, many analysts regarded the practice of psychoanalysis much like religious fundamentalists regard the Bible. In essence, psychoanalytic practice was considered to be "given" and perfect, so those who suggested new practices or ways of understanding were viewed as deviationists, not as valued innovators. Schisms and virtual excommunications were common. In contrast, today's psychoanalytic journals tend to publish works of theorists with widely diverging views even within the same issue, and dialogue rather than ritual purification is the predominant mode.[2] Moreover, a robust movement with considerable influence in the psychoanalytic community views psychoanalytic observations and practices from the vantage point of constructivism (e.g., Hoffman, 1991, 1992; Messer, Sass, & Woolfolk, 1988; Mitchell, 1993; Spence, 1982; Stern, 1992). Far from regarding psychoanalysis as fixed and unchanging, the constructivist vision highlights the multiple ways in which psychoanalysis can be viewed and challenges any fixed or given definition of psychoanalysis.

---

[2] Indeed, probably the most influential new psychoanalytic journal is titled *Psychoanalytic Dialogues*.

Although this evolving openness in psychoanalysis does not imply that psychoanalysis is in any way getting to look more like EMDR, it does mean that some of the obstacles even to considering the relation between the two approaches have diminished. Further pursuit of the question of whether aspects of EMDR might be fruitfully combined with psychoanalytic work could potentially accelerate this trend toward greater openness and, indeed, lead to deeper inquiry into the fundamental nature of both EMDR *and* pyschoanalysis.

One- and Two-Person Models

Not all trends in psychoanalytic thought and practice ease the path toward a convergence or intersection of the two approaches. Psychoanalysts have begun abandoning, to varying degrees, the original epistemological model of psychoanalysis, in which the analyst attempted to be neutral, relatively anonymous, and an observer who does not influence what is observed (see, e.g., Mitchell, 1988; Renik, 1995, 1996; Wachtel, 1987, see chapter 11). Increasingly, contemporary analysts share some version of Sullivan's (1953, 1954) idea of the analyst as a *participant*–observer. The phenomena analysts observe do not just emerge or unfold spontaneously from the patient's psyche (Wachtel, 1982b); they are not viewed in their purest, least contaminated form by analysts eliminating their own influence. Rather, the analyst's influence is an inevitable and intrinsic part of the process. The patient is always viewed and can only be viewed in relation to the analyst, who is also a part of the picture that is being observed.

In contemporary psychoanalytic discourse, the distinction between the participant–observer model and the older model is often discussed in terms of *one-person* and *two-person* models (e.g., Aron, 1996; Frank, 1999; Modell, 1984). In the one-person model, the crucial events are considered to take place within the patient's head, and the patient is observed as a kind of closed system whose properties can be studied from the outside. In the two-person model, the therapist's, or observer's, influence on the relational field is crucial. Both people, the therapist and the patient, play a role in creating the psychological phenomena—including the patient's subjective experience—that are the focus of study of the analysis.[3]

Perhaps the most dramatic and illuminating illustration of the difference between the two models is evident in the work of the late Merton

---

[3] Outside of the psychoanalytic consulting room, of course, *more* than two people can actively contribute to each other's experience. In the family, at work, among groups of friends, and even in the analyst's office if his or her practice includes work with couples, the "two"-person model must be expanded. (One may say that even in analysis, more than two people are involved because the patient's experience includes his or her memories and fantasies of interactions with people in addition to the psychoanalyst. Still, as Modell notes, there is a difference between *representations* or *fantasies* of others that reside within the mind of one person and interactions with *actual* others who have minds of their own.)

Gill, one of the most distinguished and influential analysts of recent decades. In the 1950s, Gill offered perhaps the best articulated argument in the psychoanalytic literature for the one-person model. Several decades later, he became one of the most influential proponents of the two-person model and considered appreciation of that model's implications as essential for successful psychoanalytic practice (Gill, 1954, 1982, 1994).

The embrace of a two-person model contributed to the possibilities of coherently combining psychoanalytic exploration and attention to the transference on the one hand and the use of active techniques, including EMDR, on the other (see Frank, 1999, and Wachtel, 1997, for more detail). However, it also increased the divisions between the psychoanalytic view and the EMDR perspective in certain ways. EMDR is largely practiced from a version—in this case a cognitive–behavioral version—of the one-person model. EMDR therapists are cautioned against interrupting the flow of clients' thoughts and images or imposing their ideas on clients. At the beginning of the manual used by the EMDR Institute for its Level II training workshops is a quotation from Proust: "We don't receive wisdom, we discover it for ourselves after a journey which no one can take for us or spare us, for it is a point of view about things." This is a seductively engaging quotation and does capture an important and valuable aspect of the therapeutic enterprise and of EMDR in particular. If translated from the language of literature into the language of therapy, however, it is also a statement par excellence of the one-person model. It is a model of material that emerges or unfolds from the unconscious, the model that largely guided psychoanalysis through its first 75 years.[4]

To be sure, this model does not completely capture the way EMDR is conducted. Shapiro (1995) described EMDR as "a highly interactive, client-centered procedure" (p. 119). This description reflects a dialectical polarity which is at the heart of EMDR and indeed of all good therapy (cf. chapter 8 of Wachtel, 1993). EMDR, reflecting its cognitive–behavioral origins, is highly structured. It consists of a set of protocols for different kinds of clients and problems and has a sequential, stepwise approach that is directed and overseen by the therapist. At the same time, each client's treatment is different and unpredictable, following the flow of the client's own associations and images; the therapist operates under the injunction, "Stay out of the way of the client during successful processing" (Shapiro, 1995, p. 338).

In principle, the balance between these competing visions and values can vary from client to client or from stage to stage of the therapeutic work. In addition, familiarity with therapists who practice EMDR makes it clear that individual differences among therapists are clearly evident, with

---

[4]Compare the assumptions in the quotation from Proust with the critique of the notion of therapy as a lonely journey in chapter 12 of Wachtel, 1997.

some practicing EMDR in a way that emphasizes the structured, therapist-directed flavor of cognitive–behavioral therapy (CBT) and some emphasizing more the client-directed dimension of the work. Nevertheless, my impression, both from my own training in EMDR and from my discussions with EMDR practitioners, is that EMDR tends to be undertaken more from a one-person model than a two-person model.

In part, by stating this view, I am highlighting the epistemological foundations of EMDR. The work proceeds largely from the premise that what is being processed is something inside the client, something stored in the brain from the past. This, of course, is another similarity to psychoanalysis as it has been conceptualized through most of its history, but it is also a potential point of divergence from the trends in recent psychoanalytic discourse and conceptualization that I have been discussing in this chapter.[5]

EMDR AND "WORKING THROUGH"

Contemporary versions of psychoanalysis must grapple with many of the same issues that previous psychoanalytic models had to address, such as the nature of the curative process and the nature of the "working-through" process, which was recognized by Freud rather early as a necessary supplement to the sheer attainment of insights. It is in this working-through process that EMDR may be particularly able to contribute, both to clinical effectiveness and to conceptual clarity.

The concept of *working through* is one of the most crucial in the psychoanalytic conceptualization of therapeutic change, but it has never been very clearly defined. In another work, I discussed the relationship between working through and the processes of exposure and extinction of anxiety as follows:

> Psychoanalytic accounts of working through are often rather vague. Freud sensed early that singular flashes of insight are unlikely to lead to permanent change, that something more arduous and less dramatic was usually required. This observation has been confirmed so readily in clinical practice by others that therapists reading or talking about working through feel they know precisely what is being referred to. But while the *experience* of working through is a familiar one, the pro-

---

[5] It is worth noting that the one-person model originated in part from what I have called *Freud's epistemological anxieties* (Wachtel, 1993, pp. 180–182)—his concern to defend himself against the charge that the wishes and fantasies he discovered in the course of psychoanalytic exploration were the result of suggestion. EMDR has much less of a stake in the particular content that results from using the procedure. The contribution of EMDR does not stand or fall on whether the material being processed includes thoughts stirred by the input of the therapist. The idea of processing material that has been problematically stored in the brain, however, has tended to be associated with a relatively hermetic view of that material.

cess that is represented is not nearly as clear. Psychoanalytic accounts tend to discuss it in terms of examining the newly discovered thoughts, feelings, and experiences from a variety of different perspectives until it is fully understood. The emphasis, in other words, is . . . often cognitive.

The extinction concept, together with Freud's revised theory of anxiety, suggests another explanation. Working through is needed because what is most essential in therapeutic change is the overcoming of anxieties learned early in life that are no longer appropriate (if they ever were). . . . The unlearning of these fears, however, is impeded by the avoidance they engender, which makes impossible the needed experience of encountering the source of fear and discovering it is no longer a danger. And once the therapist does manage to bring about exposure to the previously avoided cues, *repeated* exposure to them is necessary. . . . it is not enough merely to "see" what you have blinded yourself to; it is essential to see it again and again—in other words, to undergo repeated extinction trials to eliminate the anxiety associated with these cues, or, in psychodynamic terminology, to participate in working through. (Wachtel & McKinney, 1992, pp. 339–340)

These considerations have substantial relevance to EMDR in numerous respects. It is in the working-through phase of treatment that EMDR's greatest contribution may lie. Case reports and some of the preliminary research on EMDR (Marcus, Marquis, & Sakai, 1997; Rothbaum, 1997; Scheck, Schaeffer, & Gillette, 1998; Wilson, Becker, & Tinker, 1995, 1997) have suggested that EMDR may accelerate the working-through process. Moreover, EMDR and the research it has spawned and will continue to spawn may contribute to better understanding the processes implicated in working through. For example, what is the relative contribution of exposure per se and the deeply experiential conviction that develops from successfully confronting thoughts and feelings that had previously been viewed as dangerous or overwhelming? What additional contribution can be attributed to the way—in both psychoanalytic therapy and EMDR— that emotional reactions and the thoughts that are at odds with them affect each other? In the psychoanalytic tradition, there has been much discussion of the distinction between intellectual and emotional insight. It is apparent that merely *knowing* that something is no longer dangerous or is in the past does not always affect one's emotional reaction to what one fears. Could it be this is because the thoughts and the emotions are stored in different parts of the brain, and that the "working-through" process somehow brings them to bear on each other? And, in accord with some theorizing about EMDR, does the bilateral stimulation associated with EMDR contribute to reconnecting neural pathways that had become dissociated from each other? These are questions that are not only of importance to practitioners of EMDR but bear as well on our understanding of the working-through process more generally.[6]

EMDR AND PSYCHODYNAMIC EXPLORATION

The potential contributions of EMDR are not limited to the working-through phase. My own clinical experience suggests that EMDR can also contribute to the exploratory, or uncovering, aspect of the work and can foster the development of insights. To illustrate why I believe EMDR holds considerable promise in this realm, I offer the following autobiographical snippet.

My first experiences of EMDR, which occurred in the Level I and Level II trainings, intrigued me enough that I sought therapy from an EMDR practitioner in order to experience the process from the patient's perspective. It seemed to me that just as one should not practice psychoanalysis without having experienced the procedure from the other side of the couch, one should experience EMDR as a patient before using it as a therapist. My excursion into EMDR was considerably briefer than my experience in psychoanalysis, but in certain respects it took me to places I had never reached with psychoanalysis alone. One of the most illuminating examples of this occurred as I explored a disturbing memory from my childhood.

I had long harbored a memory of an act I committed as a young child. The memory involved an act of gratuitous cruelty that contrasted starkly with my preferred image of myself. In this memory, I was walking by myself in a country vacation resort where my family was staying for part of the summer. As I walked through the grass, I came upon a large bullfrog and stepped on it. In doing so, I squashed and killed it.

Fortunately for my mental stability and well-being during the years before my experience with EMDR, this was not a memory that tortured me. Unlike the disturbing memories of those with PTSD, people who encounter unbidden images with terrible regularity, the recollection of squashing the frog was by no means a regular intruder on my consciousness. At times, years could go by without my thinking of it—but when the memory did come to mind, it was a very unwelcome visitor.

Perhaps not surprisingly, the memory recurred most frequently during the years when I was in analysis. However, the analysis did little to help me either understand the memory or feel better about it. The only reason

---

[6]The issue of how much EMDR contributes beyond mere exposure remains a controversial one, with vigorous arguments offered on both sides. I am intrigued by the possibility that EMDR may allow clients to overcome anxiety and conflict more fully and rapidly, and my clinical experience suggests that this can happen. More systematic evidence is needed, however, to resolve this controversy.

it was not a real problem in my life was because I infrequently thought about it, not because it was really resolved.

In my EMDR experience, I thought it would be interesting and perhaps useful to see what would happen if I chose this memory as a target. What happened was quite fascinating. As I began to picture the image while tracking a light that was moving back and forth, the image became more vivid and detailed. I could see clearly the fence that enclosed the resort's swimming pool, and I was walking on the grass within the confines of the fence. Then I had the thought that the image could not be right; I was picturing myself as four years old, but my mother never would have let me be alone in a pool area at that age. I was unsure whether my previous images of the event had situated it in that fenced-in area, but in the very vivid image that came to me during EMDR, this seemed clearly to be where the event took place. How could this be? Anyone who knew my mother would have no doubt that she would never have let her four-year-old be alone in the pool area. Could I have been older? No, the conviction that I was four years old was, if anything, even stronger than my conviction about the event's location within the pool area. As with the location, I am not sure whether previous recollections had specified my age as 4, rather than just as a "young boy." However, as I experienced the event during EMDR, I was absolutely *certain* that I was four when it happened.

Then, suddenly, a thought came to me like a bolt of lightning: *I was four when my brother was born*. Equally suddenly, this entire disturbing memory, which had been part of my subjective life narrative for decades and had been virtually untouched by years of analysis, dissolved into a quite different picture. This was not a memory of squashing a frog; it was a memory of having wanted to squash my baby brother! It was not a memory of a real event; it was what psychoanalysts call a *screen memory*.

Now, wanting to squash one's baby brother is not exactly something to be proud of. Still, this recasting of the meaning of my memory felt to me very much like exoneration. The memory as I had experienced it for all those years indeed made me feel ashamed. The act felt sadistic, cowardly, and destructive. I had killed an innocent creature for no reason other than that no one was looking. It felt like a dark spot in my life history that indicated something troubling and specific about me. Perhaps serial killers had such events in their histories, but nice people, good people, did not![7] In contrast, my new understanding of what this memory actually represented rendered it no longer troubling (if nonetheless not conventionally "nice"). I was enough of a psychoanalyst to believe that virtually everyone had something like this in his or her history. And after all (I now

---

[7] Again, the point is not that I was constantly tortured by this memory. Generally I am a rather upbeat person with reasonably solid self-esteem. On those occasions when the memory did surface, however, it felt troubling and shameful and made me wonder about myself.

realized) it was not a memory of an actual event but of a fantasy. My brother is in fact alive and well and living in Westchester County, NY.

As I continued to process this "memory," further images arose and further understandings developed. First, I realized that the gate around the swimming pool in the memory was very likely a representation of the bars of my baby brother's crib. Then, with a chuckle, I remembered conversations my wife and I had had decades later when our son was born. When looking at him on his stomach in his crib with his legs pulled up under him, we both remarked that he looked like a frog. My brother also must have looked like a frog to me, providing the perfect image for a screen memory that was unaffected by years of analysis but resolved itself with startling immediacy during EMDR.

Anecdotal reports such as mine do not prove anything. I have no doubts that others could describe instances in which EMDR did not unravel something that psychoanalysis did. Moreover, EMDR is not the only nonpsychoanalytic method through which significant insights may be attained. Such insights can emerge even through the sensitive use of straightforward behavioral methods such as systematic desensitization (see, e.g., Wachtel, 1991a, 1997). Nonetheless, something about the experience I have reported seems to me compelling and suggests that the EMDR experience can contribute powerfully to releasing some of the stuck locks in the darker rooms of the psyche.

EMDR, PSYCHOANALYSIS, AND RESISTANCE

If EMDR may turn out to facilitate the process of working through, and even at times to deepen the insights that psychoanalytic exploration is designed to promote, there is a potential benefit as well in the opposite direction; practitioners of EMDR have much to gain from incorporating ideas and perspectives from the psychoanalytic point of view. For example, in my experience the phenomena of transference and resistance, which are at the heart of the psychoanalytic approach, are by no means absent in EMDR. I recall vividly an experience with one patient, a rather obsessive man who had great difficulty letting go or permitting certain emotions to surface. He responded to EMDR with a series of thoughts and images that are essentially summarized by, "I'm thinking that you're moving your finger in front of my eyes" or "What came to mind was that you were moving your finger back and forth."

It is not that EMDR had no value in the work with this man. In fact, later in the very same session, he had the thought, accompanied by vivid imagery, "I'm aware that I put a lid on my feelings." The thought occurred not during the formal EMDR part of the session but while we were "just talking"—that is, resuming "therapy as usual" and in the process, elaborating and exploring the clinical experience of EMDR. Shapiro has emphasized (e.g., Shapiro, 1995) and EMDR training always stresses that the practice of EMDR should not be a mechanical procedure. Part of its very essence includes using the clinical skills that mark a good clinician of any orientation. It seems to me highly unlikely that this patient would have understood as clearly at that point that he "put a lid" on his feelings had I not used EMDR in this session. At the same time, had I not brought to bear years of experience working with conflict and resistance, this session might not have moved in a direction that was therapeutically useful.

Behaviorally oriented therapists also encounter resistance and have ways of working with it; but those in the psychoanalytic tradition have paid much more careful and extensive attention to this dimension of therapeutic work and have developed theoretical concepts and clinical strategies that can add considerably to the armamentarium used by therapists of other persuasions (see Wachtel, 1982a, 1997). As a method that originated in the cognitive–behavioral realm but that simultaneously makes quite direct contact with the phenomena central to psychoanalysis, EMDR might benefit substantially from considering how adding a "psychoanalytic flavor" to EMDR could open up new possibilities.

EMDR FROM A NEW VANTAGE POINT: A PSYCHOANALYTIC PERSPECTIVE

To clarify the potential contributions a psychoanalytic perspective could make to EMDR, it is useful to look more closely at some aspects of the standard approach to EMDR that seem perfectly ordinary and scarcely worth noting to cognitive–behavioral therapists. To psychoanalytically oriented therapists, these same procedures are likely to feel like a completely unnatural way of conducting therapy and to reflect very specifically EMDR's cognitive–behavioral origins. I thus wish to consider whether certain features of EMDR, rather than being considered *intrinsic* to EMDR, might be better thought of as artifacts of the specific orientation out of which EMDR evolved.

It is important to note that referring to these features as *artifacts* does not mean that they are necessarily wrong, clinically useless, or features of EMDR that will eventually fade away. These are issues that remain to be investigated via clinical practice and systematic research. Rather, my aim is to create a kind of distance from the familiar, to introduce a new angle or perspective that can stimulate or encourage such investigation. Until now, EMDR has been so closely associated with a cognitive–behavioral vantage point that many within the movement have not thought to ask the questions being addressed in this chapter. In a sense, this discussion is similar to what psychoanalytically oriented therapists do when they attempt to make some of their patients' unexamined character traits more ego dystonic—that is, they transform what was previously taken for granted into an object of curiosity to be examined.

Treating Disorders vs. Treating Patterns of Living and Experiencing

As is typical of cognitive–behavioral approaches, especially in the more recent era of managed care and of prevalent research funding policies that parallel insurance company and medical agendas, EMDR has largely focused on treating discrete disorders.

Psychoanalysis also began with a focus on discrete disorders. The early years of psychoanalysis were very intensely focused on the elimination of hysterical and obsessional *symptoms*. However, as psychoanalysis evolved, understanding the personality context within which those symptoms arose moved to center stage. Although today relief from painful symptoms is still an important goal of psychoanalytic therapy, two characteristics in particular distinguish contemporary psychoanalytic practice quite significantly from the approach that characterized psychoanalysis in its first decades.

First, even when the focus is on symptoms, psychoanalysts usually assume that to understand and treat the symptoms adequately, their role in the patient's overall adaptation or in his or her character or personality must be understood. This tendency can be traced at least back to the work of Reich (1930) and Horney (1939, 1945, 1950). It does not just direct the therapist's attention to personality disorders (as defined by the *Diagnostic and Statistical Manual of Mental Disorders [DSM]*), which some people are deemed to manifest, and others are not. Rather, the focus is on the patient's entire way of life, on the total configuration of values, emotions, perceptual, and cognitive tendencies he or she manifests. Because everyone has such characteristics in their unique personalities, the concern with the personality context of patients' symptoms is directed toward all patients, not just those with an Axis II diagnosis.

The second (somewhat related) characteristic of contemporary psychoanalytic practice that I wish to highlight here is that the emphasis of much clinical work in this tradition is not on symptoms or specific disorders at all, but on what Sullivan (1953) has called "problems in living." Today, psychoanalytic work usually centers on tasks such as helping people with their relationships, determining how they feel about themselves and their lives, and finding meaning in their work. In the current political atmosphere, such concerns are often described disparagingly as the problems of the "worried well," in contrast to "real" disorders with specific diagnoses (and, of course, shorter and cheaper treatments). This is unfortunate not only because it reflects a set of values more relevant to corporate bottom lines than to human welfare (discussed later on) but because in fact this is a realm in which EMDR has much to contribute.

Patients' Complaints and the Larger Life Patterns in Which They Are Embedded

There is much to be said for and much to be said against the psychoanalytic idea of understanding symptoms primarily in the context of the overall organization of the personality. There is now much evidence that so-called symptoms can often be quite successfully treated without attending to any possible characterological foundations or ramifications. Behavior therapy, cognitive–behavior therapy, and EMDR all clearly accomplish this task with considerable regularity. It has been one of the continuing blind spots of many psychoanalysts that they fail to appreciate sufficiently this established fact when addressing the welfare of their patients.[8]

On the other hand, I am extremely skeptical that *all* symptoms are best treated this way. The patient's way of life and the web of relationships, assumptions, and emotional meanings that characterizes his or her individuality often play a crucial role in the patient's symptomatic complaints. Thus, aside from larger value issues (which are discussed in a later section), these matters can be crucial, even in the treatment of the patient's specific complaints.[9]

Should EMDR Be More Ambitious?

In my views regarding the question of whether therapy should address problems in living and not just *DSM*-diagnosed disorders, I differ more substantially from many (although by no means all) behavioral and cognitive–behavioral therapists and EMDR practitioners. This is one of the areas in which I believe the general purview of EMDR can be usefully and valuably extended and in which the contribution of EMDR can potentially aid therapists in addressing a broader set of psychological challenges.

The way that American psychiatry and psychology presently focus on diagnostic categories and the increasing pressure to frame evaluations of treatment in terms of specific disorders (and even essentially to equate empirical validation per se with the cognitive style of dividing the world up into discrete categories of disorder) seem to me essentially politics and economic self-interest dressed in the garb of science. There is little reason to think that nature created 377 specific psychological disorders (the total

---

[8]I am referring here to therapies such as exposure treatments for simple phobias, cognitive–behavioral treatments for panic attacks, and EMDR treatments for PTSD. Such treatments can often be successfully used with little attention to the kinds of issues to which psychoanalysts direct much of their clinical effort.

[9]It is important to note that attention to the larger context of the patient's life and the ways of thinking, feeling, and making sense of life experiences that may be the basis of specific symptomatic complaints is not necessarily alien to cognitive–behavioral therapists (e.g., Goldfried & Davison, 1994; Young, 1999).

in the current *DSM*) and then added a bit of comorbidity as a fudge factor. I am convinced that 100 years from now our lists of diagnostic categories will seem practically medieval.

The present approach to understanding psychological distress is shaped by the increasing degree to which corporations have gained control over health care and the corresponding bottom-line values that have insidiously affected our thinking about human services. Therapists have become "providers," who are as likely to attend workshops about marketing, business development, or billing software as they are to probe the nuances of their patients' or clients' lives. To accommodate the corporations' definitions of what is legitimately treatable, many therapists have accepted and even endorsed a narrow and impoverished definition of the goals of psychotherapy. It would be a shame if EMDR practitioners followed this trend because EMDR has considerable potential to expand therapists' ability to treat the problems in living that, diagnosable or not, have played such a major role in causing people to seek psychotherapy.[10]

CYCLICAL PSYCHODYNAMICS AND THE INTERACTIVE DIMENSION OF PEOPLE'S DIFFICULTIES: THE ISSUE OF ACCOMPLICES

Another consideration that points to potential variations and innovations in the practice of EMDR derives from the theoretical perspective I have called *cyclical psychodynamics* (see, e.g., Gold & Wachtel, 1993; Wachtel, 1993, 1997; Wachtel & McKinney, 1992). This theoretical approach was originally developed to provide a framework for integrating the insights and perspectives of psychoanalysis with the active intervention possibilities of behavior therapy.[11] The approach is a part of the broader

---

[10]This by no means questions the importance of providing help for people who have been traumatized by terrible events. People who have experienced rape, incest, war, or natural disasters should be among the highest priorities for receiving psychological resources. Those resources are scarce, partly because of a value orientation that emphasizes cost more than psychological experience, a value system that profit-oriented (and treatment-limiting) health maintenance organizations and managed care corporations represent par excellence. Clinicians should not have to choose between helping those who have been traumatized and enriching the lives of people who do not have "diagnosable syndromes." The real choice in allocating societal resources is, in essence, whether to address the ways in which relationships, self-esteem, and a sense of meaning and coherence contribute to the quality of life (quite apart from "disorders" per se) or to produce more sports utility vehicles, electronic doo-dads, and the like. We are prevented from seeing these alternatives by a subterfuge that persuades us that the only legitimate choices individuals or societies have are those that are provided by "the market," a mechanism that in fact precludes many of the choices that would most meaningfully address the needs of the majority of people (for an elaboration of these issues, see Wachtel, 1983, 1998).

[11]Currently, cyclical psychodynamics includes substantial emphasis on systemic perspectives as well (e.g., Wachtel & Wachtel, 1986), but that dimension is not as central to the discussion in this chapter.

"relational" trend in psychoanalysis (see chapter 15 of Wachtel, 1997), but it introduces more radical innovations in treatment technique. In addition, it spells out much more elaborately the ways in which the actual interactions between people contribute to the construction of each person's experience and the ways in which personality is continuously shaped by circular patterns in which "inner" psychological structures and inclinations and "external" events in daily life reproduce each other ad infinitum.

From the vantage point of cyclical psychodynamics, the perpetuation of maladaptive patterns and reactions (and of more salutary tendencies) is not sufficiently understood if therapists concentrate only on what has been "internalized" by their patients. The reaction tendencies manifested by patients are not simply a product of material locked in their psyche or neural patterns stored in their brain. Rather, these tendencies are maintained by the ways their impact on others leads to consequences and life experiences that confirm or strengthen the internalized inclination.

Thus, although traumas can leave powerful marks on the psyche— and even alter structures in the brain—the impact of the trauma is not limited to the deeply etched memories or the emotional reaction patterns that continue to disrupt the person's life years after the event. When, in reacting to those memories, the patient is wary with other people, is prone to emotional outbursts, has difficulty functioning effectively on the job or maintaining intimate, trusting relationships, experiences anxiety or absence of pleasure in sexual activity, or manifests the consequences of the trauma in countless other ways, those reactions have *further* impact on the patient's life.

The enduring effects of the trauma do not just reside in the patient's brain. They reside as well in his or her way of life. A way of life that may have originated from a trauma can itself become a continuing source of traumatization that further perpetuates the same problematic way of life. For example, lack of trust can deprive the traumatized individual of experiences that help make the world seem safer and kinder to most people and hence can contribute to perpetuating mistrustfulness. Unpredictable emotional outbursts can put people off or cause them to withdraw, perpetuating a state of isolation or of being treated uncaringly, which can fuel still further emotional outbursts. Wariness or avoidant behavior with regard to sex, or ambivalence deriving from the struggle between healthy desire and residual anxiety, can lead to behavior that is experienced by others as teasing or provocative and can evoke anger and even cruelty that further confirms the individual's fearfulness and creates retraumatization. The disruptive effects of trauma on the ability to concentrate or to pursue academic and career success can place the individual in continuing stress, generate further rage or depression, and even force the person to live in neighborhoods in which further traumatization is more likely. In turn such experiences further disrupt the ability to concentrate and in other ways set the stage for more of the same.

In these and other patterns, the impact of the trauma lies not just in memory or in how the experience was "stored" in the brain. It also involves *new* experiences that might not have occurred in the present if the patient had not had the earlier unfortunate experiences in the past.

This means that it is often not enough to clear the patient's mind of the anomalous residues of the past; therapists must also help patients change the current patterns that make their present lives resemble the traumatic circumstances of the past. Therapists must pay active attention not only to what patients feel, think, and remember but also to what they *do*—to the ironic ways in which reactions to the traumas of yesterday lead to behavior that increases the likelihood of further traumatization tomorrow. It also means the therapist must pay attention not only to what the patient does but to what the patient's behaviors evoke *in others*.

As I have discussed in more detail elsewhere (see, e.g., Wachtel, 1991b, 1993), problematic psychological reactions usually require "accomplices" to maintain them. Understanding the way others react to the patient is essential for fully understanding the way the past is carried forward into the present and the future—the way the problematic schemas are perpetuated. The role of accomplices is not always readily evident, however. Often, their role may be subtle and therefore difficult for the untrained eye to discern. Indeed, this is one of the reasons that more internal explanations of psychological disorders—explanations that concentrate on only a part of the maintaining influences—are so prevalent. If one looks closely and perceptively, however, it is possible to see how tendencies that may appear to be firmly internalized are in fact being maintained by actual experiences.

Using Countertransference to Alert the Therapist to the Role of Accomplices

In attempting to discern the subtle transactional patterns that maintain the patient's difficulties, it is important to be attentive to the emotional reactions the patient evokes in the therapist. Although it is one of the shortcomings of standard psychoanalytic epistemology to assume that all of the patient's emotional and behavioral inclinations and all of the reactions they evoke in others can be observed in the playing out of the transference and countertransference—such an assumption ignores the specificity of the pairing of any particular patient and any particular therapist and what they bring out in each other—it is equally wrong to ignore the powerful source of therapeutically relevant information that is offered by attention to these matters. Often, the key to seeing what is going on in the patient's daily life—to seeing how persisting emotional and behavioral reactions that may appear to be deeply rooted or indelibly etched in the patient's brain are a product of ongoing actions and reactions between the patient and the significant others in his life—lies in noticing what is going on between the patient and his or her therapist. Because the therapist is in a special position to observe the reactions of "the other" to the patient when that other is the therapist him- or herself, the perceptions and understandings engendered by attention to this dimension of what is happening in the therapy room can help to "tune" the therapist to notice aspects of what is transpiring in the patient's life outside the consulting room that the therapist might otherwise not have noticed (see, for example, Wachtel, 1997).

AN ALTERNATIVE USE OF "EMDR"

I have put quotation marks around "EMDR" in the heading of this section because, strictly speaking, the work I will describe here is *not* EMDR. As it is presently defined, and presently practiced, EMDR is a highly structured treatment with a very specific set of steps and procedures. What I present here is a way of working that is inspired by EMDR, that draws upon some of the key elements of EMDR, but it differs quite substantially from the way EMDR is most typically practiced.

This difference derives from two main sources—(a) the kinds of patients and problems on which my practice focuses and (b) my prior training in, and continuing interest in, the psychoanalytic point of view. It would certainly be too extreme to state that I am describing a "psychoanalytic EMDR," in contrast to the "cognitive–behavioral EMDR" that is presently the mainstream of EMDR work—among other objections to such a formulation, both EMDR and my own approach are integrative rather than strictly defined by either a cognitive–behavioral or a psychoanalytic polarity—but it is certainly the case that I have adapted an approach initially shaped by a cognitive–behavioral sensibility to the sensibilities that fit my own training, personality, and patient population.

I had earlier found that something similar happened when I began to incorporate the methods of behavior therapy into my work as a psychoanalytically oriented therapist. At first, my integration of the two approaches was really more a simple combination or mixture than a true synthesis. It would have been relatively easy for an observer to decide when I was being psychoanalytic in the work and when I was being behavioral. At times I would listen and make occasional interpretations, and at other times I would engage in systematic desensitization or assertiveness training in ways relatively indistinguishable from how a behavior therapist would do it. It was not long, however, before the synthesis proceeded in a more thoroughgoing way. As I put it elsewhere,

In the early stages of an integrative effort, the separate components are likely to remain discrete and identifiable. They are *combined* but not really synthesized. . . . It is not likely to be long, however, before something more interesting . . . happens. When assumptions and methods come into close contact with other assumptions and methods that were previously alien, subtle changes begin to appear in all of the constituents of the evolving synthesis. (Wachtel, 1997, p. 392)

My way of working is generally less structured than is EMDR. I do not typically use readily identifiable protocols with different patient groups. In part this decision reflects my psychoanalytic background. Psychoanalytic therapists often work in a more intuitive fashion, attending particularly to the subtle affective tones and incipient meanings that are constantly communicated by the patient, and adapting the work to the patient's individuality and the constantly fluctuating state of the therapeutic relationship.[12] Especially in my own work, which is undertaken from a more relational or participant–observer version of psychoanalytic thought rather than from the perspective of a relatively silent or neutral analyst (see chapter 11 of Wachtel, 1987 and chapter 15 of Wachtel, 1997), there is considerable interchange, and that interchange cannot be readily planned or made to conform to a manual.[13]

This does not mean that I do not use structured procedures. For many years, my work has been characterized by an integration of the psychoanalytic method and viewpoint with cognitive–behavioral techniques. Thus, including the more structured approach of EMDR in at least a part of my work fit readily within the approach I had already developed for utilizing the psychoanalytic perspective in new ways. Indeed, in certain ways including EMDR was easier. EMDR, unlike most behavioral methods, has many similarities to free association. By its very nature, it elicits "material" in a way that, for example, systematic desensitization does not. That is, the therapist using systematic desensitization *prescribes* the images to which the patient is to be exposed and attempts to create a structure in which the patient sticks only to the images that the therapist has prescribed rather than letting whatever comes up be the focus of attention. Those images may be arrived at jointly—in the cooperative endeavor between patient and therapist as they create a hierarchy—but the hierarchy itself is rather

---

[12] The point is not that therapists using EMDR are not intuitive or that they do not attend to the individuality of their patients. In certain respects, EMDR is an approach that is highly individualized. The images that the patient addresses come from the patient, not the therapist, and no two patients, even in the "same" protocol, are immersed in anything approaching the same images. At the same time, however, there is a structured regularity to the *therapist's* participation that is far greater than in psychoanalytic therapies. There are pluses and minuses in each regard. What I am emphasizing here is simply that there are differences.

[13] Contrary to what has become a recent dogma, the existence of a manual is by no means necessary for an approach to be meaningfully evaluated by systematic research (Messer & Wachtel, 1997).

linear and focused, and spontaneous departure from the hierarchically pro-grammed set of images is not encouraged.[14]

In contrast, EMDR is not prescriptive in content. The therapist indicates where to start, but from that point on, it is up to the patient. The flow of images, memories, and experiences is spontaneous and un-guided, much like the process of free association in psychoanalysis. In fact, it is more so than is typical of psychoanalytic practice today, which is increasingly adopting a more interactive, relational model that differs from the one-person model of free association that characterized psychoanalysis in its early years (see previous discussion).

Herein is one key difference between the way I have utilized a number of the elements of EMDR and the way that EMDR proper is practiced (and the reason I call my use of it "EMDR" rather than EMDR). I employ "EMDR" in the context of a therapy that is generally fairly interactive, and I am at times interactive in the "EMDR" part of the work as well. That is, sometimes the "EMDR" work I do looks just like EMDR (without the quotation marks). But sometimes I interject and interweave the work I ordinarily do as an integrative, relational psychoanalytic therapist. For example, I interpret, I help patients to structure and make sense of their thoughts, I point to conflicts of which the patient may have been unaware, I help patients to reframe their experience, and I point out potentially useful actions (see Wachtel, 1993).

In part because the goal of my work is not just to "cure" specific "dis-orders," but to help people lead fuller and more satisfying lives, I have found that I must use the elements of EMDR differently. Frequently, I incorporate "EMDR" into the ongoing flow of a largely psychodynamic therapy. Thus, usually after having earlier introduced EMDR in a more formal or structured way, I might at a certain point in the therapeutic dialogue say to the patient, "This sounds like something that would be useful to explore further with EMDR. Would you like to try it?" (At other times, I might be more inclined to say "useful to work on via EMDR" rather than "useful to explore." It depends on whether the emphasis is more on bringing out fresh material or helping the patient resolve or get past something already clearly in con-sciousness but whose troubling nature is not diminishing. Of course, these two dimensions of therapeutic work are not in opposition, but the emphasis varies from one situation to another.)

A Brief Technical Note

In using the elements of EMDR in a psychodynamic context, I have found that auditory bilateral stimulation is easier to incorporate than eye

---

[14]It should be noted, however, that systematic desensitization too can bring forth much material of psychodynamic significance when it is used within the context of an approach that is simultaneously interested in and attentive to the complex flow of subjective experience (Wachtel, 1991a; 1997).

movement. The fluid movement from conversation to "EMDR" proceeds more easily when the therapist does not have to do things such as get up and move to a position next to the patient. In addition, the transference issues are probably somewhat less problematic when the therapist is not physically moving toward or away from the patient. (If visual rather than auditory stimulation is emphasized—either because of the patient's preferences or, potentially, in light of future research findings—the use of a light bar rather than sitting near the patient and moving one's fingers would probably fit better with the approach being described here.)

Interpretation and Cognition

In using "EMDR" in a psychoanalytic context, the *cognitive* dimension of EMDR is replaced somewhat by the *interpretive* dimension of the psychoanalytic approach. The introduction of a cognitive dimension to behavior therapy not only advanced the sophistication and completeness of the behavioral point of view, but it also brought it closer in certain ways to the psychoanalytic approach. It introduced a more complex mediational model that is at least somewhat akin—though by no means equivalent—to that used in psychoanalysis. Moreover, since the assumptions that cognitive therapists thought were guiding their patients' behavior and shaping their experience were not always able to be stated by the patient—and indeed at times a good deal of therapeutic work was necessary to tease out the cognitive substructure—a rough parallel was introduced to the interpretive efforts of the psychoanalytic therapist, who was also seeking to find underlying mental structures that the patient had not been able to articulate or describe.

Because of these (interesting, yet also quite rough) parallels, it is likely that the vast majority of therapists who can imagine the possibility of integration between psychoanalytic and behavioral approaches—whether their starting point be psychoanalytic or behavioral—regard such an integration as easier and more likely to be fruitful if the behavioral end of the spectrum is in fact *cognitive*–behavioral. Although I agree with this assessment in certain respects, overall I am considerably more skeptical about this proposition than most proponents of integration (see, e.g., chapter 16 of Wachtel, 1997).

My own efforts to integrate a behavioral dimension into a psychoanalytically oriented approach stemmed in large part from dissatisfaction with what seemed to me an excessively cognitive quality to psychoanalytic practice. Although all psychoanalysts agree that therapy must not be dryly intellectual, and the distinction between intellectual and emotional insight is one of the most venerable ideas in the psychoanalytic tradition, it nonetheless seemed to me that when analysis went wrong, it was far more likely that the problem was that the therapy had lapsed into mere words, substituting ideas and thoughts for emotions and experiences. Rarely was the problem that the work had become too experiential, with insufficient talking or explanation.

Thus, what appealed to me most about behavior therapy was its emphasis on action and—although not often appreciated by analysts—on direct experience. When a cognitive dimension was introduced into behavior therapy, it seemed to me to enhance the theoretical comprehensiveness of behavior therapy, but not necessarily its suitability for integration with psychoanalysis. Psychoanalysis already *had* mediating processes built into its very heart, and in my view the psychoanalytic conceptualization of those processes was much richer. Cognitive therapy all too often seemed to embody an arid rationalism, and although there was good evidence that cognitive therapies were helpful to people, the evidence was much less clear that the specifically cognitive components added anything clinically significant to the behavioral interventions to which they were almost always linked. Moreover, I have continued to have serious questions about that branch of cognitive therapy that attempts to persuade patients that their view of the world is irrational, which implies that the therapist has a more rational view of the world than the patient does (see Wachtel, 1993, 1997).[15]

The cognitive perspective in EMDR seems to me somewhat different and less problematic. As I understand EMDR, one key aim is to overcome the dissociation between thoughts and emotions that permits people to experience for years distressing emotional reactions that are at odds with what they know or think. The person may be able to utter sentences that convey that a danger situation was long ago and no longer exists or that he or she was not at fault for what happened, yet the emotional reaction persists as if those sentences were irrelevant. Part of what EMDR seems to do is to bring into effective contact the pathways that contain the cognitive and emotional encodings of the experience so that they can influence each other. That process, as stimulated by EMDR, is very different from the syllogistic logic chopping that at times characterizes cognitive therapy.

The EMDR approach does not elevate cognition over emotion or attempt to change people's emotions by changing their sentences. Implicit in the EMDR approach as I understand it is a view similar to that of psychoanalysis—that cognition and emotion should be simultaneously

---

[15] In contrast, more constructivist versions of cognitive therapy attempt to understand in more empathic fashion the way the world looks to the patient. Rather than persuade the patient that he or she is being irrational, constructivist cognitive therapists simply point out that the way the patient has viewed matters is but one plausible way of understanding or construing the events of his or her life, and they attempt to interest patients in considering alternative ways of constructing their vision of their life and experiences. (For additional discussion about the distinction between constructivist and rationalist versions of cognitive therapy and of the relevance of this distinction to the relationship between cognitive and psychoanalytic approaches, see Wachtel, 1997, chapter 16.)

brought to bear, that it is *emotion-laden* thoughts that should be the focus of therapy and that are the center of the patient's personality and of his problems.

In certain respects, however, EMDR, reflecting its cognitive–behavioral origins, approaches cognition in a way that is harder to reconcile with the vision that guides the psychoanalytically oriented therapist. It has been my experience—no doubt reflecting in part my own predispositions and how they are communicated to the patient—that asking for the negative cognition is often not a simple and straightforward procedure, and that at times it forces the patient's experience into a Procrustean sentence structure that moves away from the patient's own way of conceiving of his or her experience. No doubt there are some people for whom a single sentence such as "I am worthless" or "I can never succeed" actually distills their experience sufficiently to be useful. But to my psychoanalytically tuned ears, this sounds more like Beck-speak or Ellis-speak, not a way of conceptualizing people's underlying psychological structures that would have much resonance for clinicians not steeped in the cognitive–behavioral worldview. I too am concerned about the underlying thoughts that accompany distressing emotions and memories, and I agree that they include very centrally self-evaluations. But they rarely, in my experience, can be well captured by a single sentence.

Interestingly, my dissatisfaction with the way cognitions are approached in EMDR stems from my very interest in EMDR as a potentially important way of bringing together thoughts and emotions that have seemed to be on their own independent tracks. Because I am skeptical that the key thoughts are as syllogistic as cognitive therapists implicitly suggest, I am concerned to bring forth a fuller and less artificially constrained sense of what those thoughts are.

Thus, in my own utilization of "EMDR," I am more open ended and nondirective in my approach to bringing out and articulating the underlying thoughts. Rather than forcing the patient to boil these thoughts down to a sentence or two, I seek a more variegated set of thoughts and images. "What else comes to mind?"—that old psychoanalytic standby—seems to me quite useful here. And I clearly convey to patients that I am not looking for a single, well-articulated sentence, but rather for a wide variety of thoughts, such as what kind of person they are, what their role in the experience was, and what their experience tells them about their life.

The search for the positive cognition has felt to me, as I have attempted it, even more artificial. Patients seem to be guessing what I am getting at, what I want from them, and largely constructing an alternative by logically inverting what they had previously said in offering me a negative cognition. Indeed, this was my own experience as a patient as well when, as noted above, I underwent (and benefited from) EMDR therapy myself.

Once again, this is not to say that I am not interested in how patients would *like* to think about themselves or about a distressing experience or life pattern on which we are working.[16] Indeed, I have my own equivalent of what EMDR therapists (*without* the quotation marks) call *installing* the positive cognition. The term *installation* grates a bit on the nerves of my psychoanalytic sensibilities; it sounds too pat and mechanical. But in fact, my clinical approach, regardless of whether I am using "EMDR," includes clinical processes that are at least first cousins of what EMDR therapists call installation. The attributional comments that have become an increasingly important part of my own clinical work (see Wachtel, 1993, especially chapter 9) entail introducing, in subtle ways that patients are more likely to embrace, a variety of alternative ways of viewing themselves and their life that I hope they will take on in place of some others that might be described as "negative." And when I employ "EMDR" within the more conversational context I am describing, I will frequently say about the patient's report after a set something like, "It sounds like what you were picturing was a way of speaking up to your husband that affirms your right to be heard" (stating it in a way that implies I agreed with this affirmation of a patient who had been telling herself she did not have such a right), or "The thoughts and images that occurred to you seem to reflect an increasing recognition that you were not responsible for the way he treated you," or "I see you were able to let yourself get more in touch with the angry feelings toward your mother that you had previously felt were unacceptable." I cannot discuss here the larger context or clinical strategy that leads to my making statements of this sort, or how they fit with the other kinds of comments that are part of my clinical approach.[17] It should be noted, however, that their functional role has much in common with what EMDR therapists call *cognitive interweave*.

The extent of the options available to therapists for putting their understanding into words—and for helping point patients toward experiencing and thinking about themselves and their lives differently—is often unrecognized or poorly understood. (See Wachtel, 1993, for a detailed examination of what therapists actually say to their patients or clients and of which kinds of statements and phrasings are therapeutic and which—all too common—ways of communicating are countertherapeutic.) I use the full range of linguistic interventions when using "EMDR" in a psychoanalytic context, moving freely back and forth from more formal EMDR sets to the dialogue that is more typical of the psychoanalytic approach.[18]

---

[16] It is important to note, by the way, that working on a distressing *experience*, as with PTSD, and working on a distressing *life pattern* or *relationship pattern*, as is the more common focus in my own practice, is not exactly the same. The variations I am discussing here probably bear more directly on the latter kind of work than on the former.

[17] See Wachtel, 1993.

[18] Thus, the interpretive therapeutic dialogue can supply the content or focus of what an

As I understand it, the "EMDR" helps bring up new material and aids in the working-through process, whereas the more dialogical and interpretive aspects of the work help focus the patient's associations,[19] reduce resistance, point the patient toward new modes of interaction with others, *and* offer a kind of psychoanalytic equivalent of (or, better, variation on) the "cognitive" dimensions of EMDR.

REMAINING QUESTIONS

Both my own clinical experience and my reading of the research literature make me very optimistic about the future prospects of EMDR. But clinical experience alone is always subject to selective perception and remembering, and the more controlled research on EMDR does leave important questions remaining. It seems to me quite well established that, for the particular clinical syndromes on which investigation has been primarily focused, EMDR has been shown to have a positive clinical effect. That is, it is clearly superior to placebo or no-treatment control groups. Less clear is whether EMDR is superior to other effective treatments or which of its multiple elements (singly or in particular combinations) are essential or offer something beyond what other treatments offer.

Shapiro (1999) has pointed out that most of the studies which have found no difference between EMDR and treatments based on exposure alone have not used clinicians who were well trained in EMDR. This is an especially important issue because EMDR is a more complex treatment than standard exposure approaches such as systematic desensitization or flooding. That, of course, is exactly what some of the critics of EMDR object to; their preference is for simple procedures that can be administered by a graduate student or a clerk as effectively as by a skilled clinician. To the degree that the same results can be obtained more cheaply and quickly without elaborate training or attention to clinical complexities, such re-

EMDR set will begin with. I might say, for example, "It sounds like what you're feeling is such and such; if that makes sense to you, can you focus on that while you have the head phones on?" Or the EMDR experience can be directed toward a transference experience, asking the patient to focus on a feeling he or she is having toward me or on an image of saying something to me that has been difficult to say. Or, as the patient reports the experiences he had during a set, I might listen to the flow of the material from the vantage point of my understanding of the patient's dynamics, and choose the point at which to say "go with that" accordingly. In all of these circumstances, I make sure, as do most therapists using EMDR, to include the affective and bodily aspects of the experience and not just the cognitive or content component.

[19] Recall here the discussions of the therapist as participant–observer, of one- and two-person models, and of the fallacy that material just "emerges" or "unfolds." Because the material that emerges is never just "spontaneous" or internally generated, but is always at least in part a product of the interaction between the two people in the room—an interaction in which the therapist inevitably "cues" the patient in a wide variety of ways—it is useful for the therapist to be able to do so in as witting and sophisticated a way as possible. The guidance provided by psychoanalytic theory is one way to maximize this.

duced treatments can be a social good, and I would agree that the burden of proof must lie with those of us who view more elaborate procedures and more complex clinical skills as necessary. But I clearly stand on the side of those who believe that reducing the clinical enterprise to a few discrete and quasimechanical procedures, capable of being administered by technicians with relatively limited training, is unwise and short-sighted social policy. I expect that well-designed research will demonstrate the significantly incremental value of more comprehensive attention to the complexities of people's difficulties and of their lives, but the research remains to be done.

Clearly, just as research is required to establish whether EMDR adds something to the clinical effectiveness of exposure alone, so too is research required to determine whether the use of "EMDR" in a psychoanalytic context adds to, subtracts from, or leaves unchanged the effectiveness of EMDR. It is my own expectation that the answer will not be unambiguous, that for some cases the presently standard approach to EMDR will prove superior and for others the kinds of variations I have been describing will prove more useful.

What is perhaps most crucial is that the experimental spirit that has characterized EMDR in its first 10 years continue. One of the sad miscarriages of psychoanalysis was its premature congealing into a "classical" or "orthodox" approach that impeded progress for many years. EMDR is still very young. The particular ideas presented in this chapter may or may not turn out to be useful. What *will* be useful is a spirit of innovation, a readiness to experiment and depart from tradition, and a sense of responsibility to evaluate the effectiveness of those departures.

REFERENCES

Arkowitz, H. (1997). Integrative theories of therapy. In P. L. Wachtel & S. B. Messer (Eds.), *Theories of psychotherapy: Origins and evolution* (pp. 227–288). Washington, DC: American Psychological Association.

Aron, L. (1996). *A meeting of minds: Mutuality in psychoanalysis.* Hillsdale, NJ: Analytic Press.

Frank, K. A. (1999). *Psychoanalytic participation: Action, interaction, and integration.* Hillsdale, NJ: Analytic Press.

Gill, M. M. (1954). Psychoanalysis and exploratory psychotherapy. *Journal of the American Psychoanalytic Association, 2,* 771–797.

Gill, M. M. (1982). *Analysis of transference.* New York: International Universities Press.

Gill, M. M. (1994). *Psychoanalysis in transition.* Hillsdale, NJ: Analytic Press.

Gold, J. R., & Wachtel, P. L. (1993). Cyclical psychodynamics. In J. Gold & G.

Stricker (Eds.), *Comprehensive handbook of psychotherapy integration* (pp. 59–72). New York: Plenum.

Goldfried, M. R., & Davison, G. C. (1994). *Clinical behavior therapy*. New York: Wiley.

Hoffman, I. Z. (1991). Toward a social–constructivist view of the psychoanalytic situation. *Psychoanalytic Dialogues, 1,* 74–105.

Hoffman, I. Z. (1992). Some practical implications of a social-constructivist view of the psychoanalytic situation. *Psychoanalytic Dialogues, 3,* 287–304.

Horney, K. (1939). *New ways in psychoanalysis*. New York: Norton.

Horney, K. (1945). *Our inner conflicts*. New York: Norton.

Horney, K. (1950). *Neurosis and human growth*. New York: Norton.

Marcus, S., Marquis, P., & Sakai, C. (1997). Controlled study of treatment of PTSD using EMDR in an HMO setting. *Psychotherapy, 34,* 307–315.

Messer, S. B. (1992). A critical examination of belief structures in integrative and eclectic psychotherapy. In J. C. Norcross & M. R. Goldfried (Eds.), *Handbook of psychotherapy integration* (pp. 130–165). New York: Basic Books.

Messer, S. B., Sass, L. A., & Woolfolk, R. L. (Eds.). (1988). *Hermeneutics and psychological theory: Interpretive perspectives on personality, psychotherapy, and psychopathology*. New Brunswick, NJ: Rutgers University Press.

Messer, S. B., & Wachtel, P. L. (1997). The contemporary psychotherapeutic landscape: Issues and prospects. In P. L. Wachtel & S. B. Messer (Eds.), *Theories of psychotherapy: Origins and evolution* (pp. 1–38). Washington, DC: American Psychological Association.

Mitchell, S. A. (1988). *Relational concepts in psychoanalysis*. Cambridge, MA: Harvard University Press.

Mitchell, S. A. (1993). *Hope and dread in psychoanalysis*. New York: Basic Books.

Modell, A. H. (1984). *Psychoanalysis in a new context*. New York: International Universities Press.

Reich, W. (1930). *Character analysis*. New York: Noonday Press.

Renik, O. (1995). The ideal of the autonomous analyst and the problem of self-disclosure. *Psychoanalytic Quarterly, 64,* 466–495.

Renik, O. (1996). The perils of neutrality. *Psychoanalytic Quarterly, 65,* 495–517.

Rothbaum, B. O. (1997). A controlled study of eye movement desensitization and reprocessing for posttraumatic stress disordered sexual assault victims. *Bulletin of the Menninger Clinic, 61,* 317–334.

Scheck, M. M., Schaeffer, J. A., & Gillette, C. S. (1998). Brief psychological intervention with traumatized young women: The efficacy of eye movement desensitization and reprocessing. *Journal of Traumatic Stress, 11,* 25–44.

Shapiro, F. (1995). *Eye movement desensitization and reprocessing: Basic principles, protocols, and procedures*. New York: Guilford Press.

Shapiro, F. (1999). Eye movement desensitization and reprocessing (EMDR): Clinical and research implications of an integrated psychotherapy treatment. *Journal of Anxiety Disorders, 13,* 35–67.

Spence, D. P. (1982). *Narrative truth and historical truth*. New York: Norton.

Stern, D. B. (1992). Commentary on constructivism in clinical psychoanalysis. *Psychoanalytic Dialogues, 2*, 331–364.

Stricker, G., & Gold, J. R. (1996). Psychotherapy integration: An assimilative, psychodynamic approach. *Clinical Psychology: Science and Practice, 3*, 47–58.

Sullivan, H. S. (1953). *The interpersonal theory of psychiatry*. New York: Norton.

Sullivan, H. S. (1954). *The psychiatric interview*. New York: Norton.

Wachtel, P. L. (1977). *Psychoanalysis and behavior therapy: Toward an integration*. New York: Basic Books.

Wachtel, P. L. (Ed.). (1982a). *Resistance: Psychodynamic and behavioral approaches*. New York: Plenum Press.

Wachtel, P. L. (1982b). Vicious circles: The self and the rhetoric of emerging and unfolding. *Contemporary Psychoanalysis, 18*, 273–295.

Wachtel, P. L. (1987). *Action and insight*. New York: Guilford Press.

Wachtel, P. L. (1991a). From eclecticism to synthesis: Toward a more seamless psychotherapeutic integration. *Journal of Psychotherapy Integration, 1*, 43–54.

Wachtel, P. L. (1991b). The role of accomplices in preventing and facilitating change. In R. Curtis & G. Stricker (Eds.), *How people change: Inside and outside therapy* (pp. 21–28). New York: Plenum Press.

Wachtel, P. L. (1993). *Therapeutic communication: Knowing what to say when*. New York: Guilford Press.

Wachtel, P. L. (1997). *Psychoanalysis, behavior therapy, and the relational world*. Washington, DC: American Psychological Association.

Wachtel, P. L. (1998). Overconsumption. In R. Keil, D. V. J. Bell, P. Penz, & L. Fawcett (Eds.), *Political ecology* (pp. 259–271). New York: Routledge.

Wachtel, P. L., & McKinney, M. (1992). Cyclical psychodynamics and integrative psychodynamic therapy. In J. Norcross & M. Goldfried (Eds.), *Handbook of psychotherapy integration* (pp. 335–370). New York: Basic Books.

Wachtel, E. F., & Wachtel, P. L. (1986). *Family dynamics in individual psychotherapy*. New York: Guilford Press.

Wilson, S. A., Becker, L. A., & Tinker, R. H. (1995). Eye movement desensitization and reprocessing (EMDR) treatment for psychologically traumatized individuals. *Journal of Consulting and Clinical Psychology, 63*, 928–937.

Wilson, S. A., Becker, L. A., & Tinker, R. H. (1997). Fifteen-month follow-up of eye movement desensitization and reprocessing (EMDR) treatment for PTSD and psychological trauma. *Journal of Consulting and Clinical Psychology, 65*, 1047–1056.

Young, J. (1999). *Cognitive therapy for personality disorders: A schema-focused approach* (3rd ed.). Sarasota, FL: Professional Resource Press.

6

EMDR AND COGNITIVE–BEHAVIOR THERAPY: EXPLORING CONVERGENCE AND DIVERGENCE

NANCY J. SMYTH AND A. DESMOND POOLE

Since first introduced by Shapiro (1989a, 1989b), eye movement desensitization and reprocessing (EMDR) has been the subject of considerable interest, debate, and controversy within the behavioral literature (Poole, De Jongh, & Spector, 1999; Rosen, Lohr, McNally, & Herbert, 1998). In this chapter, EMDR is examined from a behavioral perspective with the goal of exploring connections between it and behavior therapy. Since its initial introduction as an intervention for posttraumatic stress disorder (PTSD), EMDR has been expanded and is used to treat a range of other disorders (see Manfield, 1998). The present discussion centers on its application in the management of PTSD for two reasons: First, PTSD is the diagnostic category on which the majority of research studies have focused. Second, empirical research has determined that EMDR (Chemtob, Tolin, van der Kolk, & Pitman, 2000) and cognitive–behavioral therapy (CBT) (Rothbaum, Meadows, Resick, & Foy, 2000) are efficacious in the treatment of PTSD; they seem to be equally effective, although EMDR may be more efficient (Van Etten & Taylor, 1998).

The chapter begins with a brief consideration of the development and essential principles of behavior therapy and of the manner in which behavioral approaches have conceptualized PTSD. This context is essential to understanding how EMDR is conceptualized from a behavioral perspective. The relationship between EMDR and behavior therapy is then explored and mechanisms for its apparent effectiveness considered. Finally, contributions of behavior therapy to EMDR and of EMDR to behavior therapy are discussed, including challenges that each poses to the other.

BEHAVIOR THERAPY: AN OVERVIEW

Behavior therapy, or as it is now more commonly called, CBT,[1] is a treatment approach that reflects diverse theories and procedures, none of which has been accepted as the one unifying framework. However, over the years, behavior therapy has always retained its original firm adherence to empiricism and "the application of the experimental method to the understanding and modification of abnormalities of behavior" (Yates, 1970, p. 420). This adherence to empiricism has resulted in the incorporation of knowledge from social psychology, psychophysiology, and the cognitive sciences. In this section, a historical overview is provided of the development of cognitive–behavioral theories and techniques so that the reader can understand their relationship with EMDR and the historical context in which EMDR was developed.

Development of Behavior Therapy

Unlike some other psychotherapeutic approaches that are closely associated with the work of a single individual, views differ about the origins and essential characteristics of behavior therapy. However, there is widespread agreement that research into what is now referred to as *classical conditioning* (Pavlov, 1927, 1928) and on the principles of instrumental learning, or *operant conditioning* (Bekhterev, 1932; Skinner, 1938; Thorndike, 1913), were key elements in the development of behavior therapy. As Yates (1970) pointed out, "The experimental procedures of these workers began to be applied ... almost immediately to the area of abnormal behavior, both in a general explanatory sense and in the explanation of particular disorders" (p. 13).

For example, Watson and Raynor (1920) demonstrated that irrational fears and avoidance (i.e., phobic behavior) could be created in a child through classical conditioning. They did this by pairing the presentation of a disturbing event—a loud noise (the unconditioned stimulus, or UCS)

---

[1]The terms *behavior therapy* and *cognitive-behavior therapy* (CBT) are used interchangeably throughout this chapter.

—with a white rat (the conditioned stimulus, or CS), of which the child (Little Albert) was not initially afraid. After numerous pairings of the noise with the animal not only did the child become distressed at the sight of the animal alone, but this conditioned response (CR) showed *generalization* to other similar stimuli (i.e., other white, furry objects). Jones (1924) later demonstrated that repeated exposure to the CS in the absence of the UCS could be used to eliminate phobic behavior, or the CR, a process called *habituation*.

By the 1950s, behavior therapy really began to emerge and challenge the then accepted concept of mental disorders. It did so in different forms and with different emphases on both sides of the Atlantic. In America, many psychologists at various centers sought to apply operant conditioning techniques to clinical problems. *Operant conditioning* is the process by which an organism's actions are shaped by either *reinforcement* or *punishment*. Reinforcement, the process of rewarding behavior with positive consequences or elimination of negative stimuli, increases the likelihood an action will recur. Punishment, the process of discouraging behavior by introducing aversive consequences or removing positive stimuli decreases the likelihood behavior will be repeated. The focus of the Americans' pioneering research activity was on the analysis and modification of chronic and severe problems of hospitalized patients who would have been classified as having psychotic disorders (see Ullmann & Krasner, 1965).

In Britain, interest in behavioral approaches to the understanding and treatment of abnormal behavior was initially centered at the Department of Psychology, headed by Eysenck, at the Institute of Psychiatry in London. After Eysenck's (1952) trenchant criticism of the effectiveness of psychodynamic psychotherapy, dissatisfaction with the use of such treatment methods grew. Numerous psychologists (e.g., Jones, 1956; Meyer, 1957; Yates, 1958) began to use single-case experimental investigations to study behavioral change. However, British psychologists were less concerned than their American counterparts in just applying conditioning principles to alter behavior; they were also prepared to draw on other approaches and principles derived from the theoretical and empirical knowledge base of general psychology. Therefore, Eysenck (1964) defined behavior therapy as "the attempt to alter human behavior and emotion in a beneficial manner according to the laws of modern learning theory" (p. 1), whereas Yates (1970) argued that behavior therapy "represents (or should represent) a unique and particular way of approaching the patient.... The definition does *not* deny an important role to learning theory in many disorders of behavior, with respect both to explanation and to therapy; what it does deny is that the use of learning theory is the essence of behavior therapy" (Yates, 1975, p. 4).

During the 1950s, a theory with a different emphasis was being developed in South Africa. Wolpe, disenchanted with psychoanalytic theory and drawing on the animal research on experimental neurosis, formulated a neurophysiological theory of *reciprocal inhibition*. He postulated that the elimination of anxiety could be achieved by the repeated elicitation of a response incompatible with the fear reaction. This idea led to his development of the systematic desensitization procedure for the treatment of anxiety disorders (Wolpe, 1958). Subsequent research led to the rejection of the theoretical model on which Wolpe based systematic desensitization and also demonstrated that many of the elements of the treatment procedure, considered essential for effective treatment, were not necessary to achieve therapeutic effects (Yates, 1975).

Wolpe's pioneering work was to prove highly influential in stimulating research. Combined with Eysenck's (1952) criticisms of psychodynamic psychotherapy and the rapidly emerging emphasis on the application of a rigorous empirical approach to the study of abnormal behavior, an era of intense research on the nature and treatment of anxiety disorders began, which resulted in new behavioral treatment methods being developed, evaluated, and refined. As a consequence, today the use of, in particular, direct exposure methods are widely accepted as the treatment of choice for many anxiety disorders (Marks, 1987) although, as noted by Barlow and Hofmann (1997), relatively few patients actually receive such treatments.

By the 1970s, theoretically based research activity shifted to a more technological approach to treatment with a focus on the application of technique. For example, London (1972) argued, "The first issue is the factual one—Do they work? On whom? When? The how and why come later" (p. 919). This shift resulted in greater concern with the development of standardized approaches to treatment, the application of behavioral interventions to a range of problems, and the evaluation of the interventions' effectiveness.

During this important phase in the evolution of behavior therapy, the sophistication used to examine therapeutic effectiveness increased. Evidence was accumulated that demonstrated the effectiveness of behavioral methods in the management of a wide range of disorders and limited effectiveness with other disorders such as depression.

Development of CBT

Given the limited success of purely behavioral methods in treating depression, behavior therapists began to recognize the need to pay more attention to and place greater emphasis on the importance of their patients' attitudes, values, and beliefs. As a consequence, numerous behaviorally oriented researchers and clinicians became increasingly interested in the work of Beck and his colleagues on the cognitive theory of depression (Beck, 1967; Beck, Rush, Shaw, & Emery, 1979). In recent years, previous, more overt behavioral approaches have been merging with procedures designed to address the cognitive factors believed to contribute to the development and maintenance of emotional disturbances (e.g., Barlow, Craske, Cerny, & Klosko, 1989). The integration of cognitive concepts with behavior therapy has also stimulated a return to emphasis on the importance of theory. There is evidence of renewed interest in the value of setting up and testing specific hypotheses to elucidate the nature and causes of disorders that, in turn, can guide the development and refinement of intervention strategies (Gelder, 1997).

Numerous applications of CBT-type approaches derived from different theoretical perspectives were developed to treat various types of mental disorders. Of particular interest is the development of CBT approaches to treat PTSD.

PTSD: CBT FORMULATIONS AND TREATMENT

In 1980, PTSD was accorded the status of a formally recognized diagnostic classification when it first appeared in third edition of the *Diagnostic and Statistical Manual of Mental Disorders* (DSM–III; American Psychiatric Association, 1980). Before this, the symptoms of posttraumatic stress had long been recognized and described in the psychiatric literature, often in relation to reactions to specific types of traumatic experiences. A PTSD diagnosis is based on the presence of a constellation of symptoms that occur after exposure to a traumatic event. The symptoms include persistently reexperiencing the event, emotional numbing and avoidance of trauma-related stimuli, and symptoms of hyperarousal.

Because the diagnostic criteria for PTSD include a presumed causal environmental event, (i.e., exposure to a traumatic experience), it is not surprising that attempts to understand and treat the disorder would attract the interest of behavior therapists working with other anxiety-based disorders. Within a relatively short period after the formal recognition of PTSD as a diagnostic category, reports of the use of behaviorally oriented treatment strategies began to be described in the literature. Two conceptual models have had a significant influence on behavioral approaches: the conditioning model of Keane, Zimering, and Caddell (1985) and the emotional-processing formulation of Foa and Kozak (1986).

Keane et al. (1985) based their conceptualization of PTSD on Mowrer's (1947, 1960) two-stage model of fear and avoidance and expanded it by emphasizing the role of stimulus generalization. They postulated that exposure to a life-threatening traumatic event will condition the individual to a broad range of environmental stimuli that were present at the time and that through the mechanism of stimulus generalization, an even larger range of stimuli may elicit anxiety and PTSD symptoms. Although research on other anxiety disorders has consistently demonstrated that repeated exposure to the source of fear causes a decline in anxiety (Marks, 2000), in people with PTSD, extinction does not take place even though reexperiencing and therefore, reexposure to the original event occurs frequently. Keane et al. explained that these exposure experiences are short and incomplete, activating only a limited number of the stimuli present during the original trauma. Consequently, their treatment approach used prolonged exposure to habituate and extinguish fear responses.

Foa, Steketee, and Rothbaum (1989) developed an alternate model that was based on the work of Lang (1977, 1979), which they maintain better accounts for the full range of PTSD symptoms than Keane et al.'s (1985) conditioning model. Lang (1979) proposed that memory contains "fear structures" consisting of three separate elements containing different types of information: information about stimulus characteristics; information about verbal, physiological, and behavioral responses; and information about the meaning of the stimulus and response elements to the individual. These memory structures are considered to be programs that when activated initiate action to reduce or eliminate the experienced fear. Foa and Kozak (1986) argued that it is the interpretative, or meaning, information contained in the fear structures that is critical in activating the emotional response. When a traumatic experience is not only catastrophic but also uncontrollable and unpredictable, the individual's basic assumptions regarding safety are violated more significantly. The process creates a large and pervasive fear structure that is readily activated by a vast array of stimuli. This gives rise to responses characteristic of those with PTSD: the recurring episodes of heightened arousal, the reexperiencing of the event, and the attempts to avoid or escape situations that trigger these responses. However, because of the nature and extent of the postulated PTSD fear structure, such avoidance strategies prove unsuccessful, and the person keeps re-experiencing the event. Consequently, treatment involves prolonged exposure during which new and corrective information about the feared event or object is made available, thereby altering the estimate of the threat (Foa & Kozak, 1986; Foa, Steketee, & Rothbaum, 1989). Based on the work of Lang, Foa and colleagues have suggested that to eliminate fear, the fear structure must be activated for an extended period while new information that is incompatible with the present information is made available.

THE EMERGENCE OF EMDR

During the mid-1980s, when Keane and colleagues (Keane, Fairbank, Caddell, & Zimering, 1989) and Foa and colleagues (Foa, Rothbaum, Riggs, & Murdock, 1991) were developing CBT treatments for PTSD, Shapiro was developing eye movement desensitization (EMD). When EMD was introduced in 1989 in a controlled study (Shapiro, 1989a) as a method for treating PTSD, only one other controlled clinical outcome study had been published (Peniston, 1986). Peniston provided 45 sessions of biofeedback-assisted desensitization to Vietnam veterans and reported the treatment superior to a no-treatment control group. During 1989, three CBT studies were also published. Flooding (prolonged exposure) was compared with standard veterans' care (Cooper & Clum, 1989); both resulted in small clinical effects after 6 to 14 sessions. Flooding was compared with a wait-list control (Keane et al., 1989); small clinical effects were achieved after 14 to 16 sessions. Psychodynamic therapy, hypnotherapy, and desensitization were compared (Brom, Kleber, & Defares, 1989); small to moderate clinical treatment effects were found for all three approaches after 16 sessions.

In contrast to the preceding three studies, Shapiro (1989a) compared EMD to an exposure control and reported substantial treatment effects with EMD after only one session. She originally considered EMD a desensitization procedure and postulated that the effects might be explained in terms of a process of *reciprocal inhibition,* a process similar to one proposed by Wolpe (1958) as the basis of the therapeutic effects of systematic desensitization. Indeed, it was Wolpe (1990) who introduced EMD at the annual conference of the Association for the Advancement of Behavior Therapy.

On the basis of Pavlov's (1927) theories, Shapiro (1989a) suggested that a traumatic event causes imbalance between excitatory and inhibitory neural processes, causing information processing to be blocked and preventing resolution of the experience. She hypothesized that "the rhythmic multi-saccadic [eye] movement may be the body's automatic inhibitory (or excitation releasing) mechanism" and that "the EMD process, therefore, reciprocally inhibits the excitatory phase" (Shapiro, 1989a, p. 220). This was a *post hoc* theoretical explanation presented to account for the effects of the EMD procedure, which seemed to have rapid and lasting effects on trauma-related symptoms. Shapiro (1991) subsequently modified her theoretical explanation of the treatment process as simple desensitization to incorporate aspects of cognitive reprocessing and renamed the method eye movement desensitization *and reprocessing* (EMDR) to reflect this shift.

The origin of EMDR, which was initially presented by Shapiro (1989a) as the behavioral treatment procedure called EMD, was unusual, if not unique, in the field of behavior therapy. Rather than being derived from general psychological theory or from direct clinical observation, Shapiro reported that it was the result of personal experience and introspection. As she stated, "Careful self-examination ascertained that the apparent reason for this effect [the desensitization of the traumatic memories] was that the eyes were automatically moving in a multi-saccadic manner while the disturbing thought was being held in consciousness" (Shapiro, 1989a, p. 201).

From its onset, EMDR has been controversial. A factor in the adverse reaction to EMDR by some within the behavioral therapy community is Shapiro's (1989a) report that personal experience rather than psychological theory or clinical observation is the starting point for the development of EMDR. Academic convention dictates that an impression of scientific objectivity should be maintained. For example, the authors of this chapter did not write it in first person. However, we acknowledge that when supervising graduate students, it is not unusual to find that a personal experience has been the inspiration for a proposed research study. We also customarily encourage them to conduct a literature review to find an appropriate theoretical framework from which to derive testable hypotheses. Having done this, it is then unlikely that the final thesis or subsequent publications will refer to the original personal source of inspiration.

In fact, Shapiro (1998) has acknowledged that a subsequent literature review resulted in her discovering the research of Antrobus and his colleagues (Antrobus, 1973; Antrobus, Antrobus, & Singer, 1964) into the possible relationships between spontaneous eye movements and cognitive processes. Although it is not possible to rewrite history, if Shapiro had followed established convention and presented her treatment procedure as one that was derived from existing research rather than personal experience, it is possible that it might have been more readily accepted.

THE FORMULATION OF EMDR AND TREATMENT OF PTSD

Shapiro proposed the accelerated, or adaptive, information-processing model in an attempt to explain the reason EMDR seems to have rapid clinical results (Shapiro, 1994b, 1995, 1998, 2001). According to this model, PTSD and other mental disorders develop when the information related to a distressing experience is inadequately processed and is stored in a state-dependent fashion. The memory network becomes effectively isolated from more adaptive information and is not assimilated. During EMDR, this material is linked to more adaptive information and new associations are made, resulting in complete information processing and adaptive resolution.

In the evolution of EMD into EMDR, an eight-phase treatment protocol was developed, which has been described in detail by Shapiro (1995, 1999, 2001). It is now generally acknowledged that this multicomponent package contains numerous elements that are common in other forms of behavioral interventions. However, the inclusion of eye movements remains a pivotal (and controversial) feature of the overall procedure, although it has been suggested that forms of alternating stimuli (i.e., other than eye movements) such as finger taps (Bauman & Melnyk, 1994) and auditory tones (Shapiro, 1994a) are also therapeutically effective (Shapiro,

1995). It is hypothesized that the external stimulation enhances the information processing qualities of the treatment. As discussed in another section, various theoretical explanations have been proposed to account for the clinical findings.

THE RELATIONSHIP BETWEEN EMDR AND BEHAVIOR THERAPY

Examination of the multicomponent procedure that is contemporary EMDR (disregarding its most controversial element—i.e., eye movements or other alternating forms of stimulation)[2] reveals an overlap between EMDR and other behavior therapy interventions. The focus on the trauma image, body sensations, associated affect, and beliefs is consistent with the emotional processing (Foa & Kozak, 1986) and cognitive therapy elements of behavioral approaches to PTSD. From this perspective, EMDR might simply be considered a new comprehensive, multidimensional behavior therapy reminiscent of multimodal therapy (Lazarus, 1991, see chapter 8) that, as argued by Hyer and Brandsma (1997), combines the various elements particularly effectively and efficiently.

Another key element of EMDR, but one that is rarely highlighted in the ongoing debates about EMDR's mechanisms, is *mindful attention* ("just notice"), which has an emphasis on just letting "whatever happens, happen" (Shapiro, 1989, p. 204; 1995). This component is not unlike dialectical behavior therapy's (DBT's) "mindfulness" (Linehan, 1993a, 1993b) and the "radical acceptance" characteristic of DBT and acceptance and commitment therapy (Hayes, Strosahl, & Wilson, 1999). Most notably, this focus contrasts with the protocols for prolonged exposure, in which the therapist must be vigilant, noticing any signs of avoidance, and work with clients to ensure they remain focused on the trauma. It may be that careful attention and acceptance of "whatever happens" are more efficient strategies for accessing associated elements of the trauma-related memory structures than the procedures used in prolonged exposure and flooding.

Considered from this perspective, EMDR, minus the eye movements, can be considered a parsimonious integration of all of the core elements of old and new behavioral treatment methods. For this reason, some have noted that EMDR is just a variant of "extant behavioral treatments" and that the eye movements are superfluous (Lohr, Tolin, & Lilienfeld, 1998, p. 150). It is not surprising then that eye movements have become such a central focus in the debates about EMDR. They are the one component that does not seem to be clearly derived from existing behavior therapy

[2]Except in cases in which eye movements are being contrasted with another type of alternating stimulation (e.g., tapping, tones), from this point on the phrase *eye movements* is used to refer to *any* type of external stimulation.

procedures or from any other established theory of behavior change (Shapiro, 1995). For this reason, and because the number of controlled studies supporting EMDR's efficacy has grown, the debate in the behavioral literature has shifted from "Does EMDR work?" to "Do the eye movements make a unique contribution to EMDR's treatment outcome?" (Lohr et al., 1998; Smyth, 1999).

This is a key question for behavior therapists, because without the eye movements, EMDR may be considered merely a recombination of the various elements of CBT. However, to date, the question of whether eye movements contribute to EMDR's treatment effect has yet to be adequately investigated. Many of the dismantling studies have had serious methodological problems, and the research findings have been equivocal (Chemtob et al., 2000; Smyth, 1999).[3] As previously mentioned, Hyer and Brandsma (1997) suggested that it may be the manner in which the multiple elements of the procedure are combined rather than the eye movement component itself that renders EMDR effective. Others (e.g., Lohr et al., 1998) have argued that EMDR's treatment effects are purely the result of direct imaginal exposure.

It is certainly true that imaginal exposure is a component of EMDR, as is true of other behaviorally oriented interventions for PTSD. However, as used within the EMDR process, it differs from the prolonged exposure protocols that have been generally considered necessary for habituation of anxiety responses (Marks, 1987). For example, 20 to 25 minutes of continuous exposure has been reported to be necessary for people with specific phobias (Chaplin & Levine, 1981; Watson, Gaind, & Marks, 1978), whereas people with agoraphobia need continuous exposure for 50 to 60 minutes (Foa & Chambless, 1978; Stern & Marks, 1973) before habituation begins to occur. Studies using prolonged exposure for PTSD have typically used continuous exposure for approximately 1 hour, and the pro-

---

[3]Several studies have found no statistical differences in outcome during comparisons of eye movements and similar exposure conditions with no eye movements (e.g. Boudewyns et al., 1993; Boudewyns & Hyer, 1996; Carrigan & Levis, 1999; Devilly, Spence, & Rapee, 1998; Pitman et al., 1996; Renfrey & Spates, 1994; Sanderson & Carpenter, 1992). Other studies report treatment effects for the eye movement component (e.g. Lohr, Tolin, & Kleinknecht, 1995, 1996; Montgomery & Allyon, 1994; Wilson, Silver, Covi, & Foster, 1996). Of the latter studies, the first three are not group designs; they are representative of the behavioral tradition of single-case research.

At least three critical factors make interpretation of the components analysis virtually impossible (Smyth, 1999).

1. No effort has been made to design studies (or interpret their results) to investigate competing theories regarding the mechanisms by which eye movements might be important.
2. Sample sizes are grossly inadequate, consequently some studies (e.g., Devilly et al., 1998; Renfrey & Spates, 1994) have reported findings that seem likely to have been statistically significant if the sample sizes had been appropriate.
3. Basic methodological deficiencies are evident, such as inadequate treatment time (Carrigan & Levis, 1999; Dunn et al., 1996; Sanderson & Carpenter, 1992), omission of more than one element of the protocol in the eye movement condition (Dunn et al., 1996), and failure to follow the EMDR protocol (Carrigan & Levis, 1999; Devilly et al., 1998; Foley & Spates, 1995; Sanderson & Carpenter, 1992).

cedure is repeated during multiple sessions (Foa et al., 1991; Keane et al., 1989; Marks, Lovell, Noshirvani, Livanou, & Thrasher, 1998; Richards, Lovell, & Marks, 1994). In addition, the procedure emphasizes focusing the person's attention on the aspects of the traumatic event that provoke the greatest anxiety. Distraction is also avoided because it has been generally found to impair habituation (Rodriguez & Craske, 1993), although some conflicting research findings have been reported (Craske, 1999).

The exposure element of EMDR is, in many ways, the antithesis of what has been considered procedurally necessary for habituation. The exposure is not continuous but is provided in short bursts, and it is combined with eye movements, which are potentially distracting. In addition, rather than seeking heightened arousal, clients are instructed to "just notice" the experience and encouraged to distance themselves when high levels of emotion are aroused. In addition, no attempt is made to maintain attention on the original traumatic event. Clients are simply to "go with whatever comes up." This practice of mindful attention plus free association violates most procedural elements of exposure considered crucial in other current exposure-based behavioral treatments of PTSD; however, it should be noted that there are many procedural variations for exposure treatment when one looks beyond PTSD treatments. As noted, exposure times for the other anxiety disorders vary significantly. In addition, others (e.g., Wagner & Linehan, 1998) reported using just a few minutes of exposure to enhance new learning. These interventions might be considered brief, controlled exposures used to provide opportunities to build self-efficacy and mastery—tasks that would be consistent with Bandura's (1977) social learning theory.

To make sense out of the discrepancies that EMDR raises about dosed vs. prolonged exposure, it is helpful to differentiate between various exposure *protocols* and the *mechanism* of exposure that is thought to facilitate change (J. Herbert, Hahnemann University, personal communication, November 6, 1998). Classical conditioning posits that prolonged exposure is necessary for habituation; that is, habituation through exposure is what brings about change. Although Keane's model of PTSD is predicated on this assumption, it should be noted that Foa and colleagues (Foa & Kozak, 1986; Foa et al., 1989) consider habituation to be only part of the change process that is stimulated. They posit an information-processing mechanism of change is also necessary, noting that exposure in a safe environment allows the client to take in new information. Essentially, they propose that exposure activates two change processes—habituation and information processing:

> In addition to promoting changes in the response aspect of a fear structure via short-term physiological habituation, exposure to a feared situation changes its meaning. In other words, the threat meaning linked

to the stimulus and the response elements of the fear structure is also modified. (Foa et al., 1989, p. 169)

However, although Foa and colleagues offered this intriguing hypothesis, the procedural elements of their PTSD treatment protocol still rest, virtually exclusively, on a traditional exposure-via-habituation model. In considering mechanisms of change, one of EMDR's major contributions may be in affording support for Foa and colleagues' proposition that some mechanism other than or in addition to habituation may be involved in the success of exposure treatments.

This of course does not necessarily mean that eye movements are this mechanism. It could well be that the *combination* of active behavioral strategies, including mindful attention with acceptance of whatever emerges, better engages habituation and emotional processing. As a result, the emotional memory network may be modified more efficiently than by exposure interventions that keep attention focused on the traumatic incident alone. This change process would be consistent with the emotional processing model presented by Foa and Kozak (1986) but does highlight key procedural differences from the traditional exposure-based models of PTSD treatment.

On the other hand, if eye movements are an active element in the process of stimulating information processing, what might behavior therapists consider their mechanism of action? Shapiro originally considered the procedure to be a desensitization process that acted by reciprocal inhibition (Wolpe, 1958). The eye movements were postulated to be "the body's automatic inhibitory (or excitation-releasing) mechanism" (Shapiro, 1989a, p. 200), which permitted emotional processing that had been blocked by the traumatic experience to proceed. She subsequently moved from this initial theoretical proposal and advanced the previously mentioned accelerated information-processing model (Shapiro, 1995), which was recently renamed adaptive information processing (Shapiro, 2001). This model, although drawing to some extent from existing theory on information processing, is directed more toward hypothesized neurophysiological mechanisms presumed to underlie the therapeutic effects of EMDR rather than on the possible psychological processes involved. Shapiro (1998) has indeed acknowledged it was "formulated to explain the observed rapidity of treatment effects" (p. 147). However, as Keane (1998) pointed out, theoretical explanations of EMDR need to be integrated with existing general psychological models of psychopathology and behavioral theories of PTSD.

In fact, many researchers have sought to identify the mechanisms involved with eye movements. For example, in a study carried out to examine working memory, Andrade, Kavanagh, and Baddeley (1997) hypothesized that eye movements and other visuospatial tasks may achieve therapeutic effects by disrupting the functioning of the visuospatial sketch-pad of working memory. The obtained results supported their hypothesis. Several other authors (Armstrong & Vaughan, 1996; Dyck, 1993; Mac-Culloch & Feldman, 1996) have suggested that effects are achieved by a process of classical conditioning caused by the activation of the orienting reflex (Pavlov, 1927). MacCulloch and Feldman argued that alternating stimulation activates the orienting reflex; in the absence of external danger signals, it causes a reflex response of decreased arousal and positive physical sensations. They suggested that this process occurs in EMDR and through classical conditioning results in positive feelings becoming linked to the original stimulus (the traumatic event) and replacing the original negative emotional response. In support of this thesis, they cited the findings of Wilson, Silver, Covi, and Foster (1996), which discuss "compelled" relaxation in response to eye movement stimulation.

Becker and colleagues (Becker, Todd-Overmann, Stoothoff, & Lawson, 1998) found that eye movements function as an orienting response and allow suppressed thoughts to emerge if they are presented at an optimal speed. They noted that it was critical that the eye movements were not so fast that they distracted participants from internal experiences yet fast enough that they interfered with avoidance processes. Interestingly, they did not find that alternating tones functioned in the same way. This study highlights the need for components studies to examine variables such as the type and speed of the alternating stimulation used in EMDR. It also suggests important conceptual differences exist between an orienting response and distraction—a point that might shed a new light on the conflicting results noted previously on the role of distraction in exposure treatment (Craske, 1999).

A small but expanding body of research literature includes possible explanations for the therapeutic effects of eye movements that are based on accepted general psychological knowledge and theory—all of which are compatible with behavior therapy, especially the information-processing and cognitive therapy traditions. However, it has to be acknowledged that as yet, many questions remain unanswered regarding the essential components and methods of action of the multiple elements of EMDR.

WHAT CAN BEHAVIOR THERAPY CONTRIBUTE TO EMDR?

By now it is evident that EMDR incorporates many components of behavior therapy. In addition, the eight-phase EMDR protocol also includes the key behavioral practices of (a) assessing the current triggers for symptomatology, (b) evaluating the client's situation for problem-maintaining factors and interpersonal contingencies that discourage behavior change, (c) teaching self-control skills, and (d) having clients keep logs between sessions (Shapiro, 1995). Behavior therapy's strong empirical tradition, with its emphasis on the scientist-practitioner model and the experimental investigation of the single case, has influenced the development and practice of EMDR (see Rubin, 1999). However, behavior therapy has more to offer the EMDR practitioner.

Shapiro (1995) has discussed the importance of assigning behavioral tasks as homework in particular clinical situations. A behavioral perspective would promote this, together with ongoing systematic assessment of the client's current life, as a good general strategy for a client who had not already initiated such changes to ensure that changes observed in the treatment session were generalizing to daily life. Similarly, although Shapiro noted the importance of determining client goals, behavior therapy would place more emphasis on the importance of operationalizing them in measurable and quantifiable terms. Adopting the behavior therapists' practice of determining how often a problem occurs, when and where a problem does (and does not) occur, and a problem's intensity and duration could help EMDR therapists more precisely assess the degree of progress made in treatment. For example, although a distress rating of 0 on an EMDR target memory is important, it is also important to evaluate whether clients are making actual progress toward their identified goals. If a target memory is no longer upsetting yet no progress toward the goal has been made, this would indicate the need to reevaluate the rationale for target selection and review the treatment plan as a whole.

In addition, using the CBT procedure of *functional analysis*—sometimes called *behavior chain analysis*—can assist EMDR therapists in narrowing down target problems for intervention. Use of such analysis identifies the immediate events (or antecedents) that trigger a particular problem behavior and the sequence of reactions (e.g., thoughts, images, feelings, body sensations) that follow the trigger and culminate in the problem behavior. In addition, the immediate and long-term consequences of behavior can be identified. These data may suggest the function of a particular behavior and thus provide information that facilitates intervention.

For example, Sandy was a 35-year-old woman who had entered treatment for a problem with crack cocaine and PTSD that were related to childhood sexual abuse. Although Sandy readily identified how cocaine had negatively affected her life, she had been unable to abstain for more than 4 to 6 weeks at a time, despite completing an inpatient cocaine treatment program and attending Narcotics Anonymous regularly. A functional analysis of Sandy's relapses revealed the following pattern; pieces of the behavior chain are identified in [brackets].

Interpersonal interactions with significant others (close friends, coworkers, and parents) that involved conflict or criticism [*antecedents*, or *triggers*] evoked feelings of shame [*affect*] accompanied by strong nausea [*physiological reaction*] and negative thoughts about herself ("I'm disgusting") and hopelessness ("I'm not fixable") [key cognitions, or *schema*]. If she could not connect with a close friend when this occurred, she would drink and then use crack [*behavior*], which would help her "numb out" [*short-term consequences, reinforcing*]. However, during the relapse, Sandy often became retraumatized, either sexually or physically, experiences that intensified her PTSD symptoms and feelings of shame [*long-term consequences*]. In addition, the negative consequences of use associated with the crack relapses (e.g., stealing things, lying to others, missing work) further increased her feelings of shame [*long-term consequences*].

Tracing this pattern with Sandy helped her to understand that although her substance use temporarily reduced her feelings of shame (through negative reinforcement—the removal of a negative feeling state), the long-term consequences increased her feelings of shame, thereby increasing her vulnerability to subsequent potential shame triggers.

The data gathered in a functional analysis affect the treatment plan and have obvious relevance to the practice of EMDR. The EMDR protocol involves targeting past trauma, then present triggers, and finally future templates (Shapiro, 1995). A functional analysis assists in identifying the present triggers and the situations for which future templates will be needed. In addition, when the client's internal reactions to the triggers (affect, cognitions, sensations, and any imagery) are probed to identify the schema links between the present and the past, the functional analysis can help to identify targets for processing with EMDR. However, although the process of functional analysis (identifying behavior chains) can guide treatment planning, the targets for intervention are different for behavior therapists and EMDR therapists. Whereas behavior therapists are likely to use behavioral strategies, cognitive strategies, or both to alter current actions and beliefs, the targets for EMDR processing focus more on the affect associated with the chain of events. In addition, rather than focusing on the present behavior patterns, EMDR practitioners tend to try and elicit early experience memories associated with similar cognitions, physical sensations, and emotions.

In Sandy's case, the functional analysis suggested that interpersonal conflict with significant others would be an important target for intervention. Consequently, she was asked to recall the most recent occasion when the events in the behavior chain analysis had occurred. She described being criticized at work by her supervisor and was asked to bring an image of this into her mind and notice the associated thoughts, bodily sensations, and affect.

This event could become the target for initiating processing with the use of eye movements, although the EMDR protocol would suggest finding an earlier target when possible. As a result, rather than addressing this event, the therapist asked Sandy to recall an occasion in her early life when she had experienced similar reactions.[4] She responded by discussing a time when she was age 5 and being sexually abused by her uncle. This event became the target for EMDR because of the therapist's hypothesis that it may have been a "setting event" for the development of the cognition "I am disgusting." In reviewing this incident with Sandy, it was clear how the schema "I am disgusting" might have developed from this trauma; what was not entirely clear was the origin of "I am not fixable." Because this cognition was an important part of the present problem identified in the functional analysis, the therapist collected more contextual information about Sandy's life at the time of the abuse. What emerged was that Sandy experienced severe headaches, nausea, and urinary problems during the years her uncle abused her, but her pediatrician failed to find any treatable cause for any of these problems, despite many medical tests. In this case, information gathered during the functional analysis prompted the therapist to search further for other experiential sources for Sandy's key trauma-related beliefs. Without a functional analysis, an EMDR therapist might have stopped searching for those additional targets.

The foregoing case discussion also highlights the contributions that cognitive psychology, especially the information about schemas, can make to EMDR treatment. For example, Young's (1994, see chapter 7) schema-focused therapy provides a framework for key maladaptive schemas such as defectiveness, abandonment, emotional deprivation, mistrust and abuse, and social exclusion that can help to organize history taking and guide selection and organization of EMDR targets. Knowledge of Janoff-Bulman's (1992) work on the shattering impact of trauma on individuals' basic beliefs about life and themselves—that the world is a good, meaningful place and that the individual has worth—is critical for any EMDR therapist's understanding of the impact of trauma on a client's sense of self and the world.

Other CBT techniques that can be helpful to the EMDR therapist include *Socratic questions* and *behavioral experiments* (Beck et al., 1979). Socratic questions are questions that allow clients to come to their own conclusions. Behavioral experiments are tasks that are given to clients to carry out either during or between sessions to assess a specific belief. Socratic questions can be particularly helpful in developing cognitive interweaves when EMDR processing becomes stalled.

For example, Andrew is convinced that his wife Amy, who travels often for business, will die and not return from a business trip. During EMDR, Andrew continues to remain very fearful, despite having already processed the past underlying trauma. The following dialogue illustrates how Socratic questions can be used to elicit a cognitive interweave. In the

---

[4]This technique shares characteristics with several different theoretical approaches, including schema-focused therapy (Young, 1994) and ego state therapy (Watkins & Watkins, 1997).

following transcript, asterisks (****************) represent a set of eye movements, and comments in [brackets] indicate editorial points of interest.

Therapist: What do you feel the chance is that Amy will die? What percentage out of 100?

Andrew: 80%.

Therapist: Okay. I wonder . . . about how many times has Amy gone out of town on business in the last year?

[The therapist would choose a longer time frame if the frequency in the past year had not been very high.]

Andrew: I'm not sure . . . at least 20 times, I guess.

Therapist: All right, 20 times. And how many of those times did Amy come close to dying?

Andrew: Well . . . none, I guess.

Therapist: None at all? So what percent is that?

Andrew: Zero.

Therapist: I see . . . and what kind of things will she be doing differently on this trip that make you think this one will be more dangerous than the past trips?

Andrew: Hmmm . . . well, I guess she won't really be doing anything differently.

Therapist: Okay . . . stay with that . . .

****

Behavioral experiments are key components when clients need to acquire new experiential information from the present to evaluate whether beliefs are accurate perceptions of the world. For example, clients who believe that people will ridicule them if they faint from a panic attack might be given the assignment of taking a friend (or the therapist) to a mall and watching while the friend pretends to faint. The clients can observe whether other people's reactions match their predictions. On the basis of this experience, the clients are then free to evaluate their beliefs in light of the information they have gathered. Socratic questioning and behavioral experiments are compatible with EMDR's client-centered perspective, which highly values the idea of clients developing their own conclusions (Shapiro, 1995).

WHAT CAN EMDR CONTRIBUTE TO BEHAVIOR THERAPY?

If nothing else, EMDR provides behavior therapists with a structured method that includes many effective elements of traditional behavioral treatment with some that are used in more recent behavioral interventions developed by Linehan (1993a, 1993b) and Hayes, Strosahl, and Wilson (1999) and combined in a way that facilitates therapeutic change (Hyer & Brandsma, 1997). Although Foa and Kozak (1997) have noted that combination interventions are rarely more efficacious than an effective single intervention, this research has almost exclusively involved single-target complaints (e.g., anxiety). However, in clinical practice, clients rarely present only one target problem. A comprehensive intervention might help confront the range of problems that can accompany PTSD because they may not all respond to a single behavioral treatment method. For example, Ehlers and colleagues (1998) found that people who had been raped and rated themselves high in mental defeat and alienation on self-evaluations had inferior outcomes with exposure compared with those who rated themselves low. The findings suggest that exposure may be best suited for those with fear-related symptoms and thoughts and that cognitive restructuring might be the intervention of choice for those with mental defeat and alienation. Given that EMDR incorporates elements of exposure and cognitive restructuring, one might predict that it would be helpful for a broader range of trauma-related problems. If this hypothesis were to be confirmed, then it could follow that EMDR could be a key intervention in addressing more complex trauma reactions, such as *disorders of extreme stress, not otherwise specified* (DESNOS; van der Kolk, 1996), that are characterized by similar negative beliefs.

In addition to the advantages associated with a comprehensive, integrative treatment, some preliminary evidence has suggested that EMDR is more efficient in treating PTSD than traditional CBT. For example, a recent meta-analysis found that EMDR generally achieved treatment effects in fewer sessions than traditional CBT (Van Etten & Taylor, 1998). However, direct comparisons of EMDR and established behavioral interventions have only begun. Three such studies have found that EMDR achieved outcomes similar to CBT but did so in fewer sessions (EMDR vs. exposure —Ironson, Freund, Strauss, & Williams, 2002; EMDR vs. exposure with stress inoculation training—Lee, Gavriel, Drummond, Richards, & Greenwald, in press; EMDR vs. exposure with cognitive restructuring—Power, McGoldrick, & Brown, 1999); an additional study (Exposure + stress inoculation training + cognitive restructuring—Devilly & Spence, 1999) did not support this finding.

EMDR also encourages behavior therapists to reexamine the procedure and assumptions of exposure treatments. The practice of EMDR suggests to clients the importance of mindful attention ("just notice") and acceptance ("let whatever happen, happen"). As noted previously, these components are present in newer behavioral treatments (Hayes et al., 1999; Linehan, 1993a, 1993b). Together these treatments may comprise a new direction for cognitive interventions in behavior therapy, which have tended to focus on controlling, changing, and stopping thoughts rather than having the client simply accept them.

EMDR also offers CBT therapists a tool to help clients who have difficulty accepting what they know rationally rather than what they believe emotionally. Many of these clients may use cognitive restructuring only to later confess to their therapist that they have difficulty believing the more rational thoughts: "Intellectually, I know I'm not a failure, but it still feels like I am." The EMDR protocol allows clients to differentiate between what they *know* to be true and what *feels* true (through the validity of cognition [VoC] rating of their positive cognition). Evidence has suggested that after successful EMDR treatment, clients report congruence between these two perspectives (Shapiro, 1995). DBT practitioners who teach clients about *rational, emotional,* and *wise mind* (Linehan, 1993b) think of this process as helping clients shift from *emotional mind* to *wise mind* while synthesizing the knowledge of the *rational mind* (M. Brimo, Kaleida Health System, Buffalo, NY, personal communication, August 13, 2000). From this perspective, EMDR may offer a focused method for eliminating emotional blocks to the processing of new information or skills acquired through standard CBT.

Consider the following case in which EMDR helped to eliminate emotional blocks to integrating new skills and information. Paula, age 36 and married, was seeking treatment for a severe social phobia, alcohol dependence, and an avoidant personality disorder. She had grown up in an alcoholic family and had been frequently ridiculed and occasionally physically abused. In addition to cognitive therapy, group exposure, and social skills treatment, Paula also completed a cognitive–behavioral self-control drinking program as part of an alcohol treatment research study. Although the severity of her social phobia and alcohol use had decreased somewhat, she continued to go through cycles of binge drinking and suicidal ideation and still had no adult friends outside of her nuclear family and therapy group. Although she had learned a range of valuable skills, Paula was unable to use them at certain times. A functional analysis of these occasions indicated that one major trigger for both her drinking and suicidal ideation was her weekly weekend visits to the home of her parents, who still abused alcohol. During these visits, she felt very young, was unable to set limits with her parents, and participated in binge drinking with her parents. After leaving their home, she would return to her own home and curl up in a fetal position in the bathroom, crying and feeling suicidal. A focused assessment of this state yielded the following cognition: "I can't live separately from my parents." Paula was asked to allow herself recall a time when she was much younger and felt this same way. She discussed a day that occurred when she was 17 years old. She had told her parents that she and her boyfriend, Josh (now her husband), were going to be married. This event was identified as the target for EMDR.

Paula's target image was the moment she told her parents about her engagement. Her negative cognition was, "I can't live without mom and dad, and I have to stay with them." Her positive cognition was, "I can live and be my own person without mom and dad." She rated this cognition a VoC (validity of cognition) of 6 on a scale of 1 to 7 (possibly indicating that she had not yet totally accessed the entire memory network and that she knew this to be true rationally). Fear was her identified emotion, and she gave it a SUD (subjective units of distress) score of 9.5 on a scale of 0 to 10, although she did not exhibit much physical evidence of fear. She identified feeling the fear in her stomach and chest. During the first 40 minutes of treatment using eye movements, Paula recalled how her parents' house looked at the time of the target event, reported feeling very fearful about telling her parents of the engagement, and discussed her memory of her father's anger. After another set of eye movements, Paula looked terrified.

Therapist: What's coming up now, Paula?

Paula: (tearfully) I'm in a deep hole, trying to get out, and my parents are pulling me back in. (sounding panicky) I can't get out!

Therapist: Okay, go with that.

****

Paula: (rising voice) I'm trapped, I'm going to die, I can't get out!

Therapist: Put Josh and I outside the hole and see us grabbing your hands and pulling you out.

Paula: (look of terror on her face, fast breathing, and louder voice) I'm going to die!

****

(Her breathing subsides, and she gets quieter.)

Therapist: What are you getting now, Paula?

Paula: I'm outside the hole. I'm alive. But it's a desert out here. And I don't know if I can trust you and Josh. I feel lost.

Therapist: Okay, just stay with that.

****

(Paula visibly relaxes and smiles.)

Therapist: What's coming up now?

Paula: Now there's green grass everywhere, and a horse has popped out of the hole. (Her childhood dream was to own a horse, and her father had always denigrated the idea.) I can take my dream with me.

The session ended at this point (because of time constraints), and no final ratings of the target were made because of concerns that it would open up new associations. A week later, Paula reported that she had gone to her parents' house the evening of her EMDR session and had felt calm and in control throughout the evening. In addition, she set clear limits about drinking and for the first time left her parents' house feeling okay and free of suicidal ideation. She also stated that she felt "a new sense of self." One month later, she had made her first adult female friend, bought a horse, and begun to regularly attend Alcoholics Anonymous meetings to help her continue to abstain from drinking.

Although the session did not eliminate all of Paula's problems, it did seem to facilitate her movement past an emotionally stalled point that had not responded to traditional CBT. Having moved past this point, she was able to consolidate her gains and more systematically apply the skills she had learned through CBT. The case provides an example of what EMDR could contribute when clients have difficulty applying CBT to particular emotional states.

Another possible contribution of EMDR to behavior therapy is that it may raise the age-old issue of the relationship between "mind" and "brain" (Stickgold, Smyth, & Foster, 1999). Traditionally, behavioral theory focused on learning principles and then mental processes (the mind) without speculating on the actual physiological mechanisms of change (the brain). The eye movement component of EMDR has raised questions about what physiological process could stimulate adaptive information processing. Shapiro (1995) and others (Levin, Lazrove, & van der Kolk, 1999; Stickgold, 2002) have speculated about this question, and debates about the contribution of biological perspectives to behavior therapy are ongoing (e.g., Hayes, 2000; Tryon, 2000). Shapiro's accelerated, or adaptive, information processing model might be considered another attempt to bridge the gap between the mind and the brain. Some (e.g., Hayes, 2000) would probably consider this an example of the use of "formulaic metaphors" in psychology, and even Shapiro may agree. However, she might emphasize that the purpose of the metaphor was (and still is) to guide future research and practice.

Certainly, it can be argued that the introduction of EMDR, perhaps more than any other recent treatment approach, has helped stimulate debate about theory and increase research related to PTSD, anxiety disorders, exposure, and emotional information processing—maybe more so than any

other recent treatment approach. In addition, the interest in the eye movement component of EMDR and its possible relationship to brain functioning (e.g., Levin et al., 1999; Stickgold, 2002) may lead to further research
that begins to link "the mind" with "the brain." If so, this would have
important implications for the theoretical underpinnings of behavior
therapy.

CONCLUDING COMMENTS

EMDR has generated not only considerable interest but also debate
and controversy. Although research has indicated that EMDR is at least as
effective as other accepted behavioral methods for treating PTSD, it seems
to be more efficient. However, debate continues regarding the theoretical
basis for the therapeutic findings. Although it seems that habituation is
unlikely to be the sole mechanism of action, the means by which exposure
achieves therapeutic effects in PTSD are also subject to differing interpretations (Foa et al., 1989; Keane et al., 1985). In addition, given that cognitive restructuring interventions involving minimal or no direct exposure
achieve outcomes comparable to exposure methods (Marks et al., 1998;
Power et al., 1999), it is apparent that processes other than habituation
can be involved in treating people with PTSD.

The controversy that continues to surround EMDR seems to be generated by various issues. Among these are the original claims that it successfully desensitized traumatic memories in a single session (Shapiro,
1989a). Early studies supportive of this claim relied heavily on self-report
measures of subjective improvement. However, even recent and more
rigorously controlled trials using standardized self-reports and clinician-
administered psychometric instruments have continued to report rapid
resolution of symptoms, although it is often in the absence of change on
physiological measures (Van Etten & Taylor, 1998). Although from an
academic perspective lack of change in physiological responses may be
interesting, for clients it is likely that the experience of subjective improvement is the most important (Seligman, 1995).

A second issue that has generated negative comments involves "Shapiro's proprietarial emphasis in controlling who may use the technique with
patients" (Boudewyns & Hyer, 1996, p. 186). This is a reference to Shapiro's initial requirement that trainees sign an agreement to refrain from
training others in EMDR, an agreement that was eliminated after the publication of her book that described in detail the EMDR treatment process.
Shapiro (1996) justified her actions by stating that she was concerned
about misapplication of the procedure, which she believes has the potential
to harm as well as help clients. Regardless of the inherent merits or otherwise of the agreement, the classic work of Bartlett (1932) clearly iden-

tified the way information can be profoundly distorted through serial transmission. As noted by Barlow and Hofmann (1997), because evidence has shown that treatment outcome is correlated with the competence of therapists and their adherence to treatment protocols, the desire to ensure adequate training of clinicians in a new and novel technique is not unreasonable.

Indeed, the issue of therapeutic expertise is acknowledged by Barlow and Hofmann (1997) to be a crucial factor in the wider dissemination and availability of empirically validated psychological treatments. Referring to the American Psychological Association's (APA, 1993) task force finding that many treatments that are considered effective were not taught in APA-approved clinical psychology training programs, they recommended that "new treatment procedures with proven efficacy should be taught in workshops for continuing education credit" (Barlow & Hofmann, 1997, p. 108). It is likely that Shapiro's insistence on doing so has contributed to the development of the clear, standardized protocol that now makes up EMDR.

Although EMDR is now firmly established as an empirically supported treatment for PTSD, it continues to raise controversial questions about the nature of treatment and healing. As was observed by one of the pioneers of behavior therapy some 30 years ago:

> Nevertheless, every now and then, a procedure that has not been suggested by any basic principle does turn out to be effective. For the behaviorist, such an empirical discovery is another kind of starting point for research directed toward elucidating the mechanisms. This is a fascinating endeavor, not only because it helps to build our understanding of the universe but also because it has the practical result of shaping procedures into more efficient and economical forms. (Wolpe, 1969, p. xi)

It seems that EMDR is an example of just such a procedure. Despite failing to satisfy Yates's (1970) rigorous requirement that, to be considered a behavioral therapy, procedures should be derived from established psychological knowledge, evidence has indicated that EMDR is an effective treatment for PTSD. The challenge remains for behavioral researchers to elucidate more fully the essential components and the mechanisms underlying its effects. For behavioral therapists seeking to modify abnormal behavior, it is an additional procedure that may be used in the experimental investigation of the single case. For the therapist, this is and must remain the essence of the practice of behavior therapy.

REFERENCES

American Psychiatric Association. (1980). *Diagnostic and statistical manual of mental disorders* (3rd ed.). Washington, DC: Author.

American Psychiatric Association. (1987). *Diagnostic and statistical manual of mental disorders* (3rd ed., rev.). Washington, DC: Author.

American Psychiatric Association. (1994). *Diagnostic and statistical manual of mental disorders* (4th ed.). Washington, DC: Author.

American Psychological Association. (1993). *Task force on promotion and dissemination of psychological procedures: A report of the Division 12 Board of the American Psychological Association*. Washington, DC: Author.

Andrade, J., Kavanagh, D., & Baddeley, A. (1997). Eye movements and visual imagery: A working memory approach to the treatment of post-traumatic stress disorder. *British Journal of Clinical Psychology, 36*, 209–223.

Antrobus, J. S. (1973). Eye-movements and non-visual cognitive tasks. In V. Zikmund (Ed.), *The oculomotor system and brain functions* (pp. 354–368). London: Butterworths.

Antrobus, J. S., Antrobus, J. S., & Singer, J. L. (1964). Eye movements accompanying day-dreaming, visual imagery and thought suppression. *Journal of Abnormal and Social Psychology, 69*, 244–252.

Armstrong, M. S., & Vaughan, K. (1996). An orienting response model of eye movement desensitization. *Journal of Behavior Therapy and Experimental Psychiatry, 27*, 21–32.

Bandura, A. (1977). *Social learning theory*. Englewood Cliffs, NJ: Prentice-Hall.

Barlow, D. H., Craske, M. G., Cerny, J. A., & Klosko, J. S. (1989). Behavioral treatment of panic disorder. *Behavior Therapy, 20*, 261–282.

Barlow, D. H., & Hoffmann, S. G. (1997). Efficacy and dissemination of psychological treatments. In D. M. Clark & C. G. Fairburn (Eds.), *Science and practice of cognitive behaviour therapy* (pp. 95–117). Oxford, England: Oxford University Press.

Bartlett, F. (1932). *Remembering*. Cambridge, England: Cambridge University Press.

Bauman, W., & Melnyk, W. T. (1994). A controlled comparison of eye movements and finger tapping in the treatment of test anxiety. *Journal of Behavior Therapy and Experimental Psychiatry, 25*, 29–33.

Beck, A. (1967). *Depression: Clinical, experimental and theoretical aspects*. New York: International Universities Press.

Beck, A. T., Rush, A. J., Shaw, B. F., & Emery, G. (1979). *Cognitive therapy of depression*. New York: Guilford Press.

Becker, L., Todd-Overmann, A., Stoothoff, W., & Lawson, P. (1998, July). *Ironic memory, PTSD, and EMDR: Do eye movements hinder the avoidance process leading to greater accessibility of traumatic memories?* Paper presented at the Annual Conference of the EMDR International Association, Baltimore, MD.

Bekhterev, V. M. (1932). *General principles of human reflexology*. New York: International Universities Press.

Boudewyns, P. A., & Hyer, L. A. (1996). Eye movement desensitization and reprocessing (EMDR) as a treatment for post-traumatic stress disorder (PTSD). *Clinical Psychology and Psychotherapy, 3*, 185–195.

Boudewyns, P. A., Stwertka, S. A., Hyer, L., Albrecht, J. W., & Speer, E. V. (1993). Eye movement desensitization for PTSD of combat: A treatment outcome pilot study. *The Behavior Therapist, 16*, 29–33.

Brom, D., Kleber, R. J., & Defares, P. B. (1989). Brief psychotherapy for posttraumatic stress disorders. *Journal of Consulting & Clinical Psychology, 57*(5), 607–612.

Carrigan, M. H., & Levis, D. J. (1999). The contributions of eye movements to the efficacy of brief exposure treatment for reducing fear of public speaking. *Journal of Anxiety Disorders, 13*, 101–118.

Chaplin, E. W., & Levine, B. A. (1981). The effects of total exposure duration and interrupted versus continuous exposure in flooding therapy. *Behavior Therapy, 12*, 360–368.

Chemtob, C. M., Tolin, D. F., van der Kolk, B. A., & Pitman, R. K. (2000). Eye movement desensitization and reprocessing. In E. B. Foa, T. M. Keane, & M. J. Friedman (Eds.), *Effective treatments for PTSD: Practice guidelines from the International Society for Traumatic Stress Studies* (pp. 139–154, 333–335). New York: Guilford Press.

Cooper, N. A., & Clum, G. A. (1989). Imaginal flooding as a supplementary treatment for PTSD in combat veterans: A controlled study. *Behavior Therapy, 20*, 381–391.

Craske, M. G. (1999). *Anxiety disorders: Psychological approaches to theory and treatment.* Boulder, CO: Westview Press.

Devilly, G. J., & Spence, S. H. (1999). The relative efficacy and treatment distress of EMDR and a cognitive behavioral trauma treatment protocol in the amelioration of post traumatic stress disorder. *Journal of Anxiety Disorders, 13*, 131–157.

Devilly, G. J., Spence, S. H., & Rapee, R. M. (1998). Statistical and reliable change with eye movement desensitization and reprocessing: Treating trauma within a veteran population. *Behavior Therapy, 29*, 435–455.

Dunn, T., Schwartz, M., Hatfield, R., & Wiegele, M. (1996). Measuring effectiveness of eye movement desensitization and reprocessing (EMDR) in non-clinical anxiety: A multi-subject yoked-control design. *Journal of Behavior Therapy and Experimental Psychiatry, 27*, 231–239.

Dyck, M. J. (1993). A proposal for a conditioning model of eye movement desensitization treatment for posttraumatic stress disorder. *Journal of Behavior Therapy and Experimental Psychiatry, 24*, 201–210.

Ehlers, A., Clark, D. M., Dunmore, E., Jaycox, L., Meadows, E., & Foa, E. (1998). Predicting response to exposure treatment in PTSD: The role of mental defeat and alienation. *Journal of Traumatic Stress, 11*, 457–471.

Eysenck, H. J. (1952). The effects of psychotherapy: An evaluation. *Journal of Consulting Psychology, 16*, 319–324.

Eysenck, H. J. (1964). The nature of behaviour therapy. In H. J. Eysenck (Ed.), *Experiments in behaviour therapy* (pp. 1–15). London: Pergamon.

Foa, E. B., & Chambless, D. L. (1978). Habituation of subjective anxiety during flooding in imagery. *Behaviour Research and Therapy, 16,* 391–399.

Foa, E. B., & Kozak, M. J. (1986). Emotional processing of fears: Exposure to corrective information. *Psychological Bulletin, 99,* 20–35.

Foa, E. B., & Kozak, M. J. (1997). Beyond the efficacy ceiling? Cognitive behavior therapy in search of theory. *Behavior Therapy, 28,* 601–611.

Foa, E. B., Rothbaum, B. O., Riggs, D. S., & Murdock, T. B. (1991). Treatment of posttraumatic stress disorder in rape victims: A comparison between cognitive–behavioral procedures and counseling. *Journal of Consulting and Clinical Psychology, 59,* 715–723.

Foa, E. B., Steketee, G., & Rothbaum, B. O. (1989). Behavioral/cognitive conceptualizations of post-traumatic stress disorder. *Behavior Therapy, 20*(2), 155–176.

Foley, T., & Spates, C. R. (1995). Eye movement desensitization of public-speaking anxiety: A partial dismantling study. *Journal of Behavior Therapy and Experimental Psychiatry, 26,* 321–329.

Gelder, M. (1997). The scientific foundations of cognitive behaviour therapy. In D. M. Clark & C. G. Fairburn (Eds.), *Science and practice of cognitive behaviour therapy* (pp. 27–46). Oxford: Oxford University Press.

Hayes, S. C. (2000). Psychology and biology: A concluding comment. *The Behavior Therapist, 23,* 8–9.

Hayes, S. C., Strosahl, K. D., & Wilson, K. G. (1999). *Acceptance and commitment therapy.* New York: Guilford Press.

Hyer, L., & Brandsma, J. M. (1997). EMDR minus eye movements equals good psychotherapy. *Journal of Traumatic Stress, 10,* 515–522.

Ironson, G., Freund, B., Strauss, J. L., & Williams, J. (2002). Comparison of two treatments for traumatic stress: A community-based study of EMDR and prolonged exposure. *Journal of Clinical Psychology, 58,* 113–128.

Janoff-Bulman, R. (1992). *Shattered assumptions: Towards a new psychology of trauma.* New York: Free Press.

Jones, H. G. (1956). The application of conditioning to the treatment of a psychiatric patient. *Journal of Abnormal and Social Psychology, 52,* 414–420.

Jones, M. C. (1924). A laboratory study of fear: The case of Peter. *Pedagogical Seminar, 31,* 308–315.

Keane, T. M. (1998). Psychological and behavioral treatments for posttraumatic stress disorder. In P. Nathan & J. Gorman (Eds.), *A guide to treatments that work* (pp. 398–407). New York: Oxford University Press.

Keane, T. M., Fairbank, J. A., Caddell, J. M., & Zimering, R. T. (1989). Implosive (flooding) therapy reduces symptoms of PTSD in Vietnam combat veterans. *Behavior Therapy, 20,* 245–260.

Keane, T. M., Zimering, R. T., & Caddell, J. M. (1985). A behavioral formulation of posttraumatic stress disorder in Vietnam veterans. *The Behavior Therapist, 8,* 9–12.

Lang, P. J. (1977). Imagery in therapy: An information processing analysis of fear. *Behavior Therapy, 8*, 862–886.

Lang, P. J. (1979). A bio-informational theory of emotional imagery. *Psychophysiology, 16*, 495–512.

Lazarus, A. A. (1991). *The practice of multimodal therapy.* Baltimore, MD: Johns Hopkins University Press.

Lee, C., Gavriel, H., Drummond, P., Richards, J., & Greenwald, R. (in press). Treatment of post-traumatic stress disorder: A comparison of stress inoculation training with prolonged exposure and eye movement desensitization and reprocessing. *Journal of Clinical Psychology.*

Levin, P., Lazrove, S., & van der Kolk, B. (1999). What psychological testing and neuroimaging tell us about the treatment of posttraumatic stress disorder by eye movement desensitization and reprocessing. *Journal of Anxiety Disorders, 13*, 159–172.

Linehan, M. M. (1993a). *Cognitive–behavioral treatment of borderline personality disorder.* New York: Guilford Press.

Linehan, M. M. (1993b). *Skills training manual for treating borderline personality disorder.* New York: Guilford Press.

Lohr, J., Tolin, D., & Kleinknecht, R. (1995). Eye movement desensitization of medical phobias: Two case studies. *Journal of Behavior Therapy and Experimental Psychiatry, 26*, 141–151.

Lohr, J., Tolin, D., & Kleinknecht, R. (1996). An intensive investigation of eye movement desensitization and reprocessing of claustrophobia. *Journal of Anxiety Disorders, 10*, 73–88.

Lohr, J. M., Tolin, D. F., & Lilienfeld, S. O. (1998). Efficacy of eye movement desensitization and reprocessing: Implications for behavior therapy. *Behavior Therapy, 29*, 123–156.

London, P. (1972). The end of ideology in behavior modification. *American Psychologist, 27*, 913–920.

MacCulloch, M. J., & Feldman, P. (1996). Eye movement desensitization treatment utilizes the positive visceral element of the investigatory reflex to inhibit the memories of post-traumatic stress disorder: A theoretical analysis. *British Journal of Psychiatry, 169*, 571–579.

Manfield, P. (Ed.). (1998). *Extending EMDR.* New York: Norton.

Marks, I. M. (1987). *Fears, phobias and rituals.* Oxford, England: Oxford University Press.

Marks, I. M. (2000). Forty years of psychosocial treatment. *Behavioural and Cognitive Psychotherapy, 28*, 323–334.

Marks, I. M., Lovell, K., Noshirvani, H., Livanou, M., & Thrasher, S. (1998). Treatment of posttraumatic stress disorder by exposure and/or cognitive restructuring: A controlled study. *Archives of General Psychiatry, 55*, 317–325.

Meyer, V. (1957). The treatment of two phobic patients on the basis of learning principles. *Journal of Abnormal and Social Psychology, 55*, 59–65.

Montgomery, R. W., & Ayllon, T. (1994). Eye movement desensitization across subjects: Subjective and physiological measures of treatment efficacy. *Journal of Behavior Therapy and Experimental Psychiatry, 25*, 217–230.

Mowrer, O. H. (1947). On the dual nature of learning: A reinterpretation of "conditioning" and "problem-solving." *Harvard Educational Review, 17*, 102–148.

Mowrer, O. (1960). *Learning theory and behavior.* New York: Wiley.

Pavlov, I. P. (1927). *Conditioned reflexes* (G. V. Anrup, Trans.). Oxford, England: Oxford University Press.

Pavlov, I. P. (1928). *Lectures on conditioned reflexes* (W. H. Gantt, Trans.). New York: International Universities Press.

Peniston, E. G. (1986). EMG biofeedback—assisted desensitization treatment for Vietnam combat veterans post-traumatic stress disorder. *Clinical Biofeedback and Health, 9*, 35–41.

Pitman, R. K., Orr, S. P., Altman, B., Longpre, R. E., Poire, R. E., & Macklin, M. L. (1996). Emotional processing during eye movement desensitization and reprocessing therapy of Vietnam veterans with chronic posttraumatic stress disorder. *Comprehensive Psychiatry, 37*, 419–429.

Poole, A. D., De Jongh, A., & Spector, J. (1999). Power therapies: Evidence versus emotion. A reply to Rosen, Lohr, McNally, and Herbert. *Behavioural and Cognitive Psychotherapy, 27*, 3–8.

Power, K. G., McGoldrick, T., & Brown, K. (1999). *A controlled comparison of eye movement desensitization and reprocessing versus exposure plus cognitive restructuring versus waiting list in the treatment of post-traumatic stress disorder.* Report to Scottish Home and Health Department, Edinburgh.

Renfrey, G., & Spates, C. R. (1994). Eye movement desensitization and reprocessing: A partial dismantling procedure. *Journal of Behavior Therapy and Experimental Psychiatry, 25*, 231–239.

Richards, D. A., Lovell, K., & Marks, I. M. (1994). Post-traumatic stress disorder: Evaluation of a behavioural treatment program. *Journal of Traumatic Stress, 7*, 669–680.

Rodriguez, B. I., & Craske, M. G. (1993). The effects of distraction during exposure to phobic stimuli. *Behaviour Research and Therapy, 31*, 549–558.

Rosen, G., Lohr, J. M., McNally, R. J., & Herbert, J. D. (1998). Power therapies, miraculous claims and cures that fail. *Behavioural and Cognitive Psychotherapy, 26*, 99–101.

Rothbaum, B. O., Meadows, E. A., Resick, P., & Foy, D. W. (2000). Cognitive–behavioral therapy. In E. B. Foa, T. M. Keane, & M. J. Friedman (Eds.), *Effective treatments for PTSD: Practice guidelines from the International Society for Traumatic Stress Studies* (pp. 60–83, 320–325). New York: Guilford Press.

Rubin, A. (1999). *Empirically evaluating EMDR with single-case designs: A step-by-step guide for EMDR therapists.* New Hope, PA: EMDR Humanitarian Assistance Programs.

Sanderson, A., & Carpenter, R. (1992). Eye movement desensitization versus image confrontation: A single session crossover study of 38 phobic subjects. *Journal of Behavior Therapy and Experimental Psychiatry, 23,* 269–275.

Seligman, M. E. P. (1995). The effectiveness of psychotherapy: The *Consumer Reports* study. *American Psychologist, 50,* 965–974.

Shapiro, F. (1989a). Efficacy of the eye movement desensitization procedure in the treatment of traumatic memories. *Journal of Traumatic Stress, 2,* 199–223.

Shapiro, F. (1989b). Eye movement desensitization: A new treatment for post-traumatic stress disorder. *Journal of Behavior Therapy and Experimental Psychiatry, 20,* 211–217.

Shapiro, F. (1991). Eye movement desensitization and reprocessing procedure: From EMD to EMDR: A new treatment model for anxiety and related traumata. *The Behavior Therapist, 14,* 133–135.

Shapiro, F. (1994a). Alternative stimuli in the use of EMD(R). *Journal of Behavior Therapy and Experimental Psychiatry, 25,* 89.

Shapiro, F. (1994b). EMDR: In the eye of a paradigm shift. *The Behavior Therapist, 17,* 153–157.

Shapiro, F. (1995). *Eye movement desensitization and reprocessing: Basic principles, protocols and procedures.* New York: Guilford Press.

Shapiro, F. (1996). Eye movement desensitization and reprocessing (EMDR): Evaluation of controlled PTSD research. *Journal of Behavior Therapy and Experimental Psychiatry, 27,* 1–10.

Shapiro, F. (1998). Eye movement desensitization and reprocessing (EMDR): Accelerated information processing and affect-driven constructions. *Crisis Intervention, 4,* 145–157.

Shapiro, F. (1999). Eye movement desensitization and reprocessing (EMDR) and the anxiety disorders: Clinical and research implications of an integrated psychotherapy treatment. *Journal of Anxiety Disorders, 13,* 35–67.

Shapiro, F. (2001). *Eye movement desensitization and reprocessing: Basic principles, protocols and procedures* (2nd ed.). New York: Guilford Press.

Skinner, B. F. (1938). *The behavior of organisms.* New York: Appleton-Century-Crofts.

Smyth, N. J. (1999, November). Is EMDR Unique? In G. K. Hare (Chair), *EMDR: The search for a database on which we can all agree.* Symposium conducted at the meeting of the annual conference of the Association for the Advancement of Behavior Therapy, Toronto, Ontario, Canada.

Stern, R., & Marks, I. M. (1973). Brief and prolonged flooding: A comparison in agoraphobic patients. *Archives of General Psychiatry, 28,* 270–276.

Stickgold, R. (2002). EMDR: A putative neurobiological mechanism of action. *Journal of Clinical Psychology, 58,* 61–75.

Thorndike, E. L. (1913). *The psychology of learning.* New York: Teachers College.

Tryon, W. W. (2000). Behavior therapy as applied learning theory. *The Behavior Therapist, 23,* 131–134.

Ullmann, L. P., & Krasner, L. (Eds.). (1965). *Case studies in behavior modification.* New York: Holt.

van der Kolk, B. A. (1996). The complexity of adaptation to trauma: Self-regulation, stimulus discrimination, and characterological development. In B. A. van der Kolk, A. C. McFarlane, & L. Weisaeth (Eds.), *Traumatic stress* (pp. 182–213). New York: Guilford Press.

Van Etten, M., & Taylor, S. (1998). Comparative efficacy of treatments for post-traumatic stress disorder: A meta-analysis. *Clinical Psychology and Psychotherapy, 5,* 126–144.

Wagner, A. W., & Linehan, M. M. (1998). Dissociative behavior. *Cognitive–behavioral therapies for trauma.* New York: Guilford Press.

Watkins, J. G., & Watkins, H. H. (1997). *Ego state: Theory and therapy.* New York: W.W. Norton.

Watson, J. B., & Raynor, R. (1920). Conditioned emotional reactions. *Journal of Experimental Psychology, 3,* 1–14.

Watson, J. P., Gaind, R., & Marks, I. M. (1978). Physiological habituation to conscious phobic stimulation. *Behaviour Research and Therapy, 16,* 229–278.

Wilson, D. L., Silver, S. M., Covi, W. G., & Foster, S. (1996). Eye movement desensitization and reprocessing: Effectiveness and autonomic correlates. *Journal of Behavior Therapy and Experimental Psychiatry, 27,* 219–229.

Wolpe, J. (1958). *Psychotherapy by reciprocal inhibition.* Stanford, CA: Stanford University Press.

Wolpe, J. (1969). Foreword. In C. M. Franks (Ed.), *Behavior therapy: Appraisal and status* (pp. ix–xiii). New York: McGraw-Hill.

Wolpe, J. (1990, November). *Eye movement desensitization (EMD) procedure: A rapid treatment for anxiety and related trauma.* Clinical roundtable presented at the annual conference of the Association for the Advancement of Behavior Therapy, San Francisco, CA.

Yates, A. J. (1958). The application of learning theory to the treatment of tics. *Journal of Abnormal and Social Psychology, 56,* 175–182.

Yates, A. J. (1970). *Behavior therapy.* New York: Wiley.

Yates, A. J. (1975). *Theory and practice in behavior therapy.* New York: Wiley.

Young, J. (1994). *Cognitive therapy for personality disorders: A schema-focused approach* (Rev. ed.). Sarasota, FL: Professional Resource Exchange.

7

COMBINING EMDR AND SCHEMA-FOCUSED THERAPY: THE WHOLE MAY BE GREATER THAN THE SUM OF THE PARTS

JEFFREY E. YOUNG, WILLIAM M. ZANGWILL, AND WENDY E. BEHARY

A few days before his session, Dan had exploded—again. A disagreement with his stepdaughter had led to another outburst during which he had cursed, slammed cabinet doors, and ruined the family's weekend. After his outburst, he had sulked for hours even though, as he later admitted, he knew he was overreacting.

The opening example illustrates a problem that has long concerned and frustrated many therapists and their clients. Why do intellectual awareness and insight not produce more significant emotional and behavioral improvements? Zajonc (1980) suggested this is because emotions and cognitions are processed in different areas and by different structures in the brain. The work of LeDoux (1989), Davis (1992), and others has shown that Zajonc was right: Emotional processing occurs through specific circuitry and structures in the brain. Unfortunately, much of clinical psychology has neither understood nor sufficiently integrated the treatment implications of this area of research. This is problematic because, as Rachman (1981) stated in response to Zajonc's article, "If words and techniques which are predominantly verbal in nature are inappropriate or at least insufficient media for entering the affective system or for modifying its functioning, we need to consider alternative modes and media" (p. 285).

However, some practitioners have recognized the need for more integrative models of psychotherapy. Two of the best models are Young's (1990, 1999) Schema-Focused Therapy (SFT) and Shapiro's (1995) Eye Movement Desensitization and Reprocessing (EMDR). Although these two approaches arose from different clinical experiences and theoretical backgrounds, they are similar in that they recognize the importance of all the ways in which people process information—affectively, physiologically, through the senses, and cognitively. Each model can be tremendously beneficial to clinicians and their clients. Combining aspects of each often yields better results than using either one alone. Thus, this chapter first includes a description of Young's model and then an illustration of the way EMDR clinicians can enhance SFT by using the powerful information-processing aspects of EMDR. Last is a brief discussion of the ways SFT can also be valuable to EMDR clinicians.

THE SCHEMA-FOCUSED THERAPY MODEL

Young's SFT (1995) was developed to expand Beck's original model of cognitive therapy. According to Beck, emotional problems were a result of biased evaluations made by the client. Beck believed that these distortions were based on core assumptions made about the self and the world formed in early childhood. Thus, Beck's version of cognitive therapy focused primarily on correcting distorted patterns of thinking.

In contrast to analytic therapy, Beck's cognitive therapy assumed that these distortions could be brought into awareness relatively easily, and then challenged and corrected. Thus, his approach focused on increasing clients' awareness of disturbing cognitions and better understanding the connection between these distorted or maladaptive cognitions and painful emotions and behaviors. As awareness increased, it was assumed that clients could then test their hypotheses, gather evidence, and determine whether their cognitions were inaccurate or maladaptive. As clients disproved their mistaken underlying assumptions about themselves and the world, they could replace these mistaken assumptions with more accurate or functional ones.

Although Beck's original model has had considerable success treating people with axis I disorders, the limitations of standard cognitive therapy have become increasingly apparent as cognitive therapists have begun focusing on more chronic, characterological clients. Young (1990) noted that for Beck's model to be successful, clients had to meet the following requirements:

1. Be able to access thoughts and emotions readily.
2. Be able to identify specific life problems.
3. Have sufficient motivation to do homework assignments.

4. Have cognitions flexible enough to respond to cognitive–behavioral techniques.
5. Be able to engage in open, positive relationships with their therapist.
6. Keep any difficulties that occurred in the therapeutic relationship from becoming a major problem focus.

Unfortunately, many clients cannot meet these criteria. As Young noted, the hallmark of more difficult clients, such as those with personality disorders or who have been severely traumatized, are the very factors that make Beck's standard model of cognitive therapy less effective for these clients. These characteristics include the following:

1. Interpersonal problems that make it difficult to engage in a positive therapeutic relationship
2. Rigidity of thought, behavior, and emotion that make change difficult
3. Diffuse presentation of problems
4. Frequent avoidance of situations that might trigger disturbing thoughts, affect, and behaviors

As a result of these limitations in the standard cognitive therapy model, Young developed SFT. SFT integrates cognitive, behavioral, experiential (e.g., Gestalt), and interpersonal (e.g., object relations) techniques using the concept of an early maladaptive schema as the unifying element.

Conceptual Underpinnings

Young posited four constructs in his model: early maladaptive schemas, schema domains, schema processes, and schema modes.

Early Maladaptive Schemas

Segal (1988) conceptualized schemas as the residue of past reactions and experience that often affects subsequent perception and appraisals. In his work, Young focused on a specific subset of these schemas, which he refers to as *early maladaptive schemas*. He defined these schemas as "broad pervasive themes regarding oneself and one's relationship to others developed during childhood and elaborated throughout one's lifetime, and dysfunctional to a significant degree" (Young, 1999, p. 9). It is assumed that these schemas develop through interplay of the child's innate temperament; everyday noxious experiences with parents, siblings, and peers; and the cultural context in which the child grows up. Schemas[1] are representations

---

[1]The use of the term *schema* throughout the rest of this chapter refers to an early maladaptive schema.

of these early life experiences and serve as filters through which later experiences are processed. Thus, schemas contain patterns of distorted thinking, painful affect, and disturbing memories.

When triggered, schemas frequently generate high levels of affect. In an attempt to cope with these painful emotions, many clients develop behaviors that are ultimately self-defeating, such as addictive behaviors and avoidance. Because of the long-standing nature of many clients' problems and the painful affect associated with their schemas, SFT focuses more attention on creating affective experiences within and outside of the therapeutic relationship than does standard cognitive therapy. The model also recommends active confrontation of maladaptive cognitive and behavioral patterns.

As of this writing, Young has defined 18 early maladaptive schemas, in addition to hypothesized developmental domains (see Appendix 7.A). For example, people who were frequently criticized growing up often develop a defectiveness/shame schema with associated thoughts and feelings that they are defective, bad, or inferior and would be unlovable if exposed.

Schemas are usually perceived to be irrefutable, which makes them difficult to change. They are intrinsically linked to people's concepts of themselves and the world. Because they were formed so early in life, schemas are often ego-syntonic. Thus, even when presented with evidence that seems to contradict the schema, people often involuntarily distort data to maintain its validity. For example, one client with a defectiveness/shame schema felt more anxious after a promotion at work than before. Instead of seeing the promotion as disproving the defectiveness schema, this client felt that because the promotion made him more visible and gave him more responsibility, it would only make people realize more quickly that he was indeed the flawed, inadequate person he believed himself to be.

Schemas are triggered under conditions relevant to a particular schema (e.g., a person with a defectiveness/shame schema asking someone out on a date, someone with an abandonment/instability schema dealing with a partner leaving to go on a business trip) or biological changes such as premenstrual syndrome (PMS) or sleep deprivation.

Schema Domains and Developmental Origins

In Young's model, the 18 schemas are grouped into five broad categories representing important aspects of people's core needs. These schema domains represent five universal developmental processes that often serve as the origin of schemas when blocked. Problems occur when a specific early maladaptive schema in that domain interferes with people's attempts to meet their needs. For example, clients with abandonment/instability schemas (in the disconnection and rejection domain) feel that sooner or later they will be abandoned by the people they care about and need. Thus, in every relationship, abandonment is inevitable. Because it is only a matter of time until the abandonment occurs, clients with this schema may get anxious even when a relationship is going well. At the first sign of problems, they often become so needy and clingy or angry that they drive the other person away. Following are the five schema domains and their associated schemas.

Disconnection and rejection. This disconnection and rejection domain is characterized by the expectation that the needs for safety, security, acceptance, nurturance, stability, protection, empathy, and guidance will not be met consistently or predictably. The families of people in this domain were often detached, cold, rejecting, withholding, explosive, unpredictable, or abusive. Schemas in this domain are abandonment/instability, mistrust/abuse, emotional deprivation, defectiveness/shame, and social isolation/alienation.

Impaired autonomy and performance. Patients in the impaired autonomy and performance area have fears about themselves and the environment that make it difficult for them to separate, survive, function independently, or be successful. These schemas include dependence/incompetence, vulnerability to harm or illness, enmeshment/undeveloped self, and failure. Clients with these schemas typically grew up in an enmeshed, overprotective, or undermining family that failed to reinforce them for performing competently or neglected to foster skills needed for independent functioning.

Impaired limits. The impaired limits domain includes schemas of entitlement/grandiosity and insufficient self-control/self-discipline and pertains to a deficiency in internal limits, responsibility to others, or long-term goal orientation. Individuals with these schemas have difficulty respecting the rights of others, cooperating, making commitments, or setting and meeting realistic goals. Clients with these schemas typically come from families that were permissive, indulgent, unstructured, or felt superior to others and did not effectively discipline their children or set appropriate limits.

Other-directedness. Individuals with schemas in the other-directedness domain (which includes the schemas of subjugation, self-sacrifice, and approval/recognition-seeking) often focus excessively on the feelings, wishes, and desires of others at the expense of their own needs. This often involves the suppression of personal needs and feelings to gain approval, acceptance, love, and connection or to avoid retaliation, rejection, blame, or loss. These clients typically grew up in an environment in which acceptance was conditional and the adults' needs were more important than the child's.

Overvigilance and inhibition. Schemas in this domain include negativity/pessimism, emotional inhibition, unrelenting standards/hypercriticalness, and punitiveness. People in this domain often place excessive emphasis on controlling their natural impulses, feelings, and choices for fear of making mistakes. Their families often stressed meeting rigid, internalized rules and demanded high performance and ethical behavior, often at the expense of happiness, creative self-expression, close relationships, or health. The family atmosphere was often grim and demanding and was sometimes punitive. The family probably had an undercurrent of pessimism and worried that things would fall apart unless everyone was constantly vigilant and behaving properly.

Schema Processes

As mentioned previously, SFT is a method of treatment involving active confrontation of clients' underlying schemas and associated distorted cognitions, painful affect, and maladaptive behaviors. Treatment involves confronting clients' various maladaptive affective, cognitive, and behavioral coping strategies, which are referred to as *schema processes*. Clients engage in these processes to avoid or compensate for the painful affect associated with the triggering of schemas. The three schema processes are (a) schema avoidance, (b) maintenance, and (c) compensation. Avoidance and compensation overlap with the analytic concept of defense mechanisms.

Schema avoidance. The schema avoidance process refers to any type of attempt—through cognitive, affective, or behavioral avoidance—by clients to avoid triggering the painful affect associated with a schema. For example, clients with a vulnerability to harm and illness schema may avoid leaving home for fear they will be harmed. Of course, this avoidance precludes any possibility that clients can experience being safe in the world and thus disprove the schema.

Although avoidance behaviors can be frustrating to clinicians and clients, if clinicians understand their clients' schemas, the avoidance makes sense. For example, if clients think and feel the world is unsafe (vulnerability to harm and illness schema), it makes sense for them to stay at home. If they feel that as soon as other people realize who they really are, then the people will be disgusted, turned off, and want to leave them (defectiveness/shame and abandonment schemas), why should such clients risk being vulnerable in a relationship?

Schema maintenance. Maintenance is a process by which clients repeat old, familiar ways of thinking, feeling, and behaving (often unconsciously) to perpetuate the schema. For example, clients with a self-sacrifice schema might repeatedly get involved with people who abuse alcohol, thus perpetuating the schema involving excessively taking care of others. Maintenance is also referred to as *surrendering to the schema*.

Schema compensation. Schema compensation is a process in which clients attempt to overcompensate for or fight the schema. It is often an early attempt by children to adapt to their pain. Like the other processes, compensation is probably adaptive in childhood. However, when it persists into adulthood, it often backfires and perpetuates the schema. For example, some clients with very critical parents might become critical of others and thus be drawn to partners that they can criticize. By being around others who are even "more defective" than they are, clients decrease the risk that their own defectiveness/shame schema will be triggered. However, being with a partner they feel is defective is likely to be very unsatisfying. Thus, continuing this pattern with others later in life is likely to prevent clients from getting the closeness and connection they want and need.

Schema Modes

So far, early maladaptive schemas, schema domains, and schema processes have been discussed. The latest concept in SFT is schema modes. Although most clients have several different schemas, at any given time, some are active and others are dormant. A schema mode is the group of currently active schemas, schema processes, or both. Thus, a schema or schema process is a *trait* concept, whereas a schema mode is a *state* concept. Young defined a schema mode as a facet of self, involving a natural grouping of schemas and schema processes that has not been fully integrated with other facets (for details, see Young & Behary 1998).

APPLICATIONS OF SFT: ASSESSMENT AND EDUCATION

SFT is composed of two phases: (a) assessment and education and (b) change. As is discussed later in this chapter, EMDR is very useful in both phases. In the assessment phase, the focus is on identification and activation of each client's schemas and particular schema processes most often used, such as determining which types of problems clients are having, which underlying schemas the problems represent, and in which maladaptive ways the clients are coping with their issues.

During this phase, clinicians also educate clients about SFT and gather various types of information to understand the case. This phase includes activities common to all good psychotherapy including history taking, mental status, and problem identification. Components of this phase specific to SFT include schema identification, schema activation, schema conceptualization, and schema education.

Assessment and Education

Schema Identification

The client's schemas are identified in numerous ways. During the initial sessions, the clinicians try to identify early, ongoing patterns connected to clients' problems. Clinicians also pay close attention to inter-actions in the therapy relationship. The use of questionnaires such as the Young Schema Questionnaire (Young & Brown 1990, 1994)—a self-report inventory with items related to each schema—and the Young Parenting Inventory (Young, 1994b) are designed to help clinicians and clients iden-tify life patterns. The Multimodal Life History Inventory, which collects essential historical material (Lazarus & Lazarus, 1991), is used to collect a broad range of information as efficiently as possible. The Multimodal Life History Inventory often provides valuable positive information, such as details about educational or vocational achievements or good relationships, that can be used as evidence later in treatment to combat some of the clients' negative views of themselves, others, and the world.

Schema Activation

The goal of schema activation is to determine experientially which of the clients' schemas are most powerful (and thus need to be addressed first); to ascertain how well clients can handle affect; and, through this experiential process, to help educate clients about the emotions associated with their schemas.

Schema Conceptualization and Education

All of the material gathered during the assessment phase is integrated into an overall picture of clients' problems and shared with them. This process may occur within the first few sessions or may take several sessions, depending on how fragile, wounded, or avoidant each client is.

Before the active change phase begins, it is essential to explain to clients the initial conceptualization in schema terms: the reason they are having problems and the purpose of your recommendations. This sharing of information helps establish a collaborative relationship, enables clini-cians to get feedback from clients, and serves as a rationale for later rec-ommendations for change by the clinicians. To further clients' understand-ing of SFT, clinicians often recommend they read *Reinventing Your Life* (Young & Klosko, 1994), a self-help book based on the schema-focused approach.

At this point in treatment, clinicians have identified clients' primary schemas and coping styles (the primary schema processes they use), com-pleted a full assessment of clients' problems, established a collaborative relationship, educated clients about schemas, and helped clients to expe-rience emotionally how the schemas are affecting their lives.

Change

SFT combines cognitive, experiential, interpersonal, and behavioral techniques to produce change in many different dimensions.

Cognitive Techniques

Cognitive strategies are designed to increase clients' awareness of their distorted views of themselves and others and to gather evidence to refute these distorted viewpoints. Thus, throughout treatment, clinicians help their clients gather evidence to contradict their distortions (as embodied in the various schemas).

When asked to provide data to contradict their schemas, many clients struggle to think of contradictory information. Using information gathered from the various instruments mentioned previously and clinicians' experiences with their clients, clinicians may need to suggest examples. For example, for a client with the emotional deprivation schema, a clinician may suggest the following, "I know you feel that you never got the nurturing and understanding you needed from your parents, but how did you and your brother and sisters get along when you were growing up?"[2] As with all cognitive techniques, clinicians should introduce information that will challenge the client's current schemas.

Clinicians also should extend the progress made during the session and apply it to clients' daily environment. One of the ways this is done is with flashcards (Young & Klosko, 1994). Flashcards are used to help clients continue the process outside of the therapy session. The flashcard lists the evidence against the schema and is carried by the clients. It can be in the form of a piece of paper, an index card, or even an audiotape. Clients are encouraged to review the "evidence" daily and whenever their schemas are activated.

This frequent review of a rational response acts as a self-control device to reduce the frequency of dysfunctional behaviors and also helps clients gain some distance from and perspective about the schema and its associated thoughts, feelings, and body sensations. The flashcard thus contradicts clients' habitual ways of thinking and continues the therapy between sessions. For example, Dan, who was mentioned at the beginning of this chapter, lost his temper when he felt unappreciated and criticized. The following flashcard was developed for him to use whenever he felt that he was unappreciated or that he was about to lose his temper.

> I know what I do I will never be good enough, *but* although some people may not appreciate me, I do have people in my life who genuinely care for me and appreciate what I do. My wife thinks I am wonderful and shows her appreciation all the time. At work, I just

---

[2]SFT clinicians are always attempting to challenge clients' underlying maladaptive assumptions about themselves and the world. Like good lawyers, good clinicians never ask questions like this unless they already know that the clients have a good answer (e.g., "Well we have always been close, and I know they would be there for me if I needed them"). If clients were an only child or did not have a good relationship with their siblings, clinicians can substitute any person who did provide care and nurturing. This could include people such as grandparents, teachers, lovers, or close friends.

received an excellent evaluation and raise. Although I'll never be perfect, I have gotten better at controlling my temper and can continue to do so.

Experiential Techniques

Although cognitive techniques can be very valuable for helping correct clients' distortions, their effectiveness can be limited for the reasons mentioned at the beginning of this chapter—cognition and affect are processed in separate systems. Thus, at various points in therapy, many clients have said that they rationally "believe" the more positive cognitions they have worked on, but this belief does not seem to help how they feel or behave.

For this reason we have focused on incorporating experiential techniques into SFT and have found that they are often the most useful of all strategies. In fact, these experiential techniques are required to weaken the strength of the underlying schemas of many clients. Three of the most commonly used experiential techniques are imagery, schema dialogues, and EMDR.

Imagery. As we mentioned previously, imagery is used in the assessment phase to help clients connect present problems to past experiences and to probe for underlying schemas. In the change phase, clients work on changing unpleasant images. For example, clients with the emotional deprivation schema would be asked to close their eyes and remember an early time in their lives when they felt deprived or not understood by a parent. They are then asked and coached by the therapist to communicate their feelings and needs to the parent in the image. With as much support and coaching as clients need, they are encouraged to state their rights as children to be loved, understood, and nurtured.

Facing the painful image of a depriving parent enables clients with this schema to better understand parents' roles in the formation of their schemas and to be fairer to themselves. In EMDR terms, this process helps clients assign appropriate responsibility (i.e., to the parent) for their issues and realize that they have more choices now than they had in the past.

Schema dialogue. With schema dialogues, clients learn to confront the feelings elicited by the schema and to support and strengthen the healthy aspects of themselves. For example, clients with the defectiveness schema can be taught that although they feel defective or worthless at a core level, some part of themselves (which is called the *healthy side*), even if initially small, can integrate evidence that they are worthwhile and do not have to feel ashamed.

In the schema dialogue, clients are asked to refute the schema by providing evidence that negates it. Refuting the schema is often difficult for many clients. Therefore, clients are initially asked to role play the schema (i.e., to say out loud thoughts consistent with a particular schema).

For example, a client role playing a defectiveness schema might list some of the following statements:

1. Why do you keep trying in relationships? You know sooner or later anybody you get involved with will realize what a loser you are.
2. You're never going to be successful because you just don't have it.
3. I can't believe you haven't been found out for the fraud that you are. It is just a matter of time until you are.

Clients are usually able to play the schema side with ease. Often when they hear the statements, they begin to realize how unfair they are to themselves.

Although the initial dialogue is easy for many clients, the next phase is not. In the second phase, clients are asked to respond to a schema using their healthy side. Clients often experience more difficulty in this phase because it requires them to access information that negates the schema— information that they typically minimize. Clinicians need to coach clients by supplying them with dialogue that supports a more balanced, less pernicious view of the self. For example, Dan, who lost his temper with his stepdaughter at the beginning of this chapter, had highly critical parents. He brought up a very distressing memory of an event that occurred when he was 8 years old. In the following transcript, comments [in brackets] indicate editorial points of interest.

Therapist: Dan, bring up that image of you when you were 8 and had just finished cleaning up the house and your mother was standing there criticizing you. Tell her how you are feeling.

Dan: I don't know what to say. I know it made me feel bad when she criticized me, but she was usually right. I did make mistakes. One time, I remember she was furious because I had forgotten to clean the baseboards.

[This is an example of how hard it can be for clients to be fair to themselves in the present because of the negative beliefs contained in the schema. Dan's unrelenting standards schema is causing him to judge his 8-year-old behavior by adult standards. When something like this happens, the therapist often needs to step in and actively coach the client.]

Therapist: Tell her that you tried as hard as you could. That you are only 8 years old and that you need her support.

Dan: "Mom, I tried as hard as I could, but when you criticize me, it makes me feel like a complete failure. I'm only 8; I need you to say something nice."

This dialogue helped Dan realize that it was not his fault that his mother criticized him. Her criticism did not mean that he was defective. In this case, it means that she was unfair. These schema dialogues often help clients to both distance themselves from the schema and to realize that the schema can be changed. With sufficient practice, many clients report an increased ability to respond in healthier ways when their schemas are triggered.

Interpersonal Techniques

As analysts have discussed for decades, many of the clients' schemas emerge in the context of the therapeutic relationship. Therefore, addressing issues that emerge in the relationship between client and clinician is important for identifying and modifying those schemas. In SFT, the therapist works openly with the client on identifying and modifying schema-driven thoughts and feelings. This may involve limited self-disclosure on the therapist's part to correct distorted beliefs and expectations of clients. Although sometimes painful to hear (especially when clients are correct about something the therapist has or has not done), it is important to allow clients to express their beliefs and feelings in the sessions.

For example, any time therapists go away on vacation or to a conference, clients with an abandonment schema are likely to become very upset and angry at their therapist. Therefore, it is important to discuss these feelings during the session, not only to reassure them about their therapist's return but also to honestly talk about the therapist's need for rest and rejuvenation. To do this, SFT therapists use what Young refers to as *empathic confrontation* as their primary working stance with clients. The therapists fully acknowledge and validate clients' feelings and concerns while gently pointing out other, more accurate views. For example, a therapist going on vacation would empathize with the client's distress and pain and fully acknowledge the pain of the separation. However, in the same session the therapist would tactfully point out returning from past vacations; the therapist can also express enjoyment in working with the client (if this is true). This last bit of reassurance is crucial for clients who worry that their therapist will abandon them because the therapist does not like them.

To use interpersonal techniques appropriately, therapists need to acknowledge that they may have issues that need to be addressed. The more therapists are aware of their own schemas, the more effective their work will be. The clinical experiences of the authors of this chapter, as well as our supervision of others, strongly suggest that the clients who trouble us the most are the ones who trigger our own unresolved schemas.

Behavior Change Techniques

As important as in-session work is, the SFT therapist assumes that work needs to be done outside of the session to break self-defeating patterns of behavior such as avoidance, maintenance, and compensation. Well-established behavior change techniques such as role playing are used to provide corrective experiences for each client.

WEAVING TOGETHER SFT AND EMDR

SFT is a complete therapeutic method. As effective as it is, it can be even more effective when combined with EMDR. This section shows some of the ways in which EMDR can increase SFT's effectiveness and how the two approaches complement each other.

As we mentioned previously, SFT has two major phases: (a) assessment and education and (b) change. This section uses Dan, the man who lost his temper, to illustrate many of the ways in which EMDR can enhance the power of SFT in both phases.

Dan is a 60-year-old executive. He is seeking treatment partly because of his wife's concerns about his temper, which flared in the chapter's opening story. She reported that periodically, when things do not go his way, he becomes explosively angry. Although he has never hit his stepchildren, his violent cursing, door slamming, and hours of sulking scare her and have ruined many family gatherings. When interviewed, Dan agreed with his wife's description of his behavior but reported that he had no idea why he got so angry. He acknowledged that the intensity of his rage seemed out of proportion to what happened.

Assessment and Education

In the initial stages of treatment (assessment and education), Dan was given the Multimodal Life History Inventory, the Young Schema Questionnaire, and the Young Parenting Inventory. Information obtained from these instruments and from discussions with Dan revealed the potential presence of numerous different schemas, including defectiveness/shame, self-sacrifice, and unrelenting standards schemas. However, efforts to trigger these schemas during a session through discussion and through imagery were unsuccessful. Dan had a difficult time getting in touch with any feelings, especially those feelings involved in events from his past. "What's the point of digging up this old stuff?" was one of his responses. Thus, although he had an intellectual understanding of his issues and schemas, little if any affective connection was made. The therapist decided to try using the procedural steps from EMDR to try and increase his emotional understanding of how his past was affecting him in the present.

The EMDR procedural steps are designed to help clients access information on many different dimensions—visually, cognitively, affectively, and physiologically. Using any client problem—past, present, or future—the therapist helps clients develop a visual image of the most disturbing aspect of the problem, identify the negative cognitions clients have about themselves in regard to the problem or event, and note the emotions that are triggered and bodily responses that occur when this information is accessed. Using these different dimensions often helps clients feel the power of their schemas, thus making the education process much easier. It also allows therapists and clients to identify the most powerful (painful) schemas, check for processes such as avoidance, and alert therapists to possible modes. Because Dan had lost his temper recently, the therapist had him focus on that event and used the EMDR procedural steps:

1. Defining the problematic memory or issue:

Therapist: Dan, please describe that last time you lost your temper.

Dan: Well, the night after we had a lot of snow, my stepdaughter's car was stuck in the driveway. I offered to help her get it unstuck and went outside and started shoveling. Not only did she not come out and help but at one point, she stuck her head out the door and asked if I was done yet. When she asked that, I just lost it.

2. Obtaining a vivid picture representing the memory or issue:

Therapist: What picture represents the worst part of that incident?

Dan: I see myself standing in the driveway, sweating like crazy, as she's standing in the doorway asking if I am almost done.

3. Developing a negative cognition:

Therapist: What words go best with that picture and express your negative belief about yourself now?

Dan: I'm not good enough.

4. Developing an alternative positive cognition:

Therapist: When you bring up that picture of standing in the snow as she is asking if you're done, what would you like to believe about yourself, now?

Dan: I am good enough.

5. Rating the emotional validity of the positive cognition:

Therapist: When you think of that picture, how true do those words —"I am good enough"—feel to you now on a scale of 1 to 7, with 1 feeling completely false and 7 feeling completely true?

Dan: About a 2.

6. Helping the client access emotions:

Therapist: When you bring up that picture of your stepdaughter standing in the doorway asking if you're done yet and those words, "I'm not good enough," what emotions do you feel now?

Dan: Sheer rage . . .

7. Measuring the subjective units of disturbance (SUDS) for this issue or memory:

Therapist: And how upsetting does that incident feel to you now, on a scale of 0 to 10, with 0 being no disturbance or neutral and 10 being the most disturbance you can imagine?

Dan: About a 9.

8. Accessing body sensations:

Therapist: Where do you feel the disturbance in your body?

Dan: In my throat, chest, and gut.

For many therapists, each of Dan's responses might have engendered more questions and discussion. However, in EMDR, most of the time moving through the questions without digressing is the most effective way to help clients access the material on so many different dimensions. Naturally, time is provided to explain and discuss any questions clients have or any issues that arise before and after the EMDR process.

At this point, Dan was surprised at the amount of distress he felt. By using the EMDR procedural steps, he was able to *feel* how disturbing the event still was. The therapist continued the evaluation to determine whether this was a one-time event or part of a pattern linked to his defectiveness/shame schema. To do this, the therapist used the *floatback technique* (Browning, 1999). Similar to the *affect bridge* used in hypnosis (Watkins, 1992), this technique is designed to help clients connect present problems to past events.

Floatback Technique

SFT and EMDR assume that one of the reasons events in the present are so disturbing is that they activate previous, still painful memories. This often happens in a session when clients' responses seem out of proportion to an event they are describing, (i.e., when an event has "hit a nerve").

In SFT, the nerve is called a *schema;* in EMDR it is called *opening a childhood file folder* in which painful information resides (Shapiro, 1995). The floatback technique is a strategy for activating a specific problem as vividly as possible to determine whether a schema has been activated and a method for educating clients about the way the problem is connected to past experiences. Once the material is activated, clients are encouraged to think of other similar events. Following is additional therapy with Dan used to illustrate this technique.

> Therapist: Dan, at this point, please bring up that image of standing sweating in the driveway as your stepdaughter asks you if you're done yet—and those negative thoughts of, "I'm not good enough." Notice which emotions are coming up for you and where you are feeling them in your body. Now, just let your mind float back to an earlier time in your life when you had similar thoughts, feelings, and bodily sensations, and tell me what comes up for you.

> Dan: I see this picture of me when I was about 8 years old, cleaning the house, trying to get my mother's approval. But no matter what I did, she always found something to criticize. No matter what I did or how hard I tried, I was never good enough.

It is clear that we have activated Dan's defectiveness/shame schema as shown by the statement, "I was never good enough." By calling his attention to the different ways in which information is stored—his disturbing visual images, negative cognitions, upsetting affect, and painful body sensations—the therapist has also educated him about schemas and their pervasiveness throughout the information-processing system. Once Dan felt how upsetting these events still were to him, he needed very little additional information to be convinced about the importance of schemas. Although numerous ways can help activate clients' schemas, many therapists who combine SFT with EMDR have found the EMDR procedural step questions combined with the floatback technique to be a very effective way to do so.

Most of the time, the procedural steps activate clients' information-processing networks very effectively, and they can feel the power of a particular schema. However, some problematic clients are not initially able to tolerate affect and instead engage in significant affective and cognitive avoidance when the therapist attempts to activate their schemas. Clients may not be able to or may refuse to engage in imagery procedures or answer the therapist's questions directly. In more severe cases, clients may dissociate when painful material arises. For clients who have difficulty tolerating increased affect, other procedures borrowed from EMDR have proved to be very helpful to the SFT/EMDR clinicians; two such procedures are the *safe place exercise* and *resource development and installation (RDI).*

Safe Place Exercise

Clients using SFT and EMDR often experience a significant amount of affect in and between sessions. Clients who have been severely traumatized or who by temperament are somewhat fragile may be overwhelmed if steps are not taken to protect them. The safe place exercise is used to create an imaginary refuge for these clients. Clients simply imagine a place where they feel safe. Ideally, this place currently exists and is accessible to the client—such as a beach, on a couch with a partner or friend, or with a pet. If no such place is currently available, clients can use a safe place from the past, such as memories of being with a loving grandparent or former partner. For clients who do not have any positive memories from the past, therapists can help them create an image of the safe place that they would like to have. When painful affect becomes too intense, clients can imagine being in their safe place and decrease the pain. Having a safe place allows clients to modulate the amount of affect they are experiencing. This increased ability to tolerate affect is crucial in SFT because clients who avoid thoughts, memories, or situations that trigger their significant schemas are not likely to make much progress.

Dan's safe place was on the beach in the Caribbean with his wife. He imagined lying on the beach, listening to the sounds of the waves, and smelling the air while his whole body relaxed. After creating this image, the therapist asked him to close his eyes and vividly recall this scene to ensure that it really did make him *feel* safe and relaxed. With a broad smile on his face, Dan mentioned that the only problem with the image was that it was so nice it made him want to leave the session and go there.

Resource Development and Installation

Although the safe place helps many clients decrease anxiety, some clients do not have the ability to develop one in the initial stages of treatment. For these clients, another procedure borrowed from EMDR, Resource Development and Installation (RDI; Leeds, 1998) has been used with SFT to help them tolerate increased levels of affect and increase their feelings of self-efficacy.

In RDI, clients are initially asked to focus on the place where they have stalled and the qualities that they lack to succeed. Using a step-by-step process, clients are then asked to think of a time, either in the present or past, when they had those qualities. When clients cannot do this, they are asked to think of a person they admire, real or imaginary, who can help them surmount their problems. These images are then used to generate an image of success on cognitive, affective, and physiological levels. To enhance the power of this image, eye movements are used repeatedly. Thus, RDI combines images of success with eye movements to strengthen clients' beliefs that they can succeed. Initially, Dan could not imagine expressing his needs to anyone without being criticized or dismissed. He imagined his older sister standing with him, putting her arm around his shoulder, and giving him encouragement.

Thus, during the assessment and education phase of SFT, therapists frequently use aspects of EMDR, especially the procedural step questions and the safe place exercise, to help them determine which schemas need to be addressed, educate clients, and increase clients' ability to tolerate painful affect.

EMDR IN THE CHANGE PHASE OF TREATMENT

For many SFT clients, the change techniques described previously (e.g., flashcards, imagery, schema dialogue) are very effective. For some clients, they are not. For example, the therapist tried to use schema dialogue and asked Dan to tell his mother what he needed. With significant prompting, he was able to say the words, but he later revealed that even though he knew the words were true intellectually (i.e., that his mother should have been more supportive and less critical), he did not really *feel* the words to be true emotionally. Even after the schema dialogue was repeated several times, along with schema mode work, he still felt that on some level his mother was right—that he had not been good enough. However, when the therapist used EMDR during the same scene—his mother criticizing the efforts he had made to clean the house—Dan reported that he felt his thoughts and feelings change for the first time. At the end of the EMDR processing, Dan reported feeling much less guilt and shame and the realization that he had done the best he could. EMDR seemed to connect what he knew intellectually with what he felt emotionally.

> Therapist: Dan, bring up that picture of your mother criticizing you when you were 8 for the way you had cleaned the house; those negative thoughts that "I'm not good enough"; notice where you are feeling it in your body and follow my fingers.
>
> [set of eye movements]
>
> Dan: (turning red in the face with tears coming to his eyes) I can't believe it. No matter what I did, it was never good enough for her.

As the sets of eye movements continued, Dan's defectiveness/shame schema played itself out in numerous ways. One of the most interesting was that as he started to feel less pain from that specific event of being criticized at 8, he then blamed himself for letting it bother him so much.

Dan: What kind of wimp am I for letting this bother me so much? I mean, this was 50 years ago.

As therapy continued, Dan became increasingly aware of how unfair his situation had been; how much it still bothered him, though less so than before the EMDR; and how connected it was to his current issue of losing his temper whenever he felt criticized. (The criticism, of course, triggered his underlying feelings of defectiveness and shame, hence producing the anger.)

During the next few sessions, Dan reported several changes. For the first time, he realized, emotionally, that he had been a pretty good kid. He also reported that the event felt further away and less intrusive to him (a common response after EMDR processing). At a joint session with his wife, she reported an even more surprising event. She said that while on vacation the previous week, Dan had been late meeting her. She said that in the past, if she would have said anything at all to him about being late, he might have flown into a rage and ruined the rest of their day. This time, when she gently mentioned it, Dan apologized. He did not get angry or sulk. On hearing his wife describe this event, Dan laughed and said, "You know, she's right. In the past I probably would have blown up; but now, I wouldn't have even remembered it if she hadn't said something."

Thus, EMDR connected cognition with affect, decreasing the pain from the past event and reducing the strength of the defectiveness/shame schema. Using EMDR to make this connection allowed more adaptive information to be internalized (e.g., "My wife was a little irritated with my being late, but she does not think I am a horrible person."). Clients often report that after EMDR, their schemas feel weaker.

After the schemas have been weakened during a session, clients still need to make changes to their natural environment, which is why both EMDR and SFT have behavior change components. However, before giving an assignment to be completed outside of the session, EMDR can be used to effectively anticipate obstacles that might arise and reduce the clients' anxiety, thus improving their chances of success. Essentially, this is using EMDR for imaginal desensitization before in vivo exposure. In EMDR, this is called the *float-forward* technique (Browning, 1999).

The float-forward technique uses the previously described procedural steps with one important change. When therapists ask for the clients to think of an image involving them changing, they ask the clients to imagine the worst thing that could happen. This image is designed to uncover and successfully address any anticipatory anxieties clients may have.

This technique encourages clients to face their fears and helps them and the therapists devise solutions or better coping strategies for problems that might arise. In Dan's case, he had made a significant improvement, but he still had some anticipatory anxiety about situations regarding his blended family, especially his stepdaughter. As a holiday gathering was approaching, the therapist used the float-forward technique to have Dan picture his worst fear.

> Therapist: Dan, bring up that image of sitting around the dinner table with your family. What is the worst thing that could happen?

> Dan: I see my stepdaughter making some negative comment about the way the house looks, and I just explode. And then, everybody gets mad at me for losing my temper.

[The therapist completed the rest of the procedural steps and began eye movements with this scene.]

> Dan: I feel so hurt that she would be so critical. Doesn't she know how hard I've tried to be a good provider for her mother?

[set of eye movements]

> Dan: This is weird. She is my stepdaughter, but I'm reacting to her just the way I did to my mother. She's barely out of college and I'm trying to get her approval so that I can feel good about myself.

As the processing continued, Dan realized how old and familiar this pattern was. It connected with numerous memories in which he felt he had not been good enough—situations primarily involving his mother but also including other people (e.g., at work).

After this material had been processed, Dan reported that his anxiety about the upcoming dinner had decreased. The therapist then asked him to imagine the same scene and developed a positive future template in which he responded differently to his stepdaughter's criticism.

> Dan: I see the same scene with her criticizing the house, but this time I realize that she is really just a kid, and I don't need her approval.

Again, the therapist had Dan develop the image, elicit his negative and positive cognitions, and notice which emotions were being triggered and where he felt them in his body. The therapist then used eye movements until Dan reported, very confidently, that he could handle his stepdaughter's criticism without losing his temper. Thus, the use of EMDR helped decrease his anticipatory anxiety and was an effective cognitive rehearsal.

When clients can imagine themselves successfully completing the appropriate task, they are asked to try out the new behavior between sessions. (It is recommended that when giving behavioral assignments, both therapist and client adopt an investigative stance regarding making changes. Change is hard, and the client is unlikely to be completely successful. Setting realistic expectations and giving reassurance that change is a process and not a test can help reduce client anxiety.)

ENHANCING EMDR WITH SFT

As discussed, EMDR can be very helpful to SFT/EMDR therapists. As much as EMDR can help the SFT therapist, SFT can be equally valuable for the practicing EMDR therapist. Early recognition of clients' schemas and maladaptive coping styles enhances the effectiveness of the EMDR in various ways in every stage of EMDR treatment. For example, in the EMDR phase known as *target assessment*, therapists attempt to have clients develop appropriate negative and positive cognitions specific to each problem. However, clients often do not provide "perfect" cognitions. Knowing clients' schemas can be crucial in guiding the therapist. For example, it is recommended that therapists be more lenient and supportive of clients with a defectiveness/shame schema than they might be with other clients. Trying too hard to get a perfect cognition from these clients may activate their sense of defectiveness and inhibit EMDR processing.

Similarly, during the desensitization phase, when the bilateral stimulation has commenced, therapists periodically stop the stimulation to allow clients to report what kind of processing is occurring. During these pauses, some clients will talk for an extended period. Even experienced EMDR therapists often wonder whether they should interrupt them to resume the bilateral stimulation and if so, when to do so. SFT principles make the decision much easier. For example, if a client has an emotional deprivation schema and has seldom felt heard or understood, then it is recommended that the EMDR therapists listen longer than they might normally. On the other hand, if clients are using their words to avoid unpleasant images, affect, or cognitions, then EMDR therapists are encouraged to interrupt this avoidance process and resume processing (while providing a great deal of support, of course). Thus, the way a clinician should respond while using EMDR can be greatly facilitated by a thorough knowledge of SFT.

In summary, Zajonc and Rachman were right. Cognitive information and affective information are processed in different areas of the brain (Zajonc), and alternative modes of therapy are needed to access information across various systems (Rachman). By deliberately focusing on the various ways in which clients store and process information—through the senses, cognitively, affectively, and physiologically—Young's SFT and Shapiro's EMDR are two therapies that do just that.

APPENDIX 7.A
EARLY MALADAPTIVE SCHEMAS AND SCHEMA DOMAINS[1]

Disconnection and Rejection

The expectation that one's needs for security, safety, stability, nurturance, empathy, sharing of feelings, acceptance, and respect will not be met in a predictable manner. Typical family origin is detached, cold, rejecting, withholding, lonely, explosive, unpredictable, or abusive.

1. Abandonment/Instability (AB)

The perceived instability or unreliability of those available for support and connection. Involves the sense that significant others will not be able to continue providing emotional support, connection, strength, or practical protection because they are emotionally unstable and unpredictable (e.g., angry outbursts), unreliable, or erratically present; because they will die imminently; or because they will abandon the patient in favor of someone better.

2. Mistrust/Abuse (MA)

The expectation that others will hurt, abuse, humiliate, cheat, lie, manipulate, or take advantage. Usually involves the perception that the harm is intentional or the result of unjustified and extreme negligence. May include the sense that one always ends up being cheated relative to others or "getting the short end of the stick."

3. Emotional Deprivation (ED)

Expectation that one's desire for a normal degree of emotional support will not be adequately met by others. The three major forms of deprivation are: A. Deprivation of Nurturance: Absence of attention, affection, warmth, or companionship. B. Deprivation of Empathy: Absence of understanding, listening, self-disclosure, or mutual sharing of feelings from others. C. Deprivation of Protection: Absence of strength, direction, or guidance from others.

4. Defectiveness/Shame (DS)

The feeling that one is defective, bad, unwanted, inferior, or invalid in important respects; or that one would be unlovable to significant others if exposed. May involve hypersensitivity to criticism, rejection, and blame;

---

[1]*Note.* Copyright 1998 by Jeffrey E. Young. Previously published in *Cognitive Therapy for Personality Disorders: A Schema-Focused Approach* (3rd ed.), by J. E. Young, 1999, Sarasota, FL: Professional Resource Press.

self-consciousness, comparisons, and insecurity around others; or a sense of shame regarding one's perceived flaws. These flaws may be private (e.g., selfishness, angry impulses, unacceptable sexual desires) or public (e.g., undesirable physical appearance, social awkwardness).

5. Social Isolation/Alienation (SI)

The feeling that one is isolated from the rest of the world, different from other people, and/or not part of any group or community.

Impaired Autonomy & Performance

Expectations about oneself and the environment that interfere with one's perceived ability to separate, survive, function independently, or perform successfully. Typical family origin is enmeshed, undermining of child's confidence, overprotective, or failing to reinforce child for performing competently outside the family.

6. Dependence/Incompetence (DI)

Belief that one is unable to handle one's everyday responsibilities in a competent manner, without considerable help from others (e.g., take care of oneself, solve daily problems, exercise good judgment, tackle new tasks, make good decisions). Often presents as helplessness.

7. Vulnerability to Harm or Illness (VH)

Exaggerated fear that imminent catastrophe will strike at any time and that one will be unable to prevent it. Fears focus on one or more of the following: (A) Medical Catastrophes: e.g., heart attacks, AIDS; (B) Emotional Catastrophes: e.g., going crazy; (C): External Catastrophes: e.g., elevators collapsing, victimized by criminals, airplane crashes, earthquakes.

8. Enmeshment/Undeveloped Self (EM)

Excessive emotional involvement and closeness with one or more significant others (often parents), at the expense of full individuation or normal social development. Often involves the belief that at least one of the enmeshed individuals cannot survive or be happy without the constant support of the other. May also include feelings of being smothered by, or fused with, others OR insufficient individual identity. Often experienced as a feeling of emptiness and floundering, having no direction, or in extreme cases questioning one's existence.

9. Failure (FA)

The belief that one has failed, will inevitably fail, or is fundamentally inadequate relative to one's peers, in areas of achievement (school, career, sports, etc.). Often involves beliefs that one is stupid, inept, untalented, ignorant, lower in status, less successful than others, etc.

Impaired limits. Deficiency in internal limits, responsibility to others, or long-term goal-orientation. Leads to difficulty respecting the rights of others, cooperating with others, making commitments, or setting and meeting realistic personal goals. Typical family origin is characterized by permissiveness, overindulgence, lack of direction, or a sense of superiority—rather than appropriate confrontation, discipline, and limits in relation to taking responsibility, cooperating in a reciprocal manner, and setting goals. In some cases, child may not have been pushed to tolerate normal levels of discomfort, or may not have been given adequate supervision, direction, or guidance.

10. Entitlement/Grandiosity (ET)

The belief that one is superior to other people; entitled to special rights and privileges; or not bound by the rules of reciprocity that guide normal social interaction. Often involves insistence that one should be able to do or have whatever one wants, regardless of what is realistic, what others consider reasonable, or the cost to others; OR an exaggerated focus on superiority (e.g., being among the most successful, famous, wealthy)—to achieve power or control (not primarily for attention or approval). Sometimes includes excessive competitiveness toward, or domination of, others: asserting one's power, forcing one's point of view, or controlling the behavior of others in line with one's own desires—without empathy or concern for others' needs or feelings.

11. Insufficient Self-Control/Self-Discipline (IS)

Pervasive difficulty or refusal to exercise sufficient self-control and frustration tolerance to achieve one's personal goals, or to restrain the excessive expression of one's emotions and impulses. In its milder form, patient presents with an exaggerated emphasis on discomfort-avoidance: avoiding pain, conflict, confrontation, responsibility, or overexertion—at the expense of personal fulfillment, commitment, or integrity.

Other-Directedness

An excessive focus on the desires, feelings, and responses of others, at the expense of one's own needs—in order to gain love and approval, maintain one's sense of connection, or avoid retaliation. Usually involves suppression and lack of awareness regarding one's own anger and natural inclinations. Typical family origin is based on conditional acceptance: children must suppress important aspects of themselves in order to gain love, attention, and approval. In many such families, the parents' emotional needs and desires—or social acceptance and status—are valued more than the unique needs and feelings of each child.

12. Subjugation (SB)

Excessive surrendering of control to others because one feels coerced —usually to avoid anger, retaliation, or abandonment. The two major forms of subjugation are: A. Subjugation of Needs: Suppression of one's preferences, decisions, and desires. B. Subjugation of Emotions: Suppression of emotional expression, especially anger. Usually involves the perception that one's own desires, opinions, and feelings are not valid or important to others. Frequently presents as excessive compliance, combined with hypersensitivity to feeling trapped. Generally leads to a build-up of anger, manifested in maladaptive symptoms (e.g., passive-aggressive behavior, uncontrolled outbursts of temper, psychosomatic symptoms, withdrawal of affection, "acting out," substance abuse).

13. Self-Sacrifice (SS)

Excessive focus on voluntarily meeting the needs of others in daily situations, at the expense of one's own gratification. The most common reasons are: to prevent causing pain to others; to avoid guilt from feeling selfish; or to maintain the connection with others perceived as needy. Often results from an acute sensitivity to the pain of others. Sometimes leads to a sense that one's own needs are not being adequately met and to resentment of those who are taken care of. (Overlaps with concept of co-dependency.)

14. Approval Seeking/Recognition Seeking (AS)

Excessive emphasis on gaining approval, recognition, or attention from other people, or fitting in, at the expense of developing a secure and true sense of self. One's sense of esteem is dependent primarily on the reactions of others rather than on one's own natural inclinations. Sometimes includes an overemphasis on status, appearance, social acceptance, money, or achievement—as means of gaining approval, admiration, or attention (not primarily for power or control). Frequently results in major life decisions that are inauthentic or unsatisfying; or in hypersensitivity to rejection.

Overvigilance & Inhibition

Excessive emphasis on suppressing one's spontaneous feelings, impulses, and choices OR on meeting rigid, internalized rules and expectations about performance and ethical behavior—often at the expense of happiness, self-expression, relaxation, close relationships, or health. Typical family origin is grim, demanding, and sometimes punitive: performance, duty, perfectionism, following rules, hiding emotions, and avoiding mistakes predominate over pleasure, joy, and relaxation. There is usually an undercurrent of pessimism and worry—that things could fall apart if one fails to be vigilant and careful at all times.

15. Negativity/Pessimism (NP)

A pervasive, lifelong focus on the negative aspects of life (pain, death, loss, disappointment, conflict, guilt, resentment, unsolved problems, potential mistakes, betrayal, things that could go wrong, etc.) while minimizing or neglecting the positive or optimistic aspects. Usually includes an exaggerated expectation—in a wide range of work, financial, or interpersonal situations—that things will eventually go seriously wrong, or that aspects of one's life that seem to be going well will ultimately fall apart. Usually involves an inordinate fear of making mistakes that might lead to: financial collapse, loss, humiliation, or being trapped in a bad situation. Because potential negative outcomes are exaggerated, these patients are frequently characterized by chronic worry, vigilance, complaining, or indecision.

16. Emotional Inhibition (EI)

The excessive inhibition of spontaneous action, feeling, or communication—usually to avoid disapproval by others, feelings of shame, or losing control of one's impulses. The most common areas of inhibition involve: (a) inhibition of anger & aggression; (b) inhibition of positive impulses (e.g., joy, affection, sexual excitement, play); (c) difficulty expressing vulnerability or communicating freely about one's feelings, needs, etc.; or (d) excessive emphasis on rationality while disregarding emotions.

17. Unrelenting Standards/Hypercriticalness (US)

The underlying belief that one must strive to meet very high internalized standards of behavior and performance, usually to avoid criticism. Typically results in feelings of pressure or difficulty slowing down; and in hypercriticalness toward oneself and others. Must involve significant impairment in: pleasure, relaxation, health, self-esteem, sense of accomplishment, or satisfying relationships. Unrelenting standards typically present as: (a) perfectionism, inordinate attention to detail, or an underestimate of how good one's own performance is relative to the norm; (b) rigid rules and "shoulds" in many areas of life, including unrealistically high moral, ethical, cultural, or religious precepts; or (c) preoccupation with time and efficiency, so that more can be accomplished.

18. Punitiveness (PU)

The belief that people should be harshly punished for making mistakes. Involves the tendency to be angry, intolerant, punitive, and impatient with those people (including oneself) who do not meet one's expectations or standards. Usually includes difficulty forgiving mistakes in oneself or others, because of a reluctance to consider extenuating circumstances, allow for human imperfection, or empathize with feelings.

REFERENCES

Browning, C. J. (1999, September). Floatback and float-forward: Techniques for linking past, present and future. *EMDRIA Newsletter*, pp. 12–13.

Davis, M. (1992). Analysis of aversive memories using the fear: Potentiated startle paradigm. In L. R. Squire & N. Butters (Eds.), *Neuropsychology of memory* (2nd ed.; pp. 470–484). New York: Guilford Press.

Layden, M., Newman, C., Freeman, A., & Morse, S. B. (1993). *Cognitive therapy of borderline personality disorders*. Boston: Allyn & Bacon.

Lazarus, A. A., & Lazarus, C. N. (1991). *Multimodal life history inventory*. Champaign, IL: Research Press.

LeDoux, J. E. (1989). Cognitive-emotional interactions in the brain. *Cognition and Emotion, 3*, 267–289.

Leeds, A. M. (1998). Lifting the burden of shame: Using EMDR resource installation to resolve a therapeutic impasse. In P. Manfield (Ed.), *Extending EMDR: A casebook of innovative applications* (pp. 256–282). New York: W. W. Norton.

Rachman, S. (1981). The primacy of affect: Some theoretical implications. *Behavioural Research and Therapy, 19*, 279–290.

Segal, Z. V. (1988). Appraisal of the self-schema construct in cognitive models of depression. *Psychological Bulletin, 103*, 147–162.

Shapiro, F. (1995). *Eye movement desensitization and reprocessing: Basic principles, protocols, and procedures*. New York: Guilford Press.

Watkins, J. G. (1992). *Hypnoanalytic techniques: The practice of clinical hypnosis* (Vol. 2). New York: Irvington.

Young, J. E. (1990). *Cognitive therapy for personality disorders: A schema-focused approach*. Sarasota, FL: Professional Resource Press.

Young, J. E. (1991). *Young parenting inventory*. New York: Cognitive Therapy Center of New York.

Young, J. E. (1994a). *Cognitive therapy for personality disorders: A schema-focused approach* (Rev. ed.). Sarasota FL: Professional Resource Press.

Young, J. E. (1994b). *Young parenting inventory*. New York: Cognitive Therapy Center of New York.

Young, J. E. (1999). *Cognitive therapy for personality disorders: A schema-focused approach* (3rd ed.). Sarasota, FL: Professional Resource Press.

Young, J. E., & Behary, W. E. (1998). Schema-focused therapy for personality disorders. In N. Tarrier, A. Wells, & G. Haddock (Eds.), *Treating complex cases: The cognitive behavioural therapy approach* (pp. 310–376). West Sussex, England: Wiley.

Young, J. E., & Brown, G. (1990). Young schema questionnaire. In J. E. Young, *Cognitive therapy for personality disorders: A schema-focused approach*. Sarasota, FL. Professional Resource Press.

Young, J. E., & Brown, G. (1994). Young schema questionnaire (2nd ed.). In J. E. Young, *Cognitive therapy for personality disorders: A schema-focused approach* (Rev. ed., pp. 3–76). Sarasota, FL. Professional Resource Press.

Young, J. E., & Klosko, J. (1994). *Reinventing your life*. New York: Plume.

Zajonc, R. B. (1980). Feeling and thinking: Preferences need no inferences. *American Psychologist, 35*, 151–175.

8

EMDR: AN ELEGANTLY CONCENTRATED MULTIMODAL PROCEDURE?

CLIFFORD N. LAZARUS AND ARNOLD A. LAZARUS

In the 1960s and 1970s, behavior therapy was becoming front-page glamour. Books, articles, papers, and chapters on behavioral methods and their applications were plentiful. Workshops and seminars on systematic desensitization, assertiveness training, and other behavior therapy techniques were oversubscribed. Claims for the rapid remission of a host of ills were widely circulated. Slowly, cautionary notes crept into the literature, and disclaimers were issued. Some of the renunciations centered on technical issues. For example, the major components of imaginal desensitization were questioned, such as (a) the proclaimed need for deep muscle relaxation, (b) the painstakingly crafted hierarchies, and (c) the importance of avoiding high levels of subjective units of disturbance (SUDS) that could ostensibly result in resensitization rather than desensitization. Thus, relaxation was found to be dispensable in many cases, meticulous hierarchies proved to be a waste of time, and exposure was considered to be the sine qua non for overcoming phobic disorders.

When Lazarus and his students conducted systematic follow-up inquiries, they found a disappointingly high relapse rate in many clients who had received behavior therapy, and it was argued that "cognitive restructuring" had to be added to the usual behavioral repertoires if more durable results were to be achieved. Lazarus's book *Behavior Therapy and Beyond* (1996/1971) is arguably one of the first books on what has come to be called *cognitive–behavior therapy* (CBT). London (1964) set the stage for developing cognitive–behavioral interweaves that were based on empirical support. Additional follow-up studies revealed that even CBT often has too narrow of a focus and that for various problems, additional modalities must be included if relapses are to be prevented.

For whatever reasons, eye movement desensitization and reprocessing (EMDR) has far exceeded and eclipsed the levels of widespread acclamation and denunciation that behavior therapy ever achieved, but significant revisions are already evident. For example, the use of eye movements is no longer considered essential, and other procedural steps are also not written in concrete. For instance, a couple of years ago, when we took the EMDR Level I training, therapists were encouraged to play an essentially passive role, to let "whatever happens happen" during the processing of the client's conscious phenomena. Indeed, trainees were censured if they introduced any material other than passive reassurance to the client during the processing. It was deemed important not to muddy the waters or dilute the authenticity of the information being processed. Shapiro (personal communication, November 21, 1998) explained that the "stay out of the way" order was aimed at breaking old habits of talk therapy. However, the Level II training was more proactive, and trainees were taught to take a more vigorous role in facilitating the processing and even to introduce new material to clients during the processing stage (i.e., the "cognitive interweave," which is what multimodal therapists call *providing the client with missing information* or *correcting misinformation*; e.g., Lazarus, 1989).

If systematic data on long-term follow-ups are collected across a broad spectrum of EMDR clients, it will probably be found that a fair number will remain vulnerable to untreated excesses and deficits in their cognitive and interpersonal domains. In other words, if definitive studies show that EMDR achieves a rapid attenuation of many affective reactions, it is still essential to place it in a multimodal framework so that when necessary, all relevant modalities can be addressed, and clients can emerge equipped with substantial self-management strategies. Moreover, the reported efficacy of EMDR is probably a result of it drawing on several discrete but interrelated modalities—a central feature of the multimodal orientation.

HISTORICAL ANTECEDENTS

The multimodal therapy approach was developed at a time when many innovators in the field of psychotherapy were focusing on rather narrow treatment objectives. For many years the psychoanalytic establishment stressed insight above all else. Subsequently, behavior modifiers argued for overt responses as their major domain of clinical intervention, whereas cognitive therapists focused mainly on changing dysfunctional beliefs. When Lazarus (1996/1971) underscored the synergistic properties of combining cognitive and behavioral procedures, the behavioral community reacted most unfavorably. Thereafter, thanks mainly to the pioneering efforts of Bandura (1969), Davison (1966, 1973; Davison & Valins, 1969; Davison & Wilson, 1973), Mahoney (1974), Mischel (1968), and Meichenbaum (1974), *cognition* became incorporated into mainstream behavior modification, and the term *cognitive–behavior therapy* soon became standard fare. Of course, the seminal work spearheaded by Ellis (1962) and Beck (1967) paved the way for future developments in CBT.

The emphasis throughout CBT is basically trimodal. (This also applies to Ellis's rational–emotive behavior therapy [REBT] and Beck's cognitive therapy.) The three areas traversed are affect, behavior, and cognition (ABC). On the basis of follow-up inquiries of his clients, Lazarus (1976, 1989, 1997) concluded that unless therapists transcend the ABC paradigm, many clients are likely to relapse or achieve suboptimal therapeutic gains. Gradually, the ABC range was amplified to behavior, affect, sensation, imagery, cognition, interpersonal relationships, and drugs/biological factors (BASIC ID).

Nevertheless, examination of case histories and clinical accounts by cognitive–behavioral practitioners revealed that in addition to their emphasis on affect, behavior, and cognition, they also dealt with imagery, sensation, interpersonal relationships, and biological factors. However, they regarded imagery not as a separate modality but as part of cognition. Similarly, sensation was treated as an offshoot or concomitant of affective reactions. Thus, although these modalities were taken into account, they were not systematically or thoroughly addressed. When one's clinical template explicitly spells out seven (not three) modes for assessment and possible intervention, the net result is an approach that is more comprehensive, elegant, and far reaching. Thus, multimodal therapy (MMT) spells out the need to assess BASIC ID. Clinically, in addition to focusing on problem areas in each of the foregoing modalities, examining the transactions and interactions among the different modalities is enormously beneficial.

EMDR overlaps MMT in structure and application. Not only do the protocols and eight-phase EMDR approach specifically address the primary aspects identified by MMT as necessary for successful therapy, but the procedure itself systematically accesses behavior, affect, sensation, and imagery in a highly focused and structured manner.

A primary issue in MMT, referred to as *the ripple effect*, examines the interaction among all the modalities. What impact does a specific behavior have on the other six modalities? When affective reactions occur, what impact does this have on behaviors, sensation, images, cognitions, and so forth? This interactive process can assist the EMDR therapist with investigating the clinical picture more systematically. Familiarity with MMT will enable those who use EMDR to investigate the clinical arena more fully and systematically, identify areas that may call for EMDR processing, and recognize other modalities and techniques to be incorporated for cognitive interweaves and skill enhancement.

ELEMENTS OF THE MULTIMODAL MODEL

As mentioned, the multimodal model maintains that personality comprises seven interactive and reciprocally influential dimensions or modalities, reflected by the BASIC ID acronym. The process of multimodal assessment and therapy involves identifying specific problems or symptoms within and across an individual's BASIC ID. Problem identification is usually accomplished within the first few sessions via collaboration between the therapist and client. In addition, many clients are given a comprehensive questionnaire that taps into potential problem areas within each modality (i.e., the Multimodal Life History Inventory; Lazarus & Lazarus, 1991).

After problem identification, multimodal therapists often create modality profiles that, in addition to identified problems, also include specific therapeutic recommendations across the BASIC ID profile. In terms of the selection of therapeutic methods, the multimodal position is technically eclectic and relies heavily on empirically supported interventions regardless of the technique's theoretical underpinnings (Lazarus, 1989, 1997). Thus, MMT transcends the limitations of conventional diagnostic nomenclature as well as more narrowly focused methods of psychological therapy (C. N. Lazarus, 1991). MMT and EMDR eschew diagnostic labels and focus on characteristic behavioral, affective, sensory, and cognitive responses, which then become specific targets for intervention and reprocessing respectively.

To better demonstrate these concepts, a sample modality profile of an actual client with posttraumatic stress disorder (PTSD) is presented in Table 8.1. For illustrative purposes, the data summarized in the modality profile have been simplified. Readers interested in a more thorough discussion of MMT and the use of modality profiles are urged to peruse *Brief But Comprehensive Psychotherapy: The Multimodal Way* (Lazarus, 1997).

As Table 8.1 illustrates, the primary strength of MMT is its ability to provide therapists with a more comprehensive understanding of the factors that need to be addressed. This comprehensive biopsychosocial therapeutic approach specifies highly structured ways in which to customize treatment in a personalistic model. Its combination of comprehensiveness and rigor,

TABLE 8.1
Modality Profile of a 35-Year-Old Man With PTSD (*DSM–IV*, 309.81)

Modality	Problem	Recommendation
Behavior	Avoidance	In vivo exposure
	Inactivity	Activity scheduling
Affect	Anxiety	No direct interventions*
	Panic attacks	Possible use of psycho-tropics
	Lack of confidence	Coping imagery
Sensation	Gastrointestinal distress	Relaxation training
		Diaphragmatic breathing
	Muscle tension	Sensory refocusing
		Tension/relaxation con-trasts
	Palpitations	Slow breathing exercises
		Calming self-statements
Imagery	Intrusive images of trauma	EMDR procedures
	Images of being assaulted	Various imagery exer-cises, (again including coping imagery)
Cognition	Inadequacy or failure	Various rational–emotive behavior therapy (REBT) and cognitive therapy methods**
	"I'm going to die prema-turely."	Cognitive disputation
	"Impostor syndrome"	EMDR procedures
Interpersonal	Unassertive	Assertion skills training
Drugs/biology		
	Lacks exercise	Structured exercise pro-gram
	Uses OTC antacids	Nutritional modification
		Medical check-up

The client is a corrections officer who was injured by an inmate during a riot while at work at a state prison.

*MMT views affect as the reciprocal product of the other six modalities (i.e., BASIC I.D.), and it emphasizes that the current state-of-the-art and science of psychological treatment does not allow for direct affect modification.

**REBT, a system of cognitive–behavior therapy developed by Albert Ellis, PhD, includes various methods aimed at identifying, challenging, and ultimately replacing clients' self-defeating or irrational beliefs, which are believed to lead to improved psychosocial functioning. Similarly, cognitive therapy developed by Aaron Beck, MD, is a psychotherapeutic approach that uses various collaborative methods to help clients change dysfunctional and maladaptive cognitive patterns. Examples of specific techniques a multimodal therapist might draw from REBT and cognitive therapy include rational self-talk assignments and belief change worksheets, respectively.

which emphasizes breadth and depth of treatment, can help all therapists sharpen their critical evaluation skills. It can better focus on the needed EMDR targets and highlight various ways of strengthening the protocols.

The rigorous demarcation of pivotal events in behavior coupled with the triggers and templates of the entire BASIC ID can be invaluable for broader-based EMDR applications. It is not far fetched to claim that MMT has universal applicability because all people and problems have BASIC ID determinants. Thus, MMT can be considered a model of personality in addition to a comprehensive framework for psychological assessment and treatment. Indeed, as the sample modality profile indicates, because of its empirically driven, technically eclectic stance, the multimodal model can lead to the synergistic integration of various specific therapy methods including but not limited to REBT, cognitive therapy, and EMDR. Interestingly, although EMDR was originally limited to resolving traumas of people with PTSD and other acute stress reactions, it has recently been tremendously expanded and includes other diagnostic considerations (e.g., Shapiro, 1998). Indeed, during the several years of clinical use and field testing since its inception, EMDR has claimed broad clinical efficacy. Perhaps this augmentation renders it similar to MMT, which for more than 2 decades has underscored the limitations of conventional, less systematic, narrowly focused therapies (e.g., A. A. Lazarus, 1976; C. N. Lazarus, 1991).

Another therapeutic tool, structural profiles, needs to be appreciated (see Exhibit 8.1). People tend to favor certain modalities. Thus, the terms a *sensory reactor*, an *imagery reactor*, or a *cognitive reactor* are sometimes used. These terms do not imply that people with these labels always favor or react in a given modality but that over time, they tend to gravitate toward certain response patterns. Therefore, when a person's most highly valued representational system is visual, the person is inclined to respond to the world and organize it in terms of mental images. This information is an important factor in determining where treatment should begin. The three or four favored modalities are considered, and strategies are developed accordingly. (A 35-item Structural Profile Inventory has been developed, factor analyzed, and tested for validity and reliability; see Herman, 1992a, 1992b, 1994, and Landes, 1991. However, for most practical purposes, the simple rating scale outlined in Exhibit 8.1 will suffice.)

OVERLAPPING FEATURES OF EMDR AND MMT

In a typical MMT sequence, clients recall an intrusive and disruptive memory and are asked to sit back, relax, and think about it. Assume that the structural profile indicates high sensory proclivities. When clients indicate that the untoward memory is in focus, sensory responses are probed. Clients are asked to examine each and every sensory reaction that emerges (e.g., "Right now, I can feel a fluttering in my stomach, and my neck aches and my toes are tingling."). A modality check is then conducted. Clients are asked to think about concurrent behaviors, affective responses, associated images, cognitions, and possible interpersonal connections. The SUDS may be obtained (which is based on a scale of 0 to 10). As each area is examined, it is amplified (e.g., "Let's follow those ideas [cognitions]

EXHIBIT 8.1
Structural Profile

Following are seven rating scales that pertain to various tendencies that people have. Using a scale of 0 to 6 (6 is high—it characterizes you, or you rely on it greatly; 0 means that it does not describe you, or you rarely rely on it). Please rate yourself in each of the seven areas.

1. Behavior: How active are you? How much of a doer are you? Do you like to keep busy?

    Rating: 6 5 4 3 2 1 0

2. Affect: How emotional are you? How deeply do you feel things? Are you inclined to impassioned or soul-stirring inner reactions?

    Rating: 6 5 4 3 2 1 0

3. Sensation: How much do you focus on the pleasures and pains derived from your senses? How tuned in are you to your bodily sensations—to sex, food, music, art?

    Rating: 6 5 4 3 2 1 0

4. Imagery: Do you have a vivid imagination? Do you engage in fantasy and day dreaming? Do you think in pictures?

    Rating: 6 5 4 3 2 1 0

5. Cognition: How much of a thinker are you? Do you like to analyze things, make plans, reason things through, engage in a lot of private self-talk?

    Rating: 6 5 4 3 2 1 0

6. Interpersonal: How much of a social being are you? How important are other people to you? Do you gravitate to people? Do you desire intimacy with others?

    Rating: 6 5 4 3 2 1 0

7. Drugs/biology: Are you healthy and health conscious? Do you take good care of your body and physical health? Do you avoid overeating, ingestion of unnecessary drugs, excessive amounts of alcohol, and exposure to other substances that may be harmful?

    Rating: 6 5 4 3 2 1 0

that came up, and see where they lead to, and see how they intersect with your actions, emotions, sensations, and images."). The dynamic, interactive, reciprocal model of the multimodal approach is shown in Figure 8.1.

One of the basic beliefs evident in EMDR components involves the importance of associated imagery. Shapiro (1995) wrote, "Clinicians can often recognize important dysfunctional beliefs by determining what these associated memories have in common" (p. 78). Lazarus (1989) pointed out that, "As each image is attended to, the mosaic may begin to take shape, and some clients will report significant self-revelations" (p. 242). EMDR

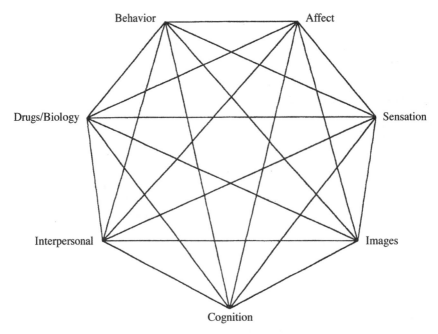

Figure 8.1. The seven major modalities of personality functioning.

emphasizes the need to focus on specific antecedent events that may have triggered untoward emotions, which is then followed by paying close attention to dominant physical sensations, predominant emotions, changes in imagery, changes in cognition, and various differential effects (Shapiro, 1995, pp. 78–88). At the very outset, the degree of overlap between EMDR and MMT is compelling (Lazarus, 1989, pp. 13–18).

Typically, EMDR therapists do not intercede very actively in clients' associated imagery, nor do they energetically question or try to intervene or modify sensory reactions or affective responses (although as discussed previously, advanced EMDR therapists are taught to "weave" in therapeutically facilitative cognitive material when faced with blocked or looped processing). However, when EMDR is not proceeding well or achieving its desired effect, the well-trained multimodal therapist shifts gears and uses a different method. Following is a clinical example (excerpted from Lazarus, 1984) in which associated imagery was the mainstay. Note the overlap with EMDR and the technical and procedural differences. What follows is a way to aid therapists in accessing previous events that (in EMDR vernacular) "need processing" and that offers a cognitive interweave for processing that has become stalled.

> Jeff: I've still been feeling uptight and depressed. I don't know what's gotten into me. I'm not doing my work properly, and everything's going to pieces.
>
> Therapist: Well, we have certainly looked into all sorts of reasons

	behind your anxiety and tension, and we have tried various methods to help you conquer your fears. Often the use of imagery helps where all other things have failed.
Jeff:	What do you mean?
Therapist:	Let me show you. Just sit back comfortably, try to relax, let your body get loose and heavy, take a few deep breaths, let the air in and out. Close your eyes, and try to imagine yourself somewhere, doing something that makes you feel very calm and peaceful. Take your time. (pause of about 1 min) What's happening? Your breathing seems to be slow and even and you appear to be relaxed. What were you picturing?
Jeff:	(opens eyes) For some reason, I saw myself on a farm watching some people milking the cows, and a lot of other pictures went flashing through my mind.
Therapist:	Such as?
Jeff:	I can't remember most of them, but a lot of things that I did as a kid came back to me. I used to love working on the farm.
Therapist:	Let's try a simple experiment. Can you get into your uptight, anxious, and depressed feelings? Try to make yourself feel really tense.
Jeff:	That's very easy for me! (after a few moments) I can feel it now. I've even got butterflies in my stomach.
Therapist:	How did you bring on the negative feelings? What ideas, thoughts, images, or pictures did you focus on?
Jeff:	I don't know.
Therapist:	(smiling) Come on. You must have thought about something. Did you think about milking cows?
Jeff:	No. (pause) I guess I just thought about being anxious, about falling apart. I wasn't thinking about anything specific.
Therapist:	Get back into those anxious feelings. Let them grow really strong. (pause) Now, as you are feeling really uptight, flash back to any scene in your past. Quick. What do you see?
Jeff:	Do you know what came to mind? For some reason I thought about the pony my father bought me when I was 10. Now what can you make of that?
Therapist:	Picture the pony as clearly as you can. Close your eyes and visualize the pony.

Jeff:	(becoming visibly upset) The pony broke his leg and they had to destroy him.
Therapist:	Are you talking about an image?
Jeff:	(weeping) No. It really happened. My oldest brother was riding him, and the pony stepped into a pothole. I'm feeling terribly anxious right now.
Therapist:	We might be on to something. Try to picture your brother riding the pony. What images do you see?
Jeff:	I can't picture that. I just draw a blank.
Therapist:	Just let yourself relax. Sit back in the chair. Let go of the tension. Breathe in and out, and each time you breathe out, feel the tension leaving your body. (30-s pause) *Now try to picture your brother riding the pony.*
Jeff:	(long pause)
Therapist:	What images do you see?
Jeff:	It's most peculiar. I can't get a clear picture of my brother. I imagine him on the pony, and then I suddenly see myself riding it. We sort of alternate.
Therapist:	Do you ever merge?
Jeff:	How do you mean?
Therapist:	In the image, are you unable to separate yourself from your brother?
Jeff:	I don't know. It's not very clear.
Therapist:	Let's try it again. Take your time, relax, settle down, breathe easy, and then try to picture your brother riding the pony.
Jeff:	(after about 30 seconds, opens eyes) Yes, we do merge. I fade in and out, and so does my brother. It's hard to tell if it's me or my brother on the pony.
Therapist:	Are we talking about the brother that died several years ago?
Jeff:	Yes. My oldest brother.
Therapist:	Let's see. He was 8 years older than you?
Jeff:	That's right. My other brothers are 6 years and 4 years younger than me. I don't see where this is leading, and I don't mean to change the subject, but I should mention that I'm feeling quite sick.
Therapist:	Where are you feeling ill?

Jeff: My head hurts, I feel dizzy, and my chest feels tight.

Therapist: Yes, you look and sound upset and anxious. But I have more than a hunch about what is going on with you. Just bear with me. How old was your brother when he died?

Jeff: Fifty-two when he had a heart attack.

Therapist: And you are now 51 years old?

Jeff: So?

Therapist: Why do you think you merged with your brother in the imagery exercise?

Jeff: What are you driving at?

Therapist: Well, we've been totally unable to explain why you suddenly started feeling anxious and depressed a few months ago. There seems to be no logical reason for it. Everything seems to be going well with you, but over the past months you have been feeling more and more upset, uptight, miserable . . .

Jeff: And you think it's tied in with my brother?

Therapist: Well, do you have any sort of gut reaction to this idea? Perhaps in many ways you overidentified with your older brother. I think that you have emulated him in many ways. Anyway, he died at 52 from a heart attack, and I think that a part of you believes that your destiny is tied up with his and that you will go the same way when you reach 52.

Jeff: That's why I'm so anxious?

Therapist: Does it sound far fetched?

Jeff: I don't know. I mean I can't say "yes" or "no."

Therapist: Let's try out some more imagery. Try to close your eyes, and relax as best as you can. (pause of about 40 s) Now picture your brother standing in front of you. See him as clearly, as vividly as possible.

Jeff: (after about 30 seconds) I can't! I think you're right. I keep seeing him change into me or me into him. Say, if this is the problem, how can I cope with it?

Therapist: Let's start with simple exercises. Relax again, close your eyes, and keep on saying inwardly to yourself over and over again: "I am not my brother; I am myself." Do this now for a few minutes.

Jeff: (after about a minute) You know, it does make me feel less anxious.

As additional facts emerged, the initial hypothesis had to be extended. Still, the imagery methods formed the thin end of a wedge that pried open a basic reason for Jeff's persistent anxiety. Imagery can often bypass verbal roadblocks and get to the root of the issue. Imagery methods can enable a therapist to side step cognitive barriers and misleading verbiage. In Jeff's case, it could probably have been advantageous at various points to use SUDS, which was devised by Wolpe and Lazarus (1966) and has become a routine measure in EMDR. Nevertheless, perhaps the most central question is whether some form of rhythm or bilateral stimulation (e.g., eye movements, alternating auditory stimulation, left-right tapping) may have enhanced, heightened, or accelerated the treatment process. According to the EMDR explanatory model (e.g., Shapiro, 1998), some form of bilateral stimulation may be necessary to produce neuronal bursts, which may accelerate the processing of salient information toward adaptive resolution. An alternative explanation is that the rhythmic stimulation in EMDR functions as an attentional focus similar to that used in hypnosis, which allows for heightened suggestibility through adaptive ideation and imagery. Perhaps future research using neuroimaging methods such as positron emission tomography (PET) or functional magnetic resonance imaging (FMRI) will address these issues.

The power of focused interventions should be underscored. Before the advent of behavior therapy, when clients complained of having phobic reactions, the most usual responses from therapists were to (a) interpret them, (b) empathize with the clients, and (c) perhaps recommend in vivo exposure. On the other hand, when using Wolpe's systematic desensitization, the phobic components were carefully dissected and placed in a meticulously constructed hierarchy and treated step by step. Most people with phobias reported rapid remission, and therapists were equipped with an efficient tool. Likewise, the concentrated, repetitive, and systematic EMDR procedure provides a highly focused sequence. Far from glossing over traumatic sequelae and symptomatic concerns, EMDR uses them as a starting point and assiduously addresses attendant associations. Herein seems to lie much of the power behind the method.

EMDR AND MMT CASE STUDY

Marge was a 22-year-old White, single woman who lived alone in an apartment and held a job as a college intake coordinator. She was referred to me (C. N. Lazarus) by a physician who said that she had medical complaints for which he could find no organic basis. As an interim measure, he had prescribed 0.25 of Xanax to be taken 3 times a day, but Marge had not taken any because she disliked taking what she regarded as unnecessary drugs. It was evident that Marge was highly anxious. A discussion with her revealed that she satisfied most generalized anxiety disorder (GAD) criteria in the fourth edition of the *Diagnostic and Statistical Manual (DSM–IV)*. She was highly irritable, constantly felt "on edge," easily fatigued, and tense, and she experienced restless sleep and frequent nightmares. These problems had developed about 10 months previously. When asked, Marge was unable to identify what had precipitated the problems and what had occurred 10 months before she sought treatment.

Marge filled out the Multimodal Life History Inventory (Lazarus & Lazarus, 1991), which yielded distinct problems across her BASIC ID. Most noteworthy were avoidant behaviors (procrastination), panic reactions, and a host of unpleasant sensory responses such as aches, pains, trembling, dizziness, and palpitations. Her nightmares usually involved faceless assailants cornering her. Marge was apt to think in all-or-none terms and to embrace perfectionistic standards. Socially, she had always been awkward and reticent. All of her few sexual experiences had been physically uncomfortable.

An obvious starting point, given her tension, irritability, and sensory discomforts, seemed to be relaxation training. A simple progressive sequence involving rhythmic diaphragmatic breathing and calming self-statements evoked an unexpected response. She started hyperventilating and began weeping. When she calmed down, she confided that she had been raped 10 months ago and described the traumatic components that made her fear for her life. It became evident that in addition to a GAD, Marge also had PTSD. Consequently, I discussed with Marge various methods and techniques that might prove helpful, including EMDR.

At our third meeting, Marge announced that she was going to be in Philadelphia for about 2 months for a clerical training course that would be followed by a recruitment assignment at a different campus. She asked if it would be all right to resume therapy after that time. When she returned, she said that she had consulted a social worker who was trained in EMDR and had received four 90-minute sessions that focused on her rape. She described it as "a weird and wonderful experience," contended that she had been "purged of the rape," and said that her nightmares, irritability, and sensory discomforts had abated. Nevertheless, she remained basically tense, a perfectionist, and socially reticent. EMDR processing of a primary event is not considered to be a complete treatment. Even after major traumas and allied issues have been resolved, other problems surely need to be addressed.

By this time, Marge was responsive to and ready for relaxation therapy, cognitive restructuring, and social skills training. She proved to be a quick learner—facile, highly motivated, proficient, and willing to take emotional risks. She achieved significant gains in eight sessions. Thus, using a football analogy, EMDR got her well beyond midfield, but EMDR plus MMT took her into the end zone. Indeed, it has been our experience that MMT and EMDR may work synergistically to enhance the efficacy of the individual approaches.

CONCLUSION

The active ingredients of many therapeutic processes remain open to conjecture. Regardless of what actually underlies the putative benefits of EMDR, its degree of overlap with many of the MMT features and components is noteworthy. In essence, EMDR is a highly systematized, elegant therapeutic package using many of the same modalities that comprise MMT. Be that as it may, MMT methods are broader and more comprehensive than the EMDR methodology. EMDR is thought of as an accelerated and facilitated information-processing therapy (Shapiro, 1998), whereas MMT is considered a theory of personality as well as a system for implementing comprehensive biopsychosocial therapy. MMT therapists can probably enhance their treatment outcomes by knowing when and how to apply EMDR, and EMDR therapists would be well advised to become proficient with the MMT framework and its many applications.

REFERENCES

Bandura, A. (1969). *Principles of behavior modification*. New York: Holt, Rinehart, & Winston.

Beck, A. T. (1967). *Depression*. New York: Hoeber-Harper.

Davison, G. C. (1966). *Differential relaxation and cognitive restructuring in therapy with a paranoid schizophrenic or paranoid state*. Proceedings of the 74th annual convention of the American Psychological Association, Washington, DC.

Davison, G. C. (1973). Counter control in behavior modification. In L. A. Hamerlynck, L. C. Handy, & E. J. Mash (Eds.), *Behavior change: Methodology, concepts, and practice* (pp. 153–167). Champaign, IL: Research Press.

Davison, G. C., & Valins, S. (1969). Maintenance of self-attributed and drug-attributed behavior change. *Journal of Personality and Social Psychology, 11*, 25–33.

Davison, G. C., & Wilson, G. T. (1973). Processes of fear-reduction in systematic desensitization: Cognitive and social reinforcement factors in humans. *Behavior Therapy, 4*, 1–21.

Ellis, A. (1962). *Reason and emotion in psychotherapy*. Secaucus, NJ: Citadel.

Herman, S. M. (1992a). A demonstration of the validity of the multimodal structural profile inventory through a correlation with the vocational preference inventory. *Psychotherapy in Private Practice, 11*, 71–80.

Herman, S. M. (1992b). Structural profile inventories: An exploratory study. *Psychotherapy in Private Practice, 11*, 85–100.

Herman, S. M. (1994). The diagnostic utility of the multimodal structural profile inventory. *Psychotherapy in Private Practice, 13*, 55–62.

Landes, A. A. (1991). Development of the structural profile inventory. *Psychotherapy in Private Practice, 9*, 123–141.

Lazarus, A. A. (1976). *Multimodal behavior therapy.* New York: Springer.

Lazarus, A. A. (1984). *In the mind's eye.* New York: Guilford Press.

Lazarus, A. A. (1989). *The practice of multimodal therapy.* Baltimore, MD: Johns Hopkins University Press.

Lazarus, A. A. (1996). *Behavior therapy and beyond.* New York: McGraw-Hill. (Original work published 1971)

Lazarus, A. A. (1997). *Brief but comprehensive psychotherapy: The multimodal way.* New York: Springer.

Lazarus, A. A., & Lazarus, C. N. (1991). *Multimodal Life History Inventory.* Champaign, IL: Research Press.

Lazarus, C. N. (1991). Conventional diagnostic nomenclature versus multimodal assessment. *Psychological Reports, 68*, 1363–1367.

London, P. (1964). *The modes and morals of psychotherapy.* New York: Holt, Rinehart, & Winston.

Mahoney, M. J. (1974). *Cognition and behavior modification.* Cambridge: Ballinger.

Meichenbaum, D. H. (1974). *Cognitive behavior modification.* Morristown, NJ: General Learning Press.

Mischel, W. (1968). *Personality and assessment.* New York: Swiley.

Shapiro, F. (1995). *Eye movement desensitization and reprocessing.* New York: Guilford Press.

Shapiro, F. (1998). *Eye movement desensitization and reprocessing: Level II training manual* (Rev. ed.). Pacific Grove, CA: EMDR Institute.

Wolpe, J., & Lazarus, A. A. (1966). *Behavior therapy techniques.* New York: Pergamon.

9

EMDR AND HYPNOSIS

STEPHEN GILLIGAN

During the past decade, EMDR has emerged as a very promising therapeutic approach for treating trauma-related problems (Shapiro, 1995; Shapiro & Forrest, 1997). It seems to allow for the integrated processing of experiential learning that has been "stuck" or "frozen" in the course of a person's experience. Although its effectiveness seems clear, many questions still remain regarding the way it works and its relationship to other therapeutic modalities. This chapter examines whether EMDR is related to a hypnotic trance and whether hypnotic forms of treatment can be used in conjunction with EMDR.

The chapter begins with a case description. General comments are made regarding the approaches of direct hypnosis, Ericksonian hypnosis, and EMDR. These three approaches are compared on three levels. Level 1 involves a special learning state that is activated when identity is destabilized. Level 2 is a symbolic–procedural level that frames the way this learning state is understood and formally developed. Level 3 involves the larger context (e.g., psychotherapy) in which the special state is used. Although all three approaches share the special learning state of Level 1, EMDR and Ericksonian hypnosis differ markedly from direct hypnosis at Levels 2 and 3. From these comparisons, a general model is proposed of the way identity moves through cycles of stability and instability during its growth and development and the role of trauma and trauma-related therapies in this growth process. The original case is then used as an example of the way Ericksonian trance work and EMDR can be woven together during clinical treatment.

CASE STUDY

Greg was a 27-year-old, college-educated man who called me for an appointment after reading an article I wrote for a local newspaper. He said that he lacked confidence and felt depressed about his life in general. He had a dead-end secretarial job at a large corporate office and few social connections. He was the youngest of four boys and grew up in an Irish-Catholic family in the Midwest. Both parents had alcoholism problems and were abusive to each other and their children; a great deal of physical violence erupted on "bad nights." Communication was often bizarre and unpredictable. Part of Greg's response was to develop dissociative skills so that he could "go away somewhere" while sitting in his room.

Greg was initially very anxious and afraid. He had only recently had (2 months previously) his first therapy experience with a psychiatrist, whose name he picked out of the phone book. The psychiatrist, described by Greg as aloof and judgmental, told Greg that he had severe characterological disorders and that long-term therapy would be needed. After eight sessions with the psychiatrist, Greg found himself more confused, frustrated, and disoriented. He wondered whether he was going crazy and asked if he could come in and talk with me about it. After suggesting that he notify his therapist he was doing this, I scheduled an appointment with him.

In the initial sessions, Greg was extremely self-critical. He described himself as "a loser," a "chickenshit," and a "fuckup." It took him a while to declare his goals for therapy, which included getting a better job, making better social connections (especially with women), and improving his feelings of self-worth.

THREE APPROACHES TO HEALING TRAUMAS

Three therapists with three distinct approaches—direct hypnosis, Ericksonian hypnosis, and EMDR—would all respond to this case uniquely. The following discussion compares and contrasts these approaches and examines whether they can be integrated.

Direct Hypnosis

Hypnosis is the mother of all modern treatment modalities (Ellenberger, 1970). Starting in the late 18th century with Mesmer; moving

10

EMDR AND EXPERIENTIAL PSYCHOTHERAPY

ARTHUR C. BOHART AND LESLIE GREENBERG

For both EMDR and experiential approaches, psychotherapy is *facilitated client self-healing*. Therapists supply interaction and procedures, but the steps of healing are generated by and emerge from the client's process. EMDR and experiential therapists would agree with Orlinsky, Grawe, and Parks (1994), who said, "we view psychotherapy as 'the activation through the process of interpersonal communication of a powerful endogenous therapeutic system that is part of the psychophysiology of all individuals and the sociophysiology of relationships (Kleinman, 1988, p. 112)" (p. 278). Based on our experience, EMDR and experiential psychotherapy have many things in common. EMDR, in many cases, seems to be quite efficient in facilitating the operation of self-healing processes found in experiential psychologies. In addition, because it can work quite rapidly, some of the self-healing processes found in experiential therapy seem to telescope so that they can be more clearly observed and studied.

This chapter compares EMDR with three experiential approaches. Although various experiential approaches exist, the chapter concentrates

We would like to thank Eugene Gendlin for reading the initial drafts and for his helpful comments on our presentation of his theories.

on Gendlin's (1996) *focusing-oriented psychotherapy* (FP), Rogers's (Bozarth, 1998) *client-centered therapy* (CCT), and Greenberg and colleagues' (Greenberg & Paivio, 1997; Greenberg, Rice, & Elliott, 1993) *process-experiential psychotherapy* (PEP) to explore similarities and differences. The exploration begins with an introduction of each approach to orient the reader.

CLIENT-CENTERED THERAPY

CCT exists both as a philosophical approach and as a particular method. As a philosophical approach, the therapist's goal is to provide a respectful, warm, empathic, and genuine *relationship*. Therapy is not intervention and is not instrumental; the therapist is not trying to make anything *happen* with the client. In fact, toward the end of his life, Rogers emphasized the genuineness of the encounter between therapist and client. He noted that in most real moments of therapy, he was not motivated to help but rather to meet the other person. "I've learned through my experience that when we can meet, then help does occur, but that's a by-product" (Rogers, in Cissna & Anderson, 1994, p. 28).

As a particular method, traditional CCT relies on a particular mode of responding. Therapists devote careful attention to what the clients are saying, try to understand, and check their understanding with empathic reflections. Originally, the responses used to check understanding were called "reflections of feeling." However, this was not an accurate term. Several research studies have found that the responses focused more on meaning than on feeling (Bohart & Greenberg, 1997). Empathic reflections are also more than paraphrasing. Usually, good empathic reflections go beyond clients' words and try to capture the gist of what they are saying. Empathic reflections help clients attend to their experience—explore it and formulate it in ways that help them empathetically understand and accept themselves, thereby helping rid themselves of dysfunctional beliefs and emotions such as shame. Empathic reflections also support the clients' own creative thinking process.

FOCUSING-ORIENTED PSYCHOTHERAPY

Focusing is a way of relating to bodily felt meanings. The process is basically one of paying attention to the middle of the body and then receptively "listening" to what comes up. Leijssen (1998) noted the following:

Therapy is restoring contact with the meaning–feeling body in which existence manifests itself, a process in which the arrested experience is touched upon again so that it can once more start moving and reveal and further unfold itself to complete its meaning. The implicit organismic experiencing, which the client feels but cannot yet express, must at one time or another become the object of attention in therapy. (p. 123)

For clients who cannot do this naturally, a training process has been devised (Gendlin, 1996). In Gendlin's FP, other techniques and procedures may be used, but their usefulness is always checked against the client's bodily felt sense. For instance, the therapist may encourage the client to imagine using a new skill, as is done in behavior therapy. However, the focus would be on the bodily felt sense the client gets while imagining using the skill. The therapist may also offer observations or alternative perspectives. However, if they do not resonate with the client's bodily felt sense of the problem, they are not pursued.

PROCESS-EXPERIENTIAL PSYCHOTHERAPY

In PEP, the therapist suggests specific tasks or procedures at specific points in the therapy process that are called *markers*. Markers are signs that the client is stuck in the processing. Three of the major tasks and their resolutions are briefly described in the following paragraphs.

First, clients may be stuck in a *split*—caught between wanting or not wanting to do something on the one hand and a self-critical *should* voice on the other. For instance, clients who want to quit their job may have a *should* voice that tells them it is irresponsible or criticizes them for being incompetent. In the *two-chair task*, clients are asked to separate the two sides of the self. The self-critical side is placed in one chair and initiates a dialogue with the other side. Therapists encourage clients to change chairs, role playing both sides. Therapists facilitate the process by encouraging clients to focus on and express feelings, wants, and needs. Gradually, the dialogue shifts. The critical side softens and shifts from saying "you should" to expressing values and fears (e.g., "I'm afraid for you"). The other side is able to move out of a defensive posture, and the two sides work toward integration.

If clients have unfinished business with a significant other, therapists have the clients sit in one chair and express their feelings, imagining that the other person is in the other chair. Then the clients change chairs and role play the other person's side. Therapists attempt to heighten feelings and help clients move from expressing secondary emotions (such as anger) to more primary emotions (such as hurt and vulnerability). After accessing primary emotions, clients become more self-accepting and assertive.

If clients are experiencing a "problematic reaction point" in which they are puzzled by one of their actions or emotional responses, therapists ask them to imagine themselves back into the scene where the puzzling emotional or behavioral reaction occurred. Then therapists help clients explore that scene vividly, going back and forth from the scene to clients' feelings, and back to the scene until a *meaning* bridge occurs and the clients suddenly recognize or understand why they had that reaction. This recognition is direct and experiential, not intellectual and conceptual. It can branch out and allow recognitions in other areas as well.

SELF-HEALING

Although all the approaches share an emphasis on self-healing, EMDR is most phenotypically similar to, first, Gendlin's FP, and second, Rogers's CCT. In all three a stepwise process that leads to naturally occurring "organic" evolution occurs. This process occurs with minimal therapist intervention and includes whatever components the client needs to resolve problematic experiences. The therapist in Greenberg's PEP intervenes more systematically. However, at a genotypic level, the underlying process of change in EMDR and PEP is similar. Both work by accessing and working with strong emotional experiences that have heretofore been disconnected and stored in the "emotional brain" (Greenberg & Paivio, 1997). This process allows more adaptive emotions to emerge (e.g., anger toward a violent childhood perpetrator instead of fear) and corrects dysfunctional beliefs (e.g., changes "I'm bad and shameful" to "I'm okay, and I'm not going to let someone abuse me like this again"). Following are examples of ways client self-healing occurs during EMDR and experiential therapy.

EMDR

Clients start by focusing on a scene involving bad feelings while keeping in mind an associated dysfunctional cognition attending to the way their body feels. They are then asked to follow the therapist's fingers (or other forms of bilateral stimulation, such as alternate tapping of the hands). The next step is guided by "what comes up" for the client. This may be an intensification of the emotion, a new part of the image, a blurring of the image, new thoughts, new emotions, new images, or new memories. The client is then told to "go with that." The process is repeated. What emerges as steps may be totally surprising and unexpected compared with the way the clients and therapists initially construe a problem. No invariant sequence exists, nor is it necessary that specific elements be included. Thus, a person may move to a resolution without accessing heavy emotions or specifically gaining a new perspective or insight.

One example involves a woman named Emily (Shapiro & Forrest,

1997). Emily sought therapy because she was having difficulty conceiving. She had been repeatedly tested and examined by physicians, and nothing could be found to be wrong. Emily had been sexually abused by her father, but she already had spent a good deal of time dealing with that in previous therapy, and it was at least partially resolved. During initial sessions, the therapist and Emily reviewed these abuse issues. Emily reported that she had also been raped by a coworker when she was age 20 at the hospital where she worked. The therapist wondered whether the rape or the childhood abuse had something to do with Emily's problem conceiving, but Emily did not seem bothered by these events. In fact, it was not the rape that bothered her so much as the way she was treated by her employers afterward. When she reported the rape, they did not initially believe her. They ordered her to see a staff psychiatrist. Emily was vague about what happened with the psychiatrist.

Emily reported that as much as she wanted to have children, she sometimes had a hard time being around them. She said that it might be because she was afraid she would molest them. This idea was what her psychiatrist had told her—it was a "medical fact" that people who were abused as children abuse their own children. The psychiatrist suggested that she never have children. Emily reported that intellectually she did not believe the psychiatrist. She researched the psychiatrist's statement and found little evidence to back it up. Nonetheless, she believed it emotionally.

At this point, the therapist started using eye movements with Emily. She had Emily focus on the scene in the psychiatrist's office. Emily relived this scene, where she had felt so sick that she had thrown up. She reported feeling sick during the EMDR. Then, as the sets of eye movements continued, she shifted from feeling sick, to feeling fear, to moaning and crying, to feeling a total loss of hope. She said, "It's like someone took my dreams and hopes and pulled them right out from under me. I wasn't the same after that" (Shapiro & Forrest, 1997, p. 62). Then, during the next set of eye movements, Emily experienced a flood of anger. She shouted out that the psychiatrist abused her. The therapist directed her to "stay with that" and initiated another set of eye movements. Next she experienced a flood of anger at her employers for making her go to the psychiatrist. After several more sets, Emily said, "How could I have believed her?" (p. 63). Finally, as they continued talking, Emily's emotions subsided. She then firmly said, "It's just not in me" (p. 63). She then rated the statement "I would never molest my children" as completely true on a 7-point scale. About 3 weeks later, Emily conceived.

In sum, the process moved from a reliving of the incident—which included the feeling of being sick—into fear, total despair, and then anger. The anger was experienced and expressed first toward the psychiatrist and then toward the hospital personnel. The process then moved into an evaluation stage in which Emily realized that she did not have to believe the psychiatrist. She then moved into a state in which she felt in her gut that she was not capable of abusing a child.

FP

A similar process is involved in Gendlin's (1996) FP. The focusing procedure is perhaps the closest analog in experiential therapy to the EMDR procedure. Following is a quote from Leijssen (1998):

> A 32-year-old woman has been depressed since the birth of her child 3 years ago. She has read a great deal about postnatal depression, but the explanations don't touch her. She thinks, "that is probably what I have," but doesn't feel that it fits. The therapist invites her to stop looking for explanations, to direct her attention toward the center of her body and remain with the question "what is really the matter with me?" Tears well up in her eyes. She wants to give an explanation for it, but the therapist encourages her to wait and remain silently attentive to her body. She spontaneously crosses her arms over the region of her abdomen and heart. The therapist lets her fully feel this gesture. Suddenly an image appears of her little daughter being carried away immediately after birth. "I don't want them to take away my daughter!" she shouts. This verbal expression is obviously right; her body recognizes that this is it, and it obviously relieves her to repeat the expression several times. But that is not all yet; further tension remains in her body. The therapist asks her to keep her attention on her body and to see what else there is. Then she sees herself standing behind glass with, in the distance, her baby in the incubator. She despairs deeply of ever being able to reach the helpless little being in the distance; she cries but with pain and anger at the gynecologist ... She now discovers that she was forced to accept the situation of leaving the child behind in the maternity ward. When, 2 weeks later, she was allowed to take the baby home, it "wasn't hers anymore." Although these were painful experiences, she now feels very relieved when bringing them into the open. For 3 years her body has carried this along without finding a proper expression for it. The woman herself had "forgotten" the events, but her body kept carrying them in the form of a depression. Now that this bodily knowledge has been opened up, the woman feels liberated. Her energy returns and, for the first time, she feels love for her daughter. (p. 122)

CCT

When one of us (A. Bohart) first saw a film of Shapiro performing an EMDR session, it reminded him of CCT except that the therapist used fingers instead of empathic responses. In CCT, clients' unfolding stepwise process is tracked by the therapist's empathic reflections. A good example is the well-known case of Gloria (Shostrom, 1965). Gloria's presenting problem was that she has lied to her daughter about her sex life, and she wanted to know if that would harm her daughter. Carl Rogers empathically listened and reflected, and Gloria moved step by step through a series of content areas, deepening her exploration as she went. Eventually she talked about a basic sense of what it was like to feel split and the problems involved in knowing when a decision is the right one. Then there was a spontaneous emergence of a completely new and apparently unrelated topic. (This was how much she liked talking to Rogers, who was so accepting, compared with her father, who was not.) This new topic led to a discussion of her feelings toward her father and her longing for someone to accept her like she wished her father had, and she had an intensely emotional moment.

Gloria did not stay on any one problem topic or approach her problem in a systematic, problem-solving way. Yet the flow of topics had an organic, or emotional, logic, similar to the flow in EMDR. Retrospectively the logic becomes clear: In various forms, Gloria is dealing with issues of self-trust and self-acceptance that are embedded in various concrete issues in her life. However, as Gendlin (1990) pointed out, it is unlikely anyone could have predicted the development of Gloria's process in advance. Yet ultimately the process was worthwhile (Bozarth, 1998). Gloria did decide to be honest with her daughter and had positive results (J. Shlien, personal communication, February, 1998).

PEP

The stepwise unfolding process that occurs for Emily during EMDR with minimal therapist intervention resembles the stepwise unfolding process noted in both FP and CCT. At a more genotypic level, the case of Emily also resembles the change process in PEP. Emily starts out feeling self-disgust (she feels sick) and fear. After she accesses these emotions, she accesses a new, more adaptive emotion of anger toward her coworkers for making her go to therapy and toward the psychiatrist. This new, more adaptive emotion leads her to spontaneously restructure her cognitions, and she shifts from believing that she could abuse her child to knowing that she would not abuse her child.

This case is similar to one reported by Greenberg and Paivio (1997). The client was a young woman who sought therapy because of relationship problems. She had been both sexually and physically abused by her parents, who had problems with alcoholism. She had been responsible for her younger siblings. She had physically abused them and had even sexually fondled her younger brother. She felt intense shame about this and thought that she "should have known better." As the therapist accessed this feeling of shame, she was able to access the pain and regret she felt about the incident and a strong positive feeling that she wanted to do the right thing. This experience helped her challenge her negative self-beliefs and move toward a more positive self-image. Later, she also accessed anger toward her parents, and this helped her further restructure her self-blame that told her she should have known better. By the end of therapy, she was sure that her regret was genuine and that she would not do such an act now. As with the case of Emily, the process moved from initial access of negative feelings, to access of more adaptive feelings, and ultimately to restructuring of dysfunctional self-beliefs.

Nature of Self-Healing

All approaches to psychotherapy ultimately rely on client self-healing (Bohart & Tallman, 1999). However, EMDR and experiential therapy place the client's self-healing process at the center of therapy. Procedures are in its service and operate primarily by helping "unstick" these processes. Clients generate the form and direction of the steps they need to move toward healing and provide the energy and investment to make the process work. They also create the solutions.

In contrast, in other approaches such as psychodynamic, cognitive, and behavioral therapies, client self-healing processes operate primarily by implementing therapist-provided corrective feedback: The therapist sets the direction of the healing and decides on the kinds of changes clients need to make. In psychoanalysis, therapists correct clients' dysfunctional modes of self-relating by providing them with corrective information in the form of interpretations. In cognitive therapy, therapists identify clients' dysfunctional beliefs and then like good teachers, provide a corrective dialogue and exercises designed to alter these dysfunctional beliefs. In behavior therapy, therapists correct dysfunctional client modes of experiencing through the use of exposure or conditioning procedures and correct dysfunctional client skills through retraining. In all of these types of therapy, therapists identify what is wrong and provide external feedback or input.

The difference between EMDR and experiential psychotherapy on the one hand and psychodynamic, cognitive, and behavioral therapies on the other is a relative one. As noted, all therapies ultimately rely on client self-healing. Nevertheless, experiential and EMDR therapists have a similar emphasis on self-healing. Following is a review of the theoretical views of self-healing and psychopathology in EMDR and experiential psychotherapy.

EMDR

EMDR's emphasis on self-healing is captured in a quote from Shapiro (1995): "There is a system inherent in all of us that is physiologically geared to process information to a state of mental health" (p. 13). Shapiro noted that this principle is derived from her application of the EMDR procedure and the results she has observed. Pathology occurs when this self-healing processing system's operation becomes blocked. EMDR is a "primarily client-centered model, which assumes that the client's shifting cognitions and levels of affect during an EMDR treatment will move to an optimal level with minimal clinician intrusion" (p. 15).

In the basic-level EMDR procedure, therapists essentially give *no* corrective feedback, suggestions, training, or instructions to clients about how to improve their behavior or ways of thinking. Instead, therapists provide a supportive prosthetic (bilateral stimulation) to facilitate the natural self-healing process. In this context, Shapiro (1995) estimated that 40% to 50% of clients are able to achieve resolution on their own. The remaining 50% to 60% of clients get stuck in their information processing and require additional assistance to move forward. This assistance, in the form of the cognitive interweave, is still relatively minimal and is an attempt to supply pieces that are missing. Shapiro explained that the things she does during the cognitive interweave are based on observations of what many clients do naturally on their own. In the cognitive interweave, brief suggestions or bits of information are provided, not so much to "correct" clients' perceptions as to shift their information processing so that it can continue on its naturally occurring self-healing course.

Shapiro offers a neuropsychological model of what she calls the *accelerated information processing* that occurs as a result of EMDR. In Shapiro's view, pathology results from memories and their associated negative cognitions and affects, which are stored in their own encapsulated neurological networks, isolated from more adaptive information. In particular, trauma is stored in nondeclarative memory in the form of images and sensations. EMDR accelerates information processing so that nondeclarative memory gets transferred and associated with declarative memory. In Shapiro's model, a trauma has various channels of associated memories. Each channel must be processed for the trauma to be fully resolved. When clients focus on their traumatic memories, sometimes unexpected other memories or experiences come up. In particular, deep emotions often surface. To resolve the problem, these associated memory channels must be "cleaned out," and clients must work through the strong emotions. These implicit, or tacit, connections emerge with therapeutic work.

In therapy, the neurological network is accessed, and the bilateral stimulation allows the encapsulated memory to be unblocked, processed, and connected to more adaptive information. Processing allows clients to adopt an adult perspective and develop positive cognitions that spread or generalize through the memory network. According to Shapiro (1995), "The outcome of an EMDR session apparently causes the linkup of the two networks, an assimilation of the painful material into its proper perspective . . . and a discharge of the dysfunctional affect, with generalization of the adaptive cognitions through the hitherto isolated material . . ." (p. 247). This process is similar to the one described by PEP therapists, in which clients access adaptive emotions and information through therapy interventions and then use them to modify maladaptive emotions and beliefs.

Experiential Therapy

CCT relies on clients as much as possible to heal themselves. FP and PEP provide a more prosthetic structure. However, similar to EMDR, the structure provided is based on an observation of what clients do well spontaneously when they are naturally self-healing. Regarding FP, Leijssen (1998) said, "A *full* felt sense usually unfolds through different *components*. . . . When the various elements do not unfold spontaneously, the therapist has to *evoke the missing components* in order for the felt sense to become fully present" (pp. 136–137). Similarly, Greenberg and his colleagues have refined the ways therapists can facilitate the healing processes that occur during two-chair, empty-chair work and systematic evocative unfolding in PEP by studying examples of when the processes work and when they do not.

A common assumption among experiential therapists is that an over-emphasis on cognitive, analytic, "top-down" processing that is disconnected from bodily experience disrupts the body's and mind's capacity for self-healing. Optimal functioning involves a dialogue between cognitive, conceptualizing activities and experiential modes of processing information, including emotion. As Gendlin (1996) noted, "Even when we want to think about a specific experience, we often leave our direct sense of it behind, to think about it. As soon as we have one thought about it, we think from that thought to another and another, without ever returning to the experience" (p. 241).

Bohart (1993), similar to Gendlin, considered the process of experiencing as implicitly rich and the source of creativity. Experiencing is an immediate, bodily, tacit, and recognitional way of knowing. It is the more primary knowing system. Conceptual knowing arises from experiential knowing and is an attempt to articulate what is first known experientially (Gendlin, 1964; Johnson, 1987; Lakoff, 1987). Experiencing is bodily felt meaning (Gendlin, 1964). Felt meanings "are tacit forms of knowing based on a bodily sense or perception of an event" (Greenberg & van Balen, 1998, p. 37). At the implicit preverbal level is an experienced complexity that can never entirely be put into words. When people speak words that stem from the experienced complexity, they are only verbalizing or symbolizing part of that complexity. Furthermore, symbolizing is not merely the act of representing what is already "there" in implicit experience. Instead, symbolizing is a creative act that generates an explicit verbal or symbolic referent. It is a *carrying forward* of what is implicitly known into a creation of new experiencing. Gendlin (1968) noted that in addition to reflecting clients' meanings, the most basic function of an empathic therapist response is to *point* at the bodily sensed implicit complexity of experiencing. This action suggests that it is paying *a certain kind of attention* to experiencing, which helps generate the carrying forward process.

The most important facet of EMDR and the experiential therapies is careful, receptive attention to experiencing, which facilitates the processing of old information and the creation of new meaning. Psychological problems result from people's inability to process incongruencies between conceptual and experiential knowing and to access relevant emotional experience. This causes them to become stuck when they run into problematic life situations. In all three therapies, primary modes of experiencing and knowing involve emotion and body sensations.

Process–experiential therapy particularly emphasizes the importance of emotion. For Greenberg and Paivio (1997), "feeling is the process of being" (p. 25). Emotions have the capacity to organize the person for adaptive action. As Greenberg and Van Balen (1998) commented:

> The problem of the origins of the wisdom of the body . . . is solved by realizing that emotion is a basic biologically adaptive system that serves an organizing function in human experience and operates by evaluating situations in relation to our well-being. (p. 53)

As with Gendlin, attention creates synthesis and development. Greenberg and Van Balen (1998) said "human beings live and grow . . . and function by attention being allocated to some aspect of the organism/environment field. . . . Attending leads to the creation of emotional meaning that organizes the person for action" (p. 53).

Greenberg and Paivio (1997) considered the primary unit of change involved in emotion to be the *emotion scheme*, which is defined as "a complex synthesis of affect, cognition, motivation, and action that provides each person with an integrated sense of him- or herself and the world, as well as with subjective felt meaning" (p. 3). Active process–experiential interventions are designed to evoke dysfunctional emotion schemes and have clients attend to, reprocess, and restructure them. Greenberg and Paivio described four types of emotional experience. Primary adaptive emotions are people's most basic healthy emotions, whereas primary maladaptive emotions are a main source of dysfunction in the emotion system. Secondary feelings are those feelings that obscure more primary feelings like anger that is expressed when hurt is primary, and instrumental feelings are those feelings expressed to influence others, such as "crocodile" tears to get sympathy.

Evoking emotion involves arousing emotional experiences related to the core themes in the counseling sessions. An important component involves an exploration and differentiation of emotional experience to access primary emotions and their associated thoughts and needs. The transformation takes place in a restructuring phase, which involves accessing core maladaptive emotion schemes and primary adaptive emotional experience that clients use to restructure the maladaptive schemes. Restructuring of activated core maladaptive emotion schemes occurs through a self-challenging of the beliefs embedded in them by newly accessed healthy emotions and needs. For example, once activated, the shame-based emotion scheme of worthlessness that results from abuse can be challenged by tapping into currently accessible anger at being violated or sadness at the loss associated with the abuse. This dialectical confrontation between the previously dominant maladaptive voices of shame and worthlessness and the newly empowered adaptive voices of anger and self-worth in the personality provides the foundation for the development of a new self-organization.

However, working with emotions involves more than mere catharsis. Although simply allowing and accepting pain is often therapeutic itself, other emotions, particularly secondary emotions such as shame, do not change merely through being experienced and expressed. Instead, the underlying maladaptive schemes must be accessed and restructured (Greenberg & Paivio, 1997).

In sum, for experiential and EMDR therapists, the primary mission of psychotherapy is to promote client self-healing. Self-healing arises in part from directing attention to tacit experiential and emotional processes. *Knowing* at this level is densely interconnected and rich. Attention directed at emotion and experiencing leads to the emergence of new, more adaptive emotional experience, new meanings, and bodily felt shifts in experiencing.

SUMMARY OF SIMILARITIES BETWEEN EMDR AND EXPERIENTIAL PSYCHOTHERAPY

- Experiential therapies and EMDR encourage clients to focus on their bodily felt experience. Looking at EMDR through the lens of Gendlin's FP, EMDR may include the focusing process that Gendlin believes is at the core of personality change. In EMDR, clients are continually being referred to imagistic and experiential aspects of their problems.
- The importance of accessing and allowing strong emotion is recognized and supported in EMDR, as it is in PEP. Staying with emotion in a supportive atmosphere can lead people to go through it productively. In trauma work, accessing strong emotion allows it to connect with cognition and allows adaptive restructuring processes to take place.

- A highly cognitive analytic mind state is discouraged. In EMDR, client-centered therapy, FP, and certain tasks in PEP, a receptive, listening, receiving, and observing mind state is promoted. If the person "stays with" experience, things emerge and shift. This is not to say that clients do not "think" but that thinking is balanced and grounded in receptive observation and tracking of holistic experience. Each approach discourages abstract intellectual speculation or unfelt narration of events. Each one emphasizes starting with experience. For example, rather than narrate a whole story, clients in EMDR are encouraged to focus on a specific scene or image; this is also true in PEP. In FP, clients are asked to pay attention to specific current bodily feeling states. In this regard, these approaches also interrupt dysfunctional self-criticism.
- Shapiro (1995) contended that EMDR accelerates information processing. However, part of the process actually involves *slowing down* processing. Clients stay with immediately available information in a step-by-step fashion, letting it change when it is ready to change. This is also true of experiential approaches. When empathic reflections are working as intended, clients move step by step. Clients do not engage in the following: "You know, I really felt let down. That *must mean* I probably *ought to* say something to her, right? Or *does it mean* that I am too vulnerable as a person?" This person leaps too quickly into analyzing what the information should or might imply, which is a typical pattern in therapy. EMDR and experiential approaches slow down intellectual, analytic processing and encourage proceeding step by step by allowing and accelerating attentive processing. The information is "dwelt upon" in an experientially immediate way. In EMDR, it seems that the provision of an attentional focus in the bilateral stimulation may dampen thinking or conceptual processing and let more information emerge from the experiential processing system.
- Both approaches also emphasize *connecting* information. Ultimately, it is the connection of cognitive, conceptual (left-brain) ways of processing information with emotional, intuitive (right-brain) information. In this regard, therapists of both approaches recognize that the body often "holds" unprocessed experience of which clients are not cognitively aware. In experiential therapies, the reason clients continue to be bothered is that the unprocessed experience signals a need for processing, just as pain signals that something is

wrong and needs to be attended to. Symptoms are part of the self-healing process.

- The intrinsic, implicit, tacit level, experience is complexly interwoven. People are intricate systems of interconnections. While therapists work with one aspect of a client's experience, new facets may emerge that do not seem to be logically connected to the presenting problem, but they may be emotionally connected. Therapy is an attempt to "right the system," not to specifically remove a symptom. Righting the system spontaneously removes symptoms and often produces other unexpected positive changes. Therapists follows clients' track of what is meaningfully and emotionally interconnected to determine what needs work.

- Processing is not complete (or even effective) unless it is accompanied by some noticeable, bodily felt shift. What is felt in the body is a major sign of success or failure. In EMDR, positive cognitions are not instilled by therapists through intellectual analysis and challenging of data or by repetitive practice (affirmations) but through a process of discovery that continues until the cognitions "feel right." The positive cognition is "installed" (Shapiro, 1995) *after* clients have already begun to think that it feels right. Regarding FP, Leijssen (1998) observed: "The client might also have a new insight about an issue, but we consider this only as a felt shift or a new step if the insight doesn't happen only in the mind but is also in some way a bodily felt resolution. As long as a feeling of tension, tightness, confusion, etc., remains . . . elements are still lacking or the proper expression has not yet been found. In that case, a friendly wait for what is still unclear or wants to move forward is indicated" (p. 138).

- The therapy process is one of *emergence*. The approaches are *discovery-oriented*. The therapist does not decide in advance what the right solution is for the client. For instance, with abuse, the client may or may not come to forgive the perpetrator. Both approaches allow for and promote unfolding of solutions in ways idiosyncratic to the well-being and experience of the particular individual.

DIFFERENCES BETWEEN EMDR AND EXPERIENTIAL PSYCHOTHERAPY

Although they have many similarities, EMDR and experiential therapy also have differences. A major difference involves the role of the relationship. In all three of the experiential approaches, the relationship is considered to be a major healing force. For example, active expression of therapists' deep empathic understanding is an important healing element. In EMDR, although therapists certainly convey respect, compassion, and acceptance to clients, they do not systematically use empathy as a therapeutic tool. In fact, Shapiro (1995) actively discouraged the use of empathic listening responses, believing that they focus clients on therapists' words rather than on the clients' own internal experience. Similarly, the genuineness of the therapist and the idea of therapy as the "meeting of persons," which was valued so much by Rogers, is also not a major component of EMDR.

A second difference is that EMDR does not rely on the articulation or symbolizing experience as an important step in the change process, which is a key component in most psychodynamic and experiential therapies. In EMDR, it is not clear that it is needed. In one of Bohart's experiences with EMDR, he initially focused on a feeling and progressively experienced bodily felt shifts toward a more benign state, without ever articulating any meaning or symbolizing his experience. Each moment in the process was one of "bare attending" to "nameless experience." Only after a shift had already occurred did he then articulate that shift in words as a change in perspective.

However, this aspect of EMDR is compatible with Gendlin's (1996) FP. Although articulating experience is a formal component of Gendlin's six steps for learning focusing (Gendlin, 1996), Gendlin seems to believe that articulation of meaning is not a necessary component of focusing but rather a by-product (E. Gendlin, personal communication, February 2, 1999). Changes in bodily felt experience are the outcome of focusing. They may or may not include the articulation or symbolization of new perspectives on experience.

A third difference is that EMDR provides a greater degree of structure and prefigures the resolution by specifying in advance the belief clients would like to have about themselves to reduce distress. This step provides both a framework for change and a sense of direction; however, it could also create a false change, or one that will not endure, especially for clients sensitive to the demands of the situation. Good EMDR therapists guard against this by asking clients whether the originally specified positive cognition fits or something better could be used. This step helps clients focus on what spontaneously emerges.

INTEGRATING EXPERIENTIAL THERAPIES WITH EMDR

Evidence reveals that EMDR, CCT, FP, and PEP all work (Elliott, 2002; Shapiro, 1995). Our informal observation is that many of the changes that occur during experiential therapies also occur during EMDR (see, for instance, Bohart, in press). Therefore, in discussing the integration of EMDR and experiential therapies, the key question becomes: "What unique contributions can each make to the other?" EMDR seems to work quickly, at least for those with specific traumas (Shapiro, 1995). EMDR can also quite efficiently access emotion. On the other hand, experiential procedures deal with the holistic meaning of clients' problems in a way that more actively involves them in meaning reconstruction activities. In addition, experiential procedures offer various opportunities for learning through doing. In sum, both therapies seem to have something to contribute to the other. The chapter includes a discussion of possibilities for incorporating EMDR into experiential work and experiential work into EMDR. Currently, the suggestions are speculative, awaiting validation and refinement through clinical experimentation and empirical investigation.

In discussing EMDR it must be clear what is mean by the term. As Shapiro (1995) conceives it, the EMDR method is a whole protocol, or whole set of protocols. A specific component, bilateral stimulation, is embedded in these protocols, but the bilateral stimulation itself can be used without the protocols. Some of the innovative work with EMDR involves using it in this way. For instance, in a book edited by Manfield (1998), eye movements are innovatively mixed in with various other kinds of therapeutic work. Therefore, the eye movement procedure, which may independently promote accelerated information processing, can be used for different purposes. First, it can be used as a process for healing trauma. Second, it can be used in any kind of therapy for purposes of access and discovery. In particular, eye movements may be a powerful way of accessing emotion. Third, eye movements in the original EMDR protocol are used to strengthen and reinforce positive cognitions. Others have used eye movements to strengthen and reinforce insights, discoveries, or positive images of the future. Furthermore, Shapiro (1995) suggested that eye movements can be used to enhance the teaching of social skills. For instance, clients can visualize enacting the requisite skill while engaging in a series of eye movements. When we discuss incorporating EMDR into experiential work, we are usually referring to the use of bilateral stimulation. When we discuss incorporating experiential work into EMDR, we are referring to incorporating experiential work into the various EMDR protocols.

Integrating Experiential Procedures Into EMDR

In what way could experiential procedures contribute to the practice of EMDR? First, they can be used when eye movements are not yet appropriate. Those therapists who use EMDR for people with dissociative disorders have suggested that eye movements cannot be used for quite a while —until clients have become stable. Experiential procedures could be beneficial in the mean time. They may help clients feel more stable and more comfortable with emotional exploration. Empathic reflections could be used to help clients gently explore and process experience, particularly clients who are feeling highly vulnerable (Greenberg et al., 1993). Empathic reflections also help clients feel understood, which can help clients feel more in control. Finally, reflections could be used to vivify experience (Greenberg et al., 1993) and bring important issues and conflicts into the forefront of clients' minds before using EMDR. Empathic reflections may provide a degree of cognitive control, which is reassuring to clients, while titrating their exposure to their own experience in a way that may increase their tolerance to later EMDR work. Similarly, the PEP problematic reaction point procedure could be used to introduce clients to the process of exploring painful or puzzling emotional scenes in a way that may help prepare them for EMDR work. Empathic reflections, focusing, and the problematic reaction point procedure all involve clients being more deliberately and cognitively active than they are in EMDR. These processes may give clients who are afraid of emotional exploration a sense of control. Finally, focusing could also help clients learn how to trust and listen to their bodily felt experience in a way that could make EMDR work better for them.

Experiential techniques also could be used to supplement EMDR. For instance, an initial stage of the EMDR protocol is getting clients to come up with a negative cognition about their problematic experience. Ideally, clients frame the cognition as a negative self-attribution, such as "I'm incompetent." However, it is not uncommon for clients to have problems framing their cognitions in this form. For instance, a client's own initial phrasing of a negative cognition might be "I can't seem to manage my finances—they always overwhelm me," but for EMDR work, the therapist wants the statement to be a negative self-attribution, such as "I am incompetent." The EMDR therapist may suggest the alternative phrasing to the client and then proceed if it is acceptable. However, no therapeutic work is done to "organically" create the phrase. Using experiential methods, this part of the therapy could be a real meaning-creation process rather than just a preliminary step. This phase could be extended with empathic reflections or focusing to help clients more naturally construct negative cognitions. Clients may come to a realization that they *feel* incompetent, and the phrase "I'm incompetent" comes more naturally. This verbalization of experience can itself be a therapeutic gain (Bohart & Tallman, 1999).

Empathic reflections may also be useful at the end of sessions. Even after attaining resolution with EMDR, some clients like to discuss what happened. Considerable evidence has shown that a significant healing factor in recovering from trauma is productive rumination and narrative reconstruction, in which clients make sense of the trauma and incorporate it into their life story (Tedeschi, Park, & Calhoun, 1998). Although EMDR moves rapidly to symptom reduction and a changed perspective, many clients still want to discuss what it all means—to trace the narrative story line and place everything into the new perspective. Empathic reflections can be very useful for this purpose.

Focusing and empathic reflections may have some unique benefits. Clients learn through the step-by-step process of listening to themselves and, facilitated by these procedures, how to process their own experience when they are not in therapy. Focusing in particular may be a useful tool to teach clients for use between EMDR sessions.

The tasks of PEP could also be used to supplement and extend EMDR work. Chair work could be used as a kind of experiential interweave. For example, having clients who were abused act out a dialogue with the abusive person might help them move forward if they are stuck in their processing. In addition, chair work may have unique benefits. For instance, when role-playing an "unfinished-business" dialogue with another person, clients get bodily and visceral feedback that should strengthen and reinforce their developing sense of self-assertiveness. Clients who were abused have the experience of defending themselves against the person who abused them in the role play. Although clients in EMDR may also become assertive, it may be beneficial to enactively and generatively practicing being assertive. Similarly, while role-playing the other person, the client may be practicing useful role-taking and empathy-building skills.

Two-chair work in which clients practice dialogue between their "should," or "critical," sides and their experiential response sides may help them learn a set of skills. They may learn how to develop a more differentiated view of their underlying needs and goals. They may also learn how to productively listen to and explore the two sides of a conflict so that they can find the best possible solution. In the two-chair and empty-chair procedure, clients may also access and learn about their deepest needs and values. These lessons seem somewhat independent of what occurs in EMDR, thus this process could be beneficial if added to EMDR work.

Integrating EMDR Into Experiential Work

CCT

Pure, traditional client-centered therapists would be unlikely to use EMDR. They object to the use of focusing and process–experiential tasks (Bozarth, 1998) because they see the procedures as therapist-imposed steps on a naturally occurring client process. Similarly, they would consider the EMDR process to be too therapist controlled.

However, if the therapist was not a purist, EMDR could profitably be incorporated into a fundamentally client-centered process of empathic listening. Clients who became stuck in the process might be asked to focus on their experience and use eye movements. Then, when they seem ready to return to the interactive self-exploration process, the therapist could once again resume empathic listening. One of us (A. Bohart) has tried this out with one willing client and has had positive results.

PEP

Eye movements could be incorporated into PEP in several ways. First, they could conceivably be added as a separate task in their own right. Research could be done to identify specific markers for their use in addition to the use of the other tasks. However, eye movements could also be incorporated *within* tasks. For instance, we have experimented with including eye movements in chair work. They have been used to enhance experiencing during chair work and reinforce a positive gain. For example, a client was exploring his feelings toward his father using the empty-chair procedure. When he made a particularly significant emotional statement, we engaged in a couple of short eye movements. This action seemed to help him sharpen his feelings. When we resumed the chair work, he quickly had a positive resolution and let go of the need to have his father's approval. His positive resolution was reinforced using eye movements, and we concluded the session with a discussion and an empathically facilitated narrative discussion.

FP

Armstrong (1998) reported on the way she integrates EMDR into her focusing-oriented approach to therapy. Basically, she uses EMDR in two ways. First, like Shapiro (1995), she suggested that some traumas are so deeply buried in the lower brain that it is difficult to access them with focusing. Even when focusing has led to other, productive changes, clients may still be left with unresolved emotions. EMDR can access and help clients reprocess those emotions. Second, EMDR can be used to jump start focusing when therapy is stuck. Armstrong argued that there should be no mechanistic incorporation of EMDR into FP on a protocol-driven basis. Instead, it is used on a sensitive, moment-by-moment basis by the therapist when appropriate. EMDR is then used in FP in a way that is similar to cognitive interweave's use in EMDR—to "unstick" client processing.

CONCLUSION

Following is a composite case example based on several individual cases to give an illustration of the way EMDR and experiential therapies can be used together.

Marshall sought therapy because he was about to get promoted at work into a position of authority. He reported having a major intense anxiety attack that had not abated since he had heard the news about 3 weeks before. He had trouble focusing on his work. At home, he felt so paralyzed by his anxiety that he had a hard time exercising or attending to anything he read or watched on television. Marshall was engaging in a lot of intellectualized self-criticism (e.g., "I should be happy," "There really must be something wrong with me to feel so anxious," "I must really be a wimp"). The therapist initially listened and responded empathically (e.g., "It's really puzzling to you: 'why am I reacting with anxiety in a situation in which I would expect myself to be happy?'" "And you really worry— this seems so severe and out of your control and so nonsensical that it might mean you have a real personality weakness," "You really think you should be facing this bravely, and instead you're overcome with anxiety").

This process temporarily relieved the anxiety. Marshall left the first session feeling a bit better and more optimistic about therapy, but at the second session, he reported that during the week the anxiety had slowly, inexorably, returned. In the second session the therapist thought EMDR might be useful. The therapist described the procedure to Marshall and asked him if he wanted to give it a try. Marshall thought it sounded interesting. The therapist engaged in the usual preliminaries (Shapiro, 1995) and then had Marshall think of the scene in which he first felt the anxiety, which was after hearing about his promotion and as he contemplated moving from his old office upstairs into his new office. Marshall reported a stress level of 9 on a 10-point scale. When asked to formulate a negative cognition, Marshall came up with, "I didn't think I really deserved the promotion. I think I've felt like I've been faking it all along—not really doing things very well, feeling like I always should have been doing things better. And I was afraid that I would be found out." In contrast to the typical EMDR procedure in which the therapist coaches the client to come up with a negative self-attribution, such as "I'm incompetent," the therapist suggested that Marshall focus on what he felt in the middle of his body when he verbalized the negative cognition. He reported having a kind of sick feeling. The therapist asked him to stay with that feeling and see what emerged. After a few moments, Marshall said, "It's like I've been faking it all along, kind of like I'm a fraud . . . that's it—I think I'm a fraud and will be found out." Using this focusing approach to help Marshall clarify the negative cognition was itself a bit of a therapeutic gain. It helped Marshall verbalize some of his experience and brought a bit of order to it. Marshall then reported that he felt a bit better. His stress level when he thought of the incident had dropped to a 6. However, 6 was still high enough to justify using the EMDR procedure. The therapist then asked Marshall to come up with a positive cognition—what he would like to believe about himself now as he thought about the incident. Marshall thought about it for a while and came up with, "I'm able." When asked how much he believed the statement, he rated it as a 3 on a 7-point scale, with 7 representing completely believable.

The therapist then had Marshall think about the scene at his desk and follow the therapist's fingers with his eyes. After the first set of eye movements, Marshall reported that the sick, anxious feeling had changed to a feeling of pure anxiety. Marshall was asked to "go with that," and a second eye movement set was performed. After this, Marshall reported that he felt sad. Another EM set was performed. He then reported both feeling sad and having thoughts about leaving his friends and moving upstairs, where he would be in a position of authority over them. Another eye movement set was performed, which led to the feeling that he did not really deserve the promotion—"Heck, there are others as good as I am." Another eye movement set was performed. He reported that some of his old friends would become critical of him for getting this promotion and moving upstairs. He would become the "enemy." Another set was performed. Marshall reported, "But heck, I really do deserve it. I work hard." Another set was performed. "Yeah. I really am a hard worker. I can be trusted." At this point he was asked how tense he was feeling, and he said he felt much better.

However, when Marshall recalled the initial scene, he still felt some tension. Another set of eye movements was initiated. After this set, Marshall reported feeling an overwhelming sense of sadness. Another set of eye movements was performed. Marshall reported that he chronically worried about his masculinity. Another set was performed. Marshall reported that he had grown up in a very tough neighborhood. His parents had been overprotective and not let him go out to play with the other kids. When he went to school, he was often teased and harassed because he was a different ethnicity than most of the kids in the school. To protect himself, he withdrew. The withdrawal had always made him wonder whether he was a coward at heart. He had handled this feeling by being quiet and keeping to himself. Another set was performed. Marshall reported feeling even greater sadness. Another set was performed. He then reported a sudden surge of anger. He was not sure what was causing the anger. Another set of eye movements was performed. "Yes. I'm mad. I'm mad at the kids that teased me, and I'm mad at my parents for overprotecting me." Another set was performed. Marshall then reported feeling great compassion toward the little kid, himself as a child, and that he wanted to comfort him and tell him that he had done his best. Another set of eye movements was performed. He reported that he wanted the best for this kid and that "this kid deserved the best." Another set was performed, after which Marshall said, "I can handle the job. I want to be promoted." At this point, recalling the original image only resulted in minimal tension (1 on the SUDS scale) and a belief of 6 on the positive cognition statement, "I'm able."

The session ended with a bit of discussion and recapitulation. Marshall wanted to talk about how the events in his childhood had influenced him. Marshall reviewed his life story and reevaluated it. The therapist listened with great interest and involvement and responded only with empathic reflections as Marshall continued his self-healing.

In the next session, Marshall wanted to work more on his fears about moving into management. In particular, he was worried about his ability to be the boss and lay down rules for others. The two-chair technique was used. In one chair, he spoke for the side, the critic, that said, "A good boss is strong and firm and lays down rules for others." In the other chair, he spoke for the side that said, "But I don't want to do that. I don't like to order others around." As the dialogue continued, the "critic" side changed from "To be a good boss, you must lay down rules" to "I worry that if you aren't stern and firm you can't be a good boss." The other side evolved to "I want people to like me." These two sides then integrated: Marshall could be a firm but empathic boss who listened to others. We then used EMDR to strengthen this new idea.

Therapy work continued for several more sessions. Marshall was interested in exploring his relationship with his father, who he thought probably provided the model for the stern boss that he thought he should be. This exploration was done through discussion and use of the empty-chair technique. Eye movements were also used periodically. Eventually, Marshall felt prepared to take on his new duties.

REFERENCES

Armstrong, M. (1998). Treating trauma with focusing and EMDR. *The Focusing Folio, 17*(1), 23–30.

Bohart, A. (1993). Experiencing: The basis of psychotherapy. *Journal of Psychotherapy Integration, 3*, 51–67.

Bohart, A. (in press). A meditation on the nature of self-healing and personality change in psychotherapy based on Gendlin's theory of experiencing. *The Humanistic Psychologist*.

Bohart, A., & Greenberg, L. S. (1997). Empathy and psychotherapy: An introductory overview. In A. Bohart & L. Greenberg (Eds.), *Empathy reconsidered* (pp. 4–31). Washington, DC: American Psychological Association.

Bohart, A., & Tallman, K. (1999). *How clients make psychotherapy work: The process of active self-healing.* Washington, DC: American Psychological Association.

Bozarth, J. (1998). *Person-centered therapy: A revolutionary paradigm.* Ross-on-Wye, England: PCCS Books.

Cissna, K. N., & Anderson, R. (1994). The 1957 Martin Buber–Carl Rogers dialogue, as dialogue. *Journal of Humanistic Psychology, 34*, 11–45.

Elliott, R. (2002). The effectiveness of humanistic therapies: A meta-analysis. In

D. J. Cain & J. Seeman (Eds.), Humanistic psychotherapies: Handbook of research and practice (pp. 57–82). Washington, DC: American Psychological Association.

Gendlin, E. T. (1964). A theory of personality change. In P. Worchel & D. Byrne (Eds.), *Personality change*. New York: Wiley.

Gendlin, E. T. (1968). The experiential response. In E. Hammer (Ed.), *Use of interpretation in treatment* (pp. 208–227). New York: Grune & Stratton.

Gendlin, E. T. (1990). The small steps of the therapy process: How they come and how to help them come. In G. Lietaer, J. Rombauts, & R. Van Balen (Eds.), *Client-centered and experiential psychotherapy in the nineties* (pp. 205–224). Leuven, Belgium: Leuven University Press.

Gendlin, E. T. (1996). *Focusing-oriented psychotherapy: A manual of the experiential method*. New York: Guilford Press.

Greenberg, L. S., & Paivio, S. C. (1997). *Working with emotions in psychotherapy*. New York: Guilford Press.

Greenberg, L. S., Rice, L. N., & Elliott, R. (1993). *Facilitating emotional change: The moment-by-moment process*. New York: Guilford Press.

Greenberg, L. S., & Van Balen, R. (1998). The theory of experience-centered therapies. In L. S. Greenberg, J. C. Watson, & G. Lietaer (Eds.), *Handbook of experiential psychotherapy* (pp. 28–60). New York: Guilford Press.

Johnson, M. (1987). *The body in the mind*. Chicago: University of Chicago Press.

Kleinman, A. (1988). *Rethinking psychiatry: From cultural category to personal experience*. New York: Free Press.

Lakoff, G. (1987). *Women, fire, and dangerous things: What categories reveal about the mind*. Chicago: University of Chicago Press.

Leijssen, M. (1998). Focusing microprocesses. In L. S. Greenberg, J. C. Watson, & G. Lietaer (Eds.), *Handbook of experiential psychotherapy* (pp. 121–154). New York: Guilford Press.

Mahrer, A. R. (1996). *The complete guide to experiential psychotherapy*. New York: Wiley.

Manfield, P. (Ed.). (1998). *Extending EMDR: A casebook of innovative applications*. New York: Norton.

Orlinsky, D. E., Grawe, K., & Parks, B. K. (1994). Process and outcome in psychotherapy—noch einmal. In A. E. Bergin & S. L. Garfield (Eds.), *Handbook of psychotherapy and behavior change* (4th ed., pp. 270–376). New York: Wiley.

Shapiro, F. (1995). *Eye movement desensitization and reprocessing: Basic principles, protocols, and procedures*. New York: Guilford Press.

Shapiro, F., & Forrest, M. S. (1997). *EMDR: The breakthrough therapy for overcoming anxiety, stress, and trauma*. New York: Basic Books.

Shostrom, E. L. (Producer). (1965). *Three approaches to psychotherapy* [Motion picture]. (Available from Psychological and Educational Films, Orange, CA).

Tedeschi, R. G., Park, C. L., & Calhoun, L. G. (Eds.). (1998). *Posttraumatic growth*. Mahwah, NJ: Erlbaum.

11

FEMINIST THERAPY AND EMDR: THEORY MEETS PRACTICE

LAURA S. BROWN

Feminist therapy is a technically eclectic, theory-driven approach to psychotherapy. It is a practice that is informed by feminist political theories and analysis, grounded in the multicultural feminist scholarship on the psychology of women and gender. The overarching goals of this approach are "to lead both therapist and client towards strategies and solutions advancing feminist resistance, transformation, and social change in daily personal life, and in relationships with the social, emotional, and political environment" (Brown, 1994, pp. 21–22). As a broadly systemic approach to understanding human behavior and behavior change, the feminist paradigm argues that individual change is unlikely when societal and environmental changes do not occur as well.

That which makes psychotherapy practice *feminist* is neither the parameters of the population with whom the therapist works nor the specific interventions used by a therapist. Instead, it is how therapists *think* about what is being done in therapy, how therapists structure the relationship of therapist and client, and how the therapy process is consciously tied to the larger social context. It is an orientation that gives its greatest attention to questions of the practitioner's epistemologies and underlying theoretical models rather than to specific techniques in practice, the nature and sort of problems being treated, or the demographic makeup of the client population.

Because of the interest of feminist therapists in social and contextual variables and the attention of feminist practice to the political nature of reality, it is unremarkable that many individuals with a history of exposure to trauma, particularly to interpersonal violence and childhood maltreatment, have sought the services of feminist therapists in the 25 or so years since feminist practice was first developed. Much trauma, especially interpersonal trauma and the trauma arising from combat and torture, occurs within a specifically political matrix. For example, crimes of violence against women, such as rape and battering, are considered by feminist theorists to be culturewide strategies within patriarchal social systems for controlling women's behavior (Lerner, 1993). Other forms of interpersonal violence, such as bias crimes against members of certain ethnic groups or against lesbians or gay men, are expressions of political viewpoints about the exclusion or lack of value of these groups. Torture is used in the service of political regimes to silence, terrorize, and control populations. The very study of trauma itself is a highly political act (Herman, 1992) because discussing human cruelty exposes how embedded it is in the core of many cultures and challenges certain hyperpatriotic worldviews.

From its inception, feminist therapists have referred in their writings to issues of working with trauma survivors. They discuss the challenges facing therapists who would like to assist these people with breaking the silence—people who have survived traumas such as rape, childhood sexual abuse, sexual harassment, discrimination, and other forms of social coercion and control that are integral to the functioning of the dominant cultures of patriarchy (Brown, 1986; Chesler, 1972; Walker, 1989). Feminist therapists have been leaders in developing modern approaches to trauma theory and treatment of the survivors of the war at home. As Herman (1992) noted, the feminist emphasis on sexual and domestic violence was one of the forces that led to the inclusion of trauma-oriented diagnoses in the *Diagnostic and Statistical Manual of Mental Disorders* (DSM; American Psychiatric Association, 1980) in 1980.

Consequently, the use of eye movement desensitization and reprocessing (EMDR) as a specific approach to working with survivors of trauma has been intriguing to many feminist therapists who work in the field of trauma because it offers a model for reducing suffering and empowering clients. EMDR seems to represent the quintessence of feminist models of practice. As a therapy approach that is driven by clients' realities, needs, and pacing, it places ultimate authority in the hands of the client, empowers clients effectively, and reduces the risk of therapists abusing their power.

Feminist therapy is also a competency-based approach to treatment, in which the therapist strives to create an egalitarian relationship with a client (Brown, 1994). In this egalitarian model, therapists work to construct a structure for therapy in which power is shared with the client and the institutionalized sources of therapists' power are interrogated and eschewed as inimical to a feminist change process. One aspect of the egalitarian model is that clients are construed as possessing expertise and authority about themselves, their lives, and their needs. Therapy then becomes a process of assisting clients with uncovering and owning that authority and competence.

EMDR has also been interesting to feminist practitioners because it seems to support this model of the therapist–client relationship. A client in EMDR ascertains the focus of the reprocessing session and determines entirely the direction in which the process will go; the role of the therapist involves skillful following, facilitation, and assistance in moving past the potential roadblocks of cognitive loops and stuck points. In EMDR as in feminist practice, the therapist and client are working to share their expertise; a therapist must learn, as feminist practice teaches, to make the client's expertise central to the success of the endeavor.

Feminist therapy theory focuses therapists' awareness on the notion that the seemingly private and highly personal transaction of psychotherapy occurs within a social and political framework that informs, transforms, or distorts the meanings given to individual experience and to the very psychotherapeutic process itself. Because EMDR attends to people's distorted beliefs in the aftermath of painful and traumatic experiences, it directly addresses and uncovers the distorted meanings given to personal experience by the social and political milieu. In feminist practice models, therapy is conceptualized not only as a discrete healing relationship between individuals but also as an experience that can cause social transformation because of the changes in attitudes and values that occur during the individual healing process. Feminist practice is among an emerging group of "critical theory" models in the behavioral and social sciences (Fox & Prilleltensky, 1997) that challenge the moral, political, and scientific status of the behavioral sciences and mental health professions while attempting to integrate those critiques into ongoing practice. Feminist practice, like other critical models, questions the sanctity of taken-for-granted notions in psychology, such as the concept of therapist or researcher objectivity or the notion of the purity of the scientific method. Feminist practice questions the regulation of *ways of knowing* in psychological science and the limitation of received knowledge to data derived solely from logical positivist empiricist paradigms. Thus, it is open to a range of methodologies (Ballou, 1990), ways of knowing (Brabeck & Brown, 1997), and different models for the therapeutic relationship itself. Feminist therapists are open to strategies for change whose efficacy and usefulness are clinically demonstrated (Lerman, 1987), as well as to those strategies developed through more formal research.

Feminist therapy, by being grounded in this critical and political analysis, aims to deprivatize the therapist's, and eventually the client's, understanding of human suffering. Feminist therapists question how each life and each pain can be manifestations of processes that are continuously extant in the layers of a larger social context. Like EMDR therapists, feminist practitioners are vitally interested in questions of how clients define what is true and in strategies for transforming clients' felt truths from disempowering to empowering verities. At the same time, feminist therapy requires that each life experience be viewed as valuable, unique, and authoritative. Clients are considered to be expert sources of knowledge regarding themselves and their cultural contexts. Because of this privileging of individual meaning and authority, combined with attention to public and political realities that inform such meaning, feminist therapy theoretically straddles the gap between positivist and postmodernist views of human behavior and change, owing allegiance to neither. Feminist practice attends to inner and outer worlds, blending dynamic and constructivist understandings of human behavior.

This chapter includes a review of certain core concepts of feminist therapy theory and an exploration of how EMDR can be integrated into feminist practice as a means of operationalizing that theory. Because feminist therapy is inherently technically eclectic, embracing interventions ranging from the psychodynamic (Alpert, 1986) to the most radically behavioral (Worell & Remer, 1992), the question to be addressed regarding EMDR as a feminist practice is whether its use in therapy supports feminist models of change. In feminist practice, that question is the boundary condition for inclusion of a strategy: Can its use promote feminist models and outcomes? Not every way of practicing therapy does this, and some strategies, particularly those that emphasize strategic approaches in which therapists intentionally use their power over the client, are per se problematic. However, EMDR seems to fall easily within the parameters of feminist practice and even in the hands of nonfeminist therapists advances the goals of feminist social and personal change that are at the core of feminist therapy models. In arguing that EMDR does support feminist strategies, this chapter explores the way feminist practice conceptualizes the notions of change and goodness of outcome. To some degree, these notions are very similar to those of nonfeminist therapies, and in other respects they are radically different.

CORE CONCEPTS IN FEMINIST THERAPY

Feminist therapy theorists have approached the task of defining the parameters of feminist therapy from these underlying assumptions regarding political analysis and knowledge generation. Several different authors (Brabeck & Brown, 1997; Brown, 1994; Lerman, 1987) have proposed a set of core concepts assumed to demarcate those parameters. Each set of criteria for feminist practice reflect shared underlying assumptions about what makes therapy practice *feminist*. An overview of these criteria sets suggests that the following core concepts are likely to be found in any therapy modality that can be a part of feminist practice.

First, such approaches to therapy explicitly link feminist political thinking to the construction of the therapy relationship. The notion that "personal is political" and therapy occurs in a larger social context are also consistent in these models. For example, during feminist therapy for a woman who is a survivor of childhood sexual abuse, feminist therapists would ground their work with the client in the knowledge that such abuse has a social function; interpretations and hypotheses that feminist therapists would offer to such clients would reflect this perspective.

Second, feminist models explicitly rely on diverse and multicultural knowledge bases. The assumption is made that knowledge of human diversity is requisite, not simply for work with "special populations" but for a complete and politically astute comprehension of the dominant group. Thus, feminist therapists who work extensively with couples become familiar with the literature on same-sex relationships, even if the bulk of their practice is with heterosexual couples. They acknowledge that same-sex couples' functioning offers valuable insights into how intimate adult pairs relate (Brown, 1986).

A third focus of these criteria is a vision of humans as competent and of distress not as psychopathology but as frequently reasonable and creative attempts to survive in oppressive conditions. Resistance is reframed as evidence of resiliency. Clients who have silenced their own knowledge of past abuses are told that such self-silencing is the way in which they were able to survive, undetected, with their knowledge until it was safe for them to speak the truth. Another common focus of these criteria for feminist practice is the attention to power in the psychotherapeutic relationship and to the creation of egalitarian modalities in which the client is explicitly empowered by all aspects of the therapeutic exchange. As one writer put it, a feminist practitioner "sets the fee as a feminist" (Luepnitz, 1988, p. 20). Feminist therapists, while explicitly acknowledging their power in the role of a therapist, structure the treatment as a joint work of two experts. The therapists are the experts in creating the conditions in which healing and change can occur; the clients are the experts on themselves, on what they want, need, feel, and value. The egalitarian framework is used as a strategy to communicate, even from the very first session, that clients are capable of knowing what they want and need to change and that the therapists' task is to assist them in uncovering and gaining access to that expertise, rather than supplanting it with the therapists' knowledge.

Finally, feminist models of practice are explicitly focused on using the therapeutic venue as a means of creating feminist consciousness in the therapist and client alike. An overarching goal of feminist practice is to create realities in which feminist consciousness, in which all humans are equally valued, becomes as much the taken-for-granted truth of life as is currently true for patriarchal realities, in which hierarchy and devaluation are the norm. Feminist practitioners know that when therapy begins, many of the people they work with will endorse some form of patriarchal consciousness because it has been the reality in which they have lived and suffered. As people experience being valued for their own expertise and let go of the patriarchal lens for self-valuation, feminist consciousness, an awareness of group membership and personal value, frequently emerges during the healing process. These critical feminist analyses of process and content in therapy tie the private and unique pains of clients and the interventions most likely to empower the clients to the public and political realities that are the crucible of the problem's formation.

In addition, the writers on criteria for feminist practice have noted that feminist therapy is not simply about working with women (Brabeck & Brown, 1997; Brown, 1994). The paradigms for understanding human experience proposed by these authors acknowledge that oppression and experiences of silencing and devaluation may occur at many points in the social and political matrix. Race, class, culture, sexual orientation, age, size, and disability, among others, are common variables along which patriarchal dichotomies of value operate to diminish quality of life and well-being and from which experience and knowledge that are usually marginalized can be derived and used. In addition, feminist conceptual frameworks imply that the experiences of the dominant—the oppressor—are as transparent to and in need of feminist analysis in therapy as are those of the oppressed. Consequently, feminist practitioners have been increasingly interested in men and in deconstructing traditional images of masculinity (Silverstein & Auerbach, 1999) to increase men's capacity for change as well.

PATRIARCHY AND ITS DISCONTENTS

To best comprehend the concepts at the core of feminist practice and then understand how EMDR can be a type of feminist practice, it is also useful to have a working definition of one of the most basic issues in feminist therapy—that is, what constitutes a patriarchy and how its effects can be detected and addressed. A goal shared by all feminist practitioners is undermining patriarchies at their most intimate levels because it is represented in the unconscious and conscious behaviors, thoughts, and feelings of most people. It is important to note that when feminist therapists refer to a *patriarchy*, they are not identifying individual men or men in general. Instead, they are referring to a very common type of social arrangement, which is potentially problematic for women and men alike, in which the following assumptions about humans and gender predominate.

The first assumption is that men and women (or, for example, "White people and Black people," or "the rich and the poor") are different in their essence, not only biologically but also "in their needs, capacities and functions. Men and women also differ in the way they were created and in the social function assigned to them by God" (Lerner, 1993, pp. 3–4). The next assumption is that men (and attributes associated with maleness [or Whiteness, or heterosexuality, or youth]) are "naturally superior, stronger, and more rational, thus designed to be dominant. . . . Women are naturally weaker, inferior in intellect and rational capacities, unstable emotionally" (p. 4). In addition, patriarchies assert that men, "by their rational minds, explain and order the world. Women by their nurturant function sustain daily life. . . . While both functions are essential, that of men is superior to that of women" (p. 4). Patriarchies convey that men have an "inherent right to control the sexuality and the reproductive functions of women" (p. 4), whereas women have no such reciprocal right. Finally, and crucially, in patriarchies, it is assumed that men speak to and for the divine deity on behalf of women and that the deity is male, even in those theologies that pay lip service to the genderless nature of the divine.

Gerda Lerner, one of the most distinguished feminist historians and theorists, writes, "Patriarchal concepts are, therefore, built into all the mental constructs of (any patriarchal) civilization in such a way as to remain largely invisible" (Lerner, 1993, p. 3). In EMDR terms, they are the true-feeling negative cognitions about the self in relationship to the world that haunt the consciousness of many individuals who have experienced trauma, maltreatment, or discrimination. Framing Lerner's observations in psychological terms, patriarchal assumptions are considered to be pervasive and often are not conscious, what Bem and Bem (1970) termed a *nonconscious ideology*. Because patriarchal constructs are so frequently not conscious, they are difficult for most people to scrutinize and critique, even when those constructs are the source of distress. For example, a client who comments that she deserved to be raped because she flirted with the man who assaulted her is voicing an ingrained patriarchal rule about women's ownership by men and the right of men to forcibly take sex from women who violate norms of female chastity. When this belief appears as the negative cognition in an EMDR processing session, it represents an exposure of patriarchal beliefs that may lie at the core of the posttrauma response.

More recent feminist thought has expanded Lerner's analysis of gender as an organizing variable in patriarchy to affirm that such nonconscious assumptions also exist about other dominant groups (e.g., Whites, upper-class people; people without disabilities) in relationship to the nondominant group (Adleman & Enguidanos, 1995). Patriarchal constructs and ways of knowing thus come to constitute "truth" in a culture and are perceived as such by members of the culture, even when those truths are disadvantageous to some individuals.

Patriarchal constructs have behavioral and intrapsychic representations, all of which can become the sources of distress or the targets of psychotherapeutic intervention. Specifically, such constructs can be internalized by people in distress and frequently become the target cognitions for EMDR. Some manifestations of patriarchy at the cultural level are overt and easy to identify, such as women's intentional and systemic exclusion from certain prestigious or well-paying activities or occupations. They are relatively simpler to modify via straightforward strategies. This type of discrimination can be dealt with through formal, legal, and systemic changes and in many instances in the United States it has begun to fade away. Still, struggles occur daily for women in certain occupations, particularly those in the traditional trades, law enforcement, and military and paramilitary settings.

Other aspects of patriarchy are apparently smaller and more subtle. They also have an impact on well-being, but taken out of context, they are not necessarily easy to identify as forms of oppression because they seem so slight. However, taken together, such "minor" social and behavioral forms of patriarchy support and enable the more overt types and constitute part of the persistent social message conveyed to people about differences in human worth and value. Some of these more subtle forms include the higher cost of women's clothing (e.g., women's cotton oxford-cloth shirts, although smaller in size than men's, cost more than men's cotton oxford-cloth shirts), the pressure on men to dissociate Eros, or desire, from emotion and to objectify sexual partners rather than relate to them, and the association of humanness with maleness in the generic masculine of language (most commonly still found in religious worship).

All of these minor factors communicate powerful metamessages about women and men and the nature of their social relationships. Sometimes a patriarchy becomes dangerous, taking the form of violence and the threat of violence targeted at girls and women and, often, gay men (who are defined in patriarchies as unmasculine and thus stripped of the privileges of their gender). Even in non-Western cultures in which patriarchies take on a less individualistic form, the devaluation of women and that which is associated with women emerges, although its lineaments may be unfamiliar to White Western observers who may mistake more communitarian cultures for nonpatriarchal ones. However, collective patriarchies, such as those of many indigenous people around the world and in North America, remain cultures in which the devaluation of the female is identifiable.

Patriarchies also affect people's attitudes and values. Beliefs about women and men's "inherent" natures, capacities, and ways of relating reflect patriarchal consciousness. The easy popularity of the notion that men and women are from different planets (Gray, 1992) is an excellent illustration of how embedded this sort of patriarchal "truth" has become. Such values can become dangerous. For example, patriarchal myths about sexual assaults and woman battering tend to place responsibility for the violence on those who were assaulted (Walker, 1989). Violence against gay men and lesbians is similarly blamed on the overt actions of the gay or lesbian person rather than on the person committing the violent act (Franklin, 1998). People of different races, who were raised in the context of White people's norms of beauty, may experience distortions of body image (Comas-Diaz & Greene, 1994). All of these attitudes and values reflect patriarchal norms and standards. Many of them are directly harmful to people, particularly when woven into the context of trauma and interpersonal violence. Even under apparently benign circumstances, these attitudes and values can be a source of self-denigration and self-loathing. For instance, the extremely high rates of disordered eating and eating-disordered beliefs among young White women seem to reflect a cultural hatred of the female body, which has curves and greater fat padding. All of these manifestations of patriarchy, behaviors and attitudes, are likely to be focuses of treatment for feminist therapists.

Feminist therapy theory posits that, in whatever shape it takes, patriarchies leave their psychological marks in the form of distortions and limitations on each person's capacity for well-being and personal power. Patriarchal patterns of thought pervade all intellectual and philosophical systems operating in a patriarchy to the point that such notions are assumed to be the truth when they are not closely examined (Lerner, 1993). These "truths" then migrate into science and into the training of mental health practitioners. For example, the presumed innate weakness of women's minds and bodies was actually taught in science lectures in many graduate psychology curricula through the beginning of the 1970s (Weisstein, 1970). Although the dangers of patriarchs to the emotional, physical, and financial well-being of White women and women and men of different races seem more obvious, there are meaningful and painful costs to most White men as well for their participation in patriarchal systems. For instance, men's higher rates of violent behaviors and incarceration or the difficulties that many men have being vulnerable in intimate relationships (Stoltenberg, 1990) are all manifestations of patriarchies.

Although gender is an almost inescapable locus of oppression in patriarchy, almost every human difference is viewed through the patriarchal lens as a form of deficiency. As Lerner (1993) noted, race, social class, and other forms of difference are epistemologically constructed in patriarchal philosophies in analogy to male–female differences. Thus, women, people of different races, people who are poor, people who have disabilities, and so on, have similar traits ascribed to them, whereas maleness, Whiteness, wealth, and physical ability also share ascriptions and stereotypes as well as levels of social desirability.

GOALS OF FEMINIST PRACTICE

Feminist therapy, as one aspect of the overall feminist movement for social change, has as a goal the subversion of patriarchal dominance as it is internalized and personified in the life of the therapist, the therapeutic relationship, and the lives of clients, colleagues, and communities. Unlike other expressions of feminism that are carried out in the more usually agreed on political arenas of legislation, the courts, and the media, feminist therapy largely concerns itself with the development of strategies for addressing oppression at the personal and intimate level. Feminist practice focuses on the many invisible and sometimes nonconscious ways in which patriarchal modes of understanding have become embedded in each person's daily life in the forms of identity development, manners of emotional expression, and experiences of personal power and powerlessness. Overt violations of personal power through interpersonal victimization, discrimination, or what Root (1992) referred to as *insidious traumatization* arising from daily small experiences of disempowerment, are considered by feminist practitioners to be prime examples of such experiences of powerlessness and can lead to distress and difficulties in life functioning. Some feminist authors have argued that certain forms of interpersonal conflict, such as sexual assault and harassment, are institutionalized strategies within patriarchal cultures for maintaining women and other marginalized groups in subordinate positions (Lerner, 1993).

DEVELOPING FEMINIST CONSCIOUSNESS

A goal of feminist practice, no matter what form that practice takes, is the development of feminist consciousness in both the therapist and the client. A corollary goal is to assist therapists and clients with taking feminist action (Brabeck & Brown, 1997) in therapy and outside of therapy as a result of participating in the therapy relationship. By *feminist consciousness*, feminist therapists refer to the following definition:

> The awareness of women that they belong to a subordinate group; that they have suffered wrongs as a group; that their condition of subordination is not natural, but is societally determined; that they must join with other women to remedy these wrongs; and finally, that they must and can provide an alternate vision of societal organization in which women as well as men will enjoy autonomy and self-determination. (Lerner, 1993, p. 14)

In practice, this definition means helping clients realize that their problems are not expressions of unique deficits or circumstances but rather are tied to group memberships and can be changed altering individual personal circumstances and the conditions of the group in the larger society.

Current feminist therapy theory expands on this definition of feminist consciousness by including an awareness of racist, classist, heterosexist, and other forms of oppression and their respective and interactive effects on human functioning (Adleman & Enguidanos, 1995; Brabeck & Brown, 1997; Brown, 1994; Greene & Sanchez-Hucles, 1997). Thus, an important aspect of any therapy practice that is feminist is its capacity to raise awareness of group membership, assign responsibility accurately for the difficulties that people have encountered in life, and challenge distorted beliefs about the lesser value of certain groups of people, particularly those groups to which clients themselves belong.

EMDR and Feminist Consciousness

EMDR may be useful in changing strongly held patriarchal beliefs and myths, particularly those that have become a part of a person's coping and adaptation to trauma and interpersonal violence. When these myths and beliefs are challenged, people are more likely to develop feminist consciousness. Patriarchal representations of reality commonly emerge during EMDR at varying stages of the treatment process. They can then become a target for processing. EMDR is a subversive strategy for creating feminist consciousness in therapy because it is a strategy that does not directly dispute the patriarchal belief. It simply invites the client to consider the possible truth of an alternative belief. Such subversive strategies are valued in feminist practice (Brown, 1994); as in the martial art of aikido, patriarchal beliefs are disempowered not through the use of greater force (itself a patriarchal change strategy) but rather through creating the opportunities for the inherent wrongfulness of the patriarchal belief systems to expose itself as the felt truth of an alternative belief emerges during treatment. EMDR is directly concerned with transforming the clients' consciousness —consciousness that relates to their experiences—through the development of the positive cognition and an increase in the validity of cognition (VoC) of the positive cognition to a level that ensures it will be stably integrated into clients' self-constructs and self-schemata. When therapists pay attention to the patriarchal undertones of a negative cognition, they can be more specific about assisting clients with disputing those in the positive cognition being developed.

Unlike more purely cognitive approaches to changing consciousness, in EMDR the reprocessing of the traumatic experience allows clients to have a felt (rather than merely a cognitive) understanding of the truth, the truth of what a feminist practitioner would identify as *feminist consciousness*. This process in turn becomes the means by which clients make serious and long-lasting challenges to their patriarchal belief systems.

When EMDR allows clients to end self-blaming behaviors—to no longer consider their traumatic experience as a result of their inherent weakness or as an expected outgrowth of membership in a devalued group—or when it allows clients to perceive themselves as powerful sources of their own transformation, then experiences that strongly resemble feminist consciousness are the consequences (sometimes unintended) of EMDR treatment. Aside from the Socratic dialogue that therapists might use during the cognitive interweave component of a reprocessing session, they do not take charge of challenging false patriarchal beliefs. Rather, clients are empowered to listen to their own answers to these questions and use them to develop a more compassionate view of themselves and a more powerful way of being. EMDR assists clients with coming to the self-realization that their negative beliefs are no longer true and is thus particularly effective at changing the "feels true" nature of patriarchal mythologies.

As alluded to in the previous paragraphs, one common locus for the exposure of patriarchal beliefs and values is in the assessment of the negative cognition at the outset of an EMDR processing session. Many negative cognitions "feel true" in part because they resonate with strongly manifested patriarchal values. At times, they are completely introjected versions of patriarchal constructs (e.g., "I was beaten because I talked back to my husband"). Because such values are so embedded in the cultural and emotional background and are often accepted as true by the larger society or clients' own particular culture of reference, the values are difficult for clients either to identify as wrong or to challenge directly. Even when direct cognitive challenges to negative cognitions are made by therapists, a process that is used by cognitive–behavioral therapists during the disputation of distorted beliefs, such challenges often fall short of resulting in permanent change because the old distorted cognitions are reinforced by the social environment. The old beliefs continue to have the emotional weight of truth. EMDR seems to assist clients with being more resilient in the face of social pressures for the status quo, clients who are attempting to develop feminist consciousness because of the way it addresses and transforms felt realities. The following case study illustrates the way this process might unfold.

Case Study

Jan, an Asian American heterosexual woman in her mid-30s sought therapy to deal with a previous sexual assault. A former boyfriend had come to her home for a social visit and forced her to have sex. Although numerous years had passed since the assault, she reported that she was still being affected by the experience, particularly in terms of her self-concept.

During the assessment of her cognitions, which took place before EMDR, Jan reported that her cognitions were variations of the same theme

—that she had no right to call this assault a *rape* because she had already had consensual sex with the man in the past and that it was her fault or her overreaction that led her to perceive this experience as an assault. Jan also had many self-deprecating and self-blaming beliefs. Because she had been sexually active with several partners, although it had always been in the context of committed relationships, she considered herself to be sexually flawed or damaged. The daughter of immigrants from an Asian country, Jan had already experienced conflicts with her family of origin about her choice to leave their home without being married and about the fact that she had lived with two of her boyfriends, including the one who had sexually assaulted her. Her negative cognition at the beginning of processing was, "If I had been a better woman, this wouldn't have happened to me."

This type of self-accusatory cognition is typical of people who have been sexually and physically abused by acquaintances (Herman, 1992; Walker, 1989). Such patriarchal dicta include the notion that an unchaste woman (who, by definition in a patriarchal system, is any woman who is sexual outside of the implied ownership context of marriage) has lost the right to sexual self-determination. Thus, an unchaste woman may not say no to a man who desires sexual activity because such a woman has no right to refuse him or be sexually self-determined.

In addition, a patriarchal principle states that a woman who has consented to sexual activity with a man once has abrogated any future rights to withdraw the consent from the same man. For example, by law in some states, a sexual assault by a husband of his wife (or in some cases, of his former wife) is not a crime because marriage or former marriage legally confers perpetual sexual access rights to the husband.

Patriarchal values are also revealed in the self-assessments of people who have been sexually assaulted. The patriarchal message is that women, being less rational than men, overreact to being forced into nonconsensual sexual activity. Because of the absence of overt violence or threat of other bodily harm, their overreaction is their perception of the sexual activity as an assault. In forensic contexts, it is extremely common for attorneys to challenge the possibility that posttraumatic stress disorder (PTSD) can develop in women who have been the targets of sexual incursions in which other violence does not occur; patriarchies do not define sexual violence as life-threatening. Instead, it is defined as a threat to the ownership rights of the man to whom the woman is connected (Robson, 1992).

The themes in Jan's negative cognitions ("I was to blame," "I overreacted," "I shouldn't have invited him in"), and those of many other people who have been sexually assaulted, clearly demonstrate to feminist practitioners how clients may have internalized patriarchal values about women and their sexuality. In turn, these beliefs have become embedded in clients' perception of themselves in relationship to the sexual assault.

Such negative cognitions reflect not only the client's interpretation of a particular traumatic event but also the cultural norms and years of socialization that preceded the trauma. Feminist practice asserts that it is necessary to consider clients' beliefs in their sociopolitical contexts. Because this kind of negative cognition reflects strongly held dominant culture values, it may be particularly resistant to change through purely cognitive methods; the context and culture continually reinforce the belief.

Attempts to find a positive cognition that contravenes this kind of patriarchal belief system may prove difficult. This is not, feminist theorists would argue, because clients are resistant to developing or unable to develop a positive cognition. A personal negative cognition that reflects the patriarchal ideology may feel so true that it is difficult to challenge or imagine differently. A feminist practitioner would not be surprised if a client had a VoC of 1 or 2 for a positive cognition related to a trauma with such inherent deep cultural symbolism. The positive cognition for a sexual assault experience, a cognition that would be likely to be an expression of feminist consciousness (e.g., that women have the right to say no, that a woman's prior sexual experiences do not strip her of the power to withhold sexual consent, that sexual assault is life threatening and not a "property crime"), may feel wrong when it challenges the truths of the dominant society.

Why is it valuable for a feminist practitioner to identify these kinds of negative cognitions as representing patriarchal messages? Why would a nonfeminist EMDR practitioner find it helpful to understand that the themes of many negative cognitions produced by clients are idiosyncratic versions of larger, very powerful cultural themes? This feminist analysis of the negative cognition emphasizes that what is being expressed is not evidence of unique client pathology nor is it simply a personal belief. It is the personal version of commonly found beliefs that are held by many individuals and strongly reinforced by many institutions of the dominant culture. A feminist analysis of the theme of a negative cognition in the case of highly meaning-laden traumatic events such as sexual and domestic assault, hate crime victimization, discrimination, or childhood maltreatment can also illuminate how and why a client in EMDR therapy may have difficulties challenging such a cognition during processing work. In addition, a feminist analysis could prepare therapists to plan to use cognitive interweave. In such cases, the client's negative cognitions not only are individual assessments about themselves in relationship to the world but also are representations of the culture itself and are being reinstated and reinforced by the culture from the minute the clients leave the therapy office to the moment they return. Even the most aware and resilient individuals are likely to be vulnerable to this sort of continual, often subtle, message about the "truths" of the world and their relationship to that world. These are the negative cognitions that seem to grow more embedded with initial processing sessions. The questions necessary to unblock these particular patriarchal loops are most effective when the therapist is aware of the cultural roots of the stuck point.

Listening to clients' self-statements and the themes of their negative cognitions with an awareness of their social and cultural context may offer a larger range of options for therapeutic interventions. In addition, identifying elements of patriarchal rules in clients' cognitions and stuck places may assist therapists with framing questions more incisively during cognitive interweave should it be needed during the reprocessing session.

For example, in Jan's case, the therapist used knowledge of the patriarchal context in the Socratic questioning of the client, subtly emphasizing the impact on Jan of patriarchal rape myths and commenting on the patriarchal themes that Jan was producing when she became stuck in loops. Rather than asking, "Why would *you* be responsible for his behavior?" the therapist asked, "Why would a *woman* be responsible for a man's sexual behavior?" The difference is subtle but meaningful; the question frames Jan as a woman with the common woman's experience rather than as an isolated individual. It taps into the nonconscious ideology of sexism and patriarchy embedded in Jan's individual belief system. Although the question continues to be open ended and offers ample room for Jan to take charge of the meaning of the reprocessing experience, the feminist frame on the question and the feminist therapist's awareness of the patriarchal messages embedded in Jan's cognitions gave her an opportunity to examine how her experience had been associated with many unwanted beliefs by prior exposures to patriarchal verities.

CREATING EGALITARIAN THERAPY RELATIONSHIPS

Another important stated goal of feminist therapy is the creation of egalitarian relationships between therapists and their clients. All forms of psychotherapy focus on the therapist–client relationship to some degree. The models of relating that emerge from feminist calls for radical rearrangements of social relationships are relevant to the therapeutic relationship in crucial ways. Critical analyses of power arrangements in psychotherapy and attempts to develop a paradigm for an egalitarian relationship are themes of feminist discourse. Feminist therapy has been uniquely attuned to the manner in which the internal, symbolic components of the interaction are shaped and colored by the signifiers of gender, race, class, and culture, which give our actions meaning in the social world. From the start, feminist therapists have struggled to make sense of a relationship whose parameters, as they are commonly defined, seem to have an inherent poor fit with the goals of feminist social change.

Psychotherapy, like other social institutions of a patriarchy, typically models a dominance–submission hierarchy of unequal power. Psychotherapy as it is currently practiced in most parts of the Westernized world is a form of relating that was created by White men, few of whom questioned the underlying assumptions about the role of the therapist as defined within patriarchal models of relating. This is true even in the face of the emerging demographics of psychotherapy practice, in which most of the therapists practicing the White-male versions of reality are actually women (and are also predominantly White). Consequently, most models of therapy invest expertise and authority in one person, in this case the therapist. A hierarchy of power and value is embedded in these models; much writing on therapy practice discusses the need for the therapist to manage and contain the client and the therapeutic process.

Power and its imbalances in therapy have proved to be especially thorny problems for feminist therapists given the inherent imbalances in therapy itself. Strategies for addressing this issue often involve the difficulties inherent to an attempt to merge two quite different epistemologies. Feminists consider individuals to be living within a social context of political meaning and are concerned with the rearrangement of social and political power. In contrast, psychotherapists have been apolitical, focusing on the transformation of individual lives as an end unto itself and paying little concern or attention to social arrangements.

Egalitarianism and asymmetry form two important competing tensions in the construction of a therapy relationship that is feminist. Feminist therapists interrogate and attempt to address the actual power arrangements present in the relationship as it exists in the present. In attempting to accomplish this goal, authors in the field of feminist therapy typically have described feminist therapy as being an "egalitarian relationship" (Brabeck & Brown, 1997; Brown, 1994). This construct is an attempt to acknowledge the lack of equality inherent in therapy and striving toward equality as an ultimate goal of the particular therapeutic exchange. Egalitarian relationships are relationships that are structured in a way that allows equality of power, in which artificial and unnecessary barriers to equality of power are removed from the process. In an egalitarian relationship, an equality of *value* exists between the participants and involves respect for each person's worth. However, some necessary asymmetry is involved in certain aspects of the exchange; these asymmetries are designed in part to empower the less powerful person but primarily to define and delineate the responsibilities of the more powerful person.

In an egalitarian psychotherapy relationship, a primary goal is for clients to realize and value their own needs, voice, and knowledge as central and authoritative in their lives. Therapists are not to supplant this knowledge with their own authority but rather to use their skills to resonate, mirror, and engage the clients in their own process and assist them with learning how such self-knowledge and self-value is obscured by patri-archal processes and institutions.

The temporary absence of absolute equality of power is punctuated and made conscious in feminist practice by the therapist's analysis of the complex and subtle power dynamics in the exchange. This process requires close attention by therapists if they are to maintain the delicate balance and not accidentally garner the powers that are typically ascribed to their role by dominant modalities and eschewed by feminist methodologies, (e.g., the power to define the *other* as pathological and the *self* as the norm). This model assumes that all human beings attempt to solve their problems, including the problem of emotional distress. The flawed solutions people present as their symptoms in therapy are no less competent and creative than are the flawed solutions practiced by therapists in their own lives, even when different social values have been assigned to those coping strat-egies. The specific details of the methodologies for achieving this balance vary for each person and situation. Each solution takes into account the powers of the therapist and the client and defines power as an infinite rather than a finite resource of multidimensional properties.

EMDR as Inherently Egalitarian

EMDR is an elegant solution to the problem of egalitarian relation-ship construction. The EMDR practitioner, although using a potentially powerful change strategy, is continuously engaging in interventions that empower clients to develop their own voices and awareness. This creation of space for clients' voices begins at the very start of the process when clients in EMDR are given explicit and careful informed consent guide-lines. Aside from feminist therapy, no other approach to treatment is as insistent on clients' informed consent as EMDR. (Discovering this fact in the EMDR training was one of the first indicators EMDR was a therapy modality that was potentially very congruent with feminist practice.) I have previously described the value of the informed consent process as a strategy for beginning to empower clients as effective decision-makers (Brown, 1994). Clients who participate in EMDR have also been routinely availed of this strategy. Their right to understand what will happen, to question and challenge the therapist, and to be an active collaborator in the therapy rather than a passive recipient of the therapist's skill are built in to the EMDR process.

At the next stage of EMDR, when therapists engage clients in de-veloping the image of the painful or traumatic event, the negative and positive cognitions, and the assessments of subjective units of disturbance (SUDS) and VoC, clients are once again empowered as the expert. Clients are asked to define and describe the scene that they would like to address rather than being told what to attend to. Clients' own subjective perceptions of the right place to begin reprocessing are honored in EMDR. Therapists do not determine which one of a series of painful events is the most painful or should be used as the starting point; clients do that. The concept of VoC also introduces clients to another frequently silenced source of voice and authority—their subjective perceptions of what "feels true." For clients who have silenced and minimized their own perceptions for long periods, the invitation to explicitly consider what feels true and how true it feels opens a door to their voice and self-knowledge, which in turn translates into increased personal power.

Case Studies

An example of the empowering effects of assessing VoC is illustrated by the following case study.

"Pam," a White woman in her mid-50s, had been in therapy for many years. Various therapists had attempted to deal with her much distorted view of her body size and shape. To an observer, she seemed to have an average or slight build, but since adolescence she had perceived herself as being extremely fat. Her self-perceptions had led to a series of self-injurious behaviors, including excessive fasting, purging, and exercise to the point of injury. She complained to her current therapist that she "knew" her body was supposed to be normal and could not comprehend her own resistance to the cognitive interventions that her last two therapists had engaged in with her.

When her therapist proposed using EMDR to target her body hatred, Pam easily identified a painful scene ("seeing myself in the mirror, the fat hanging off my thighs and stomach") and a negative cognition ("I'm disgusting"). She was also fairly adept at creating a positive cognition, "My body is okay as it is." However, when the therapist asked her to assess how true the positive statement felt, a fascinating dialogue began. Pam began by saying that she knew that this statement should feel very true because "everyone tells me it's true." However, the therapist would not allow Pam to impose others' values on herself. She told Pam that in this instance, it was extremely important for Pam to know what felt true for her and not what seemed true to anyone else.

Pam began to weep. When she was able to speak, she told her therapist that she had spent many years trying to "shut herself up" about her own feelings about her body, and she had felt "stupid" and guilty, as well as that she was a bad feminist, for loathing her body so intensely. Her previous therapists had always focused on the irrationality of her cognitions, which silenced her even more. She reported feeling astonished by the depth of her feelings after being told that what felt true to her was what was important—so important that the therapist would take extra time to discover what those feelings might be. She told the therapist that although the positive cognition she had generated corresponded with what she had been taught to say about herself, it had "less than no feeling of truth to it. It feels completely untrue."

The therapist then invited Pam to revisit her positive cognition and spend the time to develop a positive cognition that would feel true and thus would reflect her authority, voice, and expertise, not those of previous therapists, her current therapist, or anyone else. Pam changed her positive cognition to "I could learn to like my body better." She reported that this felt true at a VoC level of 2; not very true, but true enough that it reflected what was real for her.

The reprocessing component of EMDR in which clients engage in eye movements is also a stage at which clients can be empowered as their own authority. Although the number of eye movements for an initial reprocessing set or a set in which no affect is manifested is suggested to be 24, clients are also given explicit permission to shorten or lengthen the process through signaling. Additionally, EMDR therapists are trained to carefully follow clients' affect levels and extend or shorten the eye movements in response rather than to rigidly adhere to a protocol. The focus in the training of EMDR practitioners is on clients' needs and clients' pacing (which can be challenging for trainees accustomed to setting the timing of treatment in other modalities). The time that clients can spend with a particular aspect of the reprocessing thus becomes highly reflective of the clients' needs, not just of the therapists' opinions about how to focus the therapy.

The highly internal nature of the reprocessing component is another aspect of EMDR that supports the egalitarian therapy relationship. Clients decide what, if anything, to share during therapy. One of the most obviously power-imbalancing aspects of therapy is that clients are expected to expose their story and become vulnerable to therapists while the therapists are allowed to remain silent and behind the boundaries of their role. A therapy strategy in which clients interact with themselves and can limit what will be shared may significantly improve the imbalance of power. Clients who are not extremely verbal have a disadvantage in most talk therapies because they are forced into using a less desirable form of communication; these clients may feel more comfortable and centered in the milieu of EMDR because little verbalization is required. EMDR requires therapists to accept clients as they are rather than requiring them to adopt the modalities that are most favored by the therapists. Clients receive powerful authority as the experts about what can make change truly happen, a process that is consistent with feminist models of practice. The following case study is an example of the empowerment component of EMDR.

Rita was a Chicana woman who had often told her therapist that "language [i.e., the use of words] is not my native language." She had a lengthy history of depression resulting from a childhood in which she was physically abused by her family and subject to racial discrimination at school. She felt intimidated by being in therapy with a person who was not only a White man but also had an advanced degree. Therapy sessions had often consisted of Rita's halting attempts at communication, followed by anxious pauses and long silences.

When the therapist introduced EMDR to Rita, he informed her that she was free to share as much or as little of the processing with him as she would like. He emphasized that his job was to facilitate her own voyage of self-discovery, and he reminded her on numerous occasions that whatever would emerge would be true for her and would emerge at a speed that was right for her. This message given to clients by EMDR practitioners—that the content of their processing is their own truth and they are the judges of where to follow the content—is a conscious communication of respect for the client's authority, one that rarely occurs in nonfeminist practice.

Rita had lengthy, emotion-laden, and largely nonverbal processing sessions. Her stated beginning targets were various painful experiences involving degradation and humiliation. At the end of each set of eye movements, the therapist asked what Rita was experiencing. Rita realized that she did not want to speak to the therapist in detail about what had happened. He supported her in this strategy; he only asked that if she found herself stuck in a difficult place, she allow him to help her to get out, or "unstick." He also emphasized that a large part of the work would happen outside of therapy without him and encouraged her to record her dreams, thoughts, and feelings in a journal. However, he was careful to respect Rita's wishes about whether and how much she shared about her processing outside of sessions.

During a series of six EMDR therapy sessions, Rita spoke very little. However, she reported at the end of the sessions that she was feeling much less depressed. The therapist also noted that when Rita chose to speak in the therapy sessions, she was speaking more freely and easily. Rita told the therapist that it had been extremely important to her to be allowed *not* to speak. She was finally able to tell the therapist that many of her experiences of abuse and discrimination, inside and outside of her family of origin, had involved feeling ashamed about how and what she said. After silently processing these experiences in EMDR, she was significantly less afraid of speaking. She told the therapist that she had come to see herself and her words in an entirely new light during the sessions in which she had said so little.

In this case study, the client had developed a consciousness of her own worth and value, in part because the very process of therapy communicated to her that she had the expertise to know how to heal herself, and that she did not have to use a modality that made her feel victimized all over again. The therapist, by remaining in the role of facilitator, shed the power inherent in his role, gender, and cultural background and stepped aside so that Rita could take charge. EMDR and its stance of client power can be challenging for therapists who have a strong need to maintain the power of their role. It stands in sharp contrast to some approaches to therapy in which the therapist's ability to trick or manipulate the client or the therapist's omniscient interpretations of reality for the client are central to theory and practice. By the very parameters of EMDR, EMDR practitioners are required to share power in explicit ways that can lead to egalitarian relationships, even when therapists do not identify this as an explicit goal of treatment.

As described previously, feminist therapy theory emphasizes the value of the development of people's own voices and of their capacity to resist silencing. In EMDR, the voice of the client is paramount. The change strategies available through EMDR do not privilege the therapist's perceptions. The sole potential risk in this highly egalitarian modality is during the cognitive interweave, which may be necessary to assist a client in breaking a loop. EMDR practitioners are trained to use open-ended, Socratic questioning in the cognitive interweave process. When therapists carefully adhere to this strategy, it is another medium for opening up the voice of the client. However, therapists who are not explicitly feminist in their practice may inadvertently use this juncture in EMDR to insert their own perceptions and visions of what is right and true, making interpretations rather than eliciting the client's own critical thinking skills. The difficulty for some therapists to remain consistent in the client-driven nature of EMDR reflects the tendency of most therapy training to consider the therapist as the expert. Luckily, the logical consequences of failing to remain Socratic and client driven is that the interweave is less successful. Therapists who are aware of this and have the goal of remaining effective are likely to change their own behavior in a way that makes it more effective—by empowering the client in these difficult but important "stuck" points in therapy.

UNDERSTANDING THE SOCIAL MEANING OF THERAPY

Feminist therapy has been relatively unique among schools of practice in its conscious embrace of social change as a legitimate goal of the therapy process. For example, the 1990 ethical code of the Feminist Therapy Institute, which has been accepted as a standard by many other feminist practitioners, explicitly calls on feminist therapists to act as change agents in the world outside of their offices. Because of the grounding of feminist practice in political theory, feminist therapists are also specifically attentive to the ways in which a given individual's therapy experiences either support or undermine the patriarchal status quo.

EMDR now joins with the small ranks of intentionally socially conscious therapies. Francine Shapiro, the creator of EMDR, has modeled the importance of using EMDR in situations in which it is most likely to effect social change. The EMDR Humanitarian Assistance Programs (HAP) have trained therapists to use EMDR in such locations as Northern Ireland and the former Yugoslav states. The guiding principle behind HAP is the notion that ethnic hatred reflects centuries of trauma that were transmitted from one generation to the next and reenacted in the forms of ethnic violence and societal suffering. This paradigm mirrors the concept that individual human suffering is the by-product of patriarchy. By making EMDR, which is a highly effective treatment for the sequelae of trauma, available to therapists who work in these cultures, the HAP workers are using therapy as a conscious tool for social change. The HAP program pays particular attention to issues of cultural specificity that can enhance the effectiveness of EMDR itself, a framework highly consistent with feminist practice's focus on the privileging of diversity.

The rationale of HAP is that by treating the intrapsychic aspects of ethnic hatred and trauma, social change may more easily occur. Although at this point the systematic effects of the HAP trainings are only initially being studied (evaluations of their effectiveness are now taking place), the standard has been set by Shapiro and other leading EMDR trainers, practitioners, and researchers—skill in EMDR implies a willingness to commit to social justice, and psychotherapy practice can be a core component of making real and lasting social change. Other HAP projects have offered free training and treatment to people who have been terrorized or in disasters; again, the social justice emphasis is on healing people, regardless of their ability to pay, and empowering local communities through pro bono training of local therapists.

The EMDR–HAP is an example of the feminist notion that the personal is political. In this case, therapy and its effectiveness are explicitly linked to the responsibility to "do good" and "heal the world." EMDR practitioners are not simply taught to be effective in their use of this strategy. From the inception of their EMDR training, they are given the message that if they are skillful enough, they can also have the chance to create social justice by becoming part of a HAP team. Creating an explicit value for changing the world is ultimately a feminist goal for therapy.

CONCLUSION

Of course, it is possible that even skillfully practiced EMDR could not be feminist. Many therapists who come to the initial EMDR training do so in hopes of increasing their power to affect clients; their impatience with the client-driven nature of EMDR is quickly observed in the practicum component of the training workshops. EMDR training cannot and does not erase therapists' own tendencies to use their authority to overpower clients, silence clients' voices with their words, or enhance the power of their role through the knowledge of a highly effective and seemingly magical therapeutic method. Therapists who use EMDR can subtly emphasize their own importance in the process, insist on the client sharing more than is comfortable about the processing sessions, change the wording of the negative or positive cognitions, or underemphasize the value of out-of-session processing. EMDR can be practiced in very nonfeminist ways, although it seems unlikely that fidelity to the protocol would persist over time if a therapist continued to make this sort of choice in their EMDR practice.

However, as a strategy for personal transformation, EMDR seems to clearly meet the criteria for a feminist model of practice. It offers to therapists who are already feminist practitioners a modality for working with clients that fits easily and effectively into a competency-based view of clients. EMDR assists therapists in being what I have described as the "excellent copy editors, but not the authors" of our clients' narratives. The protocol for EMDR puts clients and their voices, visions, and wisdom at center stage and truly requires the therapist to follow clients' leads.

Some feminist practitioners are uncomfortable with EMDR because its mechanism of action is uncertain. They have raised concerns that it requires therapists either to offer empirically unsupported explanations, such as Shapiro's paradigm of "accelerated information processing," or to mystify the therapy process (Forrest & Gilbert, 1996). Others have expressed concerns about the structure through which EMDR is taught. Feminist practice has typically been promulgated through various informal apprenticeship models, ones that rarely involve designated trainers or experts, usually for a small or no fee. Although this is slowly changing in feminist psychology circles, a certain suspicion of apparently commercial enterprises continues to pervade much of the feminist therapy world, a world in which serious discussions were held in the not-too-distant past about whether it was ethical for feminists to charge for therapy at all. Once therapists are directly exposed to EMDR practice through training or personal experience as a client, many of these concerns do not exist. As more self-identified feminist practitioners also become trained in EMDR, it is likely that the shared epistemologies and shared social justice orientation of these schools of therapy will allow them to perceive their similarities more easily. The potential for cross-fertilization between the work of feminist therapy practice and EMDR holds promise for effective, empowering therapies that can further the feminist goal of quiet, long-lasting social revolution.

REFERENCES

Adleman, J., & Enguidanos, G. (1995). *Racism in the lives of women: Testimony, theory and guides to anti-racist practice*. Binghamton, NY: Harrington Park Press.

Alpert, J. (Ed.). (1986). *Psychoanalysis and women: Contemporary reappraisals*. Hillsboro, NJ: Analytic Press.

American Psychiatric Association. (1980). *Diagnostic and statistical manual of mental disorders* (3rd ed.). Washington, DC: Author.

Ballou, M. (1990). Approaching a feminist-principled paradigm in the construction of personality theory. In L. S. Brown & M. P. P. Root (Eds.), *Diversity and complexity in feminist therapy* (pp. 23–40). New York: Haworth.

Bem, S. L., & Bem, D. (1970). Training the woman to know her place: The power of a non-conscious ideology. In S. Fox (Ed.), *Female psychology: The emerging self* (pp. 180–191). Chicago: SRA Books.

Brabeck, M., & Brown, L. S. (1997). Feminist theory and psychological practice. In J. Worell & N. Johnson (Eds.), *Shaping the future of feminist psychology: Education, research and practice* (pp. 15–36). Washington DC: American Psychological Association.

Brown, L. S. (1986). New voices, new visions: Toward a lesbian/gay paradigm for psychology. *Psychology of Women Quarterly, 13,* 445–458.

Brown, L. S. (1994). *Subversive dialogues: Theory in feminist therapy*. New York: Basic Books.

Chesler, P. (1972). *Women and madness*. Garden City, NY: Doubleday.

Comas-Diaz, L., & Greene, B. (Eds.). (1994). *Women of color: Integrating ethnic and gender identities in psychotherapy*. New York: Guilford Press.

Feminist Therapy Institute. (1990). Feminist Therapy Institute code of ethics. In H. Lerman & N. Porter (Eds.), *Feminist ethics in psychotherapy* (pp. 37–40). New York: Springer.

Forrest, L., & Gilbert, M. S. (1996). Three widely divergent views on effective treatment of abuse. *Psychology of Women Quarterly, 20,* 612–616.

Fox, D., & Prilleltensky, I. (Eds.). (1997). *Critical psychology: An introduction*. London: Sage.

Franklin, K. (1998). Unassuming motivations: Contextualizing the narratives of antigay assailants. In G. Herek (Ed.), *Stigma and sexual orientation: Understanding prejudice against lesbians, gay men, and bisexuals* (pp. 1–23). Thousand Oaks, CA: Sage.

Gray, J. (1992). *Men are from Mars, women are from Venus*. New York: HarperCollins.

Greene, B., & Sanchez-Hucles, J. (1997). Diversity: Advancing an inclusive feminist psychology. In J. Worell & N. Johnson (Eds.), *Shaping the future of feminist psychology: Education, research, and practice* (pp. 173–202). Washington DC: American Psychological Association.

Herman, J. L. (1992). *Trauma and recovery*. New York: Basic Books.

Lerman, H. (1987). *A mote in Freud's eye: From psychoanalysis to the psychology of women.* New York: Springer

Lerner, G. (1993). *The creation of feminist consciousness.* New York: Oxford University Press.

Luepnitz, D. A. (1988). *The family interpreted: Feminist theory in clinical practice.* New York: Basic Books.

Robson, R. (1992). *Lesbian (out)law: Survival under the rule of law.* Ithaca, NY: Firebrand.

Root, M. P. P. (1992). Reconstructing the impact of trauma on personality. In L. S. Brown & M. Ballou (Eds.), *Personality and psychopathology: Feminist reappraisals* (pp. 229–266). New York: Guilford Press.

Silverstein, L. B., & Auerbach, C. (1999). Deconstructing the essential father. *American Psychologist, 54,* 397–704.

Stoltenberg, J. (1990). *Refusing to be a man.* New York: Meridian.

Walker, L. E. A. (1989). Psychology and violence against women. *American Psychologist, 44* 695–702.

Weisstein, N. (1970). Kinder kuche kirche as scientific law: Psychology constructs the female. In R. Morgan (Ed.), *Sisterhood is powerful* (pp. 205–219). New York: Vintage.

Worell, J., & Remer, P. (1992). *Feminist perspectives in therapy: An empowerment model for women.* New York: Wiley.

12

EMDR IN CONJUNCTION WITH FAMILY SYSTEMS THERAPY

FLORENCE W. KASLOW, A. RODNEY NURSE,
AND PEGGY THOMPSON

The field of family therapy seemed to coalesce around 1960, although some of the early pioneers were already conducting and writing about family systems and treating multipatient units before then (e.g., Ackerman, 1937, 1938; Bateson, 1958; Bowen, 1959). This chapter offers a brief overview of the field and then provides case studies in which EMDR is the primary treatment methodology, used within a family systems perspective, or both.

EVOLUTION OF THE FIELD

In prior writings, Kaslow (1990, 2000a) divided the stages of the family therapy field into four overlapping periods that seem to generally correspond to each of the past four decades:

1. Pioneers and renegades (Before 1969)
2. Innovators and expanders (1969–1979)

3. Challengers, refiners, and researchers (1980–1989)
4. Integrators and seekers of new horizons (1990–1999)

In each generation the leaders have tended to be charismatic, out-spoken, articulate, determined, persuasive, and convinced that their way was and is a very important one—and possibly the only right way (or at least the best way). Most leaders have become teachers and mentors; their trainees have become devoted disciples, spreading "the word according to St. X." In the family of family therapists, which began primarily in the United States and England (Guerin, 1976; Guerin & Fogarty, 1972; Kaslow, 1980; Skynner, 1976) and spread rapidly to Australia (Lang, 1982; White & Epstom, 1990), Argentina (Herscovici & Herscovici, 1999), Belgium (Elkaim, 1985, 1986), Israel (Charny, 1986, 1990, 1996; Halpern, 2001), Italy (Boscolo & Bertrando, 1992; Boscolo, Cecchin, Hoffman, & Penn, 1987; Selvini-Palazzoli, Boscolo, Cecchin, & Prata, 1978; Selvini-Palazzoli, Cirillo, Selvini, & Sorrentino, 1989), Japan (Kameguchi, 2001; Suzuki & Suzuki, 1988), and other countries around the world (Kaslow, 2000b), loyalty to one's mentor and professional family of origin has been an important trait, just as is loyalty to one's personal family of origin.

As trainees matured and integrated ideas from other theoretical schools, resultant serious disagreements with the masters were sometimes treated as acts of rebellion and disloyalty. When the theoretical family of origin remained rigidly purist, serious rifts occurred, leading to cutoffs (Bowen, 1978). Because some of the leaders and their closest disciples considered deviations heresy, those committing such acts often felt adrift and either tried to found their own theoretical school or training program or faded into semioblivion. Alliances and schisms have been as rife in one's professional family of family therapists as in any of their personal families. This is as much a part of the legacy, aura, and ethos of this field as it is of psychoanalysis, and it is important to see this as part of the background and heritage that comprise the foundation of the major varied theories of family therapy.

The pioneer leaders in the first, second, and fourth generations showed great similarities in their willingness to depart from traditional theoretical assumptions and interventions, be in the limelight and stir up controversy, and assert the enormous importance and value of their pronouncements and treatment strategies. Those leaders in the third generation were more cautious, wanting their assertions to be firmly grounded in solid research and veering away from the somewhat flamboyant stance, "It works for me and therefore is effective and really does not need replication and documentation." The thrust toward emphasizing the importance of qualitative and quantitative applied and basic research gained momentum in the 1990s and has continued unabated into the new millennium (e.g., L'Abate & Bagarozzi, 1993; Piercy & Sprenkle, 1986; Pinsof & Wynne, 1995).

Key Concepts

The major schools of family therapy and family psychology have some common assumptions. The following list includes a summary of what the first author believes these assumptions are as of this writing:

1. The family is a system in which all members (parts) have a relationship to one another and have reciprocal impact and influence. In addition, when one member changes, all others are affected and will change in response.
2. Family systems seek to maintain the status quo or homeostatic balance. However, one or more members, usually the younger ones, will attempt to disrupt the balance to make changes, which keeps the system dynamic, not static and rigid.
3. Families provide closeness, an important, vital attachment for all members. Whereas cohesiveness is to be valued, becoming too enmeshed and possessive can be detrimental. Too much chaos and detachment also are destructive. A sense of belonging to one's family of origin (and family of creation, if married) is essential for a strong sense of well-being, yet one must also be a whole, separate, individuated person within the family system.
4. Many patients fare better in treatment if their significant others are involved (when appropriate).
5. It is as important to focus on the family members' strengths and resiliencies as on their pathology, problems, conflicts, and areas of dysfunction. Some balance must be achieved among focusing on the issues they discuss, considering the way they get themselves into difficulties in relationships, listening to their narrative accounts of their own versions of their personal stories, supporting their strengths and competencies, moving forward toward problem resolution, and achieving therapeutic goals.

Various theories can be differentiated by key factors of which practitioners and patients should be aware:

1. The time frames considered most salient in treatment and the healing process (past, present, future, or all of these)
2. The importance of the therapeutic alliance
3. The way the role of the therapist is defined—for example, coach, conductor, expert, guide, participant in a dialogue, teacher, interpreter, analyst, healer, mentor, or a combination of several of these roles

4. Whether therapy should be brief, symptom-focused, or solution-focused or should involve longer term treatment that encompasses personality, situation, and relationship, as well as symptom change
5. The relevance of the larger societal context and of such factors as gender, ethnicity, and religion
6. The importance of individual and relational diagnosis as a basis for understanding and treatment
7. The role of psychological testing and other assessment instruments in formulating and validating diagnosis (Nurse, 1999; Patterson, 1999)

Various researchers and theoreticians have listed extant theories in different ways (e.g., Becvar & Becvar, 1996; Goldenberg & Goldenberg, 1996; Nichols & Schwartz, 1995). The following list encompasses the current categorization of theories as perceived by the first author. They are listed somewhat in their order of evaluation, with the exception of the *integrative model,* which is considered here to be overarching and has been evolving and ascending in importance since the 1980s. Each theory that emerged and was differentiated from the others has been integrally associated with one to three specific progenitors and reflects the personality, life history, values, and professional training of the founders but has been modified slightly over time by the disciples who have carried on the theory (for detailed summaries of theories, see Becvar & Becvar, 1996; Goldenberg & Goldenberg, 1996; Nichols & Schwartz, 1995; for in-depth discussions, see Kaslow, Kaslow, & Farber, 1999).

Various Conceptual Models

- Psychoanalytical/object relations and attachment theories
- Emotionally focused therapy
- Multigenerational family-of-origin theories
- Bowenian systems
- Contextual/relational model
- Symbolic–experiential therapy
- Communications model
- Brief family therapy
- Structural family therapy
- Strategic and Ericksonian theories
- Systemic and paradoxical theories
- Behavioral, cognitive–behavioral, and functional models
- Psychoeducational approach
- Feminist family therapy
- Narrative and social construction approaches
- Integrative, comprehensive, multimodal theories

When using an integrative approach, therapists select judiciously the theory or theories they believe not only will best illuminate understanding of a particular case, problem, person, or family but also will use concordant treatment interventions to bring about mutually agreed on personality, behavioral, and relational changes; problem resolution; and desired outcomes. It is not a purist or doctrinaire theoretical school (Kaslow, 1987; Pinsof, 1995).

EMDR AND FAMILY SYSTEMS THERAPY

Within this vast panoply of theories, where does EMDR fit? Its underlying practice rationale actually connects to several of the theories. EMDR's focus on and concern for people's historic relational past and original trauma are similar to components of multigenerational and family-of-origin approaches. From psychoanalytical family therapy comes the premise that early traumatic events or interactions became points of arrested development and need to be resolved for a healthier developmental trajectory to be embarked on. From strategic family therapy comes the importance of concentrating on the core problem identified by patients and working toward its resolution without being diverted by other issues. Having patients tell their story in their own way is derived from both psychoanalytical and narrative approaches, whereas attempting to help patients rewrite what will occur in the next chapters of their lives is an intervention strategy primarily derived from the narrative approach and social constructionist thoughts about fashioning a new reality.

Because EMDR uses theoretical constructs drawn from the several schools listed previously and from some of the others, it falls under the rubric of an *integrative* school. Following is a case study that further illuminates some of the discussed concepts.

EMDR Used to Break an Impasse: Case Study

This case study illustrates the use of EMDR in the overall process of long-term family systems therapy. The case is presented in some detail to clarify in one concrete case the numerous assumptions and factors encompassing personality, situation, and relationship, as well as symptom change. EMDR plays a pivotal role in facilitating an effective move toward retirement by well-functioning marital partners in a traditional marriage.

Details of the Case

Patrick was a high-powered executive who was accustomed to being in control and quite adept at getting things done. Having grown up in a very organized, high-achieving, traditional, patriarchal family, he was a perfectionist and driven to excel. Patrick expected no less from his wife, Pam, and his children. He demanded perfection in housekeeping and school performance, and nothing was ever quite good enough for him. He also believed that the way to be a good husband and father (an adult version of the conforming "good boy") was to follow the golden rule: treating others as he would expect to be treated by them. Of course, he demanded of himself almost complete perfection and believed others would have the same assumptions (as his father).

One side of Patrick's personality tended to ameliorate the sometimes harsh edges of his conscientious approach to life. In a business environment, Patrick could be personally warm; he was much appreciated and was known as a good listener and problem solver. He was often able to accomplish what others could not. At home (which consisted of late evenings and short weekends) his demanding and commanding but warm protective qualities were acceded to by Pam. When Pam and Patrick's children were growing up, they had initially conformed to his demands, only to rebel in their adolescence.

Pam's father had problems with drinking too heavily and possibly with alcoholism. Her family of origin had little organization, engaged in some verbal abuse, and was always struggling financially. Her mother was protective, possibly overprotective, and expected Pam to grow up as a "good girl." Pam was attracted to Patrick partly because Patrick and his family were organized and their home seemed perfectly kept, clean, and orderly. That it was a home with no alcohol problems was a relief to Pam. She wanted to please this ambitious man who was committed to being productive. His conscientious but somewhat compulsive traits helped her meet her mother's good-girl expectations and avoid the distress of the chaotic family life of her childhood.

However, as a concomitant of enjoying the organized qualities in her marriage, she spent much of their early years together accepting his judgments and criticisms and striving ever harder to meet his standards as a housewife and mother. Although Pam was able to nurture Patrick and her children (while submerging some of her underlying resentment), she reported feeling tense—that she was trying to please but unable to satisfy Patrick. Pam often thought of leaving Patrick during this early stage in their marriage, but she could think of no way to take care of herself and their children. She felt trapped, helpless, inadequate, and dependent—very much the way that she had in her family as a child. Even though he was protective and loving, Patrick's dominating behavior seemed too much for her at times. She grew panicky and experienced overwhelming anxiety. Patrick continued to gain satisfaction from his work and enjoyed being in the traditional role of good provider (Pasick, 1990). He had the added reward of being in control at home, being fatherly to his whole family—

often to Pam as well—being strict, and demanding of excellence from everyone. He believed life was going well, although he was puzzled with his wife's occasional outbursts. He tended to let these episodes pass off, in a tolerant and loving way (with a tinge of condescension), considering them reflections of her being female. Not surprisingly, Pam continued to be anxious, developed symptoms suggesting somatization, and was at times depressed. Frequently, but not always, she suppressed her anger. She sought individual psychotherapeutic help.

With the help of individual therapy fairly early in their marriage, Pam became a bit adventuresome and discovered a release by taking trips on her own. Patrick had no interest in travel for fun; travel was a part of his work. As Patrick gained more self-esteem in his world of work, he was increasingly able to tolerate Pam's need to travel. Pam's traveling helped her gain self-confidence and a moderate sense of independence. Her husband's life continued to revolve around his work. When not traveling, he left home at 5:30 a.m. and returned for dinner punctually at 7 p.m. Thus, they were able to enjoy relatively parallel lives that overlapped and "selflessly" nurture each other as they raised their children. By the time their children left home, Pam began to work outside of the house part-time, writing copy for travel advertisements and articles, which gave her additional opportunities to travel at little or no expense.

Ultimately, Pam was confronted with the fact that her husband was going to retire in 2 years. Her overwhelming anxiety returned as she thought of having her husband around to run her life every day. Again, she thought of divorce as her only way out and told Patrick so. It was then his turn to be distressed. Not wanting a divorce, he agreed to enter couple therapy. Although relieved at his agreement, she told him that he must have some individual therapy too; he needed to work on himself first. He had never felt it was necessary. Pam thought that because she had done her work on herself, it was his turn to do some changing. This attitude was a big switch from the previous stage in their marriage when she had taken all the responsibility for the problems in the relationship.

The couple first met for a planning session with their therapists (A. R. Nurse and P. Thompson) before Patrick began individual therapy. Meeting initially as a couple helped to frame their work as that of loving, caring marital partners who had developed significant personal strengths but were having trouble managing and moving past their amplified anxiety as they faced a normal relational transition into retirement. Meeting together with cotherapists emphasized that although Patrick and Pam were each individually facing the next stage in their development, this was also a next phase in their family life cycle (Schwartz & Kaslow, 1997).

This balance of acknowledging strengths on which to build treatment, accompanied by wrestling with problems, is a typical approach in family systems therapy. Pointing out the anticipated life style changes as a stimulus for symptom development and describing the changes as part of a normal adult transition (retirement in this instance) tends to ward off expending unnecessary energy on self-derogation or blaming for psychological problems; family systems therapists often frame problems with reference to family life developmental changes (Schwartz & Kaslow, 1997). In addition, encouraging the partners to unite as they face a common problem—retirement—helped this couple to "externalize" their marital problems rather than form a solely intrarelationship or interrelationship emphasis (Winslade & Monk, 2000). In this case, the goal was not only to assist them with symptom relief for the immediate present but also to help them change their relationship so that the long-term transition into retirement would have a significantly increased chance of success.

In the initial couple session, the probable use of EMDR in the individual contacts was explained. Pam was to return to individual therapy after Patrick was well into his therapy. An agreement was reached for Patrick to meet with his individual therapist (A.R.N.) immediately. The intent was to give him a chance to tell his individual story without being in the presence of his wife and with the assistance of EMDR to begin the process of helping him structure the next chapter in his marital and professional life (Shapiro, 1995; Winslade & Monk, 2000).

Although the immediate stress affecting Patrick and the resulting marital crisis stemmed from Pam's confrontation and his awareness of her distress, Patrick had his own anxieties about retirement. He had not completely revealed to Pam how worried he was about maintaining his self-esteem without being the hub of the activities of so many people. Thus, Patrick's goal in individual therapy was to gain more insight into himself and begin to deal with the causes of his marital and retirement anxieties (Levant, 1995). These goals had been made explicit in the initial couple session and were reiterated in Patrick's first individual therapy session. The individual therapy was undertaken in the overall context of the couple's agreement to return together to engage in therapy.

To increase therapist and patient understanding, the Millon Clinical Multiaxial Inventory–III (MCMI–III, Millon, Millon, & Davis, 1994) was administered to Patrick and subsequently to Pam. Although both registered as significantly anxious on this inventory, we were relieved that Patrick had mild compulsive, conforming, or conscientious trends—ones that did not suggest severe compulsive traits or a compulsive personality disorder. Likewise, Pam did not score in the personality disorder range. Her results suggested she was mildly depressed but primarily dependent and beset with anxiety. In addition, her style did not suggest that she had a personality disorder (Millon, 1996).

Although a single inventory such as the MCMI–III obviously cannot substitute for a full psychological battery of tests (Nurse, 1999), the MCMI–III was a quite useful and inexpensive immediate source of clues (hypotheses) that helped guide the first interviews, especially because they served as a cross-check for the clinical interview impressions. The MCMI–III, to some extent, is a psychological screening instrument. Had the inventory results suggested more entrenched psychopathology, we would have undertaken more psychological testing.

By comparing the MCMI–III results, which pointed to a conscientious, conforming, and controlling approach to life for Patrick and a more dependent approach for Pam, we anticipated that they might (unconsciously) be colluding with each other in maintaining a problematic dominance–submission relationship in their marriage. Although their history implied this, being informed by this initial MCMI–III inventory pattern helped us more confidently head off behavior that might have subverted the couple therapy. These inventory findings revealed that both had strong nurturing tendencies coupled with a certain passive accommodation to each other and a selfless quality (Millon, 1996). The findings also helped reinforce our alertness not only to the positive side of their caring relationship behavior but also to the lack of focus on their own individual needs—which was true not only for her, as we expected, but also for him. This less healthy aspect of their transactions was evident in the way they communicated with each other—using parental "shoulds" and "oughts" rather than expressing their individual feelings and thoughts from an "I" position (Satir, 1967). Thus, we anticipated that one of our therapeutic endeavors would be to help each of them to self-focus more effectively while expressing themselves more directly to each other.

Rewarded by the relieving effects of sharing his worries about retirement and his marriage and aided by a discussion about his personality approach (that was suggested by his inventory results), Patrick was able to tell the story of his childhood, career, and marriage. We encountered a crucial point in therapy as we introduced EMDR and he spoke with increasing tension about his father, who had been strict and rather repressive. Using EMDR, he targeted an image of his minister father and the fear and terror he experienced as a boy when he had "sinned" by defying a minor family rule. He was able to transform this perspective of himself as a sinner into that of someone who could make mistakes and still be a good person. This childhood experience seemed to have been at the core of his conscientious/conforming style.

Patrick eased the internal pressures to be perfect and without fully realizing it, he allowed himself to relax and relate to others more easily, initially at his office. He subsequently reported with some surprise that he had received positive responses from his managing team (who did not know he was in therapy). He thought that his increased flexibility, openness, and helpfulness was carrying over into his relationship with Pam and said that he felt natural and comfortable spontaneously helping more at home. Patrick believed that he was ready to meet jointly with Pam in some couple sessions.

However, when we began the couple work, little about his behavior seemed to have changed from Pam's point of view. After many years of marriage, she still saw him as critical. Even his efforts to pick up and clean around the home, which he believed were helpful and reflective of his more cooperative attitude, were interpreted by Pam as a criticism of her ability to keep house. She had always thought that the house had to be perfect for him, because in the past he had been very critical if it was not clean and neat when he returned home. She continued to live in a constant state of tension about what she thought she "should" be doing and what she thought she "should" be accomplishing during the day. Pam seemed unable to interpret Patrick's behavior in other than the old way, despite direct work on communication. Consistent with one of the principles of family systems work (noted previously), which states that a change in one member of a system affects all others, Patrick's behavior change seemed to reinforce her dysphoric, negative assumptive system (much to his dismay). Because we were unable to dislodge Pam's negative perception of Patrick's behavior, we shifted our strategy, and Pam returned to individual therapy.

Pam admitted to her individual therapist (P.T.) that she had experienced more problems since she had stopped her part-time job to have more time to prepare for selling their house the following year. She had almost daily tension headaches, particularly when she was at home, but rarely when she was away. Physicians and other health practitioners had been unable to provide sufficient relief through medication, biofeedback, or other approaches.

Pam was quite frustrated, not only because the somatically oriented health treatments had not helped her symptoms, but also because she had found her previous therapy very helpful but still could not manage her current problems. She had discovered something of the link between her family-of-origin experiences and her feelings as an adult and attitudes toward her husband. Pam had a sense of the reason she got upset, yet she was still overwhelmed with her feelings. Apparently, her self-information remained more in the cognitive realm and was not integrated emotionally. Although she had made major steps toward independence and better health, the trauma of her early life (and its link to her marriage) continued to be a source of emotional discomfort. The individual therapist (P.T.) suggested EMDR, a possibility already described in the initial couple session, with the goal of using it to help her process her emotional blocks and assist her cognitive and emotional integration.

With the introduction of EMDR, her "safe place" was a favorite vacation spot in another state. Thus, when under pressure or simply when she wanted to relax, she could imagine an experience that centered her in her present sense of self. Reassured that she could fall back on her safe place if needed, Pam and her therapist targeted her pain. Pam stated that she woke every morning with the fear that she would get headaches. During EMDR, she used this consistent pattern as her negative cognition: "I am going to get a headache." This worry was very disturbing to her and registered at a subjective unit of disturbance (SUD) level of 10—the top of the scale. She subsequently imagined herself at her computer checking e-mail and suddenly realizing how long she had been there, then thinking that she must rush to accomplish things around the house. At that point, she told herself that a headache was coming on and would get worse. However, with continued processing, Pam created her positive cognition: "I am going to have a free day" (i.e., free of headaches).

Subsequently, Pam realized that she continued to tell herself that she needed to accomplish something productive every day, but it never seemed to be enough. If she felt unproductive despite her efforts, she felt guilty and was sure she would be judged harshly. Pam projected her own internal criticisms to Patrick, who until recently had been a willing and participating partner in this seemingly unconscious dynamic process. Responding to his critical attitude and injunction to always be busy, she believed that she did not have a choice, for example, to take time to read a book. Pam felt she had to hide what she did from Patrick or explain herself. A simple "What did you do today?" continued to feel like an interrogation and a judgment rather than genuine interest in her daily experience of life, which was now often the case. The thought of not having done something productive during the day could trigger her headache-generating process. If she developed a headache, it interfered with her working, a secondary gain in the service of her rebellion. Unfortunately, the pain prevented her from really enjoying in a nonanxious way the time she spent not working. Her ending positive cognition was "I can take time for myself," with almost the highest endorsement possible, a validity of cognition (VoC) of 6 on a 7-point scale. The following week she reported that she had taken some free time without feeling guilty and that the number of headaches had markedly decreased. Pam was beginning to realize that she at least had the right and the ability to take a little time for herself.

In the next session, Pam identified her fear of getting angry or of confrontation as a situation that triggered headaches. Despite her increasing sense of agency, she still felt totally powerless when she began to experience anger and anticipated a possible confrontation with Patrick. Beginning in EMDR with an expression of this powerlessness, her images went back to her childhood and her father's periodic drunken rages, which led to her feelings of helplessness. As she worked through this family-of-origin difficulty, she developed a new positive cognition: "I have the power within me to make contact and make changes." The positive cognition at the end of the session was "I can stand up for myself." She began to own and take responsibility for herself.

Although the material she covered was much the same as the material in her previous therapy, it seemed that EMDR allowed for more integration of the cognitive and emotional aspects with the physical aspects of her previous trauma. As the integration took place, Pam became less tense, turning more of her attention to her relationship with Patrick.

At a subsequent session, Pam reported that Patrick had taken an unexpected day off because he was not feeling well. This action had caused her a good deal of anxiety, even though he had worked in his home office all day and only came out to fix his lunch. Pam had felt tense all day. She lapsed back to her experience of powerlessness. In EMDR, her quickly emerging image was of Patrick coming home unexpectedly early from a trip years ago and finding Pam and the children happily playing a game on the dining room table. He told her he did not want to see that sort of wasted time again. As she recalled this incident, she spontaneously called herself "stupid" (for letting him control her so long). Her beginning positive cognition was "I can choose to decide what to do with my life," which eventually became "I have the power to choose and be comfortable with my choices." The following week she reported that even though their home was only somewhat in order one night, when Patrick arrived home he told her that the house was fine and not to worry about it. He offered to help her pick up. She was able to view his comments positively. She felt less pressure internally and had fewer headaches. As Pam took on more self-responsibility, she was increasingly able to differentiate between her anticipation of Patrick's behavior and Patrick's actual new behavior. In a subsequent session, Pam expressed surprise at how much Patrick had changed. (We thought significant changes had been taking place for a while, as noted previously).

However, despite Patrick's changes, Pam was afraid that even though he was altering the way he related to her, the old dominating, controlling behaviors would come back. Then she recounted being frightened when she told him about a problem for which she needed a solution. He simply listened carefully and commented empathically, but Pam behaved as if he were acting in his former "take control" mode. She did not realize until later that he was just trying to be helpful. In EMDR, her negative cognition was "I am really weak for letting him control me." Her image was of herself obediently doing whatever he said over and over while being angry all along. As she worked through this feeling, her positive cognition became "I am in control of myself" and her final positive cognition was "I can choose how I respond."

Experiencing more control over herself and understanding that she would no longer automatically anticipate being overwhelmed by Patrick, Pam returned to couple therapy with her husband. He continued to stress his desire to work with her in a balanced way and demonstrated an improved ability to listen to her. He even commented that he wished he had not been so hard on their children when they were young and took steps outside of therapy to improve his relationship with them. In sessions, as they planned ahead, with us facilitating their communication, they were receptive when we would point out an occasional return of old habits of expression that tended to again place Patrick in a dominating position and Pam in a subordinate role. They became more adept at repairing instances of miscommunication in a positive way without overreacting, and they expressed that they understood each other more (see Gottman, 1994, for the importance of repair in couple relationships).

In addition to being influenced by Gottman (1994), our efforts at using communication training approaches have continued to be affected by the pioneers who examined family interactions. These researchers include Satir (1967) and her emphasis on directing immediate feeling reactions among family members in an effort to improve emotional connection and intimacy. Berne's (1961) transactional analytical approach interpreting parent, adult, and child aspects of personality still proves to be helpful in our work. Recently, we made use of a structured communication training developed with a National Institute of Mental Health (NIMH) grant and buttressed by significant research (1997). These approaches in particular have influenced our roles as therapists and as teachers of couple communication, and we incorporated these elements in our work with Pam and Patrick.

After two concluding reinforcing couple sessions, Patrick and Pam were able to make an adventure out of planning and executing their retirement over the next year. They returned some months later for one couple session just to put their thoughts together and to ensure the effectiveness of their actual transition. All had been going well, and an unexpected bonus was their improved relationship with their adult children. They attributed this later change to Patrick's sharing with his children his regrets about being such a harsh parent when they were young and to the improved communication skills Pam and Patrick were using with their children.

Assumptions

Family systems therapy with Patrick and Pam was conducted in a way that was consistent with the major assumptions of family systems presented in the beginning of this chapter. For example, their therapy was carried out with the belief that any change in either marital partner would affect the other and that the marital partner's response would in turn affect the partner initiating the change. Thus, interweaving intrapersonal with interpersonal sessions was deemed comfortable and reasonable. By having individual and couple sessions timed with reference to the changes experienced by each partner, we were able to reinforce each person's individuality while helping them find new ways to relate that fostered a closer relationship. We began treatment and continued it with the assumption that for the most efficacious treatment, both parties needed to be involved, not simply the one with the overt symptoms. Strengths and problematic aspects of their personalities were acknowledged and engaged.

Key Factors

As noted previously, several key factors differentiate the various family systems therapy approaches. Certain factors seemed most important to us in the treatment of Patrick and Pam. First, in planning treatment, we used one personality inventory, the MCMI–III, to help us formulate hypotheses about their personality structures and potential relational dynamics. The test results led to our initial elimination of the presence of any obvious major mental illness or personality disorder and the identification of severe anxiety in both (particularly Pam); the results also indicated Patrick's mild conscientious/conforming style and Pam's dependent/depressive inclinations. Although these results were drawn from a full test battery, we were able to enter treatment with hypotheses gleaned from the MCMI–III to be confirmed and modified and that provided ideas for addressing each person. In addition, by identifying a conscientious/dependent relational combination, we were alerted to a potential dominance/submission couple dynamic, both as a source of trouble and a refuge of regression or retreat by either or both. Because compulsive/conscientious and dependent styles are characterized by more emphasis on nurturing the partner than the self (Millon, 1996), we also sought opportunities to help each person be more self-aware and communicate their own desires and needs more directly.

By working with Pam and Patrick as cotherapists, our intent was to counterbalance the traditional societal gender imbalance of the overt dominance/submission relationship within which they seemed to be caught. As each of us strengthened our therapist–patient alliance with our same-gender patient, we developed a relationship with the opposite-gender person during the couple sessions and modeled effective relationship communication for them. We consider this approach to be advantageous for working with couples who exhibit some sort of imbalance, particularly gender power imbalance.

We worked with Pam and Patrick as conductors as we introduced the framework of individual and couple sessions and introduced EMDR as a specific approach for dealing with impasses or developmental arrests related to individual family-of-origin traumas. In our individual sessions and couple sessions, we functioned as interpreters and healers. In couple sessions, we also became teachers of new communication patterns. Thus, we moved from the role of conductor to interpreter/healer to teacher and continuously moved back and forth among these roles in response to the stage of the therapy.

EMDR's Role in Breaking the Couple's Impasse

Intrapersonally, EMDR with Pam helped her integrate emotional and bodily experiences with the more conscious intellectual understanding of her past. In addition to decreasing some of her physical suffering, the EMDR interventions instigated an internal change that increased her ability to accurately perceive Patrick's changing marital attitudes and behaviors, particularly his helping and listening behaviors at home. Because she already had gained some intellectual understanding of the trauma experienced in her family of origin from previous therapy, this intellectual, emotional, and bodily integration was deemed critical for changing her perception of first herself and then Patrick.

Patrick made use of EMDR to address memories of his oppressive minister father. Application of EMDR was central to his increasing general relaxation, treating himself more humanely, and consequently being able to attend to and listen to others more effectively, first at work and then with his wife. Change often starts in areas of life that are less heavily emotionally invested, such as work relationships; then the changes move to more intimate, vulnerable areas. EMDR with Patrick probably sped up the overall therapy, although his changes might also have been facilitated by other approaches had they been used; however, our experience suggests that EMDR effects changes more rapidly.

EMDR seemed to have significantly freed Patrick and Pam from the influences of their families of origin that caused or at least contributed in a major way to their overtly dominance–controlling/submissive relationship, identified on the MCMI–III. Patrick became much less controlling, and Pam became less submissive. This modification of major personality characteristics facilitated more active communication work in couple therapy and allowed them to be influenced by the subtleties of the cotherapists' gender-balanced relationship. By learning to pay more attention to their individual needs, Patrick and Pam became more open to being direct as they worked on their communication. At the same time, they still were able to nurture each other more freely without harboring stored up resentments. This change seems to reflect a modification of the overemphasis on nurturing that was identified in the MCMI–III. Because their individual changes using EMDR were synchronized with the couple therapy, each person influenced the other positively as they moved toward the same goal of vital attachment with increased closeness, a major principle of family systems therapy. The pace of change increased as each influenced the other, in keeping with the principle that family members reciprocally influence each other.

EMDR Used to Facilitate Effective Coparenting During a Divorce: Case Study

In contrast with Pam and Patrick's case, this case focuses on an immediate, symptomatic behavioral problem rather than the long-term relationship of the partners. In this case, EMDR was used to intervene with divorcing parents, Joan and Frank. EMDR with Joan allowed her to break through an emotional block that had been impeding Frank's having meaningful contact with their children.

Details of the Case

Joan and Frank both came from homes in which their parents had divorced. They had not seemed overtly damaged by these experiences (as judged by the fourth edition of the *Diagnostic and Statistical Manual of Mental Disorders [DSM–IV]*; American Psychiatric Association, 1994) but consistent with follow-up studies of children of divorce (Wallerstein, Lewis, & Blakeslee, 2000), these young adults were internally distressed and had more than the usual difficulties developing satisfactory close relationships. When they met each other and found that they could share common experiences from their families of origin, it helped them form a romantic relationship. When Joan and Frank married, they vowed that they would never divorce and cause their children to suffer as they had.

By the time Joan and Frank had three children, more and more time was taken up with raising the children. They had less and less time together. Joan worked part time and otherwise focused on mothering—no small task given that two of the children were preschoolers and one was just starting school. At home, Frank was also constantly involved with the children, especially when Joan was at her part-time job. Joan became pregnant a fourth time. Meanwhile, Frank was getting more involved in his work relationships and became romantically involved with one of his peers. Three weeks before the delivery of his fourth child, he left Joan to live with his new girlfriend. Although Joan was hurt and furious and Frank was feeling guilty, they made attempts to reconcile with the help of couple counseling. After a year, Frank was unable to give up his new girlfriend. The couple decided to divorce.

Joan continued to feel extremely hurt and betrayed and was vociferous about not wanting to allow Frank to take their children, even for occasional weekends, because they would encounter the father's new partner. Yet the children, especially the older ones, missed having more time with their father, particularly participating in activities away from home. The arrangement that evolved was barely tolerable to Joan. Frank came to Joan's home every Saturday and cared and fed the children while Joan worked a long shift. He would put the children to bed just before Joan returned, at which time he would leave and go to the home of his new partner, who lived many miles away. He also completed this round trip two Sundays each month when Joan worked. This plan had worked on an interim basis, and the couple cooperated well enough because of concern for each of their relationships with their children. However, Frank still wanted the children to visit with him in the home of his new partner and her child, especially because he and his girlfriend had committed to a long-term relationship. By this time, Joan had begun to accept that Frank was not going to return, and she began to take steps to move more into the social arena.

Both parents agreed that their relationship had deteriorated and had been unsatisfactory for several years. When Frank began to negotiate to have the children visit him at the home of his new partner, Joan found herself vehemently resisting even thinking about the idea. The prospect of a legal battle loomed, and the cooperative aspects of their child caring work disappeared under the angry storm cloud that characterized their relationship. Interestingly, Joan understood that Frank's request was reasonable and knew that the children's relationship with their father would be strengthened if some sort of agreement could be reached. In spite of this cognitive understanding, Joan felt caught in her own overwhelming anger, which fueled her adamant stand—she did not want "her" children around "that woman!"

Rather than using lawyers as gladiators who would fight for each person's respective causes in an adversarial conflict, the couple chose to enter the collaborative divorce process (Nurse & Thompson, 1999, 2000) toward the end of the year of separation (during which they participated in the couple counseling). The collaborative divorce process involves a team consisting of an attorney and a mental health coach (professional) for each partner, one child (mental health) specialist, and one financial person. All people on the patients' teams sign an agreement not to go to court but instead to work collaboratively and use their professional skills to help them be effective coparents for their children (and settle other issues such as financial and property conflicts).

As the mental health coaches in this divorce process, we (P.T. and A.R.N.) attempted during several couple sessions to assist Joan and Frank in managing their coparenting issues, especially the visitation problem that so angered Joan. Joan had not significantly shifted her position on this issue. One of us explored Joan's feelings during an individual session. She was asked whether she had ever experienced feeling this way. After thinking for quite a while, Joan responded, "Oh yes, in junior high." EMDR had been introduced to her previously and used to help her deal with anxiety at the beginning of the collaborative divorce process. She agreed with the suggestion to use EMDR to address her current feelings.

Beginning with the experiences involved in what she labeled as "marital betrayal," a term drawn from her parents' divorce, she moved from discussing the current situation to discussing her parents' divorce. With great anguish, she recalled an episode in junior high school when she had been betrayed by her best friend. This was not the same bland recollection she had mentioned previously, when she simply noted the fact that she had been betrayed by a friend; this time, she described it with intense distress and tears. Obviously, she had been greatly affected as an early adolescent by an event that would not be classified as *trauma* according to the *DSM–IV* criteria (American Psychiatric Association, 1994). As the recollection of her friend's betrayal trauma lost its intensity during EMDR, the thought of her current trauma—the marital betrayal by her husband and the other woman—was also characterized by less intensity. The thought was still difficult for her, but Joan became visibly more relaxed. At the end of the session, Joan remarked spontaneously that it would "be okay for the kids to go with their dad this weekend"—the immediate focus of disagreement for Joan and Frank.

A single EMDR session was the breakthrough that allowed successful, although difficult, negotiations between Joan and Frank as they developed their parenting plan with our assistance. Joan seemed more integrated after the EMDR session; the edge in her voice was gone, and she acknowledged for the first time that the marriage was definitely over. Frank responded to her decreased anger and acknowledgment that the marriage was over by being less defensive and more cooperative during negotiations about the children. They were able to join forces with the common goal of paying attention to their children and their needs rather than being consumed by their own internal and interpersonal conflicts.

Assumptions, Key Factors, and EMDR's Role in the Divorce Process

A timely intervention with EMDR helped reveal a major basis of Joan's extreme anger. This adolescent experience of betrayal seemed to be linked to her parents' divorce and some sort of marital betrayal in which she was traumatized as a child or adolescent. It was sufficient for the purposes of the divorce process to deal with the feeling surrounding the adolescent betrayal because this event was her direct emotional link to her contemporary conflict. Uncovering and dealing with Joan's feelings stemming from the earlier trauma was crucial to her working realistically around a major coparenting issue. Some divorce-attorney negotiations are based on the rational assumptions of interest-based negotiations (Fisher & Ury, 1981), which stress meeting the conscious individual needs of each parent to reach solutions (Winslade & Monk, 2000). Unresolved family-of-origin conflicts in our child custody evaluations, which seem to cause breakdowns in marriages, have not been explored in these divorce-attorney negotiations. In our opinion, interest-based negotiations, although pleasingly logical and practically workable for some couples whose behavior is not unduly shaped by a lack of awareness of historical traumas or blocks, are inadequate when used with other more troubled or disturbed individuals.

Had Joan been in typical individual therapy without EMDR and involved in the usual divorce process, with her lawyer handling the action in a characteristically adversarial way with Frank's lawyer, the conflict over Frank's time with the children might have escalated. If her level of anger had not been reduced through EMDR and no collaborative process had been involved, Joan's anger and Frank's retaliation could have resulted in a court settling the visitation issue; the children would have had to exist in a tension-filled, hostile environment. Thus, this particular intervention with EMDR may be considered a key feature of the brief intervention type, characteristic of some approaches in family systems therapy.

EMDR Used in a Transgenerational Transmission Process: A Case Study

This case illustrates the way a transgenerational focus in family therapy using EMDR interrupted a pattern of repeated, irrational episodes of anger that a father, George, directed toward his son. The specter of an undesired divorce stimulated George to seek help for this family problem. Like Joan and Frank's divorce case, this case study has more of a symptomatic focus.

Details of the Case

George, who was age 35, returned to psychotherapy for help with his anger because therapy sessions several years previously had helped him enough that he was able to fall in love and marry. He and his wife, Ann, had proceeded to have a very welcome son, whom George loved very much. However, by the time his son was age 3 years, George was continually feeling overwhelmed with anger at his son for very minor behavioral problems. He knew that his anger was irrational, and Ann continued to remind him of this. Finally, Ann threatened to leave George unless he "did something" about his anger. George and Ann came into our (A.R.N. and P.T.) office because they were considering family therapy. An exploration of their family relationship revealed that their marriage was generally satisfactory. George's irrational anger toward his son continued, and George was afraid that he might even become physically abusive, although it seemed that his internal controls against such striking out were adequate. George came in for a few individual sessions.

It became clear to the therapist that George had been furious with his own father as a child. He remembered his father frequently being angry with him and recalled being afraid that his father might strike him. The therapist reintroduced EMDR to George (he had discussed it briefly in the initial couple session). The therapist targeted early images of his scenes with his angry father. As he processed these images, George realized that he was feeling exactly as he had in those scenes with his father. George was reenacting with his son the unresolved trauma with his own father.

George returned for a second individual session, reporting that he had been angry with his son but only briefly. The anger was not overwhelming, and he quickly handled the problems his son presented, which sounded like normal 3-year-old difficulties. Fortuitously, George had found an opportunity to talk with his father and discovered that his dad had originally believed that tough discipline was the only way to help his son behave and grow to be a strong man. He had mistakenly expressed his love in this way. George's father said that he now realized he had been too harsh on George. George's father apologized.

In a brief family therapy session, George and Ann worked on new ways to resolve problems with their child involving the bed time routine, eating, and other areas of conflict. Ann reported that she had no more concerns about George's expressions of anger; he seemed to have ordinary parenting frustrations. George no longer worried about reacting with physical abuse.

During the last therapy session, George reflected on his subjective sense of the impact of the EMDR intervention; he recalled no dramatic changes. He said, "You know, it's stealthlike. It seems so simple, too simple. I knew what was going on [during the process], and yet the outcome was so powerful" (Nurse, 1996). In our experience, it is not unusual for patients to experience significant emotional attitude changes in connection with EMDR therapy. George's response is similar to the response of Patrick, in the first case study. Patrick was initially unaware of his change in management style, but his management group responded to the change. Lest EMDR be misconstrued as a therapy that can handle every sort of problem, it should be noted that George and Ann began couple therapy some years later. In the subsequent therapy sessions, they resolved additional issues involving communication patterns.

Assumptions, Key Factors, and EMDR's Role in Intervention With Anger

By using EMDR, the previous feelings of unresolved anger were reexperienced and processed during therapy—in a safe context. The feelings were relabeled with a new cognitive understanding. Resolving old feelings left George free to establish new parenting patterns that fit him, his marriage, and his wife. Individual therapy without EMDR might have had a similar result but would have taken much longer, possibly increasing the risk of harm to the child, injury to the father–child relationship, and the possibility of a divorce. Classic family therapy might have modified the intensity of the father–child interaction but might not have addressed the family-of-origin anger problem swiftly. Even though George's behavior might have been modified by direct behavior pattern work, if his original internalized rage had not been resolved, his anger potential might have been cued by other subsequent patterns as his child continued to grow. His development might have caused him to challenge the family patterns, which could have threatened the family system and caused George to again respond with inappropriate anger.

More traditional family systems approaches that would not resolve George's internal conflict might have caused his child to develop certain symptoms, perhaps ones that were similar to the original aggressor—George. For example, the child might have acted out in anger against other children in his preschool or later in his elementary school.

Additional Uses of EMDR With Family Systems Therapy

Sometimes EMDR is used with family systems therapy when young children have specific symptoms and come to treatment as the identified patient. Lovett presented numerous cases in her book, *Small Wonders* (1999), wherein she used EMDR directly with a symptomatic child in a family context. Family systems therapy could be an accompanying approach to EMDR used for adults to target the source of a parent's (often unconscious) message to a child. For example, in one case entitled *"Too Good" Parents* (pp. 27–28), Lovett described working with Jeff, whose father had never listened to him. When Jeff had a child, he chose to always take his child's fears seriously (probably to demonstrate to *his* son that he was listening). As a result of this decision, his son, who was age 5 when seen by Lovett, was intensely frightened by any new situation. His too-good father had inadvertently done his son a disservice by reinforcing his son's fears and not helping him develop courage and coping skills in new situations.

A family systems approach to this problem might involve initial discussions with the family that are understandable to a 5 year old, and the therapy might provide specific parenting assistance. The role of the mother and the relationship with the father might be explored in separate couple sessions to determine whether and how much the mother is colluding with the father's behavior. This would include an exploration of whether the father's behavior might also be a way of unconsciously acting out some trauma or emotional block from the wife's past. Using EMDR, the therapist could also explore any aspects in the family system that suggested emotional background factors that could be influencing the mother to cooperate with her husband's oversolicitous behavior with their son. The father might have EMDR sessions designed to target the trauma that triggered his cognition of always taking his child's fears seriously; this approach could help him replace the damaging cognition with one that is more realistic for a parent. In addition, a therapist could use EMDR with the child, in addition to sand tray (Brems, 1993) and other work.

Finally, following the principle emphasized at the beginning of this chapter—that any change by any family member affects all members— some family sessions with the 5-year-old might be held to facilitate the creation of a new level of homeostasis for the family. During the final family therapy sessions, the therapist would have an opportunity to reframe this interruption in the family's development and each member's development as fortuitous and positive for all and to indicate that working through the son's developmental problem could serve as a model for success when dealing with future family hurdles. As noted previously, family therapists not only deal with the problems but also focus on the evolving strengths within the family and its members. Sometimes individual therapy with EMDR can be a spur for using family systems therapy to deal with the systemic consequences of an individual's development. For example, when an individual who has been sexually abused and was dependent becomes more independent and less afraid because of therapy with EMDR, an intervention with the whole family unit may be required.

In family systems therapy, it is not unusual to discover that a previously overly dependent female who feels inadequate and is playing out a culturally influenced submissive role has chosen a seemingly self-assured male who is narcissistic but has internal feelings of inadequacy and likes the woman to rely on him psychologically. In fact, the man's personality organization, with his puffed-up, overly valued self-image, might have called for this kind of spouse—one who would lean on him and verify his male strength and superior, entitled stance in the world (Nurse, 1998). If his spouse becomes more independent and wants a more equal relationship, he could feel threatened, and even rejected. His response to this inner belief might be a haughty one, an "I don't need you" attitude. In turn, the woman could feel that she has been rejected and might revert to her overly dependent ways or act out, possibly resulting in endless arguments. Family systems therapy could help this couple to understand what is happening, develop new ways of relating to each other, and rebalance their relationship differently to allow for the woman's growth. EMDR could then be used to process the memories causing the husband to feel inadequate, which could create a healthier relationship.

Some families unconsciously target one child as a repository of unresolved conflicts—a parent's conflicts that stem from current issues or from the family of origin. The concept of the family "trouble-maker" is widely recognized. In a variation of the identified patient, adolescents who are "causing trouble" might be characterized by and in turn portray themselves as "the angry one" or "the drinker" who will eventually be "just like their father." In one family we treated, a young adult was told that he was destined to be like his maternal uncle, who had "gone crazy." In these situations, it may be worthwhile to consider a combination of family systems therapy and EMDR for key family members who are carrying the family message. This combination may most efficiently help the conveyers of the message to change their attitudes and may assist the family system in changing to a more effective family relational pattern that excludes transmission of the damaging message. The targeted adolescents or young adults might associate the origin of negative self-attitudes with emotionally loaded previous family situations that damaged their sense of positive self-regard and impeded their development at key points. These situations could be systematically processed with EMDR.

EMDR AND TRADITIONAL THOUGHT IN FAMILY SYSTEMS THERAPY

An element of EMDR that is consistent with at least two traditional major approaches to treating couples is the premise that past traumas interfere with current functioning, the developmental trajectory, or both. As noted previously, psychodynamic family therapy (psychoanalytical family therapy) has its origins in this premise. In multigenerational and family-of-origin approaches, this assumption is also a core premise.

Consistent with psychodynamic family therapy (psychoanalytical family therapy) and the more recently evolved narrative therapy is EMDR's provision for having the patients tell their own stories, including those from their families of origins and their experiences of the family histories. For Patrick and Pam, the telling of their stories in couple and complementary individual sessions parallels the more traditional family and couple approaches. By contrast, the stories told by Joan and Frank and by George and Ann were short; they focused, respectively, on one patient's coparenting resistance problem in divorce and the need to resolve inappropriate paternal anger.

All three of the cases may have elements of strategic therapy, but with Joan and Frank and with George and Ann, the focus was solely on managing the immediate behavioral symptom. This strategy is particularly consistent with the proclivity of strategic therapists to focus on the patient's view of a problem while avoiding being side tracked in search of a solution. The complex fabric of the longer term couple relationship of Patrick and Pam and their need to shift their relationship in a major way is more typical of integrative family and couple therapy. Pam and Patrick were involved with extensive work on family-of-origin issues and current family interaction patterns, which coalesced in ways that required various intervention approaches by the therapists—approaches involving the role of conductor, communication expert, and teacher—all of which draw on various traditional approaches for working with couples.

When EMDR is used in family therapy, people who move past their emotional blocks can change major aspects of their internal lives, marriage, and family story to adjust to the new, less emotionally loaded reality. This shift can allow them to be more open to experiencing new interactions with others in family therapy and in family life overall. From the standpoint of narrative therapists, people who are going through a divorce can reframe the history of their marriage to provide a new and broader base on which to collaborate (Winslade & Monk, 2000).

DESCRIPTION OF POSITIVE TREATMENT EFFECTS OF EMDR

The most important overall positive treatment effect of using EMDR in family therapy interventions is the incorporation of an approach that can resolve therapeutic impasses. This is particularly true for those impasses that are based on emotional blocks or traumas stemming from individual historical events—especially those related to family-of-origin experiences. Often the origins of the emotional blocks that impede improvement are those events that are mostly or totally out of the realm of awareness.

Because, understandably, therapy with couples tends to focus on the couple's history and the partners' stated views of their difficulties, individual background experiences undermining the couple's relationship are unlikely to be extensively explored, sometimes because of the need to cope with an immediate family crisis. EMDR provides an approach for quickly locating emotional blocks and trauma. In addition, it assists people with more fully experiencing pockets of affect and locating the often mistaken cognitive belief statement connected with the original experiences. They can then change the cognition to correspond with current situations that are similar in content or context to the original trauma. For example, Joan, the woman who was getting a divorce, had no conscious understanding of the original adolescent trauma that formed the basis for her extreme feelings. These feelings kept her from behaving in a way consistent with her true thoughts, which were that her children should have more exposure to her husband's new partner. This case underscores the value of using EMDR to explore contributing previous events. Joan and Frank's circumstances, which were that Frank left Joan for another woman weeks before the birth of Joan and Frank's fourth child, could have been used to "rationally" argue that the magnitude of Joan's anger was justified given the circumstances.

Another positive effect of EMDR is the speed with which it can work. For example, when Joan worked through her impeding trauma, she spontaneously volunteered to have her children get to know Frank's new partner. This was a rapid shift. Sometimes the speed has a cumulative effect, so when a partner is jarred into realizing the change the other partner has made, the person is strongly motivated, in fact impelled, to make personal changes as well. For example, Pam, who was struggling with the impending retirement of her husband, Patrick, quickly shifted her focus to herself when she finally, almost belatedly, recognized Patrick's changes in attitude and behavior. Until that point, she was adamant that she had completed her individual therapy and was not about to work more on herself. In traditional family therapy, Patrick's changes probably would have taken longer to occur, would have been much more gradual, and would not have had the same jarring impact as his EMDR-induced change.

HOW EMDR LETS FAMILY THERAPISTS USE WHAT THEY KNOW

An obvious way that EMDR allows family therapists to use what they know is that the EMDR approach can sweep away the contributing effects on the family system of recent, known traumas and also allow the patients to discover and work through formerly hidden dynamics, such as problems generated from a parent's family of origin that may be interfering with progress in family therapy. Family therapists can continue to apply their knowledge of the individual and family life cycles and of family systems. EMDR does not interfere with the process of continuing to increase understanding of the family system as it relates to the individual personality and may increase the impact of family therapy. For example, when EMDR reveals the origins of patients' communication difficulties instead of only addressing them as they exist in the present, more in-depth change is possible. This increased change is a likely outcome because EMDR family therapists are able to link the present dysfunctional interpersonal family patterns with unresolved transgenerational problems and to process them as well.

An additional benefit for family therapists trained in EMDR is that they are provided with a different conceptual approach with which to consider family members' problems in the context of the family dynamics. For example, narrative therapists can strive to increase empathy of family members for the unique base of each family member's story of reality, particularly for the emotional knots, binds, or traumas that may not have been experienced in the same way by other family members who were involved in the same events. When therapists' empathy also increases, they are more likely to develop attitudes and behaviors that strengthen their alliance with family members and deepen their understanding of the family's interactions and life course. As mentioned earlier, the quality and character of the therapeutic alliance with the family is a key factor in differentiating among family systems approaches; from our view, the establishment of a trusted alliance is of major importance in family therapy. EMDR allows therapists to obtain an increased understanding of the underlying basis of current systems issues and communication styles. This increased understanding, including the ability to jointly explore and process the etiological events, has the potential to strengthen the therapeutic alliance and sense of co-participation in the therapeutic outcomes.

HOW EMDR EXTENDS THE OUTCOMES OF FAMILY THERAPY

Using EMDR in an integral way with family therapy has the potential for uncovering and resolving various emotional binds and blocks that might never be revealed in traditional family therapy, especially when the treatment is short term and focused. When family therapy is brief and problem focused, family members have the opportunity, because of the unexpected resolution of a single issue, to appreciate that awareness can result in many changes. For example, in the future, Joan and Frank are much more likely to realize the potential power of their unresolved past issues to affect their children's lives. Thus, as already discussed, the EMDR approach with this family emphasized the development of strengths in the family—and EMDR can do the same with other families. As mentioned, a major assumption of family systems therapy is that it focuses on the healthy *and* dysfunctional aspects of the family and its members.

SUGGESTIONS FOR STRENGTHENING EMDR

Treatment outcomes may be improved by increasing EMDR therapists' awareness of the role of family interaction patterns and dynamics and the tendency of people to try to return to a steady state, or a homeostatic balance. For example, when using EMDR to help someone deal with alcoholism, it might be discovered that although the dynamic origin of the drinking was based in a rebellion against the family's authority, the drinking member can also be used as a scapegoat for other family members. The family members project negative aspects of themselves onto the person who drinks as they attempt to rescue or actively encourage that family member to drink. When the person stops drinking, understands more about the drinking problem, and develops ways of coping effectively, family members might seek out another family member (who might volunteer) to step forward and develop a drinking problem or develop other symptoms (i.e., the phenomenon of floating pathology). This process would allow family members to maintain the family balance, the same pattern of interactions but with a different identified patient. Thus, in this example (Nurse, 1990), EMDR by itself might help the initial family member to recover but not serve the family well. As a solution, EMDR therapists could be trained more routinely in family systems thinking so that they can include the family unit and relationships in their therapy.

USING EMDR TO INVESTIGATE INTERESTING AREAS IN FAMILY THERAPY

Because of its ability to quickly make patients aware of previous experiences that are contributing to their current behavior, EMDR might effectively reveal connections between patterns stemming from early childhood experiences in the family of origin and current family and parenting difficulties. Current family problems emanating from erroneous beliefs, decisions affected by previous traumatic childhood experiences, or both might be clarified with EMDR. In addition, current conflicts may be better understood using EMDR investigation if patients are unconsciously repeating their original destructive family pattern or script (e.g., drug abuse, alcoholism, the need for a family scapegoat). Viewed through the lens of EMDR, these and other dynamics could be readily considered in an investigation of a sample of families who have the same specific problem areas. In addition, EMDR could not only be used to facilitate assessments and develop an understanding of family problem areas but also be used to help determine the types of processing needed to enable patients to reach a healthier resolution of their intrapersonal and interpersonal conflicts.

CONCLUSION

The time is ripe for several studies to be conducted, such as (a) the various ways family therapists can use EMDR with couple and family therapy, (b) EMDR's utility and effectiveness in locating, targeting, and reducing barriers to more fruitful and satisfying family life, and (c) how an understanding of family dynamics, legacies, scripts, and functioning can be incorporated by EMDR specialists not previously trained in family psychology. The objectives of EMDR and family therapy are quite congruent, so at times they are used together. The combination of the two therapies, in the hands of a skilled practitioner, enhances the positive realization of the goals established collaboratively by patients and their therapists.

REFERENCES

Ackerman, N. W. (1937). The family as a social and emotional unit. *Bulletin of the Kansas Mental Hygiene Society, 12*(2).

Ackerman, N. W. (1938). The unity of the family. *Archives of Pediatrics, 55,* 51–62.

American Psychiatric Association. (1994). *Diagnostic and statistical manual of mental disorders* (4th ed.). Washington, DC: Author.

Bateson, G. (1958). *Naven* (2nd ed.). Stanford, CA: Stanford University Press.

Becvar, D. S., & Becvar, R. J. (1996). *Family therapy: A systematic integration* (3rd ed.). Needham Heights, MA: Allyn & Bacon.

Berne, E. (1961). *Transactional analysis in psychotherapy.* New York: Grove.

Boscolo, L., & Bertrando, P. (1992). The reflexive loop of past, present and future in systemic therapy and consultation. *Family Process, 31*(2), 119–130.

Boscolo, L., Cecchin, G., Hoffman, L., & Penn, P. (1987). *Milan systemic family therapy.* New York: Norton.

Bowen, M. (1959). Family relationships in schizophrenia. In A. Auerback (Ed.), *Schizophrenia: An integrated approach* (pp. 147–178). New York: Ronald.

Bowen, M. (1978). *Family therapy in clinical practice* (2nd ed.). Northvale, NJ: Jason Aronson.

Brems, C. (1993). *A comprehensive guide to child psychotherapy.* New York: Allyn & Bacon.

Charny, I. W. (1986). What do therapists worry about? A tool for experiential supervision. In F. W. Kaslow (Ed.), *Supervision and training: Models, dilemmas, and challenges* (pp. 17–28). New York: Haworth.

Charny, I. W. (1990). Marital therapy and genocide: A love of life story. In F. W. Kaslow (Ed.), *Voices in family psychology* (Vol. 1, pp. 69–90). Newbury Park, CA: Sage.

Charny, I. W. (1996). Evil in human personality: Disorders of doing harm to others in family relationships. In F. W. Kaslow (Ed.), *Handbook of relational diagnosis and dysfunctional family patterns* (pp. 479–495). New York: Wiley.

Elkaim, M. (1985). From general laws to singularities. *Family Process, 24*(2), 151–164.

Elkaim, M. (1986). A systemic approach to couple therapy. *Family Process, 25*(1), 35–42.

Fisher, R., & Ury, W. (1981). *Getting to yes: Negotiating an agreement without giving in.* Boston: Houghton-Mifflin.

Goldenberg, I., & Goldenberg, H. (1996). *Family therapy: An overview* (4th ed.). Pacific Grove, CA: Brooks/Cole.

Gottman, J. (1994). *Why marriages succeed or fail.* New York: Simon & Shuster.

Guerin, P. J. (1976). Family therapy: The first twenty-five years. In P. J. Guerin (Ed.), *Family therapy and practice* (pp. 2–22). New York: Gardner Press.

Guerin, P. J., & Fogarty, T. (1972). Study your own family. In A. Farber, M. Mendelsohn, & A. Napier (Eds.), *The book of family therapy* (pp. 445–467). New York: Science House.

Halpern, E. (2001). Family psychology in an Israeli perspective. *American Psychologist, 56*(1), 58–64.

Herscovici, P., & Herscovici, C. R. (1999). Family therapy in Argentina. In U. P. Gielen & A. L. Comunian (Eds.), *International approaches to the family and family therapy* (pp. 117–138). Padua, Italy: Unipress.

Kameguchi, K. (2001). Family psychology and family therapy in Japan. *American Psychologist, 56*(1), 65–70.

Kaslow, F. W. (1980). History of family therapy in the United States: A kaleidoscopic overview. *Marriage and Family Review, 3*(1–2), 77–111.

Kaslow, F. W. (1987). Marital and family therapy. In M. B. Sussman & S. K. Steinmetz (Eds.), *Handbook of marriage and the family* (pp. 835–860). New York: Plenum.

Kaslow, F. W. (1990). A multifaceted family psychology potpourri. In F. W. Kaslow (Ed.), *Voices in family psychology* (Vol. 1, pp. 281–322). Newbury Park, CA: Sage.

Kaslow, F. W. (2000a). Continued evolution of family therapy: The last twenty years. *Contemporary Family Therapy, 22*(4), 357–386.

Kaslow, F. W. (2000b). History of family therapy: Evolution outside of the U.S.A. *Journal of Family Psychotherapy, 11*(4), 1–35.

Kaslow, N. J., Kaslow, F. W., & Farber, E. W. (1999). Theories and techniques of marital and family therapy. In M. B. Sussman, S. K. Steinmetz, & G. W. Peterson (Eds.), *Handbook of marriage and the family* (2nd ed., pp. 767–793). New York: Plenum Press.

L'Abate, L., & Bagarozzi, D. (1993). *Sourcebook of marriage and family evaluation.* New York: Brunner/Mazel.

Lang, M. (1982). Bad therapy: A way of learning. In F. W. Kaslow (Ed.), *The international book of family therapy* (pp. 447–462). New York: Brunner/Mazel.

Levant, R. (1995). *Masculinity reconstructed: Changing the rules of manhood at work, in relationships, and in family life.* New York: Dutton.

Lovett, J. (1999). *Small wonders: Healing childhood trauma with EMDR.* New York: Free Press.

Millon, T. (1996). *Disorders of personality: DSM–IV and beyond.* New York: Wiley.

Millon, T., Millon C., & Davis, R. (1994). *Millon Clinical Multiaxial Inventory–III.* Minneapolis, MN: National Computer Systems.

Nichols, M. P., & Schwartz, R. C. (1995). *Family therapy: Concepts and methods* (3rd ed.). Boston: Allyn & Bacon.

Nurse, A. R. (1998). The dependent/narcissistic couple. In J. Carlson & L. Speery (Eds.), *The disordered couple.* New York: Brunner/Mazel.

Nurse, A. R. (1990). A curious "only" child becomes a family psychologist. In F. W. Kaslow (Ed.), *Voices in family psychology* (Vol. 2, pp. 84–98). Newbury Park, CA: Sage.

Nurse A. R. (1996). Eye movement desensitization and reprocessing: A stealth-like approach to family of origin issues. *The Family Psychologist, 12*(3), 17–19.

Nurse, A. R. (1999). *Family assessment: Effective uses of personality tests with couples and families.* New York: Wiley.

Nurse, A. R., & Thompson, P. (1999). Collaborative divorce: A new, interdisciplinary approach. *American Journal of Family Law, 13*(4), 226–234.

Nurse, A. R., & Thompson, P. (2000). Collaborative divorce: An interdisciplinary approach for resolving divorce conflicts. In L. Vandecreek & T. L. Jackson (Eds.), *Innovations in clinical practice: A source book* (Vol. 8, pp. 169–185). Sarasota, FL: Professional Resource Press.

Pasick, R. S. (1990). Raised to work. In R. S. Meth et al. (Eds.), *Men in therapy: The challenge of change.* New York: Guilford.

Patterson, T. (1999). *Couple and family clinical documentation source book.* New York: Wiley.

Piercy, F. P., & Sprenkle, D. H. (1986). *Family therapy sourcebook.* New York: Guilford Press.

Pinsof, W. M. (1995). *Integrative problem-centered therapy.* New York: Basic Books.

Pinsof, W. M., & Wynne, L. C. (1995). Special issue: The effectiveness of marital and family therapy. *Journal of Marital and Family Therapy, 21*(4), 339–614.

Satir, V. (1967). *Conjoint family therapy* (Rev. ed.). Palo Alto, CA: Science and Behavior Books.

Schwartz, L. L., & Kaslow, F. W. (1997). *Painful partings: Divorce and its aftermath.* New York: Wiley.

Selvini-Palazzoli, M., Boscolo, L., Cecchin, G., & Prata, G. (1978). *Paradox and counterparadox.* New York: Jason Aronson.

Selvini-Palazzoli, M., Cirillo, S., Selvini, M., & Sorrentino, A. M. (1989). *Family games: General models of psychotic processes in the family.* New York: Norton.

Shapiro, F. (1995). *Eye movement, desensitization, and reprocessing: Basic principles, protocols, and procedures.* New York: Guilford Press.

Skynner, R. (1976). *Systems of family and marital psychotherapy.* New York: Brunner/Mazel.

Suzuki, K., & Suzuki, K. (1988, June). *Japanese living style in therapy of families of children.* Paper presented at the annual meeting of the American Family Therapy Association.

Wallerstein, J., Lewis, J., & Blakeslee, S. (2000). *The unexpected legacy of divorce.* New York: Hyperion.

White, M., & Epstom, D. (1990). *Narrative means to therapeutic ends.* New York: Norton.

Winslade, J., & Monk, G. (2000). *Narrative mediation: A new approach to conflict resolution.* San Francisco, CA: Jossey-Bass.

13

TRANSPERSONAL PSYCHOLOGY, EASTERN NONDUAL PHILOSOPHY, AND EMDR

SHEILA KRYSTAL, JOHN PRENDERGAST, PHYLLIS KRYSTAL,
PETER FENNER, ISAAC SHAPIRO, AND KALI SHAPIRO

In his seminal work *The Perennial Philosophy*, the British philosopher and writer Aldous Huxley (1945) described an essential thread that has run through all of the world's spiritual traditions for thousands of years. He suggested that beneath the confusion of many languages, myths, rituals, and doctrines lies a core perspective that considers the phenomenal world and individual consciousness to be an expression of a Divine Ground and humanity's only purpose to be to directly know itself as this. This view has been most clearly articulated in the Eastern nondual philosophies of Advaita Vedanta, Dzogchen Tibetan Buddhism, Chan Buddhism, and Zen Buddhism. *Nondualism* literally means "not two," referring to the illusory separation of subject and object. These nondual traditions view the separate sense of self as a purely mental construct. Transpersonal philosopher Ken Wilber (1993), deeply influenced by Advaita and Dzogchen, commented, "So overwhelmingly widespread is the perennial philosophy that it is either the single greatest intellectual error ever to appear in humankind's history or it is the single most accurate reflection of reality yet to appear" (p. 214). Wilber has proposed a "perennial psychology" that describes the same perspective in the language of psychology. The roots of transpersonal psychology thus reach back into humanity's earliest yearnings for and intuitions about spiritual union. The current state of transpersonal psychology has evolved from its late 1960s origins, when it was chiefly concerned with ecstatic and mystical states of consciousness, to its current exploration of the way that authentic spirituality can be grounded in ordinary life. Eye movement desensitization and reprocessing (EMDR) can make an important contribution to addressing this issue and has a surprising capacity to liberate expansive states of awareness.

Transpersonal literally means "beyond the person." It refers to the realms of human experience that are beyond the ego or self-image. These include the collective and archetypal realms mapped by Jung and others and the illuminated states of profound mystical insight or enlightenment sometimes referred to as *pure consciousness* or *unconditioned awareness*. These higher states of consciousness have been described with remarkable consistency by many of the cross-cultural wisdom traditions. Transpersonal psychology views these higher states as the natural culmination of the human developmental process rather than as a regression to an earlier infantile stage, as some traditional psychoanalysts have theorized.

Transpersonal psychology focuses on uncovering and sustaining these higher realms of awareness as it honors the need to address and integrate prepersonal and personal developmental levels. The goal of transpersonal psychology is to help humans realize their full personal and transpersonal potential as multidimensional beings. A transpersonal approach honors and includes the personal, yet it accents one's essential or spiritual nature and places the human experience and psyche within a much broader, even boundless, framework.

Although transpersonal psychology is not confined to any specific methodology, it is characterized by a certain *context*, or space within which the therapeutic encounter occurs, as well as by a certain range of *content*. The transpersonal context is shaped by the therapist's understanding and values, as are all therapeutic approaches, but is above all influenced by the quality of the therapist's consciousness. This may be the most important contribution that a transpersonal *psychotherapist* offers—recognizing the reality and transformative power of the therapist's and client's open and spacious presence. *Transpersonal content* includes the ordinary range of thoughts, feelings, and sensations, as well as extraordinary experiences, some of which are discussed in this chapter.

Because presence is the essential element in transpersonal psychotherapy, an actual session with a client can take on almost any form. Numerous methodologies, including EMDR, may be used as skillful means to help reveal to clients their deepest truth or help them face whatever problems they have. A transpersonal therapist supports the client's transformation and transcendence according to the client's needs and the possibilities of the moment. For example, a client's attention may be fixated on a personal childhood trauma and its related negative cognitions and painful affects, which could be addressed with the use of the standard EMDR protocol. On the other hand, a client may express a yearning for greater inner freedom and peace or a desire for a greater sense of connection to the whole of life. In this case a transpersonal psychotherapist might respond through dialogue; guiding a process of subtle sensing and imagery; inviting a shared, eyes-open meditation; or introducing the transpersonal EMDR protocol described later in this chapter.

A focus on transformation brings attention to dysfunctional beliefs, unexpressed feelings, and disowned sensations with the goal of fostering greater personal integration. A focus on transcendence explores the client's fundamental nature, free of any personal history and self-image, and supports a clear vision and acceptance of things as they are. A transpersonal approach encourages and supports clients as they "disidentify," or detach, from whom they have thought themselves to be and to live freely without a self-image. For example, clients often identify themselves according to their problems, clinging to their negative self-images (e.g., "I am fatally flawed, a hopeless case") and continuing to find and generate evidence to support their constrictive beliefs rather than tolerate less self-definition. Some clients act like newly released lifetime prisoners who are reluctant to step outside the opened doors of their prison. They prefer the certitude of a familiar negative self-identity to one that is fundamentally unknown. Transpersonal psychology welcomes and values the unknown—that which the mind can neither comprehend nor control—and questions all concepts about the world or life. The existential questions "Who or what am I?" and "What is the true nature of life?" are deeply honored and directly explored.

Identification with the therapeutic roles of therapist and client can completely dissolve in the transpersonal encounter. While observing the conventional behavioral boundaries of therapy, transpersonal therapists who are intimate with their true nature consider clients to be fundamentally no different from themselves. The split between *self* and *other* may dissolve into the felt understanding of unity, or nonseparation. Therapists' nondual awareness then becomes an open invitation for clients to drop into their own natural freedoms. At such times, therapy is no different from satsang or sangha, the traditional name in Hinduism or Buddhism for "when the lovers of the truth gather together."

Transpersonal psychotherapy with a nondual emphasis could be called *satsang psychotherapy*. It seeks to stimulate an inner wisdom in an atmosphere in which the therapist rests in an open-hearted and peaceful awareness, inviting therapeutic resonance, or *entrainment*, with the client. Entrainment is the phenomenon by which consciousness is contagious. Just as one can find oneself in a bad mood in the presence of people who are depressed, one can also experience a higher-than-usual level of consciousness in the presence of people who are attuned to their deepest nature. If the therapist is a quiet, empty, and peaceful presence, it is likely that clients will discover that presence within themselves. If the therapist keeps in mind the client's essential health and the oneness of client and therapist, the client will eventually realize this reality as well. Thus, inner peace and contentment are shared. As the client and therapist sit together, the therapist recognizes that they are both students and teachers of the other. In the open space in which anything can arise, projections are seen and withdrawn, attachments and security symbols are released, and identification with a personal history ends. Beliefs, attitudes, and preferences are held more lightly. Clients begin to realize that their difficulties come from resisting or clinging to what is. As they begin to welcome whatever arrives in their life and to let go of whatever leaves their life, contentment and harmony arise. They begin to realize it is their thoughts and not the circumstances of their lives that cause suffering. Pain is a normal part of life; suffering need not be. Clients gradually learn that they are not their thoughts but are the quiet, empty awareness in which their thoughts, emotions, and sensations arise.

As the therapists remain in the quiet space between thoughts, emotions, and sensations, without analyzing or without actively doing anything except simply being, clients discover their own being. This discovery in itself heals and integrates even the clients who were the most severely abused or are the most troubled. The "doing" of psychotherapy comes from the emptiness. There is no sense of "doership" on the part of therapists during a psychotherapy session. Therapists are not busy thinking about how to "do" the therapy or about techniques appropriate for a given diagnosis. Yet appropriate techniques, guidelines, and skillful means, such as the cognitive interweave from classical EMDR and the transpersonal EMDR protocol, arise freely and spontaneously in the mind of the therapists according to the needs of the client in the moment. The experience of the therapists is intuitive and occasionally even mystical at times. This space in which the therapists find themselves then becomes an arrow that points the clients in the direction of quiet contentment.

Thus, during a session, the therapist remains in a state of nonjudgmental compassion and loving kindness, listening to the gist of the client's story but with attention on their oneness. The therapist's inner commentary is relatively silent, and little or no attention is paid to theories, diagnoses, plans of action, or any attempt to help or fix the client. Clients are considered to be already whole and perfect; they simply do not understand this yet. As long as the therapist sees this wholeness, clients eventually will too, according to their potential. Clients will come to understand that their beliefs, problems, issues, negative attitudes, and reactions are transient, ephemeral, and eventually illusory, as their own selves move into the foreground and problems recede into the background. Opinions, preferences, attachments, beliefs, and even the facts of their history become relative—just illusions masquerading as truth. Absolute truths of love, forgiveness, and nonviolence become self-evident. Clients feel grateful and appreciative as they begin to surrender to, trust, and accept life just as it is. They realize that they suffer to the degree that they are unhappy with life as it is. Their daily circumstances become opportunities for learning and growth in the University of Life. Although clients may sometimes believe that life is too much to bear, they eventually realize that they are never given more than they can handle. They realize that thoughts are mirages distracting them from who they really are, and they can choose to put their attention on the peaceful background from which thoughts arise. Clients discover that most negative reactions to situations and people are the result of the projection of their own unwelcome and often unexplored negative tendencies. They may even learn that there is no "other!"

When therapists realize that the only problem in therapy is their own belief that clients should be different or act differently and they are willing to accept clients just as they are, personality warts and all, therapy becomes a living embodiment of satsang rather than an idea or concept of therapy. Healing can occur more rapidly. Therapy guides clients as they discover and let go of attachments by no longer identifying with the layers of conditioning that obscure the real self. Clients see how thought—chiefly beliefs, concepts, and preferences—directs their lives. They first learn to change their negative beliefs into positive ones by forgiving the past, being grateful in the present, and having hope for the future. Ultimately, nondual or satsang psychotherapy can help clients develop an awareness in which all concepts are deconstructed and they realize the self as the oneness of all. The past is gone, the future is a mystery, and the now is a gift (which is why it is called "the present")!

Transpersonal psychotherapy and EMDR have overlapping sets of principles and practices, and each has something valuable to offer the other. Both share a humanistic foundation that acknowledges a natural drive toward growth and health and the constricting effects of prior conditioning. Each approach values clear self-observation, detachment, acceptance, compassionate understanding, and forgiveness. EMDR, at least as it is conventionally practiced, and transpersonal psychotherapy also have important distinctions. Although EMDR can help to foster an "observing ego," as clients simply observe their experience as it arises during the bilateral stimulation, they are not encouraged to directly question the nature of this observing self as they would in transpersonal psychotherapy. There is more or less the presumption that a "someone"—a discrete entity—is watching. EMDR, like almost all other therapies, tends to assume that the goal of therapy is to help someone become a better person by desensitizing and reprocessing dysfunctional learning experiences. In contrast, a transpersonal approach does not assume that anything is fundamentally lacking in or wrong with a client. A transpersonal therapist assists clients to see through prior conditioning, not just as a way to become better adapted and integrated but as a preliminary step to investigating the nature of awareness itself. Whereas EMDR focuses on undoing old stories (negative cognitions) and replacing them with new stories (positive cognitions), transpersonal psychotherapy with a nondual emphasis encourages the undoing of *all* stories, negative and positive, so that a client can live fully in the present without the burden and constriction of any personal narrative that identifies the self or its history. No self is required to be reconstructed because people are able to live freely and joyfully in, and as, the awareness that exists before the creation of any self-image. The true self is not a mental creation or object but is who a person already is and always will be. Unlike most conventional therapies, including EMDR, the highest goal of a transpersonal approach is not to better know oneself as an object but simply to *be*, free of any qualifications.

Although EMDR has a tightly structured protocol and strong goal orientation, it has the capacity to induce significant expansions of awareness and extraordinary, or transpersonal, content. Clients frequently report having spontaneous insights that allow them to view past traumas with clarity and detachment and sometimes to understand how the actions of those who hurt them arose out of ignorance and abuse. Forgiveness and compassion often flow out of such direct understanding, thus ending the cycle of violence and reaction, which may have been developing for many generations. EMDR clients sometimes report unusual somatic experiences, such as the openings of energy centers and the emergence of ascending or descending currents of energy along the spine. Clients also report experiences with inner guides, deceased loved ones, mythic journeys, and other imaginal representations of their spirituality without any suggestions from the therapist. They also at times report feelings of profound gratitude for life, deep joy, the sense of being interconnected with all living beings, and the sense of feeling a relationship to or identification with the divine or being.

THREE STAGES OF AWAKENING

First you are in the light. Then the light is in you. Finally, you are the light.
—Sri Sathya Sai Baba

Sathya Sai Baba, a contemporary Indian spiritual master revered by millions, has described three stages of spiritual awakening that span increasingly subtle levels of phenomena and find their completion in nondual realization. Almaas (1986), founder of the diamond approach, described the spiritual path as first a journey *to* presence (presence outside), next as a journey *with* presence (presence inside), and finally as a journey *as* presence (nondual awareness). The Sufi poets such as Rumi, Kabir, and Mirabai spoke of the experience of the lover first, then of the beloved, and finally of love itself. Jesus of Nazareth's experience paralleled these stages as well. After his baptism by John, he declared that he was the Son of God, the Father in Heaven, and His messenger. Later Jesus declared that "God, the Father, is within me." Finally he realized that "God, the Father, and I are One."

In the first stage of spiritual life, individuals experience the Divine as if it is outside of themselves. They may pray to an outside god or meditate on an exterior symbol of the divine. Those people at the second stage experience an inner voice, higher consciousness, or deeper self and source of guidance and direction that uses dreams, signs, and synchronicity (meaningful coincidence) to direct the self. People in the last stage experience a oneness best described by the five great sentences, or Mahavakyas, of the Upanishads: "Thou Art That" ("You are God"), "Aham Brahmasmi" ("I am God"), "Prajnanam Brahma" ("Pure consciousness is God"), "Ayam Atma Brahma" ("This self is Brahman"), and "Tat Twam Asi" ("That Thou Art").

Each succeeding stage incorporates the previous stages of consciousness so that ultimately all three stages can exist simultaneously. Those people in the third stage of nondual understanding can still enjoy meditating with symbols on altars, and those in the second stage may pray to an external symbol. Transpersonal psychotherapy with a nondual emphasis seeks to bring the client into the third stage. In this approach, clients are introduced to a clear and expanded way of being in which nothing needs to be added to or taken away from their experience. The psychotherapist offers clients a direct experience of the natural freedom of being and guidelines for how this experience can be deepened and extended into all areas of life. In contrast, dualistic therapies assume that the inner and outer realities must change to achieve real fulfillment. Nondualistic therapy simply dissolves the habitual tendencies to construct something that is wrong or missing and must be changed. It introduces clients to an unconditioned level of consciousness that transcends all preoccupation with getting or losing some experience of health, well-being, or happiness. In short, as clients are encouraged to explore the duality within themselves, they look for the ego and find that it does not exist. As they look outside themselves, they find only the nonduality of others and realize that all are one. Therapists who bring this nondual awareness to their practice of psychotherapy can use EMDR more efficiently, effectively, and creatively and reaffirm the cultivation of nondual awareness in the client.

Most people simply want to be free and have peace of mind. Nondual transpersonal or satsang therapy can show people that they are already free, and peace of mind is available in the space before and between thought, emotion, and sensation. EMDR can facilitate or catalyze the movement of consciousness through these three stages, particularly when the classical EMDR protocol has been used first to desensitize and reprocess old traumas and disturbing thoughts and emotions. The remainder of this chapter describes a new transpersonal EMDR protocol, presents two cases from this protocol in which clients have experiences that correspond to these levels, and offers descriptions by several noted spiritual teachers who have had limited experience with EMDR and who explore the relationship of EMDR to psychological integration and the unfolding of spiritual understanding.

TRANSPERSONAL EMDR PROTOCOL

One of the authors of this chapter (S. Krystal) has been experimenting with what is called a *transpersonal EMDR protocol*, in which EMDR represents "deconstruction and disidentification of self" and "recognition of self." After Shapiro's (1995) standard protocol has been used to desensitize and reprocess traumas, problematic personal histories, and negative emotions and beliefs, the psychological material has been processed, and the client's symptoms such as anxiety and depression have decreased, another possibility arises. When clients report that they have no more issues to work on and want to know what happens next or simply want to explore the deeper answers to the questions, "Who am I, and what is my purpose?" then the transpersonal protocol can be used. This protocol works to desensitize and decrease the compelling nature of the distractions of mind, emotion, and sensation, which take attention away from quiet awareness. This protocol can benefit clients who already have a sense of quiet and contentment after meditation or EMDR sessions or those who have had only a glimpse of their full potential. The transpersonal protocol facilitates the experience of mental quiet and cultivates the empty mental background behind thoughts, emotions, and sensations. Distractions to awareness slow down and become ephemeral. Use of the protocol can help clients let go of objects of awareness such as beliefs, expectations, preferences, and judgments that distract and prevent them from gratefully and contentedly accepting life as it is. As EMDR processes these distractions, clients report that their contentment deepens and life is more noumenal, oceanic, and magical. Awe and appreciation increase, and laughter and a sense of surprise and wonder occur more frequently. As understanding unfolds, difficulties are taken more lightly and forgiveness is easy.

The transpersonal EMDR protocol is flexible and still evolving. It is used to target compelling distractions from quiet, peaceful emptiness, and equanimity. *Contentment* is defined as the experience of well-being evoked by the reality that perpetually exists before thought arises and in between each thought, emotion, and sensation. In time, these distractions no longer distract and are discovered to be expressions of reality. Constant contentment is the ground of being but is usually in the background. The transpersonal protocol seeks to bring this contentment into the foreground of awareness and stabilize it. This protocol should be used very intuitively. It is not necessarily linear, although its steps can be described sequentially in four phases.

Phase 1: Life Review and Preparation

In the first step of Phase 1, clients are asked to review their entire life to date during long sets of bilateral stimulation. This phase can take anywhere from 10 minutes to an entire 90-minute session. It provides an overall perspective of the lessons and opportunities life has offered. This step is for clients who have already processed negative memories, beliefs, and emotions with the standard EMDR protocol. Sometimes during this step, clients discover an emotional charge in some area of life that was left unprocessed. This area becomes a target and is processed with bilateral stimulation using the standard protocol until the subjective units of disturbance scale (SUDS) score is 0 and positive cognitions are believed completely, the body scan is clear, and the client is relaxed and peaceful. Next, the life lessons are reviewed and installed more fully during bilateral stimulation.

In the second step of Phase 1, the contentment experience is discussed and defined, and clients can be taught to quiet down or meditate if they are interested in doing so. However, note that meditation is suggested and described by the therapist as "the experience of the already present essence or truth while being still and quiet" and not as a technique used to achieve something. Peace is always present—attention is just distracted from it or does not yet know how to recognize it. Peace is like room temperature, unrecognized until it is pointed out. Therapists point out this contentment with their presence while using this protocol. Quieting techniques are useful for quieting down and focusing attention. They serve as pointers, or arrows, until contentment is recognized. S. Krystal usually suggested that clients reference their prayer state if they pray or teaches them some of the centering images from *Cutting the Ties That Bind* (Krystal, 1982) such as *the triangle, hi C,* and *figure eight,* which are joint visualizations that attune the client and therapist to the symbol of their higher consciousness, or self, and help maintain therapeutic boundaries. Entrainment or therapeutic resonance is facilitated during this instruction as the therapist remains in nondual awareness, joining the client and visualizing together in this quieting step of the protocol. The experience of becoming still and content replaces the "safe place" exercise in traditional EMDR protocol.

Phase 2: Assessment

During the assessment phase of the protocol, a contentment baseline is established during a client's present level of equilibrium. First, the concept of distraction is defined and expanded. Distractions are often persistent habits of mind, obsessive and intrusive thoughts, addictions, memories, fantasies, self-talk, sleepiness, numbing out, physical pains, itches, discomforts, noises, smells or visual images, and the full gamut of emotions including strong positive ones. For example, when clients are depressed, bored, or lonely, attention may tend to reorient around what they have to look forward to in the future, such as some event, holiday, vacation, gift, or addicting substance. Distracted attention and boredom obscure present contentment. This contentment is found when a client lets go of a depressing story. The judging mind tends to orient itself around what is wrong, where a problem or flaw is, and what needs to be done, fixed, or changed. The mind's tendency to constantly ask, "How am I doing, and how do I rate?" is like constantly taking one's temperature in a vain effort to feel comfortable or content. This activity of continuously measuring and judging oneself causes more pressure and hopelessness. One's attention is taken further and further from contentment. More subtle distractions are those reference points around which awareness tends to define itself as a "me" or ground itself in the apparent safety of the known instead of abiding in the empty unknown, which is the basis of all being. For example, the belief that "this isn't enough" or that there is some experience or object needed to be happy lead attention away from the present unknown.

To establish the contentment baseline, clients are instructed to quiet down for 10 to 15 minutes and rate their level of quietness or contentment as light, medium, or deep, with light meaning the person is very distracted and deep meaning the person is not distracted at all by thoughts, emotions, or sensations. Targets for bilateral stimulation then become any distractions that take awareness away from contentment or peaceful emptiness as established by the baseline. This can include any charged emotions, physical reactions to or thoughts about those distractions.

Next, while clients are experiencing baseline contentment without any bilateral stimulation, distractions are identified and measured on a level of distraction (LOD) scale. The therapist suggests to the client to let anything come up, report it as a distraction to the quietness, and rate it on a LOD scale of 0 to 10, with 10 being totally compelling or distracting and 0 being not distracting. These distractions and their ratings are noted by the therapist for processing in the next phase of the protocol. This measurement phase lasts about 20 minutes, and no bilateral stimulation occurs during this time. During this period, the client might become bored or feel that time is being wasted because no therapy is being received, or the client may want to talk. All of these responses are considered to be distractions.

Usually clients find the very familiar flavor of their self-talk coming into the foreground with its attendant emotions. Seasoned meditators find this assessment phase familiar. New meditators may need some coaching to stay focused and give reassurance that they should report anything that comes to awareness and takes attention away from the now.

Phase 3: Processing

In the third phase of the transpersonal EMDR protocol, clients are asked to bring to mind each target identified in the assessment phase during bilateral stimulation. Saccades of eye movements, auditory tones, or hand vibrations can be used. When all previously identified targets have been processed to 0 on the LOD scale, clients are asked to return to the contentment baseline for 10 to 20 minutes without bilateral stimulation; any new distractions from contentment are noted, discussed, and then processed with bilateral stimulation. During processing, clients can report when they realize that they are distracted. Then the therapist can initiate the stimulation or clients can control the stimulation device themselves. During processing, clients' contentment baseline deepens and distractions become less frequent. Clients also notice sooner and sooner that distractions arise from and disappear back into their source—the naturally quiet, peaceful, and empty ground of being.

As distractions become 0 on the LOD scale and each target identified in the assessment phase has been processed, the contentment is measured again without stimulation. Any new distractions are noted and processed with stimulation. It is not necessary to measure every distraction on the LOD scale as the client becomes used to the protocol. Again, the therapist is depending on intuition and resonance with clients to determine when to direct clients into the measuring intellect (and out of witness consciousness, which just notices the presence of distractions) and when to just continue the bilateral stimulation. Krystal finds that she rarely asks clients to rate their level of contentment because this activity engages the relative mind to measure and judge. Supporting this kind of discrimination effectively reduces the depth of contentment and distracts from the emptiness. If clients silently meditate during bilateral stimulation, after 10 minutes the therapist can ask, "Now what distracts from contentment?" If clients answer, the therapist can say "Stay with that" and keep processing. The protocol cycles through processing distractions, measuring contentment, processing new distractions, and measuring contentment until contentment can remain distraction free for 10 minutes. Then contentment is targeted several times with stimulation to deepen it even more and the bilateral stimulation can also be used to dissolve blocking beliefs to going deeper into contentment. Next, bilateral stimulation can be used to install future templates for deep equipoise in difficult situations, relationships, and distracting environments. During installation, clients can be asked about future events that might test their equipoise. Contentment is then paired with these future images during bilateral stimulation.

Phase 4: Grounding

In the final, or fourth, phase of the transpersonal protocol, clients are grounded and asked to log in a journal or notebook any new distractions noticed between sessions. Specifically, clients are brought back to the body, time, place, and date as they plan to leave the session. Clients are encouraged to abide in their state of contentment as much as possible, noting distractions and bringing the attention back to contentment. When distractions are particularly compelling or recurrent, clients can log them to be processed in a future session.

This transpersonal protocol, if held lightly (i.e., followed loosely and intuitively), can be instructive and give some structure to an EMDR session in which clients would like to become quieter and more contented. Clients report experiencing not only a deeper and more abiding sense of contentment after EMDR sessions but also a greater sense of surprise, humor, and delight as they find themselves accepting whatever occurs as their lives unfold, welcoming what comes and letting go of what leaves.

CASE STUDIES

Two brief examples of the use of the transpersonal protocol also illustrate the three stages of consciousness described previously. These sessions used the Lapscan, which provides both visual and auditory bilateral stimulation.

The first example illustrates the experience of the divine as present "outside." "Sara," a 45-year-old woman, was referred for EMDR by her physician to resolve issues relating to her abduction and rape in a car by two men when she was in her teens. She had been in many types of therapy previously but still had symptoms of posttraumatic stress disorder (PTSD). She experienced fear and guilt and had difficulty being open with and trusting men, particularly her husband. Her responses describe her experience at the end of her first EMDR session. The traditional protocol was used in the beginning of the session, and the transpersonal protocol was introduced when the client entered into a numenous space. A series of asterisks (********) denote sets of bilateral stimulation. The therapist's interventions are in parentheses. After processing the memory of the incident, her fear and sense of being unclean, and the body sensations in her chest, solar plexus, and pelvis, and her back pain, Sara spontaneously reported the presence of angels in the car with her:

There are angels around me in the car **************** an angel took me out of the car **************** there are huge wings of the angel **************** no more men **************** it was their problem with sex not mine **************** the angel says "Don't look back, just look forward" **************** the angel is rubbing his hand down my spine **************** the pain is gone **************** don't look back **************** I can trust the angel's left hand **************** I can trust the angel's right hand **************** I can trust the universe **************** I can relax **************** I feel cleansed. (Just stay with that, and let the experience deepen.) **************** The angels are still with me **************** they are always with me **************** they always have been **************** I am safe. (Just melt into that knowing.) **************** It is very peaceful. (Just stay in this peace.) **************** ahhh **************** mmmm **************** (Can you find anything that distracts you from this?) **************** I feel completely protected **************** (Now?) **************** A vague fear about tonight in bed with C **************** (Just come back, has the peace left?) **************** I can feel the angels (Notice that the angels are still with you in your bedroom.) **************** Yes, that's fine **************** still peaceful.

Sara experienced resolution of her traumatic rape in her first EMDR session when the divine outside her took the form of angels and rescued her, healed her, and instructed her so that she could trust the outside universe. When the protocol was subtly changed, her experience of the angels developed into peace, which could then be deepened. Sara could then notice which thoughts distracted her from the peace and return her attention to it. Finally, her angels were paired with her anxious thoughts about sex, creating a future template. She was instructed at the end of the session to notice any other distractions and log them in a journal in preparation for her next session. When Sara returned for her second session, she reported that her angels were still there even in the bedroom, and she wanted to work on memories of a recent car accident that had been distracting her during the week. This change is still holding and flowering many months later.

The following case study illustrates the second stage of spiritual awakening. In the first EMDR session the traditional protocol was used to process old material. When the client's consciousness expanded, the therapist shifted to the transpersonal protocol. The client, "Jim," was a male psychotherapist who was referred for EMDR because of burnout. Jim had been meditating for years, was on a spiritual path, and had glimpses of the divine within him. In the first session a series of memories of childhood failure leading to overexertion, a sense of a pressured doership, or need to do therapy, and his current burnout were processed. His fear of not getting everything done and losing the race, tension in his chest and back, and memories of childhood sports events were targeted. After several sets of stimulation during a 45-minute period, the transpersonal protocol was introduced when Jim began to report experiencing his spiritual self. As Jim noticed distractions from this presence within him, he reported the following:

> The drive or charge around it [the memory of failure] is diminishing **************** the whole ego platform is dissolving and loosening **************** there are objective things to be done but there is a different way of holding them **************** I trust the universe to take care of it **************** whether I am recognized or not doesn't matter that much when I am in touch with my inner richness **************** nothing matters, but objectively I have to do it and I can surrender and let God do it **************** The feeling that I've got to do it all myself is still there **************** The thought that I can't win, that my will is being defeated, and I'm not getting what I want **************** It feels old and I am less than ever in the grips of it **************** My new touchstone is what I feel now when I am totally present **************** It's hard to keep the distraction in mind, it's dissolving **************** there is an emerging feeling of confidence in my own presence **************** I don't need outside confirmation of my worth **************** I have my new touchstone or tap-root access into something that is real, not others' opinions **************** I want to let go of even that and just meditate **************** I want to let go of the whole world and just let it happen **************** stop feeding the whole object relations **************** I could use a vacation **************** the only thing I can rely on is my own presence **************** it's like Oakland, there is no "there" there! **************** I want to go into the emptiness and surrender and let go of the world which is only my idea of the world **************** I want to let go of my idea of letting go of everything. (What is in the way of taking care of yourself?) **************** I have to make it all happen, unless my egoic will makes it happen, it won't happen **************** beneath egoic will that has to make it all happen is a lack of trust in the universe. (What is the lynchpin holding the egoic pattern in place?) **************** When I let go and surrender, a higher will or God comes in a way that my parents never did and I feel support even when the support doesn't look like support **************** I feel like letting go of all of these mental constructs **************** I reify enlightenment **************** I visit the country rather than thinking it's me **************** It all just feels like a thought or series of memories, like going through life wearing too tight

a raincoat **************** it falls off and I can be
****

Jim's experience during EMDR shows the progression from the second stage of awakening into glimpses of the third stage of nondual awareness. His own psychological sophistication informs his EMDR experience as he leaves behind concepts such as ego platform and objects relations and realizes that his whole reality is simply a concept. As he speaks of his higher will, or God self, and then later of the presence that is not separate from him, he moves into nondual awareness. During Jim's next two sessions, he continued to move between the two stages, establishing his awareness more and more in the nondual reality.

SPIRITUAL TEACHERS' EXPERIENCES WITH EMDR

Several of the chapter authors (P. Krystal, Fenner, the Shapiros) experienced the transpersonal protocol during two to three sessions of EMDR from varying degrees of stabilization in the nondual perspective.

Phyllis Krystal

In the early 1950s, P. Krystal developed a psychospiritual form of visualization work called *Cutting the Ties That Bind* (1982, 1990). She has been teaching this method internationally for more than 30 years to individuals and large groups, including many psychology professionals. Her work is especially useful in helping people to let go of the attachments that prevent them from fully realizing who they are. Krystal calls this divine essence the *hi C,* or *high consciousness.* She reports that her experience with EMDR pinpointed some of the periods in her life with pockets of energy that were still acting as obstacles to further development and freedom to fully express her real self in her daily life more effectively and regularly. By highlighting forgotten or suppressed events, reactions, and emotions, she was able to let go of the residue that was still inhibiting her full expression, thus further extending her previous work by this fine-tuning process. The long, 3-hour EMDR session allowed her to review her life over a span of 85 years in a detached way and to observe how everything fit together like a mosaic, similar to what people report after they have had a near-death experience.

It was helpful for her to recall each of her important relationships and her many, varied experiences, strung like beads on a connecting thread, all with the same common theme or message: not to allow herself to be judged according to other people's standards but to know who she really is—a spark of divinity. Her experiences in her work of *Cutting the Ties That Bind* (1982, 1990) had freed her from obstructions to growth and hindrances along the path to unity with the real self, which is true awakening. She had processed her memories separately at different times but had not previously considered them with an overall view that revealed them arranged as a whole pattern. The insight that the EMDR session afforded was that the repeated lessons of her life were obviously inexorably propelling her each day to rely solely on her inner source of wisdom and guidance and to detach from all outside authority or security symbols, people, and objects.

Krystal believes that EMDR can be of great assistance in uncovering early programming and in siphoning off the energy that is still contained in memories that are causing problems. EMDR can also be very useful when leading a person back into a dream to extract its message and, if advisable, to finish the dream if it ended too abruptly or sank back into the subconscious mind before it could be recorded, decoded, and applied in life. EMDR can also desensitize the strong negative emotion in some dreams and help bring insight about the dream's message to the surface.

Peter Fenner

Fenner lived as a monk for 9 years in the Tibetan Buddhist tradition and now teaches in Australia, Europe, and the United States. His perspective invites him to experience that there is nothing to gain and nothing to lose in life. He encourages and supports the work of those who are developing new therapeutic modalities that combine cutting-edge Western modalities such as EMDR with a deep understanding of Eastern nondualistic spirituality. He offers his observations about how EMDR can be enhanced through the wisdom that is contained in these traditions and how EMDR can be an aid in dissolving emotional blockages and rigid interpretations that hinder free access to unconditioned awareness. He observes that, ultimately, human suffering is caused by a core belief that separates them from everything else. No matter how much people may work at rescripting their autobiographical stories, the results are partial and of a limited duration. The ultimate resolution of suffering can only come about if people harmonize conflicting beliefs at this deeper level. EMDR can bring these deeper structures into awareness relatively effortlessly. Once they are present in consciousness, EMDR continues to break up the structure of the limiting stories.

Fenner notes that nondualistic psychotherapies extend the wisdom of nonduality directly into the therapeutic arena. Their primary aim is to introduce people to a clear and expanded way of being in which nothing needs to be added to or taken away from their experience. They offer people a direct experience of the natural freedom of being and guidelines for how this experience can be deepened and extended into all areas of life. In contrast to dualistic therapies that assume the inner or outer realities must change to achieve real fulfillment, nondualistic therapies simply dissolve the habitual tendency to construct that something is wrong or missing. They introduce people to an unconditioned level of consciousness that transcends all preoccupations with "getting it" or "losing it."

Fenner observes that some of the distinctive features of nondualistic psychotherapies are that they neither feed nor ignore people's pain and suffering. They remove the pressure for people to stay the same or be different. They allow people to enjoy the present moment without compulsively needing to process the past or fear the future. They work with what arises in the present and neither enhance nor suppress whatever arises. Finally, they neither validate nor invalidate people's experience. When these basic principles are in place, therapy automatically gravitates toward an experience of transpersonal unity in which the therapist and client transcend their identification with a fixed personality and share in an experience in which there is no boundary between self and other, inside and outside. This approach allows therapy to reach that pivotal point of final healing at which there is no one to help or be helped and nowhere to go.

Nondualistic therapies focus on introducing people to the experience of the unconditioned mind as efficiently and effortlessly as possible. Because technical methods easily condition therapists and clients, nondualistic therapies are sensitive to the potential for technical interventions to condition therapists and clients. No matter how sophisticated a therapeutic protocol and no matter how skillfully it is used, if the therapy is not infused with the wisdom of unstructured awareness, it leaves psychological residues in the form of beliefs, knowledge, and expectations. These residues continue to condition experiences of pain and pleasure, depending on whether one's experience is challenged or supported by the structure of these residues.

According to Fenner, the challenge when using EMDR is to seamlessly blend the structure and focus of EMDR with the totally open and free nature of unstructured awareness. As S. Krystal points out, this depends more than anything else on the therapist's own experience of unstructured awareness and capacity to bring it forth in the therapeutic environment. Within a nondualistic framework, a modality such as EMDR is used with an awareness of the clients' position on a continuum of contracted-to-expanded ways of being and how they are moving toward an experience of the natural freedom of being. Skillful means determine that therapists offer the highest practice genuinely possible for a client. Goal-oriented approaches are used when a higher perspective is inaccessible. EMDR is used only as long as the residues of embedded emotional reactivity continue to degrade the freedom and spaciousness of the present moment. EMDR and the vision of nonduality exist in a dance, with EMDR receding into the background as the clear light of awareness dawns and reappearing again as previous life traumas impinge on the purity of unstructured awareness.

Fenner suggests that no matter how technically skilled therapists are, they need to be totally comfortable with doing nothing other than enjoying the utter simplicity and completeness of the present moment. In this way, EMDR can make a powerful contribution to all levels of the healing process. It can help to liberate constricted energies that block access to the experience of natural freedom. It can also work at a more subtle level in releasing the beliefs that become superimposed on the experience of unconditioned mind.

Isaac Shapiro

I. Shapiro has been giving satsang internationally for more than 8 years. He sits with large groups of people while resting in his essence and through Socratic methods leads people to an understanding of who they are. This process can resemble Gestalt therapy, in which the therapist works with one member of a group individually while the rest of the group watches and does their own work on the same issues. Because all people have similar themes of suffering, the whole group can be enlightened and healed in this process. Shapiro found that as a result of three EMDR sessions in which the transpersonal protocol was used, frozen memories arose —of which he had not been previously aware—memories that were locked in the physiology and subtle concepts. Processing with bilateral stimulation added to his understanding of consciousness. He has also described the ideal state of mind and approach of an EMDR therapist. In his experience with EMDR, subconscious activities rapidly became conscious when simple eye movements were used. He easily became aware of thoughts and pictures and memories that until that moment had not been recognized and were causing some sense of discomfort. From this conscious awareness, he gained a clarity and ease that came from being free from a subconscious belief system. He enjoyed the fact that there was no prior instruction about what should happen in the sessions and no interference in the process by the therapist. The process itself allowed what was needed to be recognized and processed.

Purely mechanically, where people place their attention determines their experience. When clients believe that something is wrong with them, and the therapist agrees and tries to "help," the therapist is reinforcing the belief system without realizing it. Shapiro's experience was that EMDR allowed him to be seen without something wrong being projected onto him. By the third session, he did the eye movements and nothing registered on the screen of his awareness. His sense was that if the therapists themselves recognize the reality beyond all concepts, then they can facilitate the development of this awareness in their clients.

Shaprio often recommends EMDR to participants in satsang, especially those with a history of trauma because they tend to have unconscious patterns of functioning in a way that results in suffering. Through EMDR, they are able to examine or become conscious of memories, or frozen concepts, and understand them in the present as they really are. This facilitates the development of the ability to be present without seeing life through subconscious filters.

Kali Shapiro

K. Shapiro holds satsang internationally with her husband (I. Shapiro) and alone. She emphasizes the importance of therapist–client equality in her sessions with EMDR.

She noted that doing sessions with a person of similar understanding, in the sense that the client and therapist know who they are first, was beneficial. In this light, no confusion existed about who had the issue, and the freedom and happiness of the client were clearly not dependent on the issue solving itself. She questioned why one would address an issue in the first place if a person is free whether or not it is resolved. She decided that people address the issue, as clients and therapists, because it is there to be addressed. It arises in consciousness only so that it can be recognized. It is then addressed in the light of knowledge with whatever tool is presented in the moment, like a car jack is used for a flat tire, or in therapy, an EMDR session for a person who has been traumatized. Knowing oneself brings unconditional love, Shapiro observes, because one sees that happiness and peace do not depend on anything changing and in fact result from loving what is, as it is. It is only when people argue with reality that they suffer. Using the analogy of the flat tire, this loving surrender to what is does not mean that the tire will not get changed because the person loves what is—having a flat tire—and will therefore be content to be stranded on the highway for 50 years. It means that the person's well being is not affected by the flat tire and whether or how it is fixed. In this ease and surrender to what is, the person's experience is that the tire gets changed even more beautifully, skillfully, and happily than it ever has been before. This unconditional love of what is, therefore, is the only space in which anything can heal if it is meant to.

Only love sows love, Shapiro notes. A session with a therapist who thinks something is wrong with a client and the problem needs healing or balancing is characterized by thought and fear, not love. More accurately, fear is disguised as love and caring in an innocent and misguided attempt to love. The result of this can only be the idea that indeed something is wrong and perhaps now it is fixed. Regardless, the client's well-being depends on this healing, so the person continues to live in fear, get sick and unbalanced again, or identify with what is wrong again. When therapists avail themselves of the true understanding that results from knowing the self, the only by-product can be true healing.

This was exactly Shapiro's experience in the EMDR sessions. The healing seemed to be on a deep, cellular brain level that was completely impersonal. She enjoyed the process very much because it felt like deprogramming a computer. She noticed that many aspects of consciousness that previously arose and made trouble in the mind would simply stop arising after the EMDR sessions. Other aspects that continued to arise after the sessions were considered outside of their usual structure in that they were allowed to resolve in their own time. She did not even have to burden herself with knowing what resolved and how it resolved and in that way, the tendency to make that healing yet another ego reference point vanished. During the sessions, she had many moments when a belief would arise to be recognized during the eye movements, but in an instant it was understood to be false, so the need for it to arise again ceased. She now often recommends EMDR to people who she knows have had deeply traumatic experiences in their lives and who are not interested in resolving or who are unable to resolve their suffering by consciously processing the experiences with traditional methods.

SUMMARY

Transpersonal psychology has been strongly influenced by the nondual spiritual traditions of the East. These traditions describe a natural unconditioned state of awareness that is every human's birthright. Realization of this awareness brings peace, freedom, joy, and acceptance of life as it is. As EMDR fosters personal integration and transformation, clients sometimes report contact with this profound awareness during a session. A specialized transpersonal EMDR protocol targets distractions to this awareness and can be used once clients have sufficiently progressed with the standard protocol. The transpersonal protocol, in conjunction with the openhearted and quiet presence of the therapist, invites clients into their natural contentment. Goals, methods, and roles fall away as therapist and client discover their shared ground. The ritual of psychotherapy unfolds into satsang, the celebration of nondual awareness. Several spiritual teachers with nondual orientations confirm the value of EMDR in working with obscurations to this awareness. EMDR has a surprising and powerful contribution to make to transpersonal psychology by helping to facilitate and stabilize the experience of nondual awareness.

REFERENCES

Almaas, A. H. (1986). *Essence*. York Beach, ME: Weiser.

Huxley, A. (1945). *The perennial philosophy*. New York: Harper & Row.

Krystal, P. (1982). *Cutting the ties that bind*. York Beach, ME: Red Wheel/Weiser.

Krystal, P. (1990). *Cutting more ties that bind*. York Beach, ME: Red Wheel/Weiser.

Shapiro, F. (1995). *EMDR: Basic principles, protocols and procedures*. New York: Guilford Press.

Wilber, K. (1993). The great chain of being. In R. Walsh & F. Vaughan (Eds.), *Paths beyond ego* (pp. 214–222). New York: Tarcher/Putnam.

SUGGESTED READING

Cortright, B. (1997). *Psychotherapy and spirit*. Albany: State University of New York Press.

Fenner, P. (1994). *Intrinsic freedom*. Newton, Australia: Millenium Books.

Krystal, P. (1990). *Cutting more ties that bind*. York Beach, ME: Samuel Weiser.

Krystal, S., Slyman, S., Wager, J., Pregerson, S., & Berbower, S. (1996). Transpersonal panel presentation at the EMDR International Conference, Santa Monica, CA.

Maharaj, S. N. (1982). *I am that*. Durham, NC: Acorn Press.

Osborne, A. (1971). *The teachings of Bhagavan Sri Ramana Maharshi in his own words*. Tiruvannamalai: South India: Messrs, Rider & Company.

Parnell, L. (1996). Eye movement desensitization and reprocessing (EMDR) and spiritual unfolding. *Journal of Transpersonal Psychology, 28*(2), 129–153.

Shapiro, F., & Forrest, M. (1997). *EMDR*. New York: Basic Books.

Shapiro, I. (1997). *Outbreak of peace*. Pasenbach, Germany: Arum Publications.

Vaughan, F. (1979). Transpersonal psychotherapy: Context, content and process. *Journal of Transpersonal Psychology, 11*(2), 101–110.

Watts, A. (1961). *Psychotherapy East and West*. New York: Ballantine Books.

14

INTEGRATION AND EMDR

JOHN C. NORCROSS AND FRANCINE SHAPIRO

EMDR is a psychotherapy phenomenon that has been confronted with multiple paradoxes. Its title explicitly invokes "eye movements," but the extant research now suggests that eye movements are not the only means of invoking the central mechanism of therapeutic action (see Shapiro, 1995, 2001). The early EMDR training was criticized as closed and unduly restrictive, yet the formal training course has now been completed by more than 30,000 mental health professionals. The EMDR procedure emerged from personal observations outside the scientific academy, yet EMDR is currently the most extensively researched treatment for posttraumatic stress disorder (PTSD; Maxfield & Hyer, 2002; Van Etten & Taylor, 1998). And EMDR originated from a rather narrow behavioral orientation but has evolved into a leading integrative treatment.

It is a small wonder that EMDR has attracted enormous professional attention, both positive and negative, from disparate theoretical persuasions. It has become an informal projective measure, an inkblot test of sorts for clinicians of varying orientations.

This closing chapter is "integrative" in two distinct senses of the term. First, it is an integrative summary of the preceding chapters, a concluding reflection on and synopsis of EMDR that is based on the 13 preceding chapters. Second, it is an integrative chapter in the sense that our commitment is toward psychotherapy integration. The lens that we adopt in reviewing the book's material is a dissatisfaction with single-school approaches and a concomitant desire to look across and beyond school boundaries to determine how patients can benefit from other ways of thinking about and practicing behavior change (Norcross & Goldfried, 1992).

Although the objective is to extract and amplify salient patterns in these disparate tales, we must be selective. We cannot review all of the themes raised in a chapter of this length and in a book of such wide scope. Instead, we shall take as our organizing principle three of the questions posed to the chapter authors:

- Which elements of EMDR are representative of traditional thought in your psychotherapy system?
- How does EMDR complement or extend the outcomes of your psychotherapy system?
- How can EMDR be strengthened?

The conclusion is an examination of the integrative paths or strategies that the contributors adopt in integrating EMDR into their preferred theoretical perspectives.

We congratulate the authors for their interesting, engaging, and frequently inspiring chapters. They responded to a daunting request: to present their respective systems of psychotherapy, address five specific questions, and illustrate their systems with case examples. The written accounts are interesting not only for their idiosyncratic view of EMDR and their innovative use of the standard protocols but also for their unique writing styles and chapter structures. This is surely psychotherapy integration in process!

HOW IS EMDR REPRESENTED IN DIVERSE SYSTEMS OF PSYCHOTHERAPY?

The consensus of the contributors is that certain elements of EMDR are routinely represented in and compatible with their various therapeutic traditions. The theoretical terms, or jargon, naturally differ and can obscure overlapping principles of change—the "language problem," as it is called in psychotherapy integration. When considering the clinical phenomenon, we all perceive numerous points of meaningful contact.

From a neuropsychological perspective, van der Kolk investigates the processes and correlates of EMDR treatment. He is impressed that EMDR seems to loosen up the free associative processes, giving people rapid access to memories and images of their past, and seems to accomplish its therapeutic benefits without people having to verbalize the source of their distress.

From an integrated psychoanalytic perspective, Wachtel finds EMDR most similar to previous versions of psychoanalytic practice. EMDR is represented in its reliance on free association, attention to spontaneous patient material, relatively minimal interference by the therapist, comparative anonymity of the person of the therapist, and the curative nature of working through.

From a behavioral perspective, Smyth and Poole note a clear fit, or multiple convergences with EMDR, which are understandable in light of its behavioral origin and early behavioral formulation. Initially, the original EMD was essentially a desensitization procedure, which in the Wolpe tradition could be explained in terms of reciprocal inhibition (or counterconditioning). EMD evolved into a more integrative procedure, a multicomponent treatment package with attendant name change. Smyth and Poole characterize EMDR as "new comprehensive, multidimensional behavior therapy" if separated from its controversial component of the bilateral stimulation. Indeed, they opine that EMDR minus the eye movements "can be considered a parsimonious integration of all of the core elements of old and new behavioral treatment methods." This integration would entail, among other things, exposure to the feared stimuli, provision of new and corrective information to alter the perception of threat, instruction in self-control skills, requests to maintain logs between sessions, assessment of subjective units of disturbance scale (SUDS) scores (pre-SUDS and post-SUDS), and an emphasis on mindfulness and acceptance work that has recently infused cognitive–behavioral therapy (CBT) work.

Likewise, from their multimodal perspective, Lazarus and Lazarus rhetorically explore whether EMDR is "an elegantly concentrated multimodal procedure." They detail the overlapping features of multimodal therapy and EMDR: "At the very outset, the degree of overlap between EMDR and MMT is compelling" right down to the use of SUDS, which was originally devised by Wolpe and Lazarus.

From an experiential perspective, EMDR and psychotherapy are facilitated self-healing. Bohart and Greenberg observe a stepwise, naturally occurring, "organic" evolution. The process occurs with minimal therapist intervention. Furthermore, both therapies work by accessing and allowing strong emotional experiences, heretofore disconnected, to emerge and be replaced by more adaptive emotions and corrected dysfunctional beliefs.

From a feminist perspective, Brown suggests that the very study of trauma itself in EMDR and feminism is a highly political act. To discuss human cruelty exposes how embedded it is in the core of many cultures and the way it challenges certain world views. In many ways, Brown writes, "EMDR seems to represent the quintessence of feminist models of practice." Its work with trauma survivors is driven by clients' realities, grounded in their needs, and oriented to their pace. Both EMDR and feminist practice place authority in the hands of the clients, letting them define positive cognitions and negative cognitions for themselves. Both therapies also converge in an egalitarian and empowering therapist–client relationship. Brown highlights several elements of EMDR that empower clients to develop their own voice and awareness, in particular, an explicit and careful informed consent.

From a hypnotic perspective, Gilligan finds key similarities with EMDR in the way healing trauma proceeds. One similarity is the premise of a special learning state in which traumatic identity and disturbing experiences may be transformed into healthy, integrated states. Second, and more broadly, both approaches invoke the same basic state of accelerated learning. Third, like the experiential traditions, both approaches strongly value the client's own innate healing potentials.

From a transpersonal perspective, Krystal, Prendergast, Krystal, Fenner, and Shapiro write of EMDR's important contribution to transpersonal goals by virtue of "a surprising capacity to liberate expansive states of awareness." Mutual points of contact include facilitating transformation, a movement toward transcendence. "Each approach values clear self-observation, detachment, acceptance, compassionate understanding, and forgiveness."

Tellingly, the contributors find EMDR elements prominently represented in their psychotherapy systems without reference to the adaptive information processing (AIP) model that governs EMDR. That is, they do not encounter any practical or conceptual difficulties in establishing points of contact because of possible differences in the overarching theory of psychopathology and change. As we discuss later in this chapter, this places most of the contributors in a pragmatic mode and utilitarian blend known as *technical eclecticism*.

Another observation, or perhaps an impression, is that the chapter authors may have been pushed toward identifying EMDR elements in their practice because of the instructional set of the book. The first question posed to them was "Which elements of EMDR are representative of traditional thought?" The authors were naturally and commendably responsive to the question and wrote of their mutual points of contact. Unfortunately, in retrospect, we realize that the questions did not request parallel discussion of the elements *not* represented in their psychotherapy systems, or points of disconnect. We also wonder about how representative the authors' sentiments are of other psychotherapists. What would be the consensus if less-than-friendly authors commented on EMDR in this undertaking? This is not to say the authors were "converts," but one of the prerequisites for inclusion in this book was that the authors were clinically familiar with EMDR. Therefore, they were clearly sympathetic to EMDR. All of which is to say that the questions posed and the authors invited helped dictate the inclination to highlight similarities rather than differences.

HOW DOES EMDR COMPLEMENT OR EXTEND OUTCOMES?

Our reading and rereading of the foregoing chapters leads us to discern three recurring ways in which EMDR complements or strengthens therapy outcomes: achieving rapid results; enhancing connections or associations; and providing a structured, safe method of accessing traumatic experiences.

First, almost to a person, the contributors point to EMDR's rapid therapeutic action. For example, Lazarus and Lazarus speak of the "rapid attenuation of many affective reactions." Bohart and Greenberg write that EMDR is "efficient . . . because it can work quite rapidly." Siegel describes his impression that the method enables achievements to occur more rapidly in some situations and allows for a highly focused form of integration to occur at an accelerated rate. Wachtel, as a final example, writes that EMDR's rapid working through is its "greatest contribution."

Indeed, Young and colleagues begin their chapter with the familiar lament that insight and intellectual awareness alone do not produce significant improvement. They view EMDR as a more appropriate medium for entering the affective system and modifying its function in a rapid, action-oriented manner.

From a different angle, Smyth and Poole note that the traditional behavioral view was that prolonged exposure to the fear response (with total response prevention) was the most effective method. Instead of prolonged exposure, EMDR generates "the observed rapidity of treatment effects." They approvingly cite recent meta-analyses that show EMDR generally achieved treatment effects in fewer sessions than traditional CBT (Van Etten & Taylor, 1998). That is, EMDR provides more efficient and rapid resolution of symptoms.

Second, EMDR extends the effects of other psychotherapy approaches by enhancing connections and promoting associative insights. The contributors describe the connections in various ways but principally in terms of clinical material and neural processing.

van der Kolk, for one, writes in his chapter that "the single most remarkable feature" of the EMDR procedure is its capacity to activate a whole variety of unexpected feelings, images, and thoughts that are ordinarily not accessed in conjunction with other memories. One of his three lasting lessons about EMDR is that it seems to loosen up the free associative processes, giving people rapid access to memories and images of their past. Similarly, Wachtel believes EMDR contributes to the exploratory or uncovering aspect of the work, promoting the development of insights. His instructive autobiographical vignette of his own EMDR treatment illustrates this point. Young and his cognitive therapist colleagues embrace EMDR for its ability to access information across sensory modalities that process both cognitive and affective information. Along the identical line, Bohart and Greenberg opine that EMDR connects information; that is, it connects the cognitive, conceptual, "left-brain" ways of processing information with emotional, intuitive, "right-brain" information. Krystal and her transpersonal colleagues praise the "extraordinary content" that EMDR induces, leading to frequent spontaneous insights that allow them to view past traumas with clarity and detachment. The client connections may sometimes be spiritual or transcendent—connections with mystical sources of wisdom and guidance and the "sense of being interconnected with all living beings."

Kaslow, Nurse, and Thompson believe that EMDR helps patients make connections and rich associations of another sort. The individual resolution of traumatic experiences, which often involves a spontaneous recognition of previous interactional patterns, makes connections with conjoint family healing. Individual EMDR and family therapy are reciprocally facilitating; they build on each other, with material from one dovetailing with material from the other.

Third, EMDR provides a structured, safe procedure to access potentially toxic traumatic experiences, which seems to translate, concretely, into structure for the therapist and structure and safety for the patient. Gilligan, for one example, writes that "the efficacy of EMDR is in its development of new techniques" for resolving frozen traumatic experiences, a view endorsed in similar language by neurobiologist van der Kolk. Smyth and Poole, for another example, write that EMDR, at a minimum, provides behavior therapists with a structured method that encompasses many effective elements of behavioral treatment. Further, they point out that EMDR suggests that therapists can be less directive of clients' emotional processing during exposure once clients have been coached in mindfulness and acceptance—a point that highlights the elements emphasized by the authors of the transpersonal chapter. Lazarus and Lazarus characterize EMDR as "systematically accessing behavior, affect, sensation, and imagery in a highly focused and structured manner."

At least two authors explicate another of EMDR's many paradoxes. Wachtel discusses a dialectical polarity that is at the heart of EMDR. On one hand, EMDR is highly structured. It is approached in a sequential, manualized, stepwise fashion directed by a therapist. On the other hand, each client's experience is different and unpredictable, following the flow of the client's own association, and the therapist is enjoined to stay out of the way of the client's processing. Gilligan observes a similar pattern: The EMDR techniques are "client-centered and naturalistic yet structured and rigorous."

As a whole, the contributing authors are convinced that EMDR extends and improves existing psychotherapy systems by providing more rapid symptom resolution and more associative material in a safe and structured manner. In the words of Smyth and Poole, this speaks favorably to "the advantages associated with a comprehensive, integrative treatment."

HOW CAN EMDR BE STRENGTHENED?

The contributors' responses to another question—"What suggestions do you have for strengthening the EMDR protocols?"—were predictably predicated on the distinctive features of their own preferred theoretical orientations. What they find missing from EMDR and the ways its therapeutic outcomes can be enriched are rooted in their respective systems of psychotherapy.

In the neurophysiology tradition, van der Kolk advocates strengthening EMDR by identifying and appreciating the neurobiology of the phenomenon, largely through the methods of neuroscience. Developmental physiologist Siegel agrees but also recommends the integration of attachment theory.

In the psychoanalytic tradition, Wachtel believes that EMDR practitioners have much to gain from a psychoanalytic view. He suggests paying more attention to the conventional phenomena of transference and resistance. He would broaden the scope from treating disorders to treating patterns of living and experiencing. He also suggests increasing attention paid to the cyclical psychodynamics of trauma: "Persisting emotional and behavioral reactions that may appear to be deeply rooted or indelibly sketched in the patient's brain are a product of ongoing actions and reactions between the patient and the significant others in his life." Wachtel would also be wary of asking clients to develop negative cognitions in ways that would force them into a Procrustean sentence structure, thus moving patients away from their own construal of the experience. In his own practice of EMDR, Wachtel is more open ended and nondirective in accessing and articulating underlying thoughts.

In the behavioral tradition, Smyth and Poole advocate for theoretical explanations of EMDR to be integrated with existing psychological models of psychopathology and behavioral theories of PTSD. They invoke Haye's (2000) objection that hypothesized biological models offer little more than "formulaic metaphors." Moreover, they seek continual identification through research studies of the mechanisms involved with bilateral stimulation: What are the essential components and methods of action in the multiple elements that constitute EMDR? Smyth and Poole also argue that behavior therapy has more to offer EMDR. For example, therapists could assign behavioral tasks for homework whenever a client has not already instituted such self-changes or routinely use functional analysis to narrow the target problems for EMDR.

Young and colleagues suggest that schema-focused therapy can augment EMDR. Specifically, they believe that early recognition of clients' schemas enhances the effectiveness of EMDR. For example, knowledge of schemas can help shape the positive cognitions (PCs) and negative cognitions (NCs), thereby helping practitioners determine how much clients should be encouraged to talk between bilateral stimulations.

In the multimodal tradition, Lazarus and Lazarus contend that when long-term data are collected on a broad spectrum of EMDR clients, a fair number of them will remain vulnerable to untreated problems in their cognitive and interpersonal domains. Accordingly, they argue that all relevant modalities should be addressed, not just rapid attenuation of affective reactions. Although briefly addressed in the EMDR protocol, all of the modalities may not be systematically or thoroughly treated. EMDR and multimodal therapy share many overlapping features, but Lazarus and Lazarus maintain that multimodal therapy is "broader and more comprehensive" than EMDR.

In the experiential tradition, Bohart and Greenberg consider therapeutic relationships to be central, a major healing force. They encourage EMDR clinicians to invoke more empathic listening responses, especially at the end of a session, and to concentrate on the genuineness of the person of the therapist. In addition, they recommend using experiential procedures that offer various opportunities for learning through doing—for example, the empty-chair method for resolution of unfinished business and the two-chair dialogue for resolution of splits.

In the feminist tradition, Brown reminds us "that individual change is unlikely when societal and environmental changes do not occur as well." Although EMDR and feminist therapy converge in uncovering painful and traumatic experiences, social justice is not a specific and explicit component of the EMDR protocol. At the same time, the EMDR Humanitarian Assistance Programs (see Appendix B) places it among the "small ranks of internationally socially conscious therapies." In other words, the "personal is political" lies within the EMDR humanitarian programs, not the therapy per se.

In the hypnotic tradition, Gilligan would strengthen EMDR by combining it with hypnosis. It is not clear under which circumstances he would do so, but a combined approach would allow the therapy to be creatively adapted to the client rather than forced to follow a fixed protocol.

Kaslow, Nurse, and Thompson voice a similar refrain: Individual therapy and family therapy can be mutually enriched. Specifically, taking account of the family context augments the general effectiveness of EMDR. According to systems theory, changes in the family affect the individual; likewise, the successful use of EMDR with an individual will result in changes in family relationships.

In the transpersonal tradition, Krystal and associates recommend that EMDR's methodological protocol and goal achievement be moderated toward some therapeutic ends. EMDR practitioners, they believe, "need to be totally comfortable with doing nothing other than enjoying the utter simplicity and completeness of the present moment." The challenge is to seamlessly blend the structure and focus of EMDR with the open and free nature of unstructured awareness.

The contributors present a series of illuminating and sage recommendations for enriching EMDR protocols. All merit serious consideration. At the same time, we would issue two cautions.

A first caution is that expanding the traditional protocol risks loss of coherence. As any psychotherapy approach expands, it encounters inevitable trade-offs in the service of becoming more comprehensive or eclectic (Messer, 1992). For example, EMDR became more integrative by bringing cognitive and affective processes into its purview but did so at the expense of clearly measurable goals and specifiable environmental triggers. Likewise, the EMDR practitioners who adopt Krystal and colleagues' suggestion that they become more comfortable with "doing nothing" may well benefit, but they also decrease the rapid, action-oriented appeal of EMDR. Or therapists who wisely examine the broader systemic world of the client in detail will necessarily temper their focus on the individual's symptom reduction if restricted to the same number of sessions.

An open system such as EMDR allows for the synergistic effects of additional therapy methods and relationship stances. At least two of the seasoned contributors to this book have cautiously adapted EMDR's standard protocol—Wachtel and his "EMDR" and Krystal and her "transpersonal" adaptation—but they note that their adaptations alter the coherence and goals of the standard protocol.

Put another way, EMDR's flexibility, which is recognized by many of the chapter authors, is both an opportunity and a challenge. At times, practitioners use the standard protocol for rapid symptom reduction, and other times the procedures are used more fluidly for different goals. Although dozens of standardized measures are available to track changes in overt symptoms, few are available to measure personal growth and the capacity for joy and bonding. The artistry of the therapeutic process is to encourage change in all domains. The integrative artistry is to know when and how such multidimensional gains can be accomplished (Norcross & Beutler, 1997). Quantifying multidimensional change and developing a core outcome battery suitable for practitioners of diverse orientations are challenging goals indeed (Shapiro, 2001; Strupp, Horowitz, & Lambert, 1997).

The second caution is that EMDR cannot be all things to all people. To be sure, it is an open and evolving approach to psychotherapy that is extremely appealing to practitioners of diverse persuasions, but to try to accommodate all perspectives or minimize all genuine differences is to cultivate a bland and defensive approach that stands for little. EMDR is more than a pitiful (if courageous) Charlie Brown caricature. Finding the balance in the assimilation–accommodation dialectic is the true and, we believe, attainable goal.

WHITHER INTEGRATION

In this book's title and in the preface, Shapiro invokes the metaphor of a prism. EMDR is described and presented through the various hues of diverse psychotherapy systems. The entire range of theoretical orientations is akin to the rainbow of colors produced by Newton's prism. Each color is an integral part of the whole, white light; each psychotherapy system is a vital contributor to the healing process.

EMDR began in the behavioral or cognitive–behavioral tradition and has evolved into an integrative approach. Siegel defines *integration* as the functional coupling of distinct elements into a coherent whole. How does one couple these distinct elements into a coherent whole? How does one integrate the constituent colors of the prism into a gleaming white?

Multiple routes or paths can lead to integration, be it neural integration, individual integration, or in this case, psychotherapy integration. The four most popular routes to psychotherapy integration *are technical eclecticism, theoretical integration, common factors*, and *therapeutic complementarity* (Norcross & Arkowitz, 1992). All four directions are represented in this volume, and all are characterized by a desire to enhance therapeutic efficacy and efficiency by looking beyond the confines of single theories and the restricted techniques traditionally associated with those theories. They do so, however, in rather different ways and at different levels.

Technical Eclecticism

The plurality of the book contributors favors a technically eclectic approach toward EMDR; that is, the chapter authors selectively employ EMDR as the best treatment for the person and the problem in specific cases. As Shapiro notes in chapter 2, "the model is not the method." A connection does not necessarily exist between the underlying theory and its clinical utility. Proponents of technical eclecticism use procedures drawn from different sources without necessarily subscribing to the theories that spawned them. Independent of the information processing model, EMDR procedures can be used within the practitioner's preferred framework.

The father of technical eclecticism, Arnold Lazarus (with his son, Cliff) writes tellingly of the synergistic properties of combining procedures (in contrast to smushing divergent theories). He argues that clinicians can probably enhance their treatment outcomes by knowing when and how to apply EMDR. Like other valuable methods, it has its place in the clinical repertoire.

Several other contributors similarly integrate EMDR into their repertoire. Smyth and Poole conceptualize EMDR as an effective package of methods largely hailing from the behavioral tradition. This package can be used profitably for the treatment of PTSD and, in concert with other methods, possibly other disorders. Noting that schema-focused therapy and EMDR are each integrative treatments in their own rights, Young and his associates believe that the two approaches can enrich each other by borrowing methods from one another as indicated for a particular person. For example, using the EMDR procedural steps—accessing client material on the visual, cognitive, affective, and physiological dimension—can help increase the patient's emotional understanding of how past events are impacting him in the present. The safe place exercise is used to create an imaginary refuge for clients who have been traumatized. In her opening sentence, Brown explicitly describes her integrative path: "Feminist therapy is a technically eclectic, theory-driven approach to psychotherapy." It is able to incorporate a multitude of specific methods. Reiterating the eclectic mantra, Krystal writes that an actual session of transpersonal therapy "can take on almost any form. Numerous methodologies, including EMDR, may be used as skillful means to help reveal to clients their deepest truth."

Theoretical Integration

Several contributors attempt a grander from of synthesis—integrating the underlying theories of psychotherapy. Theoretical integration entails a commitment to a conceptual or theoretical creation beyond the technical blend of methods. The result is not a simple combination or harmonious complement but a new, emergent theory that is more than the sum of its parts.

Shapiro offers an adaptive information-processing model that she characterizes as an attempt at "a common language." However, as with any theory, the language and concepts will not satisfy everyone. Wachtel observes that integrations have their unique flavors, and they usually reflect the original orientation of the theorists before they developed a more integrative point of view. Although EMDR is clearly an integrative approach, it is one with a cognitive–behavioral flavor. The term *processing*, for example, is intentionally generic and inclusive but as with any field-specific language, one would need to stretch the standard dictionary definition of *information* to encompass the entire experiences targeted by psychotherapists. Nor would all neurobiologists and psychotherapists concur with Shapiro's identification (see chapter 2) of "an intrinsic information-processing system." The AIP model, like all ambitious integrative models, has little direct evidence that establishes its validity or accuracy. Rather, models are clinical heuristics. Over time the therapies they spawn can be refined, tested, and as the evidence indicates, modified or even discarded, but initially they are best viewed speculatively or, as Shapiro has stated, as "written on rubber."

van der Kolk offers a tentative neurobiological integration of PTSD. He believes that trauma-related reactions become deeply imprinted on people's minds, and successful treatment depends on accessing the subcortical nature of traumatic memories. "In large part, treating PTSD consists," van der Kolk writes, "of helping patients overcome the traumatic *imprints* that dominate their lives, which are the sensations, emotions, and actions that are not relevant to the demands of the present but are triggered by current events that keep reactivating old, trauma-based states of mind."

He reviews research, including some of his own, showing that high levels of arousal interfere with frontal lobe function and that reexperiencing a traumatic experience affects Broca's area functioning. Particularly implicated is the limbic system. "Because PTSD creates a type of frozen sensory world, the therapeutic challenge is to open patients' minds to new possibilities so that they can encounter new experiences with openness and flexibility rather than interpreting the present as a continuous reliving of the past." Trauma is not primarily imprinted on people's consciousness but in their sensate experiences. "The single most remarkable feature" of the EMDR procedure, van der Kolk argues, is its capacity "to activate a wide variety of unexpected sensations, feelings, images, and thoughts that are ordinarily not accessed in conjunction with other memories." He posits that effective treatments such as EMDR invoke a common pathway to change not readily accessed by traditional insight-oriented procedures.

Siegel ambitiously attempts to integrate neurobiology, complexity theory, and attachment research. His theory is

> Therapeutic interventions that enhance neural integration and collaborative interhemispheric function may be especially helpful in moving unresolved traumatic states toward resolution. . . . the EMDR method may be selectively activating representational processes that are dominant in each hemisphere. Their simultaneous activation may cause the brain to link these otherwise isolated processes into a functional whole.

For example, EMDR may activate neurobiological mechanisms by directing the patient to think about the traumatic experiences, and the bilateral stimulation may stimulate integration of left- and right-hemisphere processing. In sum, EMDR promotes neural integration.

Common Factors

The third approach to psychotherapy integration seeks to determine the core ingredients that different therapies have in common. The eventual goal is to create a more parsimonious and efficacious treatment that is based on those commonalities. In this volume, the authors of two chapters adopt this integrative tack.

Bohart and Greenberg emphasize the many common features in EMDR and experiential therapy despite the models' disparate vocabularies. Both facilitate self-healing processes. Both involve a sequence of reliving the incident or trauma, experiencing and expressing the trauma, and moving into a self-correcting, adaptive state. In both EMDR and experiential therapy the cognitive restructuring follows after the emotional restructuring; although spontaneous restructuring may well occur along with emotional changes in EMDR, the positive cognition is specifically addressed, or "installed," only after it feels right for the patient. Both therapies share an emphasis on trusting the client's process, the centrality of emotion, focusing on bodily felt experience, accessing strong emotions, and connecting information from cognitive, conceptual ways of processing and emotional, intuitive ways of processing. In fact, Bohart writes that the first time he saw EMDR being practiced, it reminded him of client-centered therapy, except that the therapist used finger movements instead of empathic responses.

Gilligan draws on both common factors and technical eclecticism in his chapter. The core commonalities between hypnosis and EMDR may constitute the active ingredients. Conceptually, a "special learning state" is accessed and activated, and the traumatic experiences are transformed into integrated states. Both systems emphasize the innate healing capacities of humans and seek to provide a safe place in which clients can learn to trust these capacities. Procedurally, EMDR and hypnosis share a number of specific conditions. These include direct and experiential access to the core experiences, the acquisition of relaxation, as well as dual attention to the interior experience and outer environment. Because of these similarities, several forms of hypnosis and EMDR can be used within the same therapy.

Therapeutic Complementarity

Even those skeptical about the value of the "technique melding" of technical eclecticism and the "theory smushing" of theoretical integration can be enthusiastic about therapeutic complementarity. Here, genuine differences among psychotherapy systems are acknowledged and respected, but the theoretical schools are complementary, not contradictory. Allegedly rival schools of psychotherapy are not viewed as an adversity but as a healthy diversity.

In chapter 2, Shapiro views traditional psychotherapies as complementary in the various phases of EMDR. For example, symptom alleviation would be most consistent with a cognitive–behavioral formulation, whereas processing of earliest memories and "insight" are more characteristic of the psychodynamic tradition. Similarly, therapists attending to clients' cognitions, behaviors, affects, and physical sensations are seen as complementary, not antagonistic. The means of obtaining distance and mastery from traumatic material—imagery (train, movies, watching it from high or distance), deep breathing, prompts to "blank it out," and instructions to verbalize their experience—work together in multisensory channels. Complementary, not contradictory, goals.

Each psychotherapy orientation has its particular domain of expertise, and the complementary approach maximizes the expertise in a particular stage of therapy or toward a specific goal of therapy. Wachtel, for example, aims for a complementary perspective on EMDR. He demonstrates the compatibility of EMDR's more active working-through process with psychoanalytic uncovering or insight. Kaslow, Nurse, and Thompson, for another example, write of the articulation of EMDR with family therapy. When individual psychopathology is so extreme that repetitive negative family interactions are created, then individual EMDR sessions are undertaken with a primary goal of modifying both the family system and the individual's internal processing—what Kaslow et al. classify as individually focused family interventions. These goals are complementary and synergistic. Adopting systems theory, Kaslow and colleagues note that changes in the family will impact the individual, and reciprocally the successful application of EMDR with an individual will result in changes in family relationships—complementarity in practice.

In practice, the distinctions among technical eclecticism, theoretical integration, common factors, and therapeutic complementarity are probably not immediately apparent. What the clinician does—and more important, what the patient experiences—might be quite similar in all four integrative paths. Few clients experiencing an "integrative" therapy with EMDR would be able to distinguish among the four paths (Norcross & Arkowitz, 1992).

At the same time, sound practice and scientific advance demand that clinicians attend to their underlying methodologies. We should be thoughtful and judicious in the way we integrate lest we deteriorate into a syncretic muddle in which we "fly by the seats of our pants" without proper rationale or empirical verification. Although EMDR is an integrated treatment that draws from the major psychotherapy traditions, clinicians should be careful and avoid uncritical and haphazard deviations from standard protocols. These protocols have been evaluated by controlled research and have demonstrated positive and rapid effects.

For any trained EMDR clinician, the challenge is to be educated and aware of all the cards in the EMDR deck. Then if something is modified or eliminated, clinicians are knowledgeable about their benefits, risks, and possible compensations. If something is added to the standard EMDR protocol, then the clinician is knowledgeable about the proven benefits of the original and casts a critical eye to the outcomes. In all cases, deviations from the standard protocol should be empirically evaluated. Integration is sought for the enhancement of psychotherapy effectiveness, applicability, and efficiency, not merely for integration's sake.

CONCLUDING COMMENTS

Of diverse voices is sweet music made
So in our life the different degrees
Render sweet harmony among these wheels
—Dante (*Paradiso* Canto VI)

We began this chapter with a series of paradoxes concerning EMDR, and it strikes us as fitting to conclude with two others concerning the nature of psychotherapy integration as it applies to this book and EMDR.

The first paradox is that encouraging an integrative process is, in the short run, frequently at odds with a coherent integrative product. The process of welcoming diverse voices is loud, quarrelsome, and confusing—in a word, messy. Readers of this compendium surely experienced this on occasion—so many perspectives, so much disagreement, so many languages. It can leave one feeling exhausted and overwhelmed, like a general session of the United Nations, but it simultaneously leaves one energized and strengthened. In the long run, the messy process is the life blood of an integrative product. All of the major systems of psychotherapy add to the therapeutic armamentarium, enrich our understanding of EMDR, and produce the process and outcome research. One cannot integrate what one does not know. Long live messy process toward an integrative end!

The second and ultimate paradox of integration is that diverse voices create the sweetest music. EMDR is enriched by seeking disparate and critical but informed voices on EMDR. Each theoretical orientation possesses its own strengths and expresses a textured understanding of the human experience. To offer comprehensive health to the populace, to afford clients an adaptive personality within a healthy and balanced system, clinicians need to enlist the respective contributions of the major systems of psychotherapy (Prochaska & Norcross, 2002; Shapiro, 1995, 2001).

We echo Wachtel's comment that the contributors' particular ideas in this volume may or may not prove clinically useful or empirically supported. Surely not all of these rich impressions, reconceptualizations, and hunches will prove valid. But what most surely will be useful in the long run are transtheoretical dialogue, a spirit of innovation, and a sense of responsibility to evaluate the effectiveness of those innovations. Then diverse voices will combine to create a sweet harmony, and then the entire spectrum of color will meld into the whole and radiant white light.

REFERENCES

Hayes, S. C. (2000). Psychology and biology: A concluding comment. *The Behavior Therapist, 23,* 8–9.

Maxfield, L., & Hyer, L. A. (2002). The relationship between efficacy and methodology in studies investigating EMDR treatment of PTSD. *Journal of Clinical Psychology, 58,* 23–42.

Messer, S. B. (1992). A critical examination of belief structures in integrative and eclectic psychotherapy. In J. C. Norcross & M. R. Goldfried (Eds.), *Handbook of psychotherapy integration* (pp. 130–168). New York: Basic Books.

Norcross, J. C., & Arkowitz, H. (1992). The evolution and current status of psychotherapy integration. In W. Dryden (Ed.), *Integrative and eclectic psychotherapy: A handbook* (pp. 1–40). London: Open University Press.

Norcross, J. C., & Beutler, L. E. (1997). Determining the therapeutic relationship of choice in brief therapy. In J. N. Butcher (Ed.), *Personality assessment in managed health care: A practitioner's guide* (pp. 42–60). New York: Oxford University Press.

Norcross, J. C., & Goldfried, M. R. (Eds.). (1992). *Handbook of psychotherapy integration.* New York: Basic Books.

Prochaska, J. O., & Norcross, J. C. (2002). *Systems of psychotherapy: A transtheoretical analysis* (5th ed.). Pacific Grove, CA: Brooks/Cole.

Shapiro, F. (1995). *Eye movement desensitization and reprocessing: Basic principles, protocols and procedures.* New York: Guilford Press.

Shapiro, F. (2001). *Eye movement desensitization and reprocessing: Basic principles, protocols and procedures* (2nd ed.). New York: Guilford Press.

Strupp, H. H., Horowitz, L. M., & Lambert, M. J. (Eds.). (1997). *Measuring patient changes in mood, anxiety, and personality disorders: Toward a core battery.* Washington, DC: American Psychological Association.

Van Etten, M. L., & Taylor, S. (1998). Comparative efficacy of treatments for posttraumatic stress disorder: A meta-analysis. *Clinical Psychology and Psychotherapy, 5,* 126–144.

APPENDIX A
EVALUATIONS OF EMDR

Eye movement desensitization and reprocessing (EMDR) has a broad base of published case reports and controlled research that supports its use in the treatment of trauma. The current treatment guidelines from the International Society for Traumatic Stress Studies have designated EMDR as an efficacious treatment for posttraumatic stress disorder (PTSD) (Chemtob, Tolin, van der Kolk, & Pitman, 2000; Foa, Keane, & Friedman, 2000), as has the United Kingdom Department of Health (2001) (see Shapiro, 1999, 2001, 2002, for procedures, protocols, theories, and a comprehensive discussion of clinically valid research criteria; see Shapiro & Forrest, 1997, for a comprehensive narrative of cases and in-session transcripts, and see *EMDR for Trauma* in the American Psychological Association Psychotherapy Videotape series; see also Perkins & Rouanzoin, 2002, for a contemporary overview, and see Appendix C for a review of commonly asked questions and suggested research parameters).

PTSD CONTROLLED RESEARCH

The research that introduced EMDR to the professional community (Shapiro, 1989a) was one of the first controlled studies to be published on the treatment of PTSD. It appeared the same year as the first controlled studies that assessed exposure therapy (Cooper & Clum, 1989; Keane, Fairbank, Caddell, & Zimering, 1989) and psychodynamic therapy and hypnosis (Brom, Kleber, & Defares, 1989) for PTSD treatment. The two exposure studies reported that combat veterans experienced an approximately 30% symptom reduction after 8 to 15 sessions. Psychodynamic therapy and hypnosis were reported to have small to moderate effects on 60% of the patients. Although the Shapiro (1989a) study was hampered by the lack of standardized measures and independent assessment, the clinical outcomes were substantial and attracted great attention, particularly after reports of Wolpe's success with the method (Wolpe, 1990; Wolpe & Abrams, 1991).

Three years after the introduction of EMDR to the clinical scene (Shapiro, 1989a), the dearth of controlled outcome studies for the treatment of PTSD was highlighted by Solomon, Gerrity, and Muff (1992), whose review of the research literature revealed only six (nonpharmacological) studies. Solomon et al. concluded that all of the experiments they evaluated "suffer from methodological limitations" and that "further research is needed before any of these approaches can be pronounced effective as lasting treatments of PTSD" (p. 637). In fact, although it has been inferred by some that EMDR had been promoted over previously validated cognitive–behavioral treatments for trauma (e.g., Herbert et al., 2000; Lohr, Tolin, & Lilienfeld, 1998), there were no well-established, empirically validated treatments for PTSD as late as 1998 (see Chambless et al., 1998; for a comprehensive review of misconceptions found in a variety of review articles see Perkins & Rouanzoin, 2002).

In 1995, the APA Division 12 (Clinical Psychology) initiated a project to set standards for establishing the degree to which extant therapeutic methods were supported by solid empirical evidence. In 1998, independent reviewers (Chambless et al., 1998) using these guidelines placed EMDR on a list of empirically validated treatments as "probably efficacious for civilian PTSD." At the same time, exposure therapy (e.g., flooding) and stress inoculation therapy (SIT) were described as "probably efficacious for PTSD," whereas no other therapies were judged to be empirically supported by controlled research for people with PTSD. In 2000, on the basis of further studies, the International Society for Traumatic Stress Studies treatment guidelines designated EMDR as efficacious for PTSD (Chemtob et al., 2000; Shalev, Friedman, Foa, & Keane, 2000). A meta-analysis of all psychological and drug treatments for PTSD reported: "The results of the present study suggest that EMDR is effective for PTSD, and that it is more efficient than other treatments" (Van Etten & Taylor, 1998, p. 140; see also Allen, Keller, & Console, 1999; Feske, 1998; Lipke, 1999, 2000; Maxfield & Hyer, 2002; Spector & Read, 1999; Spates, Waller, & Koch, 2000).

As of this writing, approximately 11 randomized controlled studies of various cognitive behavioral therapy (CBT) treatments for PTSD have been published (for a complete review see Rothbaum, Meadows, Resick, & Foy, 2000), one controlled study of hypnosis and psychodynamic therapy has been published (Brom et al., 1989), and 16 randomized controlled studies of EMDR have been published, including six published controlled comparisons of EMDR therapy and CBT. The combat veteran studies of all treatments have been generally hampered by methodological problems (Feske, 1998; Shapiro, 1999, 2001; Solomon et al., 1992), but the civilian studies across treatments indicate clear findings. Exposure therapy and stress inoculation therapy were shown to be essentially equivalent to each other, and both were superior to supportive counseling or a wait list (Foa, Rothbaum, Riggs, & Murdock, 1991; Foa et al., 1999). Likewise, exposure and cognitive therapy were equivalent but superior to relaxation (Marks, Lovell, Noshirvani, Livanou, & Thrasher, 1998).

In all but one of the studies that assessed EMDR treatment of civilians with PTSD, it was found superior to control conditions such as active listening and HMO treatment, and relatively equivalent to versions of cognitive behavior therapy. Comparisons of EMDR with non-CBT treatments have indicated substantial differences on most measures. For instance, Scheck, Schaeffer, and Gillette (1998) reported much larger effects in the EMDR condition than the active listening control, with the EMDR group coming to within one standard deviation of the norm in two treatment sessions. A study (Marcus, Marquis, & Sakai, 1997) in a Kaiser Permanente hospital compared EMDR with standard outpatient care consisting of cognitive, psychodynamic, or behavioral individual therapy plus combinations of group therapy and medication. EMDR was found to be superior on multiple measures and resulted in more rapid and greater elimination of PTSD diagnosis. A 77% elimination of PTSD in people who had multiple traumas and a 100% elimination of PTSD in people who had single traumas was reported in a mean of 6 EMDR treatment hours. Similar results (an 84% to 90% elimination of PTSD in three 90-minute sessions) were indicated in comparisons with wait list controls (Rothbaum, 1997; Wilson, Becker, & Tinker, 1995, 1997) (see Appendix C and Chemtob et al., 2000; Maxfield, 1999; Maxfield & Hyer, 2002; Shapiro, 2001, for additional reviews).

Nine outcome comparisons of EMDR with CBT treatments of PTSD have been published, including six controlled studies and three nonrandomized studies. These studies generally reported equivalent effects on most measures (e.g., Ironson, Freund, Strauss, & Williams, 2002; Lee, Gavriel, Drummond, Richards, & Greenwald, in press; Vaughan, Armstrong, et al., 1994). In numerous studies, EMDR was found to be superior to the CBT treatment on measures of PTSD intrusion symptoms (e.g., Lee et al., in press; Rogers et al., 1999; Vaughan, Armstrong, et al., 1994). Two nonrandomized controlled comparisons of CBT treatment and EMDR with civilian populations have been conducted. In one of these (Sprang, 2001), EMDR was superior to CBT on almost all measures; on the other (Devilly & Spence, 1999), the CBT treatment was superior (see Appendix C for additional discussion, including studies that have not yet received peer review).

EMDR has been reported as having greater efficiency than the CBT treatments (i.e., fewer treatment sessions, less homework needed for clinical effects for EMDR, or both). For instance, Lee et al. (in press) reported superior effects on one measure at posttest and slight superiority on all measures at follow-up for EMDR compared with a combination of exposure and stress inoculation therapy. However, EMDR required 3 hours of homework compared with 27 hours for the control condition. In a study comparing prolonged exposure with EMDR, Ironson et al. (2002) reported that seven of the ten people in the EMDR group reached a 70% reduction in symptoms in three sessions compared with two of the twelve participants in the exposure condition.

EMDR has not been compared with hypnosis or psychodynamic therapy. The only study (Brom et al., 1989) to evaluate these other approaches found equal effects for both treatments and systematic desensitization. Small to moderate effects on 60% of the patients were reported after 12 to 18 sessions. Comparisons of EMDR with the new briefer psychodynamic therapies and the potential of additional integration through process analyses is greatly desired.

EMDR studies with combat veterans are hampered by insufficient treatment (e.g., two sessions or treating only one or two memories) for this complex population. The only randomized study using the suggested minimum treatment time (Shapiro, 1995, 2001) indicated that 77% of treated Vietnam veterans no longer had PTSD after the 12 sessions (Carlson, Chemtob, Rusnak, Hedlund, & Muraoka, 1998; see also Lipke, 2000; Silver & Rogers, 2001). However, even some of the studies with brief EMDR trials have shown effects comparable to longer trials of CBT (Boudewyns & Hyer, 1996; Pitman et al., 1996a, 1996b).

Brief descriptions of the published studies follow (see also Appendix C; see Maxfield & Hyer, 2002, for a comprehensive review of the studies' methodological strengths and weaknesses; for suggested parameters to strengthen future research comparing EMDR to other PTSD treatments, see Chemtob et al., 2000; Maxfield & Hyer, 2002; Shapiro 2001, 2002).

The following randomized controlled studies investigated EMDR treatment of civilians with PTSD:

1. *Chemtob, Nakashima, Hamada, and Carlson (2002)*. The effects of three sessions of EMDR with children experiencing psychological effects from Hurricane Iniki were evaluated using a lagged-groups design. Thirty-two children who had not responded to previous treatments and met the criteria for the classification of PTSD were randomly assigned to treatment and delayed treatment conditions. The children had shown no improvement 3.5 years after the hurricane and a year after the most recent attempts at treatment. Clinical improvements were reported in both groups on measures of PTSD symptoms, anxiety, and depression, and they had a 53% decrease in PTSD diagnosis after treatment. These changes remained stable at a 6-month follow-up. In addition to the substantial reduction of PTSD symptoms, the children had a marked reduction in visits to the school nurse in the year after the EMDR treatment as compared with previous years. This is the first controlled study investigating the treatment of disaster-related PTSD and the first controlled study investigating the treatment of children with PTSD.

2. *Edmond, Rubin, and Wambach (1999)*. Although this study did not use cases of diagnosed PTSD, the effectiveness of EMDR was tested with adult female survivors of childhood sexual abuse. Fifty-nine women were assigned randomly to

one of three groups: (a) individual EMDR, (b) routine individual treatment, or (c) delayed treatment control. At a 3-month follow-up, EMDR participants scored significantly better than routine individual treatment participants on two of the four measures, with large effect sizes suggestive of clinical significance.

3. *Ironson et al. (2002).* This controlled community-based study compared EMDR and prolonged imaginal exposure therapy. Both therapies produced a significant reduction in PTSD and depression symptoms, and the effects were maintained at a 3-month follow-up. The drop-out rate was less in the EMDR group. Furthermore, EMDR proved more efficient: Seven out of ten EMDR participants achieved a 70% reduction in symptoms in three active treatment sessions, whereas only two out of nine persons in the prolonged exposure condition achieved the same level of symptom reduction (i.e., 70% of EMDR vs. 29% of prolonged exposure participants). This is the only study to date to control for the effects of homework because equivalent exposure homework was given in each condition. Acceptable fidelity was reported, and treatment effects were stable at follow-up.

4. *Lee et al. (in press).* EMDR was compared with a treatment protocol that combined stress inoculation therapy and prolonged exposure (SITPE). The 24 participants each met *Diagnostic and Statistical Manual of Mental Disorders* (third edition, revised—DSM–IIIR) criteria for PTSD and were randomly assigned to one of the treatment conditions. Participants were also their own wait list controls. Outcome measures included self-report and observer-rated measures of PTSD and self-report measures of depression. After treatment, EMDR and SITPE produced significant improvement with equivalent effects, except that EMDR participants had significantly greater improvement on PTSD intrusive symptoms. Effects were maintained at a 3-month follow-up, with those in the EMDR condition showing greater gains. EMDR was found to be more efficient than SITPE because it required less homework (an average of 3 hours compared with 28 hours per SITPE). High fidelity to treatment was reported for both conditions.

5. *Marcus et al. (1997, 2001).* Sixty-seven individuals diagnosed with PTSD were treated in a controlled study funded by Kaiser Permanente Hospital. EMDR was found to be superior to standard Kaiser Care, which consisted of cognitive, psychodynamic, or behavioral individual therapy plus com-

binations of group therapy and medication. An independent evaluator assessed participants with multiple self-report measures of PTSD symptoms, depression, and anxiety and with a structured interview. The clients were evaluated before treatment, after three sessions, and after treatment. There was faster and more complete recovery from PTSD in the EMDR condition (50% after three sessions and 77% after treatment with 100% of those who experienced single traumas) compared with the standard care group (20% after three sessions and 50% after treatment). Follow-up evaluations reported maintenance or increase of treatment effects. The EMDR treatment providers were reported as having adequate preassessed fidelity.

6. *Renfrey and Spates (1994).* Although designed as a component analysis, this study is included since it used a sufficient number of sessions to assess clinical outcomes. Twenty-three PTSD participants were evaluated in a study that compared (a) EMDR with eye movements initiated by tracking a clinician's finger, (b) EMDR with eye movements engendered by tracking a light bar, and (c) EMDR using fixed visual attention. All three conditions produced positive changes on measures of PTSD and general symptoms, with an elimination of PTSD diagnosis in 85% of the eye movement groups, and 57% of the fixation group. The eye movement conditions were termed "more efficient" by the researchers given the use of fewer treatment sessions to achieve effects. This study is hampered by a small number of participants (six to seven in each posttest cell), making statistical significance improbable for a component analysis of this kind. No fidelity checks were reported.

7. *Rothbaum (1997).* This controlled study of people who had been raped compared EMDR to a wait-list condition and found that after three EMDR treatment sessions, 90% of the participants no longer met full criteria for PTSD, compared with 12% of those on the wait list. Results were evaluated on instruments measuring posttraumatic stress, depression, and dissociation by an independent assessor. Results were also clinically significant, with the mean scores of EMDR participants decreasing to within the normal range. Treatment effects were maintained at a 3-month follow-up. Delayed treatment of the wait-list group resulted in a replication of effects. Acceptable fidelity to treatment was reported by an external assessor.

8. *Scheck et al. (1998).* Sixty females ages 16 to 25 who were

screened for high-risk behavior and a traumatic history were randomly assigned to two sessions of either EMDR or active listening; 77% of them were diagnosed with PTSD by a blind independent assessor. Both treatments resulted in significant improvement on measures of PTSD, depression, anxiety, and self-concept. The effects of EMDR were significantly greater than those from active listening on all measures except self-concept. Before treatment, the means of all measures were more than one standard deviation above the mean (above the 84th percentile) for normative comparison groups. After the brief treatment, the EMDR participants came within the first standard deviation on all five measures. Fidelity to treatment was previously assessed for some of the clinicians in the study. Treatment effects were maintained at the follow-up.

9. *Shapiro (1989a)*. The initial controlled study of 22 individuals who had been raped or molested or were combat victims compared EMDR with a modified flooding procedure that was used as a placebo to control for exposure to the memory and to the attention of the researcher. Positive treatment effects were obtained for the treatment and delayed treatment conditions on subjective units of disturbance scale (SUDS) and behavioral indicators, which were independently corroborated at 1- and 3-month follow-up sessions. This study is hampered by the lack of standardized measures and the possibility of experimenter effects because the researcher and treating clinician were the same.

10. *Vaughan, Armstrong, et al. (1994)*. In a controlled comparative study, 36 participants with PTSD were randomly assigned to treatments of (a) imaginal exposure, (b) applied muscle relaxation, and (c) EMDR. Treatment consisted of four sessions, with 60 and 40 minutes of additional daily homework for a 2- to 3-week period for the imaginal exposure and muscle relaxation groups, respectively, and no additional homework for the EMDR group. All treatments led to significant decreases in PTSD symptoms for participants in the treatment groups as compared with those on a waiting list. A comparison between treatment groups found a significantly greater reduction of PTSD intrusive symptoms after treatment for the EMDR group. At follow-up, 70% of participants in all treatment groups no longer met PTSD diagnostic criteria. No fidelity checks were reported.

11. *Wilson, Silver, Covi, and Foster (1996)*. In a controlled study, 18 participants with PTSD were randomly assigned to eye-

movement, hand-tap, and exposure-only groups. Significant differences were found using physiological measures (including galvanic skin response, skin temperature, and heart rate) and the SUDS indicator. The results revealed that in the eye movement condition only, participants experienced a one-session desensitization of distress and an automatically elicited and seemingly compelled relaxation response, which arose during the eye movement sets. High fidelity to treatment had been previously assessed. The study is hampered by the lack of standardized diagnostic and assessments of symptoms.

12. *Wilson, Becker, and Tinker (1995, 1997)*. A controlled study randomly assigned 80 participants who had been traumatized (46% of whom had been diagnosed with PTSD) to treatment or delayed-treatment EMDR conditions and to one of five clinicians. Significant differences were found between the EMDR and wait-list groups after 30 and 90 days on standardized measures of PTSD symptoms, depression, and anxiety. This improvement was also clinically significant, with the means of the EMDR condition moving into a normal range on all measures. Treatment effects were replicated with treatment of the wait list. Effects were equally large regardless of whether the participant was diagnosed with PTSD. High fidelity to treatment had been previously assessed for many of the participating clinicians. In a 15-month follow-up study, it was determined that treatment effects had been maintained and that there was an 84% reduction in PTSD diagnosis compared to pre-treatment.

The following randomized controlled studies investigated EMDR treatment of combat veterans with PTSD:

1. *Boudewyns, Stwertka, Hyer, Albrecht, and Sperr (1993)*. A pilot study randomly assigned 20 chronic inpatient veterans to EMDR, exposure, and group therapy conditions and found significant positive results from EMDR for self-reported distress levels and therapist assessment. No changes were found in standardized and physiological measures, a result attributed by the authors to insufficient treatment time considering the secondary gains of the participants who were receiving compensation. Results were considered positive enough to warrant further extensive study, which was funded by the Veteran's Administration (VA). No fidelity check was reported for the study.

2. *Boudewyns and Hyer (1996)*. Sixty-one combat veterans with

chronic PTSD were randomly assigned to one of three conditions: (a) group therapy, (b) group therapy plus EMDR, or (c) group therapy plus EMDR with eyes closed (EC). In addition to group therapy, veterans in the EMDR and EC conditions received five to seven EMDR or EC sessions in which one or two memories were treated. This study was hampered by the limited treatment time, which was insufficient for processing multiple traumatic memories. Participants in all three conditions improved significantly, with no group differences, as revealed by a structured interview measuring PTSD symptoms. Participants in the EC and EMDR conditions showed superior improvement on mood and physiological measures compared with group therapy controls. This study indicated that the addition of EMDR or EC to group treatment may improve outcome. In this second study, fidelity to treatment was reported as variable by an external assessor, and clients were assessed by a blind independent evaluator.

3. *Carlson et al. (1998)*. This study randomly assigned 35 Vietnam combat veterans with PTSD to (a) EMDR, (b) biofeedback relaxation, or (c) wait list/routine VA clinical care. After a full course of treatment (12 sessions), the EMDR participants showed substantial clinical improvements, with several becoming symptom free. EMDR was superior to control conditions on PTSD and depression measures; no differences were noted among treatment groups on physiological measures. Positive clinical fidelity to treatment was externally assessed, and no one dropped out of the EMDR group during treatment. Treatment effects were maintained at a 9-month follow-up. This is the only study of combat veterans to achieve acceptable fidelity and use the number of EMDR sessions suggested for this population (Shapiro, 1995).

4. *Jensen (1994)*. This controlled study compared the EMDR treatment of 25 Vietnam combat veterans with PTSD with a nontreatment control group and found small but statistically significant differences after two sessions for in-session distress levels as measured using SUDS but no differences on global measures such as the Structured Interview for Posttraumatic Stress Disorder. The intern-researchers reported fidelity checks of low adherence to the EMDR protocol and skill of application, which indicated their inability to make effective use of the method to resolve the therapeutic issues of their participants. The study is also hampered by an insufficient amount of treatment time for these veterans, who had experienced multiple traumas.

5. *Pitman et al. (1996b).* In a controlled component analysis study of 17 chronic outpatient veterans, using a crossover design, participants were randomly divided into two EMDR groups, one using eye movement and a control group that used a combination of forced eye fixation, hand taps, and hand waving. Six sessions were administered for a single memory in each condition. Both groups showed significant moderate decreases in self-reported distress, intrusion, and avoidance symptoms. Fidelity was judged as variable by an external assessor. The study is additionally hampered by the small sample and treating only one or two memories in a population, which has experienced multiple traumas.

6. *Rogers et al. (1999).* Two groups of combat veterans received a single session of exposure or EMDR focusing on their most disturbing event. Both groups showed improvement on the Impact of Event scale specific to the treated incident. The EMDR treatment resulted in greater positive changes in the level of in-session distress and self-monitored intrusive recollections. This study was designed as primarily a process report to compare both methods. Clinicians were trained in both procedures and used standardized manuals, but no fidelity checks were reported.

Following are case series and uncontrolled studies that investigated EMDR treatment for symptoms of PTSD:

1. *Silver, Brooks, and Obenchain (1995).* An analysis of an inpatient veteran PTSD program ($n = 100$) compared EMDR, biofeedback, and relaxation training and found EMDR to be vastly superior to the other methods on seven of eight measures. Although hampered by a nonrandomized design, this study constitutes the only field study evaluating EMDR in comparison with other standardized treatments typically used by practicing clinicians in a VA setting.

2. *Lipke (1995).* Greater positive effects using EMDR compared with other treatment methods were reported by 76% of 445 respondents to a survey of trained clinicians who had treated more than 10,000 clients. Only 4% found fewer positive effects with EMDR.

3. *Grainger, Levin, Allen-Byrd, Doctor, and Lee (1997).* A study of 40 Hurricane Andrew survivors found significant differences on the Impact of Event scale and SUDS indicator in a nonrandomized comparison of EMDR and nontreatment conditions. Although hampered by a nonrandomized design,

this is one of the few field studies evaluating the effects of treatment on a population who had experienced a disaster.

4. *Lazrove, Kite, Triffleman, McGlashan, and Rounsaville (1998).* This open trial research study at the Yale Psychiatric Clinic provided three sessions of EMDR to eight adults with chronic PTSD. There was statistically significant improvement on all measures after treatment. Although one participant dropped out very early in the study, of the seven participants who completed treatment (including mothers whose children had been killed in auto accidents by drunk drivers), none met PTSD criteria at a 2-month follow-up.

5. *Devilly, Spence, and Rapee (1998).* This component study compared (a) EMDR with (b) an analogue treatment without eye movement and (c) a support control condition, by assessing treatment effects on 51 Vietnam combat veterans. After treatment, all groups showed significant and moderate improvements on measures of PTSD, depression, anxiety, and problem coping. No statistical differences were found among the three groups. Measures of reliable change indicated that 67% of the EMDR group, 42% of the EMDR with eyes fixed group, and 10% of the standard care group had reliably improved after treatment on a PTSD measure. This study is hampered by having afforded only two sessions of treatment to this population who had experienced multiple traumas. Fidelity to treatment was questionable based on the described procedures. A 30% drop-out rate was reported.

6. *Devilly and Spence (1999).* This nonrandomized civilian study compared EMDR with a CBT protocol designed and implemented by the primary researcher. Although based on the work of Foa et al. (1991), as noted in the study, additional CBT techniques were added to protocols researched in previous controlled studies. Not only did this study report that the CBT protocol was more effective than EMDR, very poor effects were achieved in the EMDR condition. After nine EMDR sessions, only a 36% remission of PTSD was achieved. The description of EMDR provided in this study has numerous deviations from standard practice.

7. *Sprang (2001).* Fifty clients with PTSD and complicated mourning (traumatic grief) received either EMDR or guided mourning treatment in this multisite, nonrandomized community study. Guided mourning is a CBT treatment often and successfully used for individuals who have been unable to cope with the traumatic death of a loved one. EMDR significantly reduced symptoms more than the CBT treat-

ment on behavioral measures and on four of five psychosocial measures, including a measure of PTSD symptoms. EMDR was more efficient, creating change at an earlier stage and requiring fewer treatment sessions.

EVALUATIONS OF DIVERSE CLINICAL COMPLAINTS

EMDR is conceptualized as a treatment for the experiential contributors to disorders. Expanding the standard protocols (Shapiro, 1995, 2001), additional applications have been developed in direct clinical practice by experts and consultants in various specialty areas. As with all clinical treatments for most of these disorders, little controlled research has been conducted, a state of affairs evident in an evaluation conducted by a task force set in motion by the Clinical Division of the American Psychological Association (Chambless et al., 1998). It revealed that only about a dozen complaints, such as specific phobias and headaches, had empirically well-supported treatments. In addition, many of the treatments listed as "empirically validated" had not been evaluated for the degree to which they provided substantial clinical effects. This means that practicing clinicians of all orientations are insufficiently guided by research in most of their treatment choices. Therefore, it is hoped that the additional EMDR applications will become as widely investigated by controlled research as has been the case for PTSD.

Suggested parameters are briefly reviewed in Appendix C and more thoroughly delineated in Shapiro (2001, 2002). To aid researchers in identifying protocols available for study and to assist clinicians in obtaining supervision for proposed applications, published materials and conference presentations are listed in the following part. Many presentations have been taped and are available from the conference coordinators. Presenters may also be accessed directly through the EMDR International Association (see Appendix B).

Positive therapeutic results with EMDR have been reported with a wide range of populations. However, as previously noted, most of the clinical disorders listed have no empirically validated treatments, and widespread investigation with controlled research is needed in all orientations (see Chambless et al., 1998). EMDR clinical applications are based on the information-processing model (see chapter 1 and Shapiro, 2001), which posits that the reprocessing of experiential contributors can have a positive effect in the treatment of various disorders. To date, although numerous controlled studies have supported EMDR's effectiveness in the treatment of PTSD, other clinical applications are based on clinical observations and are in need of additional investigation.

1. *Combat veterans from Desert Storm, the Vietnam War, the Korean War, and World War II who were formerly treatment resistant and who no longer experience flashbacks, nightmares, and other PTSD sequelae* (Blore, 1997a; Carlson, Chemtob, Rusnak, & Hedlund, 1996; Carlson et al., 1998; Daniels, Lipke, Richardson, & Silver, 1992; Lipke, 2000; Lipke & Botkin, 1992; Silver et al., 1995; Silver & Rogers, 2001; Thomas & Gafner, 1993; White, 1998; Young, 1995).

2. *People with phobias and panic disorder who report a rapid reduction of fear and avoidance behaviors* (De Jongh & Ten Broeke, 1998; De Jongh, Ten Broeke, & Renssen, 1999; De Jongh, van den Oord, & Ten Broeke, in press; Doctor, 1994; Feske & Goldstein, 1997; Goldstein, 1992; Goldstein & Feske, 1994; Kleinknecht, 1993; Nadler, 1996; O'Brien, 1993). Some controlled studies of people with spider phobias have revealed comparatively little benefit from EMDR (e.g., Muris & Merckelbach, 1997; Muris, Merkelbach, Holdrinet, & Sijsenaar, 1998; Muris, Merckelbach, van Haaften, & Nayer, 1997), but evaluations have been confounded by lack of fidelity to the published protocols (De Jongh et al., 1999; Shapiro, 1999). One evaluation of panic disorder with agoraphobia (Goldstein, de Beurs, Chambless, & Wilson, 2000) also reported limited results (for a comprehensive discussion, see Shapiro, 2001, 2002).

3. *Crime victims and police officers who are no longer disturbed by the after effects of violent assaults and the stressful nature of their work* (Baker & McBride, 1991; Kleinknecht & Morgan, 1992; McNally & Solomon, 1999; Page & Crino, 1993; Shapiro & Solomon, 1995; Solomon, 1995, 1998; Wilson, Becker, Tinker, & Logan, 2001).

4. *People relieved of complicated grief or excessive grief from the loss of a loved one or to line-of-duty deaths, such as engineers who are relieved of the guilt caused by one of their trains unavoidably killing pedestrians* (Lazrove et al., 1998; Puk, 1991b; Shapiro & Solomon, 1995; Solomon, 1994, 1995, 1998; Solomon & Kaufman, 1994; Sprang, 2001).

5. *Children healed of the symptoms caused by the trauma of assault or natural disaster* (Chemtob et al., 2002; Cocco & Sharpe, 1993; Datta & Wallace, 1994, 1996; Greenwald, 1994, 1998, 1999; Lovett, 1999; Pellicer, 1993; Puffer, Greenwald, & Elrod, 1998; Shapiro, 1991; Tinker & Wilson, 1999).

6. *People who have been sexually assaulted but are able to lead normal lives and have intimate relationships* (Edmond et al., 1999; Hyer, 1995; Ironson et al., 2002; Parnell, 1994, 1999;

Puk, 1991b; Rothbaum, 1997; Scheck et al., 1998; Shapiro, 1989b, 1991, 1994; Wolpe & Abrams, 1991).

7. *People who have had accidents or surgeries or who have been burned and who were once emotionally or physically debilitated but are now able to resume productive lives* (Blore, 1997b; Hassard, 1993; McCann, 1992; Puk, 1992; Solomon & Kaufman, 1994).

8. *People with sexual dysfunction who are able to maintain healthy sexual relationships* (Levin, 1993; Wernik, 1993).

9. *Clients at all stages of chemical dependency, and pathological gamblers who show stable recovery and a decreased tendency to relapse* (Henry, 1996; Shapiro & Forrest, 1997; Shapiro, Vogelmann-Sine, & Sine, 1994; Vogelmann-Sine, Sine, & Smyth, 1999).

10. *People with dissociative disorders who progress at a faster rate than that achieved by traditional treatment* (Fine, 1994; Fine & Berkowitz, 2001; Lazrove, 1994; Lazrove & Fine, 1996; Marquis & Puk, 1994; Paulsen, 1995; Rouanzoin, 1994; Twombly, 2000; Young, 1994).

11. *People with performance anxiety and those seeking performance enhancement in business, the performing arts, school, and sport activities who have benefited from EMDR* (Crabbe, 1996; Foster & Lendl, 1995, 1996, in press; Maxfield & Melnyk, 2000).

12. *People with somatoform disorders who have attained a rapid relief of suffering* (Brown, McGoldrick, & Buchanan, 1997; Grant & Threlfo, in press).

13. *Clients with other diagnoses, including personality disorders or complex PTSD, who substantially benefit from EMDR* (Allen & Lewis, 1996; Cohn, 1993; Fensterheim, 1996; Forbes, Creamer, & Rycroft, 1994; Korn & Leeds, in press; Manfield, 1998; Marquis, 1991; Parnell, 1996; 1999; Puk, 1991a; Shapiro & Forrest, 1997; Spates & Burnette, 1995; Spector & Huthwaite, 1993; Vaughan, Wiese, Gold, & Tarrier, 1994; Wolpe & Abrams, 1991).

MECHANISMS OF ACTION

Various Possibilities

Now that EMDR's efficacy in the treatment of PTSD has been recognized (Chambless et al., 1998; Foa et al., 2000; United Kingdom Department of Health, 2001; Van Etten & Taylor, 1998), attention is focused on identification of EMDR's mechanisms of action. As noted in the International Society for Traumatic Stress Studies (ISTSS) treatment guideline summary: "Research suggests that EMDR is an effective treatment for PTSD. Whether its efficacy stems from the fact that it is yet another variant of exposure therapy (with some ingredients of cognitive therapy) or that it is based on new principles is unclear" (Shalev et al., 2000, p. 366).

The possibility that EMDR could be a "variant of exposure therapy" is of particular interest because EMDR's use of exposure is antithetical to traditional practice—it calls for interrupted rather than prolonged exposure with elements of free association (Rogers et al., 1999; Rogers & Silver, 2002; Shapiro, 1995, 1999, 2001), both of which are inconsistent with the principle and practice long espoused in the exposure literature (Boudewyns & Hyer, 1990, 1996; Chaplin & Levine, 1981; Chemtob et al., 2000; Eysenck, 1979; Foa, Steketee, & Rothbaum, 1989; Keane & Kaloupek, 1982; Lyons & Scotti, 1995; Marks, 1972; Marks et al., 1998; Rachman, 1978). As noted in the ISTSS *Practice Guidelines*:

> The finding that a procedure employing multiple, brief, interrupted exposures to traumatic material can be efficacious calls for a reexamination of traditional theoretical notions that prolonged, continuous exposure is required (Eysenck, 1979). Further investigation of such issues promises to deepen our understanding of trauma treatment mechanisms. Additional properly designed dismantling studies also need to be conducted in order to identify what components of EMDR are beneficial. Ideally, such studies should be conducted with patients who are likely to be responsive to treatment (e.g., single trauma, more acute), because it is difficult to compare differences in induced changes in minimally responsive patients. (Chemtob et al., 2000, pp. 151–152)

Future research is needed to determine the relative contributions of various EMDR components, such as prescribed client preparation procedures, sensory alignment, exposure, free association, cognitive therapy elements, and dual-attention stimulation (e.g., eye movements, taps, tones), as well as the many components identified by the contributors to this volume. It is assumed that each of these components contributes to information processing in distinct and various ways (Shapiro, 1999, 2001). However, as with any complex treatment, the elimination of a single component is likely to have comparatively little effect, and the importance of a given component is likely to vary with different clinical populations and the psychological domain being measured. These fine discriminations can only be made by means of controlled studies in which the *overall* treatment effects are maximized (Kazdin & Bass, 1989). Such studies are important both to identify mechanism of actions and to develop the most robust and efficient procedures for clinical use (for a comprehensive discussion of methodological issues, suggested research parameters, and control conditions, see Shapiro, 2001).

Dual-Attention Stimulation

The dual-attention stimulation component in EMDR was introduced on the basis of empirical observation. The eye movements seemed to have a direct effect on cognitive processes (Shapiro, 1989b, 1995, 2001) based on personal experience and in a subsequent controlled experiment (Shapiro, 1989a). However, it was discovered by various trained EMDR clinicians in 1990, before any other controlled research appeared, that various types of stimulation (hand taps and tones) also had a positive clinical effect (Shapiro, 1991, 1994, 1995, 2001). Therefore, despite the unfortunate name of the method, alternate forms of stimulation were included in the treatment process.

Initial single-participant design experiments tested the eye movements and supported their clinical use (see following discussion). Subsequently, many hypotheses were developed to explain their effects. However, it is important to note that the theories were not limited to eye movements and also explained the effectiveness of the other types of stimulation used clinically. A brief review of some of the theories, current research, and parameters for future research are listed in the following paragraphs; however, for a comprehensive discussion of these topics, see Shapiro, 2001.

Theories

There is much conjecture about the possible neurobiological role of eye movements and other dual-attention stimuli. Correlations between eye movements and shifts in cognitive content and attribution have been documented in studies since the 1960s (e.g., Antrobus, 1973; Antrobus, Antrobus, & Singer, 1964; Drake, 1991; Drake & Seligman, 1989). Numerous hypotheses attempt to explain how eye movements could contribute to information processing within the EMDR procedures, including (a) disruption of the function of the visuospatial sketch pad and interference with working memory (Andrade, Kavanaugh, & Baddeley, 1997; Kavanaugh, Freese, Andrade, & May, 2001); (b) elicitation of an orienting response that stimulates an instinctive affect of interest, safety, or excitement or that evokes an alternative physiological state (Armstrong & Vaughan, 1996; Lipke, 2000; MacCulloch & Feldman, 1996); (c) evocation of a relaxation or inhibitory response (Shapiro, 1989a; Wilson et al., 1996); (d) activation of neurological processes that mimic rapid eye movement (REM) sleep-type functions and its information-processing mechanisms (Stickgold, 2002); (e) distraction that acts as an unreinforced extinction trial (Dyck, 1993); (f) evocation of a physiological state that titrates the emotional overload, encourages client engagement and processing, or both (Shapiro, 2001; Teasdale, 1999; van den Hout, Muris, Salemink, & Kindt, 2001); and (g) effects of cognitive loading (Becker, Nugent, & Tinker, 2000;

Becker, Todd-Overmann, Stoothoff, & Lawson, 1998). Although systematic research can best investigate these neurobiological speculations, biological science has not yet developed the precise tools needed to identify and measure the specific physiological elements that contribute to psychological change for EMDR or any form of psychotherapy. Although preliminary single photon emission computed tomography (SPECT) studies have indicated pre-post changes after EMDR treatment (Lansing, Amen, & Klindt, 2000; Levin, Lazrove, & van der Kolk, 1999), they do not shed light on the mechanism by which these changes occur. It is suggested that additional studies should take into account the variety of neurobiological hypotheses that have been advanced (e.g., see chapters 3 and 4, and Bergmann, 1998, 2000; Lipke, 2000; MacCulloch & Feldman, 1996; Servan-Schreiber, 2000; Stickgold, 2002). These hypotheses are particularly relevant to the choice of control conditions and the targets selected for evaluation.

Component Analyses

Numerous studies have been conducted to investigate the role of eye movements in EMDR. Although these have been summarized and cited in the review literature (Chemtob et al., 2000; Feske, 1998; Lohr et al., 1998; Lohr, Kleinknecht, Tolin, & Barrett, 1995), the lack of adherence to previously delineated standards (Shapiro, 1995, 1999, 2001) has resulted in ongoing confusion, inaccurate interpretations, and inconclusive results (Chemtob et al., 2000; Feske, 1998; Perkins & Rouanzoin, 2002). The confusion has been increased by the misreporting of some data (for comprehensive reviews, see Lipke, 1999; Perkins & Rouanzoin, 2002).

For example, the Lohr et al. (1998) review mistakenly asserted that early, single-subject designs were not supportive of the eye movement component, whereas the contrary is actually the case in three of the four component studies cited. In one of these studies, Montgomery and Ayllon (1994) concluded: "The data indicate that with PTSD subjects the use of short duration repeated exposure and cognitive restructuring alone were insufficient for positive treatment gain" (p. 228). They further stated that for five of six subjects, the addition of eye movements "resulted in the significant decreases in self-reports of distress previously addressed. These findings are reflected by decreases in psychophysiological arousal" (p. 228). In fact, all but one of the single-subject design studies with diagnosed populations have indicated support for the eye movement component (Cerone, 2000; Lohr, Tolin, & Kleinknecht, 1995, 1996; Montgomery & Ayllon, 1994).

1. *Controlled component analyses with diagnosed participants:* Controlled clinical outcome component analyses have been hampered by the use of inappropriate populations (i.e., the use of

subclinical or multiply traumatized populations), inadequate treatment doses (e.g., the use of only two sessions, or the treatment of only one memory in combat veterans who have experienced multiple traumas—e.g., Boudewyns & Hyer, 1996; Boudewyns et al., 1993; Devilly et al., 1998; Pitman et al., 1996b), and an insufficient number of participants to achieve statistical power (Kazdin & Bass, 1989). Nevertheless, *all* controlled component analysis studies that used EMDR procedures with diagnosed populations other than combat veterans who had experienced multiple traumas have indicated some positive effects in support of the dual-attention component (Feske & Goldstein, 1997; Renfrey & Spates, 1994; Wilson et al., 1996). However, more research is needed because unfortunately, many of these studies have various methodological problems (Feske, 1998; Shapiro, 1996, 2001, 2002).

2. *Controlled component analyses with subclinical participants:* The study of the impact of any component of a complex clinical method should use diagnosed populations rather than subclinical participants who will probably achieve good treatment outcomes with less powerful therapies, making it difficult or impossible to measure the effect of the one component. Furthermore, in any clinical study, it is important to use adequate fidelity checks to make sure the method is being appropriately applied (Foa & Meadows, 1997; Maxfield & Hyer, 2002). The component studies with nonclinical participants that failed to find differences between conditions (e.g., Dunn, Schwartz, Hatfield, & Wiegele, 1996) were further hampered by their use of truncated or omitted standard EMDR protocols (Fensterheim, 1996; Shapiro, 1995, 1999, 2001). For example, two studies (Carrigan & Levis, 1999; Sanderson & Carpenter, 1992) provided less than 5 minutes of eye movements, rather than the 40 to 50 minutes that is the standard application. In another study (Bauman & Melnyk, 1994) the control condition that was assumed to be a placebo treatment was actually a stimulus that has already been successfully used by EMDR practitioners as clinically effective alternatives to eye movements (i.e., hand taps; Shapiro, 1991, 1994, 1995). In designing studies, it is important that the proper control condition be used (Shapiro, 2001).

3. *Controlled studies of the eye movement component in isolation:* Controlled studies of the eye movement component in isolation (unmasked by the rest of the EMDR procedures) have indicated that this dual-attention stimulation may disrupt the

visuospatial template of working memory (Andrade et al., 1997; Kavanaugh et al., 2001) These studies have found that eye movements decrease the vividness of memory images and their associated affect. It seems that etiological, autobiographical memories may be particularly affected by the dual stimulation component, whereas secondary memories born of second-order conditioning may be equally affected by the rest of the EMDR procedures (Shapiro, 2001, 2002).

4. *Recommendations for additional research:* Various components are hypothesized to have different effects depending on the population, condition, and psychological domain being tested. Although component analyses are relatively scarce and few approaches have been examined in this way, adequate study can assist in refining extant methods. Some components may have positive effects on particular psychological outcomes, whereas others may assist to enhance client compliance by reducing distress or increasing efficiency. Therefore, it is suggested that all components of EMDR be appropriately tested (see Shapiro, 2001, for a detailed examination of extant component analyses, testable hypotheses, and suggested control conditions).

REFERENCES

Allen, J. G., Keller, M. W., & Console, D. (1999). *EMDR: A closer look.* New York: Guilford Press.

Allen, J. G., & Lewis, L. (1996). A conceptual framework for treating traumatic memories and its application to EMDR. *Bulletin of the Menninger Clinic, 60,* 238–263.

Andrade, J., Kavanagh, D., & Baddeley, A. (1997). Eye-movements and visual imagery: A working memory approach to the treatment of post-traumatic stress disorder. *British Journal of Clinical Psychology, 36,* 209–223.

Antrobus, J. S. (1973). Eye movements and non-visual cognitive tasks. In V. Zikmund (Ed.), *The oculomotor system and brain functions* (pp. 354–368). London: Butterworths.

Antrobus, J. S., Antrobus, J. S., & Singer, J. (1964). Eye movements, accompanying daydreams, visual imagery, and thought suppression. *Journal of Abnormal and Social Psychology, 69,* 244–252.

Armstrong, M. S., & Vaughan, K. (1996). An orienting response model of eye movement desensitization. *Journal of Behavior Therapy and Experimental Psychiatry, 27,* 21–32.

Baker, N., & McBride, B. (1991, August). *Clinical applications of EMDR in a law enforcement environment: Observations of the psychological service unit of the L.A.*

County Sheriff's Department. Paper presented at the Police Psychology (Division 18, Police & Public Safety Sub-section) Mini-Convention at the American Psychological Association annual convention, San Francisco, CA.

Bauman, W., & Melnyk, W. T. (1994). A controlled comparison of eye movement and finger tapping in the treatment of test anxiety. *Journal of Behavior Therapy and Experimental Psychiatry, 25*, 29–33.

Becker, L. A., Nugent, N. R., & Tinker, B. (2000, September). *What about the eye movements in EMDR?* Paper presented at the annual meeting of the EMDR International Association, Toronto, Canada.

Becker, L. A., Todd-Overmann, A., Stoothoff, W., & Lawson, T. (1998, July). *Ironic memory, PTSD, and EMDR: Do eye movements hinder the avoidance process leading to greater accessibility of traumatic memories?* Paper presented at the annual meeting of the EMDR International Association, Baltimore.

Bergmann, U. (1998). Speculations on the neurobiology of EMDR. *Traumatology, 4* (1). Retrieved March 7, 2002, from http://www.fsu.edu/~trauma/art1v4i1.html

Bergmann, U. (2000). Further thoughts on the neurobiology of EMDR: The role of the cerebellum in accelerated information processing. Retrieved March 7, 2002, from http://www.fsu.edu/~trauma/v6i3/v6i3a4.html

Blore, D. C. (1997a). Reflections on "a day when the whole world seemed to be darkened." *Changes: An International Journal of Psychology and Psychiatry, 15*, 89–95.

Blore, D. C. (1997b). Use of EMDR to treat morbid jealousy: A case study. *British Journal of Nursing, 6*, 984–988.

Boudewyns, P. A., & Hyer, L. A. (1990). Physiological response to combat memories and preliminary treatment outcome in Vietnam veteran PTSD patients treated with direct therapeutic exposure. *Behavior Therapy, 21*, 63–87.

Boudewyns, P. A., & Hyer, L. A. (1996). Eye movement desensitization and reprocessing (EMDR) as treatment for post-traumatic stress disorder (PTSD). *Clinical Psychology and Psychotherapy, 3*, 185–195.

Boudewyns, P. A., Stwertka, S. A., Hyer, L. A., Albrecht, J. W., & Sperr, E. V. (1993). Eye movement desensitization and reprocessing: A pilot study. *Behavior Therapist, 16*, 30–33.

Brom, D., Kleber, R. J., & Defares, P. B. (1989). Brief psychotherapy for posttraumatic stress disorders. *Journal of Consulting and Clinical Psychology, 57*, 607–612.

Brown, K. W., McGoldrick, T., & Buchanan, R. (1997). Body dysmorphic disorder: Seven cases treated with eye movement desensitization and reprocessing. *Behavioural and Cognitive Psychotherapy, 25*, 203–207.

Carlson, J. G., Chemtob, C. M., Rusnak, K., & Hedlund, N. L. (1996). Eye movement desensitization and reprocessing treatment for combat PTSD. *Psychotherapy, 33*, 104–113.

Carlson, J. G., Chemtob, C. M., Rusnak, K., Hedlund, N. L., & Muraoka, M. Y.

(1998). Eye movement desensitization and reprocessing for combat-related posttraumatic stress disorder. *Journal of Traumatic Stress, 11,* 3–24.

Carrigan, M. H., & Levis, D. J. (1999). The contributions of eye movements to the efficacy of brief exposure treatment for reducing exposure treatment for reducing fear of public speaking. *Journal of Anxiety Disorders, 13,* 101–118.

Cerone, M. R. (2000, November). *EMDR treatment of combat-related guilt: A study of the effects of eye movements.* Poster presented at the annual meeting of the International Society for Traumatic Stress Studies. San Antonio, TX.

Chambless, D. L., Baker, M. J., Baucom, D. H., Beutler, L. E., Calhoun, K. S., Crits-Christoph, P., et al. (1998). Update on empirically validated therapies, II. *The Clinical Psychologist, 51,* 3–16.

Chaplin, E. W., & Levine, B. A. (1981). The effects of total exposure duration and interrupted versus continuous exposure in flooding therapy. *Behavior Therapist, 12,* 360–368.

Chemtob, C. M., Nakashima, J., Hamada, R. S., & Carlson, J. G. (2002). Brief treatment for elementary school children with disaster-related posttraumatic stress disorder: A field study. *Journal of Clinical Psychology, 58,* 99–112.

Chemtob, C. M., Tolin, D. F., van der Kolk, B. A., & Pitman, R. K. (2000). Eye movement desensitization and reprocessing. In E. A. Foa, T. M. Keane, & M. J. Friedman (Eds.), *Effective treatments for PTSD: Practice guidelines from the International Society for Traumatic Stress Studies* (pp. 139–155, 333–335). New York: Guilford Press.

Cocco, N., & Sharpe, L. (1993). An auditory variant of eye movement desensitization in a case of childhood post-traumatic stress disorder. *Journal of Behavior Therapy and Experimental Psychiatry, 24,* 373–377.

Cohn, L. (1993). Art psychotherapy and the new eye treatment desensitization and reprocessing (EMD/R) method, an integrated approach. In E. Dishup (Ed.), *California art therapy trends* (pp. 275–290). Chicago, IL: Magnolia Street Publisher.

Cooper, N. A., & Clum, G. A. (1989). Imaginal flooding as a supplementary treatment for PTSD in combat veterans: A controlled study. *Behavior Therapy, 20,* 381–391.

Crabbe, B. (1996, November). Can eye-movement therapy improve your riding? *Dressage Today,* 28–33.

Daniels, N., Lipke, H., Richardson, R., & Silver, S. (1992, October). *Vietnam Veterans' treatment programs using eye movement desensitization and reprocessing.* Symposium presented at the International Society for Traumatic Stress Studies annual convention, Los Angeles.

Datta, P. C., & Wallace, J. (1994, May). *Treatment of sexual traumas of sex offenders using eye movement desensitization and reprocessing.* Paper presented at the eleventh annual Symposium in Forensic Psychology, San Francisco.

Datta, P. C., & Wallace, J. (1996, November). *Enhancement of victim empathy along with reduction of anxiety and increase of positive cognition of sex offenders after treatment with EMDR.* Paper presented at the EMDR Special Interest Group at the annual convention of the Association for the Advancement of Behavior Therapy, New York.

De Jongh, A., & Ten Broeke, E. (1998). Treatment of choking phobia by targeting traumatic memories with EMDR: A case study. *Clinical Psychology and Psychotherapy, 5*, 264–269.

De Jongh, A., Ten Broeke, E., & Renssen, M. R. (1999). Treatment of specific phobias with eye movement desensitization and reprocessing (EMDR): Research, protocol, and application. *Journal of Anxiety Disorders, 13*, 69–85.

De Jongh, A., van den Oord, H. J. M., & Ten Broeke, E. (in press). Efficacy of eye movement desensitization and reprocessing (EMDR) in the treatment of specific phobias: Four single-case studies on dental phobia. *Journal of Clinical Psychology.*

Devilly, G. J., & Spence, S. H. (1999). The relative efficacy and treatment distress of EMDR and a cognitive behavioral trauma treatment protocol in the amelioration of post traumatic stress disorder. *Journal of Anxiety Disorders, 13*, 131–157.

Devilly, G. J., Spence, S. H., & Rapee, R. M. (1998). Statistical and reliable change with eye movement desensitization and reprocessing: Treating trauma within a veteran population. *Behavior Therapy, 29*, 435–455.

Doctor, R. (1994, March). *Eye movement desensitization and reprocessing: A clinical and research examination with anxiety disorders.* Paper presented at the 14th annual meeting of the Anxiety Disorders Association of America, Santa Monica, CA.

Drake, R. A. (1991). Processing persuasive arguments: Recall and recognition as a function of agreement and manipulated activation asymmetry. *Brain and Cognition, 15*, 83–94.

Drake, R. A., & Seligman, M. E. P. (1989). Self-serving biases in causal attributions as a function of altered activation asymmetry. *International Journal of Neuroscience, 45*, 199–204.

Dunn, T. M., Schwartz, M., Hatfield, R. W., & Wiegele, M. (1996). Measuring effectiveness of eye movement desensitization and reprocessing (EMDR) in non-clinical anxiety: A multi-subject, yoked-control design. *Journal of Behavior Therapy and Experimental Psychiatry, 27*, 231–239.

Dyck, M. J. (1993). A proposal for a conditioning model of eye movement desensitization treatment for posttraumatic stress disorder. *Journal of Behavior Therapy and Experimental Psychiatry, 24*, 201–210.

Edmond, T., Rubin, A., & Wambach, K .G. (1999). The effectiveness of EMDR with adult female survivors of childhood sexual abuse. *Social Work Research, 23*, 103–116.

Eysenck, H. (1979). The conditioning model of neurosis. *Behavioral and Brain Sciences, 2*, 155–199.

Fensterheim, H. (1996). Eye movement desensitization and reprocessing with complex personality pathology: An integrative therapy. *Journal of Psychotherapy Integration, 6*, 27–38.

Feske, U. (1998). Eye movement desensitization and reprocessing treatment for posttraumatic stress disorder. *Clinical Psychology: Science and Practice, 5*, 171–181.

Feske, U., & Goldstein, A. (1997). Eye movement desensitization and reprocessing treatment for panic disorder: A controlled outcome and partial dismantling study. *Journal of Consulting and Clinical Psychology, 65*, 1026–1035.

Fine, C. G. (1994, June). *Eye movement desensitization and reprocessing (EMDR) for dissociative disorders.* Presentation at the Eastern Regional Conference on Abuse and Multiple Personality. Alexandria, VA.

Fine, C. G., & Berkowitz, A. S. (2001). The wreathing protocol: The imbrication of hypnosis and EMDR in the treatment of dissociative identity disorder and other maladaptive dissociative responses. *American Journal of Clinical Hypnosis, 43*, 275–290.

Foa, E. B., Dancu, C. V., Hembree, E. A., Jaycox, L. H., Meadows, E. A., & Street, G. P. (1999). A comparison of exposure therapy, stress inoculation training, and their combination in reducing posttraumatic stress disorder in female assault victims. *Journal of Counseling and Clinical Psychology, 67*, 194–200.

Foa, E. B., Keane, T. M., & Friedman, M. J. (2000). Guidelines for treatment of PTSD. *Journal of Traumatic Stress, 13*, 539–588.

Foa, E. B., & Meadows, E. A. (1997). Psychosocial treatments for posttraumatic stress disorder: A critical review. *Annual Review of Psychology, 48*, 449–480.

Foa, E. B., Rothbaum, B. O., Riggs, D., & Murdock, T. (1991). Treatment of posttraumatic stress disorder in rape victims: A comparison between cognitive–behavioral procedures and counseling. *Journal of Consulting and Clinical Psychology, 59*, 715–723.

Foa, E. B., Steketee, G., & Rothbaum, B. O. (1989). Behavioral/cognitive conceptualizations of post-traumatic stress disorder. *Behavior Therapy, 20*, 155–176.

Forbes, D., Creamer, M., & Rycroft, P. (1994). Eye movement desensitization and reprocessing in posttraumatic stress disorder: A pilot study using assessment measures. *Journal of Behavior Therapy and Experimental Psychiatry, 25*, 113–120.

Foster, S., & Lendl, J. (1995). Eye movement desensitization and reprocessing: Initial applications for enhancing performance in athletes. *Journal of Applied Sport Psychology, 7*(Suppl.), 63.

Foster, S., & Lendl, J. (1996). Eye movement desensitization and reprocessing: Four case studies of a new tool for executive coaching and restoring employee performance after setbacks. *Consulting Psychology Journal, 48*, 155–161.

Foster, S., & Lendl, J. (in press). Peak performance EMDR: Adapting trauma treatment to positive psychology outcomes. *EMDR International Association Newsletter: Special Issue.*

Goldstein, A. (1992, August). *Treatment of panic and agoraphobia with EMDR: Preliminary data of the Agoraphobia and Anxiety Treatment Center, Temple Univer-*

sity. Paper presented at the fourth World Congress on Behavior Therapy, Queensland, Australia.

Goldstein, A. J., de Beurs, E., Chambless, D. L., & Wilson, K. A. (2000). EMDR for panic disorder with agoraphobia: Comparison with waiting list and credible attention-placebo control condition. *Journal of Consulting and Clinical Psychology, 68*, 947–956.

Goldstein, A., & Feske, U. (1994). Eye movement desensitization and reprocessing for panic disorder: A case series. *Journal of Anxiety Disorders, 8*, 351–362.

Grainger, R. D., Levin, C., Allen-Byrd, L., Doctor, R. M., & Lee, H. (1997). An empirical evaluation of eye movement desensitization and reprocessing (EMDR) with survivors of a natural catastrophe. *Journal of Traumatic Stress, 10*, 665–671.

Grant, M., & Threlfo, C. (in press). EMDR in the treatment of chronic pain. *Journal of Clinical Psychology.*

Greenwald, R. (1994). Applying eye movement desensitization and reprocessing to the treatment of traumatized children: Five case studies. *Anxiety Disorders Practice Journal, 1*, 83–97.

Greenwald, R. (1998). Eye movement desensitization and reprocessing (EMDR): New hope for children suffering from trauma and loss. *Clinical Child Psychology and Psychiatry, 3*, 279–287.

Greenwald, R. (1999). *Eye movement desensitization and reprocessing (EMDR) in child and adolescent psychotherapy.* New York: Jason Aronson Press.

Hassard, A. (1993). Eye movement desensitization of body image. *Behavioural Psychotherapy, 21*, 157–160.

Henry, S. L. (1996). Pathological gambling: Etiological considerations and treatment efficacy of eye movement desensitization/reprocessing. *Journal of Gambling Studies, 12*, 395–405.

Herbert, J. D., Lilienfeld, S. O., Lohr, J. M., Montgomery, R., O'Donohue, W. T., Rosen, G. M., et al. (2000). Science and pseudoscience in the development of eye movement desensitization and reprocessing: Implications for clinical psychology. *Clinical Psychology Review, 20*, 945–971.

Hyer, L. (1995). Use of EMDR in a "dementing" PTSD survivor. *Clinical Gerontologist, 16*, 70–73.

Ironson, G. I., Freund, B., Strauss, J. L., & Williams, J. (2002) A comparison of two treatments for traumatic stress: A pilot study of EMDR and prolonged exposure. *Journal of Clinical Psychology, 58*, 113–128.

Jensen, J. A. (1994). An investigation of eye movement desensitization and reprocessing (EMD/R) as a treatment for posttraumatic stress disorder (PTSD) symptoms of Vietnam combat veterans. *Behavior Therapy, 25*, 311–326.

Kavanaugh, D. J., Freese, S., Andrade, J., & May, J. (2001). Effects of visuospatial tasks on desensitization to emotive memories. *British Journal of Clinical Psychology, 40*, 267–280.

Kazdin, A. E., & Bass, D. (1989). Power to detect differences between alternative treatments in comparative psychotherapy outcome research. *Journal of Consulting and Clinical Psychology, 57,* 138–147.

Keane, T. M., Fairbank, J. A., Caddell, J. M., & Zimering, R. T., (1989). Implosive (flooding) therapy reduces symptoms of PTSD in Vietnam combat veterans. *Behavior Therapy, 20,* 245–260.

Keane, T. M., & Kaloupek, D. G. (1982). Imaginal flooding in the treatment of a posttraumatic stress disorder. *Journal of Consulting and Clinical Psychology, 50,* 138–140.

Kleinknecht, R. A. (1993). Rapid treatment of blood and injection phobias with eye movement desensitization. *Journal of Behavior Therapy and Experimental Psychiatry, 24,* 211–217.

Kleinknecht, R. A., & Morgan, M. P. (1992). Treatment of post-traumatic stress disorder with eye movement desensitization and reprocessing. *Journal of Behavior Therapy and Experimental Psychiatry, 23,* 43–50.

Korn, D. L., & Leeds, A. M. (in press). Preliminary evidence of efficacy for EMDR resource development and installation in the stabilization phase of treatment of complex posttraumatic stress disorder. *Journal of Clinical Psychology.*

Lansing, K. M., Amen, D. G., & Klindt, W. C. (2000, November). *Tracking the neurological impact of CBT and EMDR in the treatment of PTSD.* Paper presented at the annual meeting of the Association for the Advancement for Behavior Therapy, New Orleans, LA.

Lazrove, S. (1994, November). *Integration of fragmented dissociated traumatic memories using EMDR.* Paper presented at the 10th annual meeting of the International Society for Traumatic Stress Studies, Chicago.

Lazrove, S., & Fine, C. G. (1996). The use of EMDR in patients with dissociative identity disorder. *Dissociation, 9,* 289–299.

Lazrove, S., Kite, L., Triffleman, E., McGlashan, T., & Rounsaville, B. (1998). The use of EMDR as treatment for chronic PTSD-encouraging results of an open trial. *American Journal of Orthopsychiatry, 69,* 601–608.

Lee, C., Gavriel, H., Drummond, P., Richards, J., & Greenwald, R. (in press). Treatment of post-traumatic stress disorder: A comparison of stress inoculation training with prolonged exposure and eye movement desensitization and reprocessing. *Journal of Clinical Psychology.*

Levin, C. (1993, July/August). The enigma of EMDR. *Family Therapy Networker,* 75–83.

Levin, P., Lazrove, S., & van der Kolk, B. A. (1999). What psychological testing and neuroimaging tell us about the treatment of posttraumatic stress disorder (PTSD) by eye movement desensitization and reprocessing (EMDR). *Journal of Anxiety Disorders, 13,* 159–172.

Lipke, H. (1995). EMDR clinician survey. In F. Shapiro (Ed.), *Eye movement desensitization and reprocessing: Basic principles, protocols and procedures* (1st ed., pp. 376–386). New York: Guilford Press.

Lipke, H. (1999). Comments on "thirty years of behavior therapy . . ." and the promise of the application of scientific principles. *The Behavior Therapist, 22,* 11–14.

Lipke, H. (2000). *EMDR and psychotherapy integration: Theoretical and clinical suggestions with focus on traumatic stress.* New York: CRC Press.

Lipke, H., & Botkin, A. (1992). Brief case studies of eye movement desensitization and reprocessing with chronic post-traumatic stress disorder. *Psychotherapy, 29,* 591–595.

Lohr, J. M., Kleinknecht, R. A., Tolin, D. F., & Barrett, R. H. (1995). The empirical status of the clinical application of eye movement desensitization and reprocessing. *Journal of Behavior Therapy and Experimental Psychiatry, 26*(4), 285–302.

Lohr, J. M., Tolin, D. F., & Kleinknecht, R. A. (1995). Eye movement desensitization of medical phobias: Two case studies. *Journal of Behavior Therapy and Experimental Psychiatry, 26,* 141–151.

Lohr, J. M., Tolin, D. F., & Kleinknecht, R. A. (1996). An intensive investigation of eye movement desensitization of claustrophobia. *Journal of Anxiety Disorders, 10,* 73–88.

Lohr, J. M., Tolin, D. F., & Lilienfeld, S. O. (1998). Efficacy of eye movement desensitization and reprocessing: Implications for behavior therapy. *Behavior Therapy, 29,* 123–156.

Lovett, J. (1999). *Small wonders: Healing childhood trauma with EMDR.* New York: Free Press.

Lyons, J. A., & Scotti, J. R. (1995). Behavioral treatment of a motor vehicle accident survivor: An illustrative case of direct therapeutic exposure. *Cognitive and Behavioral Practice, 2,* 343–364.

MacCulloch, M. J., & Feldman, P. (1996). Eye movement desensitization treatment utilizes the positive visceral element of the investigatory reflex to inhibit the memories of post-traumatic stress disorder: A theoretical analysis. *British Journal of Psychiatry, 169,* 571–579.

Manfield, P. (Ed.). (1998). *Extending EMDR: A casebook of innovative applications.* New York: Norton.

Marcus, S., Marquis, P., & Sakai, C. (1997). Controlled study of treatment of PTSD using EMDR in an HMO setting. *Psychotherapy, 34,* 307–315.

Marcus, S., Marquis, P., & Sakai, C. (2001). *Three- and six-month follow up of EMDR treatment of PTSD in an HMO setting.* Paper submitted for publication.

Marks, I. M. (1972). Flooding (implosion) and allied treatments. In W. S. Agras (Ed.), *Behavior modification: Principles and clinical applications* (pp. 151–213). Boston: Little, Brown.

Marks, I. M., Lovell, K., Noshirvani, H., Livanou, M., & Thrasher, S. (1998). Treatment of posttraumatic stress disorder by exposure and/or cognitive restructuring: A controlled study. *Archives of General Psychiatry, 55,* 317–325.

Marquis, J. N. (1991). A report on seventy-eight cases treated by eye movement desensitization. *Journal of Behavior Therapy and Experimental Psychiatry, 22,* 187–192.

Marquis, J. N., & Puk, G. (1994, November). *Dissociative identity disorder: A common sense and cognitive–behavioral view.* Paper presented at the annual meeting of the Association for Advancement of Behavior Therapy, San Diego, CA.

Maxfield, L. (1999). Eye movement desensitization and reprocessing: A review of the efficacy of EMDR in the treatment of PTSD. *Traumatology, 5*(4). Retrieved March 7, 2002, from www.fsu.edu/trauma/a1v5i4.htm

Maxfield, L., & Hyer, L. A. (2002). The relationship between efficacy and methodology in studies investigating EMDR treatment of PTSD. *Journal of Clinical Psychology, 58,* 23–41.

Maxfield, L., & Melnyk, W. T. (2000). Single session treatment of test anxiety with eye movement desensitization and reprocessing (EMDR). *International Journal of Stress Management, 7,* 87–101.

McCann, D. L. (1992). Post-traumatic stress disorder due to devastating burns overcome by a single session of eye movement desensitization. *Journal of Behavior Therapy and Experimental Psychiatry, 23,* 319–323.

McNally, V. J., & Solomon, R. M. (1999, February). The FBI's critical incident stress management program. *FBI Law Enforcement Bulletin,* 20–26.

Montgomery, R. W., & Ayllon, T. (1994). Eye movement desensitization across subjects: Subjective and physiological measures of treatment efficacy. *Journal of Behavior Therapy and Experimental Psychiatry, 25,* 217–230.

Muris, P., & Merckelbach, H. (1997). Treating spider phobics with eye movement desensitization and reprocessing: A controlled study. *Behavioral and Cognitive Psychotherapy, 25,* 39–50.

Muris, P., Merkelbach, H., Holdrinet, I., & Sijsenaar, M. (1998). Treating phobic children: Effects of EMDR versus exposure. *Journal of Consulting and Clinical Psychology, 66*(1), 193–198.

Muris, P., Merckelbach, H., van Haaften, H., & Nayer, B. (1997). Eye movement desensitization and reprocessing versus exposure in vivo. *British Journal of Psychiatry 171,* 82–86.

Nadler, W. (1996). EMDR: Rapid treatment of panic disorder. *International Journal of Psychiatry, 2,* 1–8.

O'Brien, E. (1993, November/December). Pushing the panic button. *Family Therapy Networker,* 75–83.

Page, A. C., & Crino, R. D. (1993). Eye-movement desensitization: A simple treatment for post-traumatic stress disorder? *Australian and New Zealand Journal of Psychiatry, 27,* 288–293.

Parnell, L. (1994, August). *Treatment of sexual abuse survivors with EMDR: Two case reports.* Paper presented at the 102nd annual meeting of the American Psychological Association, Los Angeles.

Parnell, L. (1996). Eye movement desensitization and reprocessing (EMDR) and spiritual unfolding. *The Journal of Transpersonal Psychology, 28,* 129–153.

Parnell, L. (1999). *EMDR in the treatment of adults abused as children.* New York: Norton.

Paulsen, S. (1995). Eye movement desensitization and reprocessing: Its use in the dissociative disorders. *Dissociation, 8,* 32–44.

Pellicer, X. (1993). Eye movement desensitization treatment of a child's nightmares: A case report. *Journal of Behavior Therapy and Experimental Psychiatry, 24,* 73–75.

Perkins, B., & Rouanzoin, C. (2002). An examination of misinformation regarding eye movement desensitization and reprocessing (EsMDR): Points of confusion. *Journal of Clinical Psychology, 58,* 77–97.

Pitman, R. K., Orr, S. P., Altman, B., Longpre, R. E., Poire, R. E., Macklin, M. L., et al. (1996a). Emotional processing and outcome of imaginal flooding therapy in Vietnam veterans with chronic posttraumatic stress disorder. *Comprehensive Psychiatry, 37,* 409–418.

Pitman, R. K., Orr, S. P., Altman, B., Longpre, R. E., Poire, R. E., & Macklin, M. L. (1996b). Emotional processing during eye-movement desensitization and reprocessing therapy of Vietnam veterans with chronic post-traumatic stress disorder. *Comprehensive Psychiatry, 37,* 419–429.

Puffer, M. K., Greenwald, R., & Elrod, D. E. (1998). A single session EMDR study with twenty traumatized children and adolescents. *Traumatology, 3(2).* Retrieved March 7, 2002, from http://www/fsu.edu/~trauma/v3i2art6.html

Puk, G. (1991a, November). *Eye movement desensitization and reprocessing: Treatment of a more complex case, borderline personality disorder.* Paper presented at the annual meeting of the Association for Advancement of Behavior Therapy, New York.

Puk, G. (1991b). Treating traumatic memories: A case report on the eye movement desensitization procedure. *Journal of Behavior Therapy and Experimental Psychiatry, 22,* 149–151.

Puk, G. (1992, May). *The use of eye movement desensitization and reprocessing in motor vehicle accident trauma.* Paper presented at the eighth annual meeting of the American College of Forensic Psychology, San Francisco.

Rachman, S. (1978). *Fear and courage.* New York: Freeman.

Renfrey, G., & Spates, C. R. (1994). Eye movement desensitization and reprocessing: A partial dismantling procedure. *Journal of Behavior Therapy and Experimental Psychiatry, 25,* 231–239.

Rogers, S., & Silver, S. M. (2002). Is EMDR an exposure therapy? A review of trauma protocols. *Journal of Clinical Psychology, 58,* 43–59.

Rogers, S., Silver, S., Goss, J., Obenchain, J., Willis, A., & Whitney, R. (1999). A single-session, controlled group study of flooding and eye movement desensitization and reprocessing in treating posttraumatic stress disorder among Vietnam war veterans: Preliminary data. *Journal of Anxiety Disorders, 13,* 119–130.

Rothbaum, B. O. (1997). A controlled study of eye movement desensitization and reprocessing for posttraumatic stress disordered sexual assault victims. *Bulletin of the Menninger Clinic, 61,* 317–334.

Rothbaum, B. O., Meadows, E. A., Resick, P., & Foy, D. W. (2000). Cognitive–

behavioral therapy. In E. B. Foa, T. M. Keane, & M. J. Friedman (Eds.), *Effective treatments for PTSD: Practice guidelines from the International Society for Traumatic Stress Studies* (pp. 60–83, 320–325). New York: Guilford Press.

Rouanzoin, C. (1994, March). *EMDR: Dissociative disorders and MPD.* Paper presented at the fourteenth annual meeting of the Anxiety Disorders Association of America, Santa Monica, CA.

Sanderson, A., & Carpenter, R. (1992). Eye movement desensitization versus image confrontation: A single-session crossover study of 58 phobic subjects. *Journal of Behavior Therapy and Experimental Psychiatry, 23,* 269–275.

Scheck, M. M., Schaeffer, J. A., & Gillette, C. S. (1998). Brief psychological intervention with traumatized young women: The efficacy of eye movement desensitization and reprocessing. *Journal of Traumatic Stress, 11,* 25–44.

Servan-Schreiber, D. (2000). Eye movement desensitization and reprocessing: Is psychiatry missing the point? *Psychiatric Times, 17,* 36–40.

Shalev, A. Y., Friedman, M. J., Foa, E. B., & Keane, T. M. (2000). Integration and summary. In E. A. Foa, T. M. Keane, & M. J. Friedman (Eds.), *Effective treatments for PTSD: Practice guidelines from the International Society for Traumatic Stress Studies* (pp. 359–379). New York: Guilford.

Shapiro, F. (1989a). Efficacy of the eye movement desensitization procedure in the treatment of traumatic memories. *Journal of Traumatic Stress, 2,* 199–223.

Shapiro, F. (1989b). Eye movement desensitization: A new treatment for post-traumatic stress disorder. *Journal of Behavior Therapy and Experimental Psychiatry, 20,* 211–217.

Shapiro, F. (1991). Eye movement desensitization & reprocessing procedure: From EMD to EMDR—A new treatment model for anxiety and related traumata. *Behavior Therapist, 14,* 133–135.

Shapiro, F. (1994). Eye movement desensitization and reprocessing: A new treatment for anxiety and related trauma. In L. Hyer (Ed.), *Trauma victim: Theoretical and practical suggestions* (pp. 501–521). Muncie, IN: Accelerated Development Publishers.

Shapiro, F. (1995a, September/October). Doing our homework. *Family Therapy Networker,* 49.

Shapiro, F. (1995b). *Eye movement desensitization and reprocessing: Basic principles, protocols and procedures* (1st ed.). New York: Guilford Press.

Shapiro, F. (1996). Eye movement desensitization and reprocessing (EMDR): Evaluation of controlled PTSD research. *Journal of Behavior Therapy and Experimental Psychiatry, 27,* 209–218.

Shapiro, F. (1999). Eye movement desensitization and reprocessing (EMDR) and the anxiety disorders: Clinical and research implications of an integrated psychotherapy treatment. *Journal of Anxiety Disorders, 13,* 35–67.

Shapiro, F. (2001). *Eye movement desensitization and reprocessing: Basic principles, protocols and procedures* (2nd ed.). New York: Guilford Press.

Shapiro, F. (2002). EMDR twelve years after its introduction: A review of past, present, and future directions. *Journal of Clinical Psychology, 58,* 1–22.

Shapiro, F., & Forrest, M. (1997). *EMDR*. New York: Basic Books.

Shapiro, F., & Solomon, R. (1995). Eye movement desensitization and reprocessing: Neurocognitive information processing. In G. Everley (Ed.), *Innovations in disaster and trauma psychology, Vol. 1* (pp. 216–237). Elliot City, MD: Chevron Publishing.

Shapiro, F., Vogelmann-Sine, S., & Sine, L. (1994). Eye movement desensitization and reprocessing: Treating trauma and substance abuse. *Journal of Psychoactive Drugs, 26,* 379–391.

Siegel, D. J. (in press). The developing mind and the resolution of trauma: Some ideas about information processing and an interpersonal neurobiology of psychotherapy. In F. Shapiro (Ed.), *EMDR as an integrative psychotherapy approach: Experts of diverse orientations explore the paradigm prism*. Washington, DC: American Psychological Association Press.

Silver, S. M., Brooks, A., & Obenchain, J. (1995). Eye movement desensitization and reprocessing treatment of Vietnam War veterans with PTSD: Comparative effects with biofeedback and relaxation training. *Journal of Traumatic Stress, 8,* 337–342.

Silver, S., & Rogers, S. (2001). *Light in the heart of darkness: EMDR and the treatment of war and terrorism survivors*. New York: Norton.

Solomon, R. M. (1994, June). *Eye movement desensitization and reprocessing and treatment of grief*. Paper presented at fourth international conference on Grief and Bereavement in Contemporary Society, Stockholm, Sweden.

Solomon, R. M. (1995, February). *Critical incident trauma: Lessons learned at Waco, Texas*. Paper presented at the Law Enforcement Psychology Conference, San Mateo, CA.

Solomon, R. M. (1998). Utilization of EMDR in crisis intervention. *Crisis Intervention, 4,* 239–246.

Solomon, R. M., & Kaufman, T. (1994, March). *Eye movement desensitization and reprocessing: An effective addition to critical incident treatment protocols*. Paper presented at the fourteenth annual meeting of the Anxiety Disorders Association of America, Santa Monica, CA.

Solomon, S. D., Gerrity, E. T., & Muff, A. M. (1992). Efficacy of treatments for posttraumatic stress disorder. *Journal of the American Medical Association, 268,* 633–638.

Spates, C. R., & Burnette, M. M. (1995). Eye movement desensitization and reprocessing: Three unusual cases. *Journal of Behavior Therapy and Experimental Psychiatry, 26,* 51–55.

Spates, C. R., Waller, S., & Koch, E. I. (2000). A critique of Lohr, Tolin, and Lipke's commentary: Of messages and messengers. *The Behavior Therapist, 23,* 148–154.

Spector, J., & Huthwaite, M. (1993). Eye-movement desensitization to overcome post-traumatic stress disorder. *British Journal of Psychiatry, 163,* 106–108.

Spector, J., & Read, J. (1999). The current status of eye movement desensitization and reprocessing (EMDR). *Clinical Psychology and Psychotherapy, 6,* 165–174.

Sprang, G. (2001). The use of eye movement desensitization and reprocessing (EMDR) in the treatment of traumatic stress and complicated mourning: Psychological and behavioral outcomes. *Research on Social Work Practice, 11*, 300–320.

Stickgold, R. (2002). Neurobiological concomitants of EMDR: Speculations and proposed research. *Journal of Clinical Psychology, 58*, 61–75.

Teasdale, J. D. (1999). Emotional processing, three modes of mind and the prevention of relapse in depression. *Behaviour Research and Therapy, 37*(Suppl. 1), 53–77.

Thomas, R., & Gafner, G. (1993). PTSD in an elderly male: Treatment with eye movement desensitization and reprocessing (EMDR). *Clinical Gerontologist, 14*, 57–59.

Tinker, R. H., & Wilson, S. A. (1999). *Through the eyes of a child: EMDR with children.* New York: Norton.

Twombly, J. H. (2000). Incorporating EMDR and EMDR adaptations into the treatment of clients with dissociative identity disorder. *Journal of Trauma and Dissociation, 1*, 61–81.

United Kingdom Department of Health. (2001). *Treatment choice in psychological therapies and counselling evidence based on clinical practice guideline.* London: Author. Retrieved March 7, 2002, from http://www.doh.gov.uk/mentalhealth/treatmentguideline/

van den Hout, M., Muris, P., Salemink, E., & Kindt, M. (2001). Autobiographical memories become less vivid and emotional after eye movements. *British Journal of Clinical Psychology, 40*, 121–130.

van der Kolk, B. A. (in press). Beyond the talking cure: Somatic experience and subcortical imprints in the treatment of trauma. In F. Shapiro (Ed.), *EMDR as an integrative psychotherapy approach: Experts of diverse orientations explore the paradigm prism.* Washington, DC: American Psychological Association.

Van Etten, M. L., & Taylor, S. (1998). Comparative efficacy of treatments for posttraumatic stress disorder: A meta-analysis. *Clinical Psychology and Psychotherapy, 5*, 126–144.

Vaughan, K., Armstrong, M., Gold, R., O'Connor, N., Jenneke, W., & Tarrier, N. (1994). A trial of eye movement desensitization compared to image habituation training and applied muscle relaxation in post-traumatic stress disorder. *Journal of Behavior Therapy and Experimental Psychiatry, 25*, 283–291.

Vaughan, K., Wiese, M., Gold, R., & Tarrier, N. (1994). Eye-movement desensitization: Symptom change in post-traumatic stress disorder. *British Journal of Psychiatry, 164*, 533–541.

Vogelmann-Sine, S., Sine, L. F., & Smyth, N. J. (1999). EMDR to reduce stress and trauma-related symptoms during recovery from chemical dependency. *International Journal of Stress Management, 6*, 285–290.

Wernik, U. (1993). The role of the traumatic component in the etiology of sexual dysfunctions and its treatment with eye movement desensitization procedure. *Journal of Sex Education and Therapy, 19*, 212–222.

White, G. D. (1998). Trauma treatment training for Bosnian and Croatian mental health workers. *American Journal of Orthopsychiatry, 63*, 58–62.

Wilson, D., Silver, S. M., Covi, W., & Foster, S. (1996). Eye movement desensitization and reprocessing: Effectiveness and autonomic correlates. *Journal of Behavior Therapy and Experimental Psychiatry, 27*, 219–229.

Wilson, S. A., Becker, L. A., & Tinker, R. H. (1995). Eye movement desensitization and reprocessing (EMDR) treatment for psychologically traumatized individuals. *Journal of Consulting and Clinical Psychology, 63*, 928–937.

Wilson, S. A., Becker, L. A., & Tinker, R. H. (1997). Fifteen-month follow-up of eye movement desensitization and reprocessing (EMDR) treatment for PTSD and psychological trauma. *Journal of Consulting and Clinical Psychology, 65*, 1047–1056.

Wilson, S. A., Becker, L. A., Tinker, R. H., & Logan, C. R. (2001). Stress management with law enforcement personnel. A controlled outcome study of EMDR versus a traditional stress management program. *International Journal of Stress Management, 8*, 179–200.

Wolpe, J. (1990, November). *Eye movement desensitization (EMD) procedure: A rapid treatment for anxiety and related trauma.* Clinical roundtable presented at the annual conference of the Association for the Advancement of Behavior Therapy, San Francisco.

Wolpe, J., & Abrams, J. (1991). Post-traumatic stress disorder overcome by eye movement desensitization: A case report. *Journal of Behavior Therapy and Experimental Psychiatry 22*, 39–43.

Young, W. (1994). EMDR treatment of phobic symptoms in multiple personality. *Dissociation, 7*, 129–133.

Young, W. (1995). EMDR: Its use in resolving the trauma caused by the loss of a war buddy. *American Journal of Psychotherapy, 49*, 282–291.

APPENDIX B
EMDR RESOURCES

EMDR HUMANITARIAN ASSISTANCE PROGRAMS

EMDR Humanitarian Assistance Programs (HAP) is an international volunteer network of therapists committed to providing an opportunity, worldwide, for people who have been traumatized to experience comprehensive healing.

Funded by private donations, HAP therapists travel to inner-city agencies, war-torn regions, disaster sites, and developing nations offering free and low-cost training to local mental health professionals. Newly trained therapists receive ongoing professional guidance from HAP volunteers as they start using EMDR with people who have been traumatized in their own communities.

EMDR–HAP has provided services and training for therapists in Zagreb and Sarajevo, Northern Ireland, Kenya, The Ukraine, Colombia, El Salvador, Serbia, Hungary, Turkey, India, the Middle East, and Bangladesh. Efforts in the United States include training therapists in inner cities, treating survivors and witnesses of urban violence, and exploring the way EMDR can break the cycle of violence by working within the prison system.

EMDR–HAP volunteers provide free direct services to survivors of natural and manmade disasters. After the Oklahoma City bombing, HAP volunteers provided 700 hours of free treatment to 250 people who were in severe emotional pain. Currently a network of clinicians provides pro bono services to victims, families, rescue workers, and others who were involved in the September 11, 2001, attacks on the World Trade Centers and the Pentagon.

EMDR–HAP volunteers increase awareness about posttraumatic stress disorder (PTSD) through the speakers bureau. EMDR–HAP representatives speak at conferences and to health care provider groups and community service organizations, spreading the word about EMDR's effectiveness in treating PTSD, a disorder than can persist for decades when it goes untreated.

EMDR–HAP is a 501 (C)(3) nonprofit organization. All volunteers are trained in the EMDR methodology and are licensed in the mental health field. Each therapist donates at least 1 week per year of therapy or training time to make healing available to those who can least afford to pay for treatment. HAP coordinates efforts and provides modest accommodations and travel expenses to treatment locations.

Contact information for the EMDR Humanitarian Assistance Programs:
Office location: 50 West Bridge St., New Hope, PA
Mailing address: PO Box 723, New Hope, PA 18938 or PO Box 52164, Pacific Grove, CA 93950
Telephone: (215) 862-4310, *Fax:* (215) 862-4312
Web site: http://www.emdrhap.org
E-mail address: HAPnewhope@aol.com

EMDR INTERNATIONAL ASSOCIATION

About the Association

The EMDR International Association (EMDRIA) is a 501 (C)(6), nonprofit, professional membership organization. The association's mission is to "establish, maintain and promote the highest standards of excellence and integrity in ... EMDR ... practice, research, and education." The purpose of the organization is to foster ongoing education, research, and development regarding EMDR and to offer continued professional and educational support of EMDR practitioners. Members are mental health professionals who have participated in formal training in EMDR and are using it clinically or for research purposes. The organization offers its members opportunities to learn of new applications, concerns, and research through meetings, articles, audiotapes of EMDR conference presentations, a research discussion list, a list of all approved programs, and newsletters. Client brochures and information packets are available to members. The quarterly newsletters and annual conferences disseminate clinical results, new protocols, innovations, relevant theories, and information on opportunities for international collaboration regarding clinical and research interests. At this time, EMDRIA has affiliated organizations throughout the world.

EMDRIA is the ongoing support system for EMDR trained practitioners and provides the mechanism for the continued development of EMDR in a professional manner. Through EMDRIA, practitioners have access to the latest clinical information and research data on EMDR.

Contact information for the EMDR International Association:
Mailing address: PO Box 141925, Austin, TX 78714-1925
Telephone: (512) 451-5200, *Fax:* (512) 451-5256
Web site: http://www.emdria.org
E-mail address: emdria@aol.com

TRAINING AVAILABILITY

An unfortunate side effect of the widespread media attention surrounding EMDR has been that a number of untrained clinicians and laypersons are using their version of the method with clients. In addition, various workshops in "eye movement therapy" have been springing up all over the country. In all the instances that have been reported, the eye movements are being used without the procedures, protocols, or safeguards that represent EMDR. We feel strongly that clients need to be protected from the potential dangers of the misuse of this therapy. The EMDR International Association acts as a clearinghouse for pertinent information and maintains a directory of all programs approved to educate clinicians in the EMDR methodology (as described in this volume). An EMDRIA committee currently evaluates both university courses and responsible training programs. University courses and training centers that meet these standards have their graduates eligible for membership in EMDRIA. To obtain information regarding the professional guidelines, eligibility requirements, and alternative training programs, please contact EMDRIA.

APPENDIX C
COMMONLY ASKED QUESTIONS
ABOUT EMDR AND SUGGESTIONS
FOR RESEARCH PARAMETERS

LOUISE MAXFIELD

WHAT IS EMDR?

Eye movement desensitization and reprocessing (EMDR) is a psychotherapy treatment that was originally designed to alleviate the distress associated with traumatic memories (Shapiro, 1989a, 1989b). Shapiro's (2001) *adaptive information-processing model* posits that EMDR facilitates the accessing and processing of disturbing memories to bring them to an adaptive resolution. After successful treatment with EMDR, affective distress is relieved, negative beliefs are reformulated, and physiological arousal is reduced. During EMDR, the client attends to emotionally disturbing material in brief sequential doses while simultaneously focusing on an external stimulus. Therapist-directed lateral eye movements are the most commonly used external stimulus, but various other stimuli including hand tapping and audio stimulation are often used (Shapiro, 1991). Shapiro (1995) hypothesized that EMDR facilitates the accessing of the traumatic memory network so that information processing is enhanced, with new associations forged between the traumatic memory and more adaptive memories or information. These new associations are thought to result in complete information processing, new learning, elimination of emotional distress, and development of cognitive insights. EMDR uses a three-pronged protocol: (1) The past events that have laid the groundwork for dysfunction are processed, forging new associative links with adaptive information; (2) the current circumstances that elicit distress are targeted, and internal and external triggers are desensitized; and (3) imaginal templates of future events are incorporated to assist the client in acquiring the skills needed for adaptive functioning.

WHAT IS THE THEORETICAL BASIS FOR EMDR?

Shapiro (1995) developed the *accelerated information-processing model* to describe and predict EMDR's effect. More recently, Shapiro (2001) expanded this into the *adaptive information-processing model* to broaden its applicability. She hypothesized that humans have an inherent information-processing system that generally processes the multiple elements of experiences to an adaptive state in which learning takes place. She conceptualized memory as being stored in linked networks that are organized around the earliest related event and its associated affect. Memory networks are understood to contain related thoughts, images, emotions, and sensations. The information-processing model hypothesizes that if the information related to a distressing or traumatic experience is not fully processed, the initial perceptions, emotions, and distorted thoughts are stored as they were experienced at the time of the event. Shapiro argued that such unprocessed experiences become the basis of current dysfunctional reactions and are the cause of many mental disorders. She proposed that EMDR successfully alleviates mental disorders by processing the components of the distressing memory. These effects are thought to occur when the targeted memory is linked with other more adaptive information. When this occurs, learning takes place and the experience is stored with appropriate emotions that are able to guide the person in the future.

Suggested Research

Research is needed to test predictions made by the information-processing model. The hypothesis that treating etiological events will resolve core pathology could be evaluated with outcome measures evaluating personality, interpersonal qualities, affect control, and sense of identity. The hypothesis that EMDR enhances information processing can be tested by process research evaluating the in-session elicitation of new material and determining whether and how this new material predicts resolution of the targeted memories.

IS EMDR A ONE-SESSION CURE?

No, EMDR is not a one-session cure. When Shapiro (1989a) first introduced EMDR into the professional literature, she included the following caveat: "It must be emphasized that the EMD procedure, as presented here, serves to desensitize the anxiety related to traumatic memories, not to eliminate all PTSD symptomatology and complications, nor to provide coping strategies to victims" (p 221). This first study focused on one memory, with effects measured by changes in the subjective units of disturbance scale (SUDS). Researchers consistently report similar effects for EMDR with SUDS measures of in-session anxiety. Since that time, EMDR has evolved into an integrative approach that addresses the full clinical picture. Two studies (Lee, Gavriel, Drummond, Richards, & Greenwald, in press; Rothbaum, 1997) indicated an elimination of diagnosis of posttraumatic stress disorder (PTSD) in 83% to 90% of civilian participants after four to seven sessions. Other studies using participants with PTSD (e.g., Ironson, Freund, Strauss, & Williams, 2002; Scheck, Schaeffer, & Gillette, 1998; Wilson, Becker, & Tinker, 1995) found significant decreases in a wide range of symptoms after three or four sessions. The only study (Carlson, Chemtob, Rusnak, Hedlund, & Muraoka, 1998) of combat veterans to address the multiple traumas of this population reported that 12 sessions of treatment resulted in a 77% elimination of PTSD. Clients with multiple traumas; complex histories of childhood abuse, neglect, and poor attachment; or both may require more extensive therapy, including substantial preparatory work in Phase 2 of EMDR (Korn & Leeds, in press; Maxfield & Hyer, 2002; Shapiro, 2001).

Suggested Research

It is recommended that outcome studies compare EMDR with other PTSD treatments using the complete three-pronged protocol and 12 or more sessions, with a session-by-session evaluation of recovery patterns. A wide range of psychometrics should be used to evaluate the process of change in overt symptoms, quality of life, and personal development parameters. An evaluation of client factors such as trauma history should be analyzed to determine their possible effects on treatment length and course.

IS EMDR AN EFFICACIOUS TREATMENT FOR PTSD?

Yes, EMDR is an efficacious treatment for PTSD. EMDR is the most researched psychotherapeutic treatment for PTSD. Twenty controlled outcome studies have investigated the efficacy of EMDR in PTSD treatment. Sixteen of these studies have been published, and the preliminary findings of four have been presented at conferences. Studies using wait-list controls found EMDR to be superior; six studies compared EMDR with treatments such as biofeedback relaxation (Carlson et al., 1998), active listening (Scheck et al., 1997), standard care (group therapy) in a Veterans Administration (VA) hospital (Boudewyns & Hyer, 1996), and standard care (various forms of individual therapy) in a Kaiser health maintenance organization (HMO) facility (Marcus, Marquis, & Sakai, 1997). These studies all found EMDR to be superior to the control condition on measures of posttraumatic stress.

Seven randomized clinical trials have compared EMDR with exposure therapies (Ironson et al., 2002; McFarlane, 1999; Rothbaum, 2001; Taylor, Thordarson, et al., 2001; Vaughan et al., 1994) and with cognitive therapies plus exposure (Power, McGoldrick, & Brown, 2001). These studies have found EMDR and the cognitive–behavioral therapy (CBT) control to be relatively equivalent; EMDR was superior in two studies on measures of PTSD intrusive symptoms, and CBT was superior in the study by Taylor, Thordarson, and colleagues (Taylor, Thordarson, et al., 2001) on PTSD symptoms of intrusion and avoidance. Two controlled studies without randomization were conducted; one (Devilly & Spence, 1999) found the CBT condition to be superior to EMDR, and the other (Sprang, 2001) found EMDR to be superior to the CBT control on multiple measures.

Two studies found EMDR to be more efficient than the CBT control condition, with EMDR using fewer treatment sessions to achieve effects (Ironson et al., 2002; Power et al., 2001). Two studies that compared treatment response on a session-by-session basis (Taylor, Thordarson, et al., 2001) and at midpoint (Rothbaum, 2001) reported that EMDR did not result in more rapid treatment effects than exposure. However, in both studies the exposure treatment sessions were supplemented with 1 hour of daily homework, whereas the EMDR condition was implemented without homework. The only study to control for the ancillary effects of homework (Ironson et al., 2002) supplemented exposure and EMDR treatments with the same number of hours of exposure homework. Most studies noted that because EMDR has minimal homework requirements, the overall treatment time is much shorter for EMDR (e.g., Lee et al., in press; Vaughan et al., 1994). Treatment effects have generally been well maintained.

The efficacy of EMDR in the treatment of PTSD is now well recognized. In 1998, independent reviewers (Chambless et al., 1998) for the American Psychological Association (APA) Division of Clinical Psychology placed EMDR, exposure therapy, and stress inoculation therapy on a list of empirically supported treatments as "probably efficacious"; no other therapies for any form of PTSD were judged to be empirically supported by controlled research. In 2000, after the examination of additional published controlled studies, the treatment guidelines of the International Society for Traumatic Stress Studies gave EMDR an A/B rating (Chemtob, Tolin, van der Kolk, & Pitman, 2000), and EMDR was found efficacious for treating PTSD. The United Kingdom Department of Health (2001) has also listed EMDR as an efficacious treatment for PTSD.

Foa, Riggs, Massie, and Yarczower (1995) suggested that exposure therapy may not be very effective for clients whose prominent affect is anger, guilt, or shame. Reports by clinicians treating combat veterans (e.g., Lipke, 1999; Silver & Rogers, 2001) have indicated that EMDR may be effective with such PTSD presentations. A preliminary study found that EMDR reduced symptoms of guilt in combat-related PTSD (Cerone, 2000). Taylor, Thordarson, and colleagues (Taylor, Thordarson, et al., 2001) reported equivalent and significant effects for exposure therapy and EMDR on reducing symptoms of anger and guilt.

Suggested Research

Although EMDR and CBT treatments are relatively equivalent in the treatment of PTSD symptoms, comparisons of clinical and client factors are recommended. This includes the comprehensive evaluation of clinical factors such as length of treatment, attrition, maintenance, and generalization of effects and the assessment of client factors such as symptom severity, affective presentation, comorbid disorders, and the presence of complex PTSD. Additional research in actual field settings is suggested to increase external validity. Specific attention should be paid to client compliance (Scott & Stradling, 1997) and the effects of various treatments on the therapists (Marks, Lovell, Noshirvani, Livanou, & Thrasher, 1998). It is also recommended that a wide range of psychometrics evaluating more than simple symptom reduction be included.

ARE TREATMENT EFFECTS MAINTAINED OVER TIME?

Twelve studies involving participants with PTSD assessed treatment maintenance by analyzing differences in outcome between posttreatment and follow-up. Follow-up times have varied and include periods of 3, 4, 9, and 15 months and 5 years after treatment. Treatment effects were maintained in eight of the nine studies with civilian participants; one study (Devilly & Spence, 1999) reported a trend for deterioration. Of the three studies with combat veteran participants, only one (Carlson et al., 1998) provided a full course of treatment (12 sessions). This study found that treatment effects were maintained at 9 months. The other two studies provided limited treatment: Devilly, Spence, and Rapee (1998) provided two sessions and moderate effects at posttest were not maintained at follow-up. Pitman et al. (1996) treated only two of multiple traumatic memories, and treatment effects were not maintained at a 5-year follow-up (Macklin et al., 2000). It seems that the provision of limited treatment may be inadequate to fully treat the disorder, resulting in remission of the partial effects originally achieved.

Suggested Research

Future research should investigate whether any client factor (e.g., symptom severity, affective presentation, comorbid disorders, complex PTSD) predicts sustained effects. An assessment of treatment factors (e.g., length of preparation, length of treatment, treatment compliance, treatment response, symptom reduction) would also assist in the evaluation of the maintenance of effects. It is further recommended that studies use longer follow-up periods to better ascertain the long-term effects of treatment.

IS EMDR EFFECTIVE IN THE TREATMENT OF PHOBIAS, PANIC DISORDER, OR AGORAPHOBIA?

Much anecdotal information has indicated that EMDR is effective in the treatment of specific phobias. Unfortunately, the research that has investigated EMDR treatment of phobias, panic disorder, and agoraphobia has not provided strong empirical support for such applications. Although these results are partly a result of methodological limitations in the various studies, it is also possible that EMDR may not be consistently effective for treating these disorders. De Jongh, Ten Broeke, and Renssen (1999) theorized that because EMDR is a treatment for distressing memories and related pathologies, it may be most effective in treating anxiety disorders that follow a traumatic experience (e.g., dog phobia after a dog bite) and less effective for those of unknown onset (e.g., snake phobia).

The only randomized trials evaluating EMDR treatment of specific phobias were a series of experiments on the treatment of spider phobia (Muris & Merckelbach, 1997; Muris, Merkelbach, Holdrinet, & Sijsenaar, 1998; Muris, Merckelbach, van Haaften, & Nayer, 1997). These studies have indicated that EMDR was less effective than in vivo exposure therapy in eliminating spider phobia. Research has yet to determine if these results can be generalized to other types of phobias or phobias in general. Methodological limitations of these studies include failure to use the full EMDR treatment protocol (Shapiro, 1999) and confounding of effects by using the exposure treatment protocol as the posttreatment assessment. When the full EMDR phobia protocol was used in case studies of medical and dental phobias (DeJongh & Ten Broeke, 1998; De Jongh et al., 1999; De Jongh, van den Oord, & Ten Broeke, in press), good results were achieved.

Clinical utility is an important consideration in treatment selection. The application of in vivo exposure may be impractical for clinicians who do not have easy access to feared objects (e.g., spiders) in their office settings, and some phobias are limited to specific events (e.g., thunderstorms) or locations (e.g., bridges). EMDR may be a more practical treatment than in vivo exposure, and the in vivo aspect can often be added as homework (De Jongh et al., 1999).

Three studies have investigated EMDR treatment of panic disorder in those with and without agoraphobia. The first two studies were preliminary (Feske & Goldstein, 1997; Goldstein & Feske, 1994) and provided a short course (six sessions) of treatment for panic disorder. The results were promising but limited by the short course of treatment. Feske and Goldstein wrote, "Even 10 to 16 sessions of the most powerful treatments rarely result in a normalization of panic symptoms, especially when these are complicated by agoraphobia" (p. 1034). The EMDR effects were generally maintained at the follow-up. A third study (Goldstein, de Beurs, Chambless, & Wilson, 2000) was conducted to assess the benefits of a longer treatment course. However, this study changed the target population and treated patients with agoraphobia. Participants who had panic disorder with agoraphobia did not respond well to EMDR. Goldstein (quoted in Shapiro, 2001) suggested that these participants needed more extensive preparation than was provided in the study to develop anxiety tolerance. The authors suggested that EMDR may not be as effective as CBT in the treatment of panic disorder with and without agoraphobia; however, no direct comparison studies have yet been conducted.

Suggested Research

Studies are needed to make direct comparisons of EMDR and CBT in the treatment of panic disorder with and without agoraphobia. It is recommended that studies use participants with traumatically induced disorders, such as a driving phobia after a car accident. Future studies could determine whether EMDR treatment would be inappropriate for certain populations with phobias. The possibility that a combination of EMDR and in vivo exposure may be more effective than either alone should be investigated, with a focus on outcome, efficiency, and attrition. In the treatment of agoraphobia, future research could examine the utility of developing anxiety tolerance before EMDR treatment. Appropriate fidelity should be assessed to include procedural adherence and the incorporation of the full phobia protocol (Shapiro, 2001).

IS EMDR USED FOR EVERY CLINICAL DISORDER?

No, EMDR is not used for every clinical disorder. EMDR was developed as a treatment for traumatic memories, and research has demonstrated its effectiveness in the treatment of PTSD. Shapiro (2001) stated that it should be helpful in reducing or eliminating other disorders that originate following a distressing experience. For example, Brown, McGoldrick, and Buchanan (1997) achieved successful remissions in five of seven consecutive cases of people with body dysmorphic disorder after one to three EMDR sessions that processed the etiological memory. Similarly, some researchers have reported elimination of phantom limb pain after EMDR treatment of the etiological memory and the pain sensations (Vanderlaan, in press; Wilensky, 2000; Wilson, Tinker, Becker, Hofmann, & Cole, 2000). It is not anticipated that EMDR will be able to alleviate symptoms arising from physiologically based disorders such as schizophrenia or bipolar disorder. However, there are anecdotal reports of people with such disorders being treated successfully with EMDR for distress related to traumatic events.

In addition to studies assessing the effectiveness of EMDR in the treatment of PTSD, phobias, and panic disorders, some preliminary investigations have indicated that EMDR might be helpful for people with other disorders, such as dissociative disorders (e.g., Fine & Berkowitz, 2001; Lazrove & Fine, 1996; Paulsen, 1995), performance anxiety (Foster & Lendl, 1996; Maxfield & Melnyk, 2000), body dysmorphic disorder (Brown et al., 1997), pain disorder (Grant & Threlfo, in press; Ray & Zbik, 2001), and personality disorders (e.g., Korn & Leeds, in press; Manfield, 1998). These findings are preliminary, and additional research is required before any conclusions can be drawn. In this textbook, applications of EMDR are described for complaints such as depression (Shapiro, chapter 1), attachment disorder (Siegel, chapter 4), social phobia (Smyth, see chapter 6), anger control (Young, chapter 7), generalized anxiety disorder (Lazarus, see chapter 8), distress related to infertility (Bohart, chapter 10), body image disturbance (Brown, chapter 11), marital discord (Kaslow, chapter 12), and existential angst (Krystal, chapter 13); all such applications should be considered in need of controlled research for comprehensive examination.

Suggested Research

It is recommended that research evaluate the effectiveness of the standard EMDR protocol with such clinical complaints before or in addition to testing any modification of the protocol. This evaluation will determine whether adjustments in preparation, targets, or process are useful.

CAN EMDR'S EFFECTS BE ATTRIBUTED TO PLACEBO OR NONSPECIFIC EFFECTS?

No, EMDR's effects cannot be attributed to placebo or nonspecific effects. Numerous studies have found EMDR to result in an outcome that is superior to placebo treatments and treatments not specifically validated for PTSD. EMDR has outperformed active listening (Scheck et al., 1998); standard outpatient care consisting of individual cognitive, psychodynamic, or behavioral therapy in a Kaiser Permanente hospital (Marcus et al., 1997); and relaxation training with biofeedback (Carlson et al., 1998). EMDR has been found to be relatively equivalent to CBT therapies in seven randomized clinical trials that compared the two approaches. Because the treatment effects are large and clinically meaningful, it can be concluded that EMDR is not a placebo treatment. For example, in a meta-analysis of PTSD treatments, Van Etten and Taylor (1998) calculated the mean effect sizes on self-report measures for placebo and control conditions as 0.43, as 1.24 for EMDR, and as 1.27 for CBT (p. 135). Several studies (e.g., Taylor, Thordarson, et al., 2001) have measured the credibility of the treatments being provided as a way to determine whether EMDR elicited more confidence from clients, thereby producing larger effects; no study found EMDR to be more or less credible. Because EMDR is not more credible than these other therapies, it seems that the effects cannot be attributed to suggestion or a heightened placebo effect.

Suggested Research

Assessments of credibility should be standard practice in all treatment outcome studies.

WHAT HAVE META-ANALYSES REVEALED ABOUT EMDR?

Three meta-analyses have evaluated EMDR outcomes. Van Etten and Taylor (1998) examined responses to psychotherapeutic and pharmacological treatments of PTSD. They reported that EMDR and exposure therapies achieved similar outcomes and were superior to other psychotherapeutic treatments. In their analysis, they noted that the EMDR studies had used fewer sessions (4.3) to achieve the same level of results produced by more exposure sessions (10.4). They concluded that their results "suggest that EMDR is effective for PTSD, and that it is more efficient than other treatments" (p. 140). However, direct comparisons of efficiency are better made within a single study with the same population by analysis of session-to-session response.

The Davidson and Parker (2001) meta-analysis evaluated outcomes in 34 different EMDR studies. This was a thorough and comprehensive meta-analysis, although some studies were overlooked. They concluded that EMDR was superior to no-treatment and nonspecific treatment controls and equivalent in outcome to exposure and other CBT approaches. As discussed previously, such findings are consistent with those in the EMDR literature. Unfortunately, in their investigation of the eye movement component, Davidson and Parker did not distinguish between clinical dismantling studies and component action studies. In addition, they did not distinguish between analogue studies that used partial EMDR done for 15 minutes with normal students and dismantling studies with multiple sessions for people with chronic PTSD. This lack of distinction created large variability in the meta-analysis and made it difficult to find effects. However, they noted that their data indicated that the comparison effect size between EMDR with eye movements and EMDR without eye movements was "marginally significant if one examines only clinical populations satisfying [DSM] diagnostic criteria" (p. 311). However, even this evaluation failed to assess whether the length of treatment offered to the participants with PTSD was clinically adequate to reveal differential main effects.

The outcomes of EMDR studies vary considerably, with a wide range of outcomes reported and with the efficacy of EMDR varying across studies. In a meta-analysis, Maxfield and Hyer (2002) sought to determine whether differences in outcome were related to methodological differences. All published PTSD treatment outcome studies were reviewed to identify methodological strengths and weaknesses and were rated using the gold standard (GS) scale (adapted from Foa & Meadows, 1997). Then the relationship between methodological rigor and effect sizes in these studies was examined. Results indicated a significant relationship between scores on the GS scale and effect size, with more rigorous studies reporting larger effect sizes. It seemed that methodological rigor removes noise and thereby decreases error measurement, allowing for the more accurate detection of true treatment effects. It should be noted that the association between methodology and outcome is purely correlational and may actually be the effect of some unknown third variable. However, it can be argued that when considering the aggregate evidence for the efficacy of EMDR, greater weight may be given to those studies with better methodology because they seem more likely to reveal accurate outcomes.

Suggested Research

Future research can use meta-analyses to assess potential predictors of treatment outcome. Factors that could be examined include number of sessions, client characteristics, chronicity and severity of symptoms, type of diagnosis, and comorbidity. A meta-analysis of research investigating the eye movement component is needed to determine whether outcome differs according to study type. This analysis might assist in developing a more complete understanding of the role of dual attention in EMDR.

IS FIDELITY TO TREATMENT IMPORTANT?

Yes, fidelity to treatment is important. Treatment fidelity is considered one of the gold standards of clinical research (Foa & Meadows, 1997). Clearly, if the treatment being tested does not adhere to the standard protocol, then the treatment being examined is not the standard treatment; the study will have poor validity, and the results may not be informative about the actual treatment. Treatment fidelity has been a subject of much controversy (Greenwald, 1996; Perkins & Rouanzoin, 2002; Rosen, 1999). Evidence has shown that EMDR is a robust treatment that is not affected by certain changes to protocol; for example, variations in the eye movement or stimulus component do not seem to interfere with outcome (Renfrey & Spates, 1994). On the other hand, evidence has shown that truncating the procedure may result in poor outcomes; for example, an analysis (Shapiro, 1999) of the procedures used in the EMDR phobia studies found that those omitting more than half of the EMDR phases achieved poor outcomes compared with those using the full protocol. In a methodological meta-analysis, Maxfield and Hyer (2002) found a significant positive correlation between pre-post effect size and assessments of fidelity. Specifically, those studies with fidelity assessed as adequate tended to have larger effects than those with fidelity assessed as variable or poor or that was not assessed.

Suggested Research

A measure of treatment fidelity needs to be developed that has good interrater reliability. The relationship between ratings on this measure and ratings of treatment effect can then be specifically examined. Furthermore, scores can be developed for the integrity of treatment received by each client, and this variable can be entered into analyses to determine the extent to which fidelity contributed to treatment outcome.

WHAT ELEMENTS OF EMDR CONTRIBUTE TO ITS EFFECTIVENESS?

EMDR is a complex therapeutic approach that integrates elements of many traditional psychological orientations and combines them in structured protocols. These elements include psychodynamic (Fensterheim, 1996; Solomon & Neborsky, 2001; Wachtel, chapter 5), cognitive behavioral (Smyth & Poole, chapter 6; Wolpe, 1990; Young, Zangwill, & Behary, chapter 7), experiential (e.g., Bohart & Greenberg, chapter 10), physiological (Siegel, chapter 4; van der Kolk, chapter 3), and interactional therapies (Kaslow, Nurse, & Thompson, chapter 12). Consequently, EMDR contains many effective components, all of which are thought to contribute to treatment outcome.

Marks et al. (1998) proposed that emotion can be conceptualized as a "skein of responses" viewed as "loosely linked reactions of many physiological, behavioural, and cognitive kinds" (p. 324). They suggested that different types of treatment weaken different strands within the skein of responses, and "some treatments may act on several strands simultaneously" (p. 324). EMDR is a multicomponent approach that works with strands of imagery, cognition, affect, somatic sensation, and related memories. This complexity makes it difficult to isolate and measure the contribution of any single component, especially because different clients with the same diagnosis may respond differently to different elements.

Shapiro's (2001) information-processing model conceptualizes EMDR as working directly with cognitive, affective, and somatic components of memory to forge new associative links with more adaptive material. Numerous treatment elements are formulated to enhance the processing and assimilation needed for adaptive resolution, including (a) linking of memory components, (b) mindfulness, (c) free association, (d) repeated access and dismissal of traumatic imagery, and (e) eye movements and other dual-attention stimuli:

- *Linking of memory components.* The client's simultaneous focus on the image of the event, the associated negative belief, and the attendant physical sensations may forge initial connections among various elements of the traumatic memory, thus initiating information processing.
- *Mindfulness.* Mindfulness is encouraged by instructing clients to "just notice" and "let whatever happens, happen." This cultivation of a stabilized observer stance in EMDR seems similar to processes advocated by Teasdale (1999) to facilitate emotional processing.
- *Free association.* During processing, clients are asked to report on any new insights, associations, emotions, sensations, and images that emerge into consciousness. This nondirective free association method may create associative links between the original targeted trauma and other related experiences and information, thus contributing to processing of the traumatic material (Rogers & Silver, 2002).
- *Repeated access and dismissal of traumatic imagery.* The brief exposures of EMDR provide clients with repeated practice in controlling and dismissing disturbing internal stimuli. This may provide clients with a sense of mastery, contributing to treatment effects by increasing their ability to reduce or manage negative interpretations and ruminations.
- *Eye movements and other dual-attention stimuli.* Many theories have been developed about how and why eye movements may contribute to information processing; these are discussed in detail in the following paragraphs.

Suggested Research

To determine the contribution of the relevant components, it is recommended that future dismantling studies use more rigorous methodology (Maxfield & Hyer, 2002), a sample large enough to provide adequate power, and control conditions that are distinct from eye movements and theoretically meaningful. As of this writing, no randomized clinical dismantling study has provided a full course of treatment to a large sample of clinically diagnosed participants.

IS EMDR AN EXPOSURE THERAPY?

A standard treatment for anxiety disorders involves exposing clients to anxiety-eliciting stimuli. It has sometimes been assumed that EMDR uses exposure in this traditional manner and that this accounts for EMDR's effectiveness. Some reviewers have stated, "Had EMDR been put forth simply as another variant of extant treatments, we suspect that much of the controversy over its efficacy and mechanisms of action could have been avoided" (Lohr, Lilienfeld, Tolin, & Herbert, 1999, p. 201). However, such a perspective ignores important elements of the EMDR procedure that are antithetical to exposure theories; in other words, the theories predict that if these EMDR elements were used in exposure therapy, a diminished outcome would result (Rogers & Silver, 2002). These elements include frequent brief exposures, interrupted exposure, and free association. Exposure theorists Foa and McNally (1996) wrote: "Because habituation is a gradual process, it is assumed that exposure must be prolonged to be effective. Prolonged exposure produces a better outcome than does brief exposure, regardless of diagnosis" (p. 334). However, EMDR uses extremely brief, repeated exposures (i.e., 20 to 50 seconds). Other theorists (Marks et al., 1998) stated that exposure should be continual and uninterrupted: "Continuous stimulation in neurons and immune and endocrine cells tends to dampen responses, and intermittent stimulation tends to increase them" (p. 324). EMDR, on the other hand, interrupts the internal attention repeatedly to ask "What do you get now?" Exposure therapy is structured to inhibit avoidance (Lyons & Keane, 1989) and specifically prohibits the client from reducing "anxiety by changing the scene or moving it ahead quickly in time to skim over the most traumatic point" (p. 146) to extinguish the anxiety. However, free association to whatever enters the client's consciousness is an integral part of the EMDR process.

Certainly, theories explicating exposure therapy fail to explain the treatment effects of EMDR, with its brief, interrupted exposures and its elicitation of free association. In addition, there appears to be a difference in the treatment processes of EMDR and exposure therapy. During exposure therapy, clients generally experience long periods of high anxiety (Foa & McNally, 1996), whereas EMDR clients generally experience rapid reductions in SUDS levels early in the session (Rogers et al., 1999). This difference suggests the possibility that EMDR's use of repeated, short, focused attention may invoke a different mechanism of action than that of exposure therapy, with its continual, long exposure.

Suggested Research

Research is needed to examine the role of exposure in the treatment of people with PTSD, perhaps by comparing standard EMDR with a modified EMDR protocol in which the amount of exposure is predetermined. Likewise, standard exposure therapy could be compared with a variant in which exposure is interrupted using an EMDR-type procedure in which free association is elicited. Such research will be helpful for identifying some of the core mechanisms that are active in PTSD treatment. Physiological measures taken during each condition (Wilson, Silver, Covi, & Foster, 1996) may reveal potentially fruitful information regarding the physiological mechanisms of action and response during the process of change.

ARE EYE MOVEMENTS CONSIDERED ESSENTIAL TO EMDR?

Although eye movements are often considered its most distinctive element, EMDR is not a simple procedure dominated by the use of eye movements. It is a complex psychotherapy, containing numerous components that are considered to contribute to treatment effects. Eye movements are used to engage the client's attention to an external stimulus while the client is simultaneously focusing on internal distressing material. Shapiro described eye movements as "dual-attention stimuli"—to identify the process in which the client simultaneously attends to external and internal stimuli. Therapist-directed eye movements are the most commonly used dual-attention stimulus, but various other stimuli, including tactile and auditory stimulation, are often used. The use of such alternate stimuli has been an integral part of the EMDR protocol for more than 10 years (Shapiro 1991, 1993).

Suggested Research

All the outcome research in EMDR treatment has used eye movements as the dual-attention stimulus. It is recommended that clinical dismantling studies investigate whether the effects of eye movements and the other dual-attention stimuli, such as tactile stimulation and tones, differ and to determine whether certain kinds of dual-attention stimuli are more helpful for some types of clients. Other aspects of dual-attention stimuli such as speed, intensity, and bilaterality, also need to be studied. It is important that component studies have sample sizes sufficient to ensure adequate statistical power.

WHAT HAS RESEARCH DETERMINED ABOUT EMDR'S EYE MOVEMENT COMPONENT?

In 1989, Shapiro (1995) noticed that the emotional distress accompanying disturbing thoughts disappeared as her eyes moved spontaneously and rapidly. She began experimenting with this effect and determined that when others moved their eyes, their distressing emotions also dissipated. She conducted a case study (1989b) and a controlled study (1989a), and her hypothesis that eye movements were related to desensitization of traumatic memories was supported. The role of eye movements had been previously documented in connection to cognitive processing mechanisms. A series of systematic experiments (Antrobus, Antrobus, & Singer, 1964) revealed that spontaneous eye movements were associated with unpleasant emotions and cognitive changes.

Twenty published studies have investigated the role of eye movements in EMDR. Studies have typically compared EMDR with eye movements to a control condition in which the eye movement component was modified (e.g., EMDR with the eyes focused and unmoving). Four types of studies have been conducted: (a) case studies, (b) dismantling studies using clinical participants, (c) dismantling studies using nonclinical analogue participants, and (d) component action studies in which eye movements are examined in isolation.

Case Studies

Four case studies evaluated the effects of adding eye movements to the treatment process, and three of them demonstrated an effect for eye movements. Montgomery and Ayllon (1994) found eye movements to be necessary for EMDR treatment effects in five of six civilian clients with PTSD. They wrote that the addition of the eye movement component "resulted in the significant decreases in self-reports of distress previously addressed. These findings are reflected by decreases in psychophysiological arousal" (Montgomery & Ayllon, 1994, p. 228). Lohr, Tolin, and Kleinknecht (1995) reported that "the addition of the eye movement component appeared to have a distinct effect in reducing the level of [SUD] ratings" (p. 149). When Lohr, Tolin, and Kleinknecht (1996) treated two participants with claustrophobia, substantial changes in disturbance ratings were achieved only after eye movements were added to an imagery exposure procedure that used the brief, frequent exposures of EMDR. The fourth study (Acierno, Tremont, Last, & Montgomery, 1994) did not use standard

EMDR protocol for phobias or the standard procedures for accessing the image, formulating the negative belief, or eliciting new associations. In addition, the participant was instructed to relax between sets of eye movements until the SUDS rating was reduced to baseline, a procedure not used in EMDR. The procedures used in this study did not eliminate the phobia, and no effect was found for the eye movement condition.

Clinical Dismantling Studies With Diagnosed Participants

Four controlled dismantling studies have been conducted with participants who had PTSD, and two studies have been conducted with participants who were diagnosed with other anxiety disorders. These studies tended to show that EMDR with eye movements was slightly better than EMDR with modifications; however, such comparisons were not usually statistically significant, and results were equivocal. For example, Devilly et al. (1998) reported rates of reliable change of 67% for the eye movement condition, compared with 42% of the condition without eye movements. Renfrey and Spates (1994) reported a decrease in PTSD diagnoses of 85% for eye movement conditions and 57% for the group without eye movements. These studies were unfortunately limited by severe methodological problems, including inadequate statistical power. For example, each condition in the Renfrey and Spates (1994) PTSD study included six or seven people. The participants in the other three PTSD studies (Boudeywns & Hyer, 1996; Devilly et al., 1998; Pitman et al., 1996) were combat veterans who received only three sessions or treatment of only two traumatic memories. Such an inadequate course of treatment produced only moderate effect sizes; therefore, a much larger sample would be required to provide adequate statistical power for the detection of any possible differences among groups. There has yet to be a single rigorous dismantling study with a sample size adequate to assess treatment effects.

Clinical Dismantling Studies With Analogue Participants

The controlled studies that used analogue participants with nonclinical anxiety found no effect for eye movements. These analogue studies, which typically used normal college student participants, had many problems. The EMDR protocol was often truncated (e.g., Carrigan & Levis, 1999; Sanderson & Carpenter, 1992), resulting in poor construct validity and making interpretation of results problematic. It is also unlikely that the responses of analogue participants can be generalized to people with chronic PTSD, a disorder that seems resistant to placebo effects (Solomon, Gerrity, & Muff, 1992; Van Etten & Taylor, 1998). Analogue participants responded well to EMDR without eye movements, a procedure with numerous active components. The minimal distress of the analogue participants was relieved with minimal treatment, and the assessment of differences between the eye movement condition and condition without eye movements was limited by a floor effect. Consequently, it may not have been possible to detect differences between conditions.

Component Action Studies

Component action studies test eye movements in isolation. These studies typically provide brief sets of eye movements (not EMDR) to examine their effects on memory, affect, cognition, or physiology. The purpose is to investigate the effects of moving the eyes (not EMDR), and eye movements are compared with control conditions such as imaging and tapping. For example, participants might be asked to visualize a memory image, then to move their eyes briefly, and then to rate the vividness of the image. This action permits a pure test of the specific effects of eye movements and lack of eye movements without the added effects of the active ingredients of the other EMDR procedures. The studies have generally used nonclinical participants and a within-subject design, which compares the differences in each individual's responses to the various conditions. This design reduces the variance of subjective responding and eliminates possible floor effects.

Findings from these studies suggest that eye movements may have an effect on physiology by decreasing arousal (e.g., Barrowcliff, MacCulloch, & Gray, 2001; Wilson et al., 1996) and on memory processes by enhancing semantic recall (Christman & Garvey, 2000). Four studies (Andrade, Kavanagh, & Baddeley, 1997; Kavanaugh, Freese, Andrade, & May, 2001; Sharpley, Montgomery, & Scalzo, 1996; van den Hout, Muris, Salemink, & Kindt, 2001) have demonstrated that eye movements decrease the vividness of memory images and their associated emotions. No (or minimal) effect has been found for tapping conditions. These studies suggest that eye movements may make a contribution to treatment by decreasing the salience of the memory and its associated affect.

DO EYE MOVEMENTS CONTRIBUTE TO OUTCOME IN EMDR?

Much confusion tends to result when the findings of the three types of previously discussed component studies are combined. Because these studies differ substantially in design, purpose, participants, and outcome measures, they have produced a wide range of results. In dismantling studies with analogue participants, eye movements do not contribute to outcome, possibly because of a floor effect. In clinical dismantling studies with diagnosed participants, a consistent insignificant trend for a treatment effect was found. In the component action studies, a consistent significant effect for eye movements in isolation was found in reducing the vividness of and affect associated with autobiographical memories; it is possible that such effects may contribute to treatment outcome. In the Davidson and Parker (2001) meta-analysis, no effects were found for EMDR with eye movements compared with EMDR without eye movements when all types of studies were included. However, when the results of the clinical dismantling studies were examined, EMDR with eye movements was significantly superior to EMDR without eye movements.

Various reviews of the related eye movement research have provided a range of conclusions. Some reviewers (e.g., Lohr et al., 1999; Lohr, Tolin, & Lilienfeld, 1998) stated that no compelling evidence has shown that eye movements contribute to outcome in EMDR treatment, and the lack of unequivocal findings has led some reviewers to dismiss eye movements altogether (e.g., McNally, 1999). Other reviewers (e.g., Chemtob et al., 2000; Feske, 1998; Perkins & Rouanzoin, 2002) identified methodological failings (e.g., lack of statistical power, floor effects) and called for more rigorous study.

Suggested Research

Research is needed to answer questions about the role of eye movements and other dual-attention stimuli. It is recommended that clinical dismantling studies use a large sample of participants with PTSD (related to a single trauma) to investigate whether EMDR with eye movements is more effective than EMDR without dual-attention stimuli. As of this writing, no study like this has been conducted (see Shapiro, 2001, for specific recommendations for research designs).

WHAT ARE SOME HYPOTHESIZED MECHANISMS OF ACTION FOR EYE MOVEMENTS IN EMDR?

A commonly proposed hypothesis for the mechanism of action for eye movements in EMDR is that dual-attention stimulation elicits an orienting response. The orienting response is a natural response of interest and attention that results when attention is drawn to a new stimulus. Three different models can be used to conceptualize the role of the orienting response in EMDR: cognitive/information processing (Andrade et al., 1997; Lipke, 1999), neurobiological (Bergmann, 2000; Servan-Schreiber, 2000; Stickgold, 2002), and behavioral (Armstrong & Vaughan, 1996; MacCulloch & Feldman, 1996). These models are not exclusive; to some extent, they view the same phenomenon from different perspectives. Barrowcliff et al. (2001) posited that the orienting in EMDR is actually an "investigatory reflex" that results in a basic relaxation response after determination that there is no threat; this relaxation contributes to outcome through a process of reciprocal inhibition. Others have suggested that the inauguration of an orienting response may disrupt the traumatic memory network, interrupting previous associations to negative emotions and allowing for the integration of new information. It is also possible that the orienting response induces neurobiological mechanisms that facilitate the activation of episodic memories and their integration into cortical semantic memory (Stickgold, 2002). All of this is purely speculative, and research is needed to test these hypotheses.

Several research studies (e.g., Andrade et al., 1997; Kavanaugh et al., 2001; van den Hout et al., 2001) have indicated that eye movements and other stimuli have an effect on perceptions of the targeted memory, decreasing image vividness and associated affect. Two possible mechanisms have been proposed to explain how this effect may contribute to EMDR treatment. Kavanaugh et al. (2001) hypothesized that this effect occurs when eye movements disrupt working memory, which decreases vividness and results in decreased emotionality. They further suggested that this effect may contribute to treatment as a "response aid for imaginal exposure" (p. 278) by titrating exposure for those clients who are distressed by memory images or affect. van den Hout et al. (2001) hypothesized that eye movements change the somatic perceptions accompanying retrieval, leading to decreased affect and therefore decreasing vividness. They proposed that this effect "may be to temporarily assist patients in recollecting memories that may otherwise appear to be unbearable" (p. 129). This explanation has many similarities to reciprocal inhibition.

Suggested Research

Research investigating mechanisms of action should be driven by hypotheses, with outcomes evaluated in relation to the hypothesis being tested (see Shapiro 2001, for examples of suggested research designs).

REFERENCES

Acierno, R., Tremont, G., Last, C., & Montgomery, D. (1994). Tripartite assessment of the efficacy of eye-movement desensitization in a multi-phobic patient. *Journal of Anxiety Disorders, 8,* 259–276.

Andrade, J., Kavanagh, D., & Baddeley, A. (1997). Eye-movements and visual imagery: A working memory approach to the treatment of post-traumatic stress disorder. *British Journal of Clinical Psychology, 36,* 209–223.

Antrobus, J. S., Antrobus, J. S., & Singer, J. L. (1964). Eye movements accompanying daydreaming, visual imagery, and thought suppression. *Journal of Abnormal and Social Psychology, 69,* 244–252.

Armstrong, M. S., & Vaughan, K. (1996). An orienting response model of eye movement desensitization. *Journal of Behavior Therapy and Experimental Psychiatry, 27,* 21–32.

Barrowcliff, A. L., MacCulloch, M. J., & Gray, N. S. (2001, May). *The de-arousal model of eye movement desensitization and reprocessing (EMDR), Part III: Psychophysiological and psychological concomitants of change in the treatment of posttraumatic stress disorder (PTSD) and their relation to the EMDR protocol.* Paper presented at second annual meeting of the EMDR Europe, London.

Bergmann, U. (2000). Further thoughts on the neurobiology of EMDR: The role of the cerebellum in accelerated information processing. *Traumatology, 6* (3). Retrieved March 15, 2002, from http://www.fsu.edu/~trauma/v6i3/v6i3a4.html

Boudewyns, P. A., & Hyer, L. A. (1996). Eye movement desensitization and reprocessing (EMDR) as treatment for post-traumatic stress disorder (PTSD). *Clinical Psychology and Psychotherapy, 3,* 185–195.

Brown, K. W., McGoldrick, T., & Buchanan, R. (1997). Body dysmorphic disorder: Seven cases treated with eye movement desensitization and reprocessing. *Behavioural and Cognitive Psychotherapy, 25,* 203–207.

Carlson, J. G., Chemtob, C. M., Rusnak, K., Hedlund, N. L., & Muraoka, M. Y. (1998). Eye movement desensitization and reprocessing for combat-related posttraumatic stress disorder. *Journal of Traumatic Stress, 11,* 3–24.

Carrigan, M. H., & Levis, D. J. (1999). The contributions of eye movements to the efficacy of brief exposure treatment for reducing exposure treatment for reducing fear of public speaking. *Journal of Anxiety Disorders, 13,* 101–118.

Cerone, M. R. (2000, November). *EMDR treatment of combat-related guilt: A study of the effects of eye movements.* Poster presented at the annual meeting of the International Society for Traumatic Stress Studies, San Antonio, TX.

Chambless, D. L., Baker, M. J., Baucom, D. H., Beutler, L. E., Calhoun, K. S., Crits-Christoph, P., et al. (1998). Update on empirically validated therapies. *The Clinical Psychologist, 51,* 3–16.

Chemtob, C. M., Nakashima, J., & Carlson, J. G. (2002). Brief-treatment for elementary school children with disaster-related PTSD: A field study. *Journal of Clinical Psychology, 58,* 99–112.

Chemtob, C. M., Tolin, D. F., van der Kolk, B. A., & Pitman, R. K. (2000). Eye movement desensitization and reprocessing. In E. B. Foa, T. M. Keane, & M. J. Friedman (Eds.), *Effective treatments for PTSD: Practice guidelines from the International Society for Traumatic Stress Studies* (pp. 139–155, 333–335). New York: Guilford Press.

Christman, S., & Garvey, K. (2000, November). *Episodic versus semantic memory: Eye movements and cortical activation.* Poster presented at the 41st annual meeting of the Psychonomic Society, New Orleans, LA.

Davidson, P. R., & Parker, K. C. H. (2001). Eye movement desensitization and reprocessing (EMDR): A meta-analysis. *Journal of Consulting and Clinical Psychology, 69,* 305–316.

De Jongh, A., & Ten Broeke, E. (1998). Treatment of choking phobia by targeting traumatic memories with EMDR: A case study. *Clinical Psychology and Psychotherapy, 5*, 1–6.

De Jongh, A., Ten Broeke, E., & Renssen, M. R. (1999). Treatment of specific phobias with eye movement desensitization and reprocessing (EMDR): Protocol, empirical status, and conceptual issues. *Journal of Anxiety Disorders, 13*, 69–85.

De Jongh, A., van den Oord, H. J. M., & Ten Broeke, E. (in press). Efficacy of eye movement desensitization and reprocessing (EMDR) in the treatment of specific phobias: Four single-case studies on dental phobia. *Journal of Clinical Psychology*.

Devilly, G. J., & Spence, S. H. (1999). The relative efficacy and treatment distress of EMDR and a cognitive behavioral trauma treatment protocol in the amelioration of post traumatic stress disorder. *Journal of Anxiety Disorders, 13*, 131–157.

Devilly, G. J., Spence, S. H., & Rapee, R. M. (1998). Statistical and reliable change with eye movement desensitization and reprocessing: Treating trauma with a veteran population. *Behavior Therapy, 29*, 435–455.

Fensterheim, H. (1996). Eye movement desensitization and reprocessing with complex personality pathology: An integrative therapy. *Journal of Psychotherapy Integration, 6*, 27–38.

Feske, U. (1998). Eye movement desensitization and reprocessing treatment for posttraumatic stress disorder. *Clinical Psychology: Science and Practice, 5*, 171–181.

Feske, U., & Goldstein, A. (1997). Eye movement desensitization and reprocessing treatment for panic disorder: A controlled outcome and partial dismantling study. *Journal of Consulting and Clinical Psychology, 36*, 1026–1035.

Fine, C. G., & Berkowitz, A. S. (2001). The wreathing protocol: The imbrication of hypnosis and EMDR in the treatment of dissociative identity disorder and other maladaptive dissociative responses. *American Journal of Clinical Hypnosis, 43*, 275–290.

Foa, E. B., & McNally, R. J. (1996). Mechanisms of change in exposure therapy. In R. M. Rapee (Ed.), *Current controversies in the anxiety disorders* (pp. 329–343). New York: Guilford.

Foa, E. B., & Meadows, E. A. (1997). Psychosocial treatments for posttraumatic stress disorder: A critical review. *Annual Review of Psychology, 48*, 449–480.

Foa, E. B., Riggs, D. S., Massie, E. D., & Yarczower, M. (1995). The impact of fear activation and anger on the efficacy of exposure treatment for posttraumatic stress disorder. *Behavior Therapy, 26*, 487–499.

Foster, S., & Lendl, J. (1996). Eye movement desensitization and reprocessing: Four cases of a new tool for executive coaching and restoring employee performance after setbacks. *Consulting Psychology Journal: Practice and Research, 48*, 155–161.

Goldstein, A. J., de Beurs, E., Chambless, D. L., & Wilson, K. A. (2000). EMDR for panic disorder with agoraphobia: Comparison with waiting-list and credible attention-placebo control condition. *Journal of Consulting and Clinical Psychology, 68,* 947–956.

Goldstein, A., & Feske, U. (1994). Eye movement desensitization and reprocessing for panic disorder: A case series. *Journal of Anxiety Disorders, 8,* 351–362.

Grant, M., & Threlfo, C. (in press). EMDR in the treatment of chronic pain. *Journal of Clinical Psychology.*

Greenwald, R. (1996). Is EMDR being held to an unfair standard? Rejoinder to Van Ommeren (1996). *Professional Psychology: Research and Practice, 28,* 306.

Ironson, G. I., Freund, B., Strauss, J. L., & Williams, J. (2002). A comparison of two treatments for traumatic stress: A pilot study of EMDR and prolonged exposure. *Journal of Clinical Psychology, 58,* 13–128.

Kavanaugh, D. J., Freese, S., Andrade, J., & May, J. (2001). Effects of visuospatial tasks on desensitization to emotive memories. *British Journal of Clinical Psychology, 40,* 267–280.

Korn, D. L., & Leeds, A. M. (in press). Preliminary evidence of efficacy for EMDR resource development and installation in the stabilization phase of treatment of complex posttraumatic stress disorder. *Journal of Clinical Psychology.*

Lazrove, S., & Fine, C. G. (1996). The use of EMDR in patients with dissociative identity disorder. *Dissociation, 9,* 289–299.

Lee, C., Gavriel, H., Drummond, P., Richards, J., & Greenwald, R. (in press). Treatment of post-traumatic stress disorder: A comparison of stress inoculation training with prolonged exposure and eye movement desensitization and reprocessing. *Journal of Clinical Psychology.*

Lipke, H. (1999). *EMDR and psychotherapy integration.* Boca Raton, FL: CRC Press.

Lohr, J. M., Lilienfeld, S. O., Tolin, D. F., & Herbert, J. D. (1999). Eye movement desensitization and reprocessing: An analysis of specific versus nonspecific factors. *Journal of Anxiety Disorders, 13,* 185–207.

Lohr, J. M., Tolin, D. F., & Kleinknecht, R. A. (1995). An intensive investigation of eye movement desensitization of medical phobias. *Journal of Behavior Therapy and Experimental Psychiatry, 26,* 141–151.

Lohr, J. M., Tolin, D. F., & Kleinknect, R. A. (1996). An intensive investigation of eye movement desensitization of claustrophobia. *Journal of Anxiety Disorders, 10,* 73–88.

Lohr, J. M., Tolin, D. F., & Lilienfeld, S. O. (1998). Efficacy of eye movement desensitization and reprocessing: Implications for behavior therapy. *Behavior Therapy, 29,* 123–156.

Lyons, J. A., & Keane, T. M. (1989). Implosive therapy for the treatment of combat-related PTSD. *Journal of Traumatic Stress, 2,* 137–152.

MacCulloch, M. J., & Feldman, P. (1996). Eye movement desensitization treatment utilizes the positive visceral element of the investigatory reflex to inhibit the memories of post-traumatic stress disorder: A theoretical analysis. *British Journal of Psychiatry, 169,* 571–579.

Macklin, M., Metzger, L. J., Lasko, N. B., Berry, N. J., Orr, S. P., & Pitman, R. K.

(2000). Five-year follow-up study of eye movement desensitization and reprocessing therapy for combat-related posttraumatic stress disorder. *Comprehensive Psychiatry, 41,* 24–27.

Manfield, P. (Ed.). (1998). *Extending EMDR.* New York: Norton.

Marcus, S. V., Marquis, P., & Sakai, C. (1997). Controlled study of treatment of PTSD using EMDR in an HMO setting. *Psychotherapy, 34,* 307–315.

Marks, I. M., Lovell, K., Noshirvani, H., Livanou, M., & Thrasher, S. (1998). Treatment of posttraumatic stress disorder by exposure and/or cognitive restructuring: A controlled study. *Archives of General Psychiatry, 55,* 317–325.

Maxfield, L., & Hyer, L. A. (2002). The relationship between efficacy and methodology in studies investigating EMDR treatment of PTSD. *Journal of Clinical Psychology, 58,* 23–41.

Maxfield, L., & Melnyk, W. T. (2000). Single session treatment of test anxiety with eye movement desensitization and reprocessing (EMDR). *International Journal of Stress Management, 7,* 87–101.

McFarlane, A. (1999, November). *Comparison of EMDR with CBT in PTSD patients.* Paper presented at the annual meeting of the International Society for Traumatic Stress Studies, Miami, FL.

McNally, R. J. (1999). On eye movements and animal magnetism: A reply to Greenwald's defense of EMDR. *Journal of Anxiety Disorders, 13,* 617–620.

Montgomery, R. W., & Ayllon, T. (1994). Eye movement desensitization across subjects: Subjective and physiological measures of treatment efficacy. *Journal of Behavior Therapy and Experimental Psychiatry, 25,* 217–230.

Muris, P., & Merckelbach, H. (1997). Treating spider phobics with eye movement desensitization and reprocessing: A controlled study. *Behavioral and Cognitive Psychotherapy, 25,* 39–50.

Muris, P., Merkelbach, H., Holdrinet, I., & Sijsenaar, M. (1998). Treating phobic children: Effects of EMDR versus exposure. *Journal of Consulting and Clinical Psychology, 66,* 193–198.

Muris, P., Merckelbach, H., van Haaften, H., & Nayer, B. (1997). Eye movement desensitization and reprocessing versus exposure in vivo. *British Journal of Psychiatry, 171,* 82–86.

Paulsen, S. (1995). Eye movement desensitization and reprocessing: Its cautious use in the dissociative disorders. *Dissociation, 8,* 32–44.

Perkins, B., & Rouanzoin, C. (2002). An examination of misinformation regarding eye movement desensitization and reprocessing (EMDR): Points of confusion. *Journal of Clinical Psychology, 58,* 77–97.

Pitman, R. K., Orr, S. P., Altman, B., Longpre, R. E., Poire, R. E., & Macklin, M. L. (1996). Emotional processing during eye-movement desensitization and reprocessing therapy of Vietnam veterans with chronic post-traumatic stress disorder. *Comprehensive Psychiatry, 37,* 419–429.

Power, K. G., McGoldrick, T., & Brown, K. (2001, May). *A controlled trial of eye movement desensitization and reprocessing versus imaginal exposure and cognitive restructuring, versus waiting-list control in posttraumatic stress disorder.* Paper presented at the European Society for the Study of Traumatic Stress, Edinburgh, Scotland.

Ray, A. L., & Zbik, A. (2001). Cognitive behavioral therapies and beyond. In C. D. Tollison, J. R. Satterthwaite, & S. W. Tollison (Eds.), *Practical pain management* (3rd ed.; pp. 189–208). Philadelphia: Lippincott.

Renfrey, G., & Spates, C. R. (1994). Eye movement desensitization and reprocessing: A partial dismantling procedure. *Journal of Behavior Therapy and Experimental Psychiatry, 25*, 231–239.

Rogers, S., & Silver, S. M. (2002). Is EMDR an exposure therapy? A review of trauma protocols. *Journal of Clinical Psychology, 58*, 43–59.

Rogers, S., Silver, S., Goss, J., Obenchain, J., Willis, A., & Whitney, R. (1999). A single session, controlled group study of flooding and eye movement desensitization and reprocessing in treating posttraumatic stress disorder among Vietnam War veterans: Preliminary data. *Journal of Anxiety Disorders, 13,* 119–130.

Rosen, G. R. (1999). Treatment fidelity and research on eye movement desensitization and reprocessing (EMDR). *Journal of Anxiety Disorders, 13,* 173–184.

Rothbaum, B. O. (1997). A controlled study of eye movement desensitization and reprocessing for posttraumatic stress disordered sexual assault victims. *Bulletin of the Menninger Clinic, 61,* 317–334.

Rothbaum, B. O. (2001, November). Prolonged exposure versus EMDR for PTSD rape victims. In P. A. Resick (chair), *Three clinical trials for the treatment of PTSD: Outcome and dissemination.* Paper presented at the annual meeting of the Association for the Advancement of Behavior Therapy, Philadelphia.

Sanderson, A., & Carpenter, R. (1992). Eye movement desensitization versus image confrontation: A single-session crossover study of 58 phobic subjects. *Journal of Behavior Therapy and Experimental Psychiatry, 23*, 269–275.

Scheck, M. M., Schaeffer, J. A., & Gillette, C. S. (1998). Brief psychological intervention with traumatized young women: The efficacy of eye movement desensitization and reprocessing. *Journal of Traumatic Stress, 11*, 25–44.

Scott, M. J., & Stradling, S. G. (1997). Client compliance with exposure treatments for posttraumatic stress disorder. *Journal of Traumatic Stress, 10,* 523–526.

Servan-Schreiber, D. (2000). Eye movement desensitization and reprocessing: Is psychiatry missing the point? *Psychiatric Times, 17,* 36–40.

Shapiro, F. (1989a). Efficacy of the eye movement desensitization procedure in the treatment of traumatic memories. *Journal of Traumatic Stress Studies, 2,* 199–223.

Shapiro, F. (1989b). Eye movement desensitization: A new treatment for posttraumatic stress disorder. *Journal of Behavior Therapy and Experimental Psychiatry, 20,* 211–217.

Shapiro, F. (1991). Stray thoughts. *EMDR Network Newsletter, 1,* 1–3.

Shapiro, F. (1993). Eye movement desensitization and reprocessing (EMDR) in 1992. *Journal of Traumatic Stress Studies, 6,* 417–421.

Shapiro, F. (1995). *Eye movement desensitization and reprocessing: Basic principles, protocols and procedures* (1st ed.). New York: Guilford Press.

Shapiro, F. (1999). Eye movement desensitization and reprocessing (EMDR): Clinical and research implications of an integrated psychotherapy treatment. *Journal of Anxiety Disorders, 13*, 35–67.

Shapiro, F. (2001). *Eye movement desensitization and reprocessing: Basic principles, protocols and procedures* (2nd ed.). New York: Guilford Press.

Sharpley, C. F., Montgomery, I. M., & Scalzo, L. A. (1996). Comparative efficacy of EMDR and alternative procedures in reducing the vividness of mental images. *Scandinavian Journal of Behaviour Therapy, 25*, 37–42.

Silver, S., & Rogers, S. (2001). *Light in the heart of darkness: EMDR and the treatment of war and terrorism survivors.* New York: Norton.

Solomon, M., & Neborsky, R. J. (Eds.). (2001). *Short-term therapy for long-term change.* New York: Norton.

Solomon, S. D., Gerrity, E. T., & Muff, A. M. (1992). Efficacy of treatments for posttraumatic stress disorder. *Journal of the American Medical Association, 268*, 633–638.

Sprang, G. (2001). The use of eye movement desensitization and reprocessing (EMDR) in the treatment of traumatic stress and complicated mourning: Psychological and behavioral outcomes. *Research on Social Work Practice, 11*, 300–320.

Stickgold, R. (2002). EMDR: A putative neurobiological mechanism of action. *Journal of Clinical Psychology, 58*, 61–75.

Taylor, S., Thordarson, D., Maxfield, L., Wilensky, M. S., Ladd, W. G., Lanius, U. F., et al. (2001, July). *EMDR, exposure therapy, and relaxation training for PTSD: A controlled outcome study.* Paper presented at the World Congress meeting of the Association for the Advancement of Behavior Therapy, Vancouver, Canada.

Teasdale, J. D. (1999). Emotional processing, three modes of mind and the prevention of relapse in depression. *Behaviour Research and Therapy, 37*(Suppl. 1), 53–77.

United Kingdom Department of Health. (2001). *Treatment choice in psychological therapies and counselling evidence based clinical practice guideline.* London: Author. Retrieved March 15, 2002, from http://www.doh.gov.uk/mentalhealth/treatmentguideline/

van den Hout, M., Muris, P., Salemink, E., & Kindt, M. (2001). Autobiographical memories become less vivid and emotional after eye movements. *British Journal of Clinical Psychology, 40*, 121–130.

Vanderlaan, L. (in press). The resolution of phantom limb pain in a 15-year old girl using eye movement desensitization and reprocessing. *EMDR Clinician.*

Van Etten, M. L., & Taylor, S. (1998). Comparative efficacy of treatments for posttraumatic stress disorder: A meta-analysis. *Clinical Psychology and Psychotherapy, 5*, 126–144.

Vaughan, K., Armstrong, M., Gold, R., O'Connor, N., Jenneke, W., & Tarrier, N.

(1994). A trial of eye movement desensitization compared to image habituation training and applied muscle relaxation in post-traumatic stress disorder. *Journal of Behavior Therapy and Experimental Psychiatry, 25,* 283–291.

Wilensky, M. (2000). Phantom limb pain. *EMDRAC Newsletter, 4*(2).

Wilson, D., Silver, S. M, Covi, W., & Foster, S. (1996). Eye movement desensitization and reprocessing: Effectiveness and autonomic correlates. *Journal of Behavior Therapy and Experimental Psychiatry, 27,* 219–229.

Wilson, S. A., Becker, L. A., & Tinker, R. H. (1995). Eye movement desensitization and reprocessing (EMDR) treatment for psychologically traumatized individuals. *Journal of Consulting and Clinical Psychology, 63,* 928–937.

Wilson, S. A., Tinker, R., Becker, L. A., Hofmann, A., & Cole, J. W. (2000, September). *EMDR treatment of phantom limb pain with brain imaging (MEG).* Paper presented at the annual meeting of the EMDR International Association, Toronto, Canada.

Wolpe, J. (1990). *The practice of behavior therapy* (4th ed.). New York: Pergamon Press.

AUTHOR INDEX

SUBJECT INDEX

Adaptive resolution, 9, 13–14
  requirements for, 32
Adherence to treatment regimen
  EMDR outcomes, 402–403
  PTSD treatment, 66
Affective functioning
  assessment phase of treatment, 36–37
  bottom-down processing, 70–71
  in change process, 42, 144–145, 168–169, 250
  cognitive functioning and, 30, 96, 108, 168–169, 181
  definition of emotion, 96
  in EMDR model of pathology, 29–30
  in emergence of traumatic memory, 58–60
  in emergence of unprocessed childhood memories, 11–12
  emotion schemes, 249–250
  in experiential therapies, 249–250
  hemispheric development in brain and, 91
  impaired response flexibility and, 116–117
  as integrative process, 108
  in interpersonal relationships, 98
  journal of emotional experiences, 40
  memory processes in, 60
  neurophysiology of, 68–70, 96–97, 110, 181
  regulation in PTSD, 69, 96
  sensate experience in, 68–69
  somatic manifestations, 30
  top-down processing, 70–71
Agoraphobia, 160, 398–399
Amygdala, 65
Anxiety
  behavior theory/therapy, 153–154
  multimodal therapy with EMDR, 220–222
  patient's description of symptoms, 19
Applications of EMDR, generic, 4, 12–17, 27, 168, 399–400
  See also EMDR and different orientations

Assessment
  baseline data, 35, 36–37
  behavioral techniques relevant to EMDR, 164–166, 169–170
  client history, 31–34
  of client readiness for memory processing, 34–35
  family systems therapy, 296–297, 302, 315
  goals, 35–37
  of lifetime patterns of dysfunction, 33
  of mid-session therapeutic progress, 39
  in multimodal therapy, 212, 214–215
  in re-evaluation phase of therapy, 41
  in schema-focused therapy, 187–188, 193–195, 201
  in transpersonal EMDR, 328–329
  validity of cognition, 36, 39–40
Attachment
  complexity theory, 99
  developmental significance, 86–87
  disorganized/disoriented, 91–92, 99
  in therapeutic change, 98, 106–107
  trauma effects, 91–92
  unresolved/disorganized, 92
Attentional processes
  awareness of physical symptoms in processing, 37
  in desensitization phase of therapy, 38
  EMDR mechanism of action, 28, 107–109, 161
  in experiential therapy, 249
  in transpersonal assessment, 328–329
Avoidance behavior
  conditioning research, 152–153
  as schema process, 186
  in trauma therapy, 67
  in treatment, 34

Behavior chain analysis, 164–166
Behavior therapy
  assessment techniques, 164–166
  change mechanism, 345
  compatibility with EMDR, 158, 159–163, 343, 347

429

Behavor therapy (*continued*)
    concept of psychopathology in, 153–154
    in EMDR treatment techniques, 41, 163–167
    psychoanalytic therapy and, 124–125, 137–138, 140–141, 143–144
    PTSD conceptualization, 151–152
    technical and theoretical evolution, 152–154, 209
    use of EMDR in, 168–172
    See also Cognitive–behavioral approach
Bilateral stimulation, 111–115, 142–143, 254
    mechanism of action, 220
    in transpersonal EMDR, 327, 329–330
    variables in administration, 163
Bipolar disorder, 399–400
Body dysmorphic disorder, 16–17, 399, 400
Body scan, 40
Broca's area, 60, 65

Change mechanisms and processes
    as adaptive resolution, 9, 13–14, 32
    attachment processes in, 98, 106–107
    attentional mechanisms in, 28, 107–109, 161
    in behavior therapy, 345
    in bilateral stimulation, 220
    client attention to physical symptoms in, 37
    clinical significance of eye movements, 159–160, 162–163, 373–375, 404–405, 406–407, 409–410
    in cognitive–behavioral approaches to PTSD, 155–156
    cognitive component, 143–147, 181, 182
    development of feminist consciousness in, 273–274
    dual-attention stimuli mechanism of action, 372–375
    in EMDR, 8–9, 10, 13–14, 17–18, 27, 28–30, 42–43, 77–80, 101–102, 107–108, 129, 157, 158–159, 162–163, 172, 220, 229, 235–236, 246–248, 345–347, 352, 370–375, 393–394, 403–405, 410–411
    emotional regulation in, 71

in experiential approach, 239, 242, 248–250
in family systems therapy, 291, 301–302, 303, 310
in feminist therapy, 266
generalization of therapeutic effects, 32
habituation in, 161–162
in hypnotherapy, 230–231, 232
identity destabilization in, 234–235
imaginal exposure in, 160–161, 405–406
information processing models, 91, 101–102, 111, 161–162
integrative aspects of EMDR, 342–344, 345–347, 351–352
learning in, 51
maintenance of therapeutic benefits, 40, 41, 397–398
mindful attention in, 159
narrative construction in, 91, 95, 311
neurophysiology, 95–96, 115–117, 342
ordered chaos model, 234
placebo effects, 400–401
processing of dysfunctional memories, 12–13, 30
psychoanalytic conceptualization, 61–62, 127, 129–130
rapid effects of EMDR, 27, 51–52, 172, 312–313, 345
reciprocal inhibition theory, 154
representational integration in, 110–111, 112–113, 114–115
as restructuring of emotion schemes, 249–250
retraumatization in, 67
in schema-focused therapy, 184, 188–193, 198–201
self-healing, 239, 242, 246–250
self-love in, 50
special learning state in, 230–232, 234–236
spontaneous processing in, 42–43
therapeutic relationship in, 78–80
transition from childish to adult perspective in, 46
in transpersonal psychology, 321–323, 335, 337–338
treatment closure, 40–41
as working through, 130–131
Chaos theory, 234
Childhood experience
    of caregiving, 63

in model of psychopathology, 10–11,
12
in neurobiological development, 86–
87, 88–89
parent-child interaction, 99
schema formation and maintenance,
183–187
traumatic, 13, 14–15
Child patient, EMDR with, 309–310
Cholinergic system, 78
Client-centered therapy
eye movement procedures in, 256–257
mechanism of change, 242
process and technique, 240, 244–245
therapeutic relationship in, 240
See also Experiential approaches
Cognitive–behavioral approach
in EMDR practice, 134–135
guided mourning treatment, 367–368
multimodal focus, 211
origins of EMDR in, 123, 124, 143,
144
psychoanalytic approach and, 143–144
PTSD outcome studies, 358, 359, 367–
368, 395–396
PTSD treatment, 151, 155–156
technical and theoretical evolution,
152, 154–155, 209–210, 211
See also Behavior therapy
Cognitive functioning
affective functioning and, 30, 96, 108,
168–169, 181
in change processes, 143–147, 181,
182
early maladaptive schema formation,
183–184
in EMDR model of pathology, 42
in EMDR treatment, 144–145
hemispheric development in brain and,
90–91
installation of positive beliefs, 39–40
neurophysiology, 90
patriarchal constructs in, 271
rationalizing irrational behavior, 58
schema formation, 92–93
schema processes, 186–187
Cognitive interweave, 43, 146
case studies, 43–51
Cognitive theory/therapy
in EMDR model of change, 29, 30
in EMDR treatment techniques, 41
limitations, 182–183

psychopathology conceptualizations,
182
schema-focused therapy and, 182–183,
189–190
treatment goals, 182
See also Cognitive–behavioral approach
Complexity theory, 98–99
Conditioning
conceptual evolution, 152–153
in EMDR model of change, 29, 163
in PTSD pathogenesis, 155–156
Construction of meaning, 57
process, 62–63
See also Narrative construction
Constructivism, 126
Countertransference, 139–140
Couples work, 310, 311–312
Cyclical psychodynamic approach, 125,
137–140

Depression, 16, 400
Desensitization
clinical origins, 154
in EMDR, 28, 37–39, 201
need for relaxation in, 209
patient schema considerations, 201
Development, psychological
complexity theory, 98–99
conceptualizations of mind, 90
cycles of identity in, 233–234
determinants, 86–87
implications for trauma treatment, 104
integrated process, 100–101
interpersonal relationships in, 63, 87,
88–89, 90
memory capacity, 93
neurobiology, 86–89, 93
schema formation, 92–93, 183–187
self-organizing systems for, 100
See also Childhood experiences; Personality development
Diagnostic classification
PTSD, 155
treatment focus on, 135, 136–137
Dialectical behavior therapy, 159
Dissociation
attachment experience and, 99
in disorganized/disoriented attachment,
91–92
as failed integration, 101
trauma response, 58

Generalization of therapeutic effects, 32
Genetics, developmental significance of, 88, 89
Genograms, 33, 34
Gestalt therapy, 336
Grief work, 369
Group therapy
    PTSD outcome studies, 364–365
    transpersonal approach, 336–337
Guided imagery, 34, 40

Habituation, 153
    in classical conditioning, 161
    in EMDR treatment, 160–161
    as mechanism of change, 161–162
Helplessness, 9–10, 16
Humanitarian assistance programs, 284
Hypnotherapy, 41, 62
    change mechanism, 230–231, 232, 235–236, 344
    direct hypnosis, 225, 226–227
    EMDR and, 230–232, 235–238, 344, 353
    Ericksonian, 225–226, 227–229, 231
    identity destabilization in, 233
    process and technique, 226–229, 236–237
    PTSD treatment, 59, 358, 359–360
    sociocultural context, 232
Hysteria, 61

Imaginal exposure, 160–161, 405–406
    in multimodal therapy, 216–220
    PTSD outcome studies, 361, 363
    relaxation in, 209
    in schema-focused therapy, 190
Information processing
    experiential model of change, 251–252
    in interpersonal communication, 98
    model of change, 8–9, 27, 28–29, 51–52, 74, 91, 101–102, 108, 111, 161–163, 229, 247–248, 251–252, 393–394, 404
    model of personality, 12
    model of psychopathology, 7–8, 8, 16, 17, 31–32, 101–102, 229, 394
    neurobiology, 90, 91, 247–248
    potential for theoretical integration, 351–352

in PTSD pathogenesis, 156, 158
response flexibility in, 115–117
spontaneous processing in therapy, 42–43
transition from childish to adult perspective, 46
trauma effects, 104–105
unprocessed childhood events, 11
Informed consent, 279
Insight, 42, 130, 131–133
Interpersonal relations
    assessment, 164–165
    developmental significance, 63, 87, 88–89, 90
    emotional experience and, 98
    information processing in, 98
    integration in, 100
    in maintenance of traumatization, 138–139
    neurobiology of, 87
    patriarchal constructs in, 270–271, 272
    schema manifestations, 184–185, 186–187
    See also Family systems therapy
Interpretation, in psychodynamic therapy, 143
    with EMDR techniques, 146–147

Journal of emotional experiences, 40

Language
    capacity to describe experience, 248–249
    clinical significance, 30, 145, 253
    effects of trauma, 66–67
    in resolution of traumatic experience, 61–62, 65–67
    therapeutic transition from childish to adult speech, 46
Learning theory, 161
    in behavior therapy, 153
Lightstream technique, 34
Limbic system, 96–97
    in trauma response, 65
Locus of control, 48, 79
    in unprocessed childhood events, 11

Meditation, 17
    in transpersonal EMDR, 327

Memory
  accuracy of, 57
  associative nature, 17–18
  autobiographical, 60, 91, 109, 114, 115
  brain function in, 60–61, 90, 91, 92,
      93–96, 108, 114, 115
  in construction of meaning, 57
  dreaming and, 94–95
  in EMDR model of change, 12–13,
      404
  in EMDR model of psychopathology,
      9–10, 42
  episodic, 93
  explicit, 92, 93, 94, 108
  focal attention and, 107–108
  implicit, 60, 92
  in intense emotional experience, 60
  in posttraumatic stress disorder, 7–8,
      57–58
  as process, 57
  representational integration in, 114–
      115
  screen, 132
  semantic, 93
  targeting of, for treatment, 32–33, 34,
      35–36
  trauma response, 60, 95
  unprocessed childhood events, 11–12
  working, 107–108
Meta-analysis studies of EMDR, 401–402
Mindful attention, 159, 161, 404
Mother Theresa, 4
Multimodal therapy, 41–42
  clinical strengths, 212–213
  EMDR and, 211–212, 213–222, 343,
      348
  process and technique, 212, 214–215
  PTSD, 212
  rationale, 211
  technical and theoretical evolution,
      210–211

Narrative construction
  in change process, 91, 95, 311
  in EMDR, 324
  failed integration as result of trauma,
      101, 106
  in family systems therapy, 311
  neurophysiology, 91, 95
  in PTSD, 58–59, 60–61
  schema formation and, 93

Narrative therapy, 311, 313
Neural maps, 90, 108
Neurophysiology, 5
  bilateral stimulation effects, 220
  brain structure, 87–88
  cholinergic system, 78
  developmental model, 86–89
  of dual-attention stimuli, 372–373
  in EMDR mechanisms of change, 32,
      73, 247–248, 342
  of emotional processing, 68–70, 96–
      97, 110, 181
  experience-dependent development,
      88–89
  hemispheric development in brain,
      90–91
  of information processing, 90, 91
  of interpersonal experience, 87
  manifestations of unprocessed child-
      hood memories, 16
  of memory, 90, 91, 92, 93–96, 108,
      114, 115
  psychotherapy outcomes, 95–96
  reciprocal inhibition theory, 153–154
  of representational processes, 109
  subcortical involvement in trauma
      memory, 59–61
  trauma experience, 87, 89, 91, 95–96,
      97–98, 104–105
  trauma processing, 64–66
  trauma resolution, 117–118, 352
Nonverbal communication, 98

Panic disorder, 369, 398–399
Pathogenesis
  behavioral conceptualizations, 153–
      154
  chaos theory, 234
  cognitive theory, 182
  conditioning model, 153
  cyclical psychodynamic conceptualiza-
      tion, 138–139
  diagnostic classification and, 136–137
  earlier life experiences in, 8, 10–11, 12
  early maladaptive schema formation in,
      183–184
  EMDR concepts, 8, 9–10, 16, 17, 29–
      30, 42, 157, 229, 247
  information processing model, 7–8, 16,
      17, 42, 52, 101–102, 247
  integration and, 95, 100–101

PTSD outcome studies, 359–360
See also Psychoanalytic theory/therapy
PTSD. See Posttraumatic stress disorder

Rape, 9–10, 168
   EMDR treatment outcome studies, 362, 363
   feminist therapy, 274–277
   transpersonal therapy case study, 330–331
Rapid effects of EMDR, 27, 51–52, 172, 312–313, 345
Rapid eye movement sleep, 78
   in memory process, 94
Reciprocal inhibition theory, 153–154
   as EMDR mechanism, 157
Relaxation techniques, 40
   in desensitization, 209
   in multimodal therapy, 221
   PTSD outcome studies, 361, 363, 365, 366
Religion and spirituality, 4, 6–7
   nondual philosophies, 319, 324–325, 334–335, 338
   process of spiritual awakening, 324–325
   transpersonal psychology and, 319–320, 338
Research needs, 4–5, 52–53, 147–148, 173, 394, 395
   EMDR component analysis, 375, 404–405, 406–407, 410
   family systems therapy and EMDR, 315
   meta-analysis, 401–402
   neurophysiology of therapeutic change, 95–96
   panic disorder treatment with EMDR, 399
   PTSD treatment, 397
   sensory stimulation component of EMDR, 112, 163
   stability of EMDR effects, 397–398
   treatment fidelity, 403
Resistance, in psychoanalytic theory/practice, 133–134
Resource development and installation procedure, 34–35, 197–198

Safe place exercise, 34, 197, 327
Schema-focused therapy, 166

assessment and education phase, 187–188, 193–195
behavior change techniques, 193
change process, 188–193, 198–201
EMDR and, 181–182, 187, 193–201, 347–348, 351
etiological concepts, 183–187
flashcard use, 189
floatback technique, 195–196
role-play in, 190–191
theoretical development, 182–183
therapeutic relationship, 188, 192
treatment focus, 184, 186
See also Schema formation
Schema formation, 92–93, 166
   avoidance process, 186
   compensation process, 186–187
   domains of, 184–186, 202–207
   early maladaptive, 183–184, 202–207
   maintenance, 186
   resistance to change, 184
   schema modes, 187
   See also Schema-focused therapy
Schizophrenia, 399–400
Self-concept
   early maladaptive schema formation, 184
   therapy as pathologizing, 336, 337
   in transpersonal concept of change, 321, 322–323
Self-efficacy beliefs
   in desensitization phase of therapy, 38
   maintenance of therapeutic benefits, 40
   in preparation phase of therapy, 34
Self-love, 50
Sexual dysfunction, 370
Sociopolitical context
   feminist concept of patriarchy, 268–271, 272, 276–277
   of feminist therapy, 265–266, 267–268, 283–284
   of trauma, 264
Socratic questioning, 166–167
Somatic symptoms, 11, 21
   associated with unprocessed memories of childhood, 15–16
   body scan phase of treatment, 40
   client awareness, 37
   clinical significance, 30, 37
   in PTSD, 64, 65
   in trauma, 67–68
Somatoform disorders, 370

ABOUT THE EDITOR

Francine Shapiro, PhD, the originator and developer of EMDR, is a senior research fellow at the Mental Research Institute in Palo Alto, California. She is the founder and president emeritus of the EMDR Humanitarian Assistance Programs, a nonprofit organization that coordinates disaster response and pro bono training worldwide. She has served as advisor to a wide variety of trauma treatment and outreach organizations and journals.

Dr. Shapiro has been an invited speaker on EMDR at many major psychology conferences, including two divisions of the American Psychological Association and the American Psychological Society Presidential Symposium on PTSD. She has written and coauthored numerous articles, chapters, and books about EMDR, including *Eye Movement Desensitization and Reprocessing, EMDR,* and *EMDR as an Integrative Psychotherapy Approach.* She is a recipient of the Distinguished Scientific Achievement in Psychology Award presented by the California Psychological Association.